People and Computers XI

Springer-Verlag London Ltd.

M.A. Sasse, R.J. Cunningham and
R.L. Winder (Eds)

People and Computers XI

Proceedings of HCI '96

Springer

Angela Sasse, MSc
University College London
Gower Street, London WC1E 6BT, UK

Jim Cunningham, BE, M Eng Sc
Imperial College of Science, Technology and Medicine
Queens Gate, London SW7 2BZ, UK

Russel Winder, BSc, PhD
University College London
Gower Street, London WC1E 6BT, UK

ISBN 978-3-540-76069-6 ISBN 978-1-4471-3588-3 (eBook)
DOI 10.1007/978-1-4471-3588-3

Originally published by Springer-Verlag Berlin Heidelberg New York in 1996

Cover design by Simon Buckingham Shum and Fox Design

Typeset by *Winder.*

34/3830-543210 Printed on acid-free paper

Contents

Preface: Maturing Nicely

With this volume, which contains all the submitted full papers selected for presentation at the conference and some of the invited papers of HCI'96, we are starting the second decade of annual conferences of the British HCI Group (A Specialist Group of the British Computer Society). This warrants a brief reflection on the state of the conference and the direction in which it is developing.

In their editorial for the proceedings HCI'85, Peter Johnson and Stephen Cook (1985) stated that:

> "the aim of the conference and the group was to bring together researchers, designers and users of computer systems to discuss and exchange views on the quality of user interfaces".

Growing attendance at the conferences and membership of the group over the past decade have affirmed the need for such a forum.

It is an indication of continuity in HCI research that of the contributors to the HCI'85 proceedings, 4 have a full paper in this volume (Jim Alty, Peter Johnson, John Long, and Alistair Sutcliffe), one is an HCI'96 keynote speaker (Alison Kidd) and 4 served as members of the HCI'96 Conference Committee 11 years on (Gilbert Cockton, Alan Dix, Harold Thimbleby and Bob Spence).

At the same time, the papers in this volume and the overall conference programme reflect a development of HCI which has taken place over the past decade. From a forum of researchers from a range of disciplines in 1985 (Psychology, Computer Science, Ergonomics/Human Factors and Electrical Engineering) exchanging views, the conference has moved to become a showcase of an established discipline at work. Methods and tools, which were the focus of the early years, have moved out into the hands of practitioners who are providing feedback on their applicability to a range of design problems. The industrial and short papers at HCI'96 provide many examples of this, and it is valuable feedback which not only leads to changes in the tools and methods themselves, but also helps to refine and consolidate the theoretical framework of HCI itself.

In their preface to the HCI'95 proceedings, Mark Kirby, Alan Dix & Janet Finlay (1995), identified the challenge that constantly emerging technologies posed to HCI. They suggest that, since new technologies require new approaches, HCI may be denied the opportunity to consolidate its knowledge into established principles, guidelines and tools. Work on relatively new technologies such as CSCW, multi- and hypermedia, which are is well represented in this volume, shows that existing HCI knowledge and tools can provide a good starting point to analyse and shape emerging technologies into usable and useful systems. At the same time, this work generates indeed new findings, methods and tools which need to be integrated in the disciplinary knowledge base.

HCI's focus has been extended from the user interface (screen displays and input/output devices) to a more holistic view which considers the user, the task to be performed, the system to be used for that purpose, in a particular environment. This holistic view can only be obtained through user involvement in the design process, and the papers by Caroline Axtell, Chris Clegg & Patrick Waterson, Simon Buckingham Shum et al. and Stephanie Wilson et al. cover research and application issues arising from user involvement.

This extension will not go far enough for Thomas Green (1995), who, in his invited paper at HCI'95, proposed a move on to "computerless HCI", a discipline which can be applied to any complex information-based artifact. The papers under Fundamental Design Issues in this volume aim to address more general principles such as style (Phil Gray & Steve Draper), games metaphors (Kostas Stathis & Marek Sergot) and the use of 3-D (Alistair Sutcliffe & Uma Patel), though there is still a preference for computer-based implementations to illustrate the principles. In the papers under Specific Design Issues, the system still takes centre stage. In our view, this does not signify lack of progress: the benefit of HCI research which leads to the development of systems for user groups such as visually impaired students (described in the paper by Carol Linehan & John McCarthy) is self-evident.

Rather than being an indication of conflicting developments, the fact that HCI research is able to develop its theory base and solve practical usability problems at the same time is, in our view, the mark of a discipline which is maturing nicely. HCI will continue to address both general and specific design problems, and these two strands should continue to inspire each other, rather than dispute each other's worth.

Another notable development is that, even though HCI'96 is the conference of the British HCI Group, it has become very much an international conference. The papers in this volume report HCI research conducted in Europe, US, Canada and Australia as well as the UK. The conference committee and the British HCI Group are extremely pleased at this development, which reflects a growth in the international reputation of the conference. It also seems to reflect strong international research collaboration in HCI, which is also encouraging. But, as Donald Day's paper reminds us, despite international research collaboration and globally marketed systems, HCI has yet to establish what usability may mean for cultures other than our own, 'Western' one.

Regular attendees of the HCI conferences and others in possession of past proceedings will note that we start the second decade of conferences with a new publisher: HCI proceedings are now published by Springer-Verlag London. We are looking forward to as fruitful a collaboration with Springer as we have had over the last 10 years with Cambridge University Press (CUP). We, on behalf of everyone involved in the last decade of HCI conferences, wish to thank CUP for having published the proceedings on those 10 occasions.

Finally some thought about the selection of papers to be included in the proceedings from those that were submitted. All submitted papers were refereed by 2–3 reviewers (all HCI researchers and practitioners) and a member of the conference committee — the lists of committee members and reviewers appears immediately after this Preface. We, the editors, would like to express our gratitude to all the reviewers for finding the time in to undertake the reviews, and for providing us with candid and thoughtful feedback which made the selection of the final 23 papers from 60 submissions easier.* In the few cases where there was disagreement between the reviewers' reports, the final decision on a paper was made by the Technical Programme Chairs. Perhaps more importantly, constructive feedback helped many of the authors to produce the final version you find in this volume.

Martina Angela Sasse
Jim Cunningham
Russel Winder

London, June 1996

References

Green, T. R. G. (1995), Looking through HCI, *in* M. A. R. Kirby, A. J. Dix & J. E. Finlay (eds.), "People and Computers X (Proceedings of HCI'95)", Cambridge University Press, pp.21–36.

Johnson, P. & Cook, S. (1985), Editorial, *in* P. Johnson & S. Cook (eds.), "People and Computers: Designing the Interface (Proceedings of HCI'85)", Cambridge University Press, pp.x–xv.

Kirby, M. A. R., Dix, A. J. & Findlay, J. E. (1995), Preface: Enjoying the Journey, *in* M. A. R. Kirby, A. J. Dix & J. E. Finlay (eds.), "People and Computers X (Proceedings of HCI'95)", Cambridge University Press, pp.ix–x.

*For those fascinated by statistics and who have noticed that there are in fact 24 papers in this proceedings, the extra one — the paper by Victoria Bellotti — is one of the invited papers.

The Conference Committee

Conference Chairs	Bob Spence (*Imperial College, London*)
	Russel Winder (*University College, London*)
Technical Programme Chairs	Jim Cunningham (*Imperial College, London*)
	Martina Angela Sasse (*University College, London*)
A/V Equipment	Huw Dawkes (*Imperial College, London*)
Demonstrations	Lisa Tweedie (*Imperial College, London*)
Doctoral Workshop	Chris Johnson (*University of Glasgow*)
Exhibition	Richard Wilson
European Liaison	Philippe Palanque (*LIS/Université Toulouse*)
Industry Day	Rory Channer (*Thames Water*)
Organization Overviews	Gilbert Cockton (*University of Glasgow*)
Posters	Ann Blandford (*Middlesex University*)
Publicity	Simon Buckingham Shum (*Open University*)
Publisher Liaison	Dan Diaper (*University of Liverpool*)
Secretariat	Jeremy Pitt (*Imperial College, London*)
Short Papers	Harold Thimbleby (*Middlesex University*)
Social Program	Stephanie Wilson (*Queen Mary and Westfield College, London*)
Strategic Planning	Ian Benest (*University of York*)
Treasurer	Pauline Smith (*Loughborough University*)
Tutorials	Sandra Foubister (*Heriot-Watt University*)

The Advisory Committee

Chair	Patrick Purcell (*Imperial College, London, UK*)
	Bob Anderson (*Rank Xerox Research Centre, UK*)
	Richard Bolt (*MIT Media Lab, USA*)
	Rory Channer (*Thames Water, UK*)
	Peter Cochrane (*BT Research Labs, UK*)
	Ken Dye (*Microsoft, USA*)
	Greg Garrison (*Reuters, UK*)
	Richard Gregory (*Bristol University, UK*)
	Simon Hakiel (*IBM Research Labs, UK*)
	David King (*BBC Research, UK*)
	Brenda Wroe (*NatWest Group Usability Services, UK*)

The Reviewers

Jim Alty (*Loughborough University, UK*)
Anne Anderson (*HCRC, University of Glasgow, UK*)
Woody Barfield (*University of Washington, USA*)
Thomas Berlage (*GMD, Schloss Birlinghoven, Germany*)
Charles Brennan (*BT Laboratories, UK*)
Stephen Brewster (*University of Glasgow, UK*)
Fred Brigham (*Philips Eindhoven, Netherlands*)
Steven Clarke (*University of Glasgow, UK*)
Clare Davies (*De Montfort University, UK*)
Donald Day (*University of New South Wales, Australia*)
Paul Dourish (*Apple Computer Inc., USA*)
Radka Dvorak (*Queen Mary and Westfield College, UK*)
Jonathan Earthy (*Lloyd's Register of Shipping, UK*)
Alistair Edwards (*University of York, UK*)
David Fulton (*University College London, UK*)
Bill Gaver (*Royal College of Art, UK*)
Stephen Gale (*AIT Ltd., UK*)
Simon Grant (*Ispra (VA), Italy*)
Martin Hofmann (*SAP AG Walldorf (Baden), Germany*)
Ismail Ismail (*University College London, UK*)
David Jennings (*David Jennings Associates, UK*)
Chris Johnson (*University of Glasgow, UK*)
Hilary Johnson (*Queen Mary and Westfield College, UK*)
Peter Johnson (*Queen Mary and Westfield College, UK*)
Pat Jordan (*Philips Eindhoven, Netherlands*)
Hermann Kaindl (*Siemens AG, Austria*)
Darryn Lavery (*University of Glasgow, UK*)
John R Lee (*University of Edinburgh, UK*)
Gary Legg (*GEC-Marconi Naval Systems, UK*)
Paul Luff (*University of Surrey, UK*)
Neil Maiden (*City University, UK*)
Stella Mills (*Cheltenham and Gloucester College of Higher Education, UK*)
Shailey Minocha (*Technische Universität Braunschweig, Germany*)
Andrew Monk (*University of York, UK*)
Alan Newell (*University of Dundee, UK*)
Tim Norman (*Queen Mary and Westfield College, UK*)
Bashar Nuseibeh (*Imperial College, UK*)
Fabio Paterno' (*CNUCE-CNR, Italy*)
Matthias Schneider-Hufschmidt (*Georgia Tech, USA*)
Brian Shackel (*Loughborough University, UK*)
Steve Somerville (*Queen Mary and Westfield College, UK*)
Alistair Sutcliffe (*City University, UK*)

Kathy Thomas (*National Physical Laboratory, UK*)
Richard Thomas (*University of Western Australia, Australia*)
Philip Turner (*University of Glasgow, UK*)
David Usher (*InterAction of Bath Ltd., UK*)
John Waterworth (*Umea University, Sweden*)
George R S Weir (*University of Strathclyde, Glasgow, UK*)
Silvia Wilbur (*Queen Mary and Westfield College, UK*)
Peter Wright (*University of York, UK*)

Fundamental Design Issues

Towards the Total Quality Interface — Applying Taguchi TQM Techniques within the LUCID Method

Andy Smith & Lynne Dunckley

Department of Computing, University of Luton, Park Square, Luton, Bedfordshire LU1 3JU, UK.

Tel: *+44 1582 34111*

Fax: *+44 1582 489212*

EMail: *andy.smith@luton.ac.uk*

Juran defines quality as being 'fit for purpose or use'. It follows clearly from this that an effective interface is an essential ingredient in a quality software product. Whilst the discipline of Human Computer Interaction is maturing quickly, there still remains only limited support for *designing in* quality rather than *evaluating it afterwards*. In this paper the authors present the results of a pilot study within the first stage in the development of the LUCID (Logical User Centred Interface Design) method which attempts to integrate a number of human factor tools within a quality framework. Particularly they focus on the phases which adopt the Taguchi Method for designing quality into products and processes. By adopting such techniques within a practical example, the authors demonstrate how the use of a scientific experimental design strategy, together with conventional statistical tools can assist the selection of the optimum user interface.

Keywords: Taguchi, user centred design, interface design, total quality management.

1 Introduction

1.1 Aims

Designing, maintaining and operating complex computer systems has become a major task both for computer specialists and for the users of their systems. At the same time computers have become so pervasive in every day life that failure or malfunction of software systems can increasingly be life threatening. There have been a number of recent cases where under situations of stress computer users have misunderstood computer output or been unable to operate software successfully. Juran (1979) defines quality as being 'fit for purpose or use'. Clearly there are still cases where the software product is not fit for the purpose.

Whilst Hartson & Boehm-Davis (1993) in a review of user interface development processes and methodologies, recognize that "in one sense considerable progress has been made" they also identify a number of specific key research areas where there remains the need for 'real breakthroughs'. In terms of iterative methodologies Hartson & Boehm-Davis (1993, p.109) state that:

1. "research in the area of formative evaluation needs to focus on iterative evaluation techniques that, in fact, lead to a convergence on a good or at least an improved design"

2. "there is especially a need for techniques that can assign credit and blame, pinpointing why user performance is not up to expected levels in terms of specific interface flaws and shortcomings".

The objective of this paper is to investigate the application of the Taguchi method derived from the philosophy of Total Quality Management within the context of human computer interface design. In order to address issues such as those identified by Hartson & Boehm-Davis, the method suggested proposes to exploit the systems and tools developed recently for rapid prototyping but follows an entirely different philosophy and practical approach.

1.2 Iterative Prototyping

It is widely recognized that the process of determining user requirements for information systems is plagued with uncertainty, ambiguity and inconsistency. In current approaches to rapid prototyping an iterative approach is adopted through the construction of software prototypes for proposed systems. The general procedure followed has been to use rapid prototyping with incremental change based around continuous studies of the prototypes in use in authentic tasks. Often prototyping approaches include a parallel design phase in which several alternatives are explored at the same time. Detailed user interface design often involves prototyping the interface with reference to guidelines and check lists such as those suggested by McGinley & Hunter (1992), Mayhew (1992), or Whiteside et al. (1988). One issue which makes interface design so difficult is the extremely large number of variables (design factors) which effect the resultant usability. Prototyping, in whatever form, as currently practised will identify some, but not all, of these variables. There is limited formality in identifying and investigating how each individual variable alters the end product.

1.3 Usability Engineering

Hewett (1986) emphasizes that interactive systems should be designed iteratively and distinguishes between formative and summative methods for interface evaluation.

Nielsen (1993) describes a life cycle of usability engineering within which usability inspection techniques are adopted. Usability inspection methods are now being widely adopted in large software development organizations. Microsoft and other companies are known to have embraced heuristic evaluation and other inspection methods in recent years (Nielsen, 1995). Heuristic evaluation is the most informal method and involves having usability specialists judge whether each dialogue element follows established usability principles. Other inspection methods include Cognitive Walkthroughs (Wharton et al., 1994), Pluralistic Walkthroughs (Bias, 1994), Feature Inspection (McGinley & Hunter, 1992), Consistency Inspection (Wixon et al., 1994) and Standards Inspection (Wixon et al., 1994). There is evidence, however (Dillon et al., 1993; Smith & Dunckley, 1995), within the mainstream software development community that whilst awareness of such methods is increasing, their adoption remains largely superficial. Whilst usability engineering and inspection methods, if adopted, have been shown to enhance usability, they do not ensure the production of the most usable interface.

1.4 Taguchi Methods and LUCID

The Taguchi approach presented here provides a semi-formal method for interface design and selection, and can be integrated into a range of current approaches. Implemented as part of the developing LUCID methodology it can be used at the early stages of software design, when it would involve brainstorming between users and designers, refinement of ideas, and the selection of alternative design options. Through the use of such a method the designer has a much higher degree of certainty that the interface developed is the most usable one possible, rather than the most usable one met so far.

2 Taguchi Design Method

Taguchi methods were developed by Genichi Taguchi in Japan and their use has spread to both the USA and Europe where, through the use of experimental design, aspects of quality can be pushed back from inspection to design. Taguchi aims to shift resources to the creative design process rather than relying on inspection methods to ensure quality.

Taguchi's ideas for TQM fall into two principal, and related, areas known as the *loss function* and *off-line quality control* (Dale & Plunkett, 1990). The majority of the applications of Taguchi methods are within production control where he defines the quality of a product to be 'the loss imparted to society from the time the product is shipped'. Among the losses, Taguchi includes consumers' dissatisfaction, warranty costs, loss of reputation and loss of market share. In order to investigate quality a quality characteristic (e.g. strength) is identified and losses occur not only when a product is out of a permissible range for the quality characteristic, but when it deviates from its target value. Quality, as defined by Taguchi, is achieved by minimizing deviation rather than mere conformance to specification. As a result emphasis is given to off-line quality control. Here we are concerned with the process of optimizing production processes and product factors (such as the quality of materials, or the temperature of production) in such a way as to minimize item to item variation in the product and performance. Underlying the Taguchi method is the concept that quality is affected by two types of factor: internal or control factors (such as materials) which can be controlled easily and external noise factors (such as maintenance of equipment) which cannot be controlled easily.

The search for the optimum production process often involves conducting a number of experiments where each of the control factors are systematically changed. Taguchi developed a number of tools to enable engineers and designers to improve processes and products. The technique for systematic investigation of conditions is based on the Factorial design method first introduced by Fisher in the 1920's and extensively applied in agrarian and social sciences. However the Taguchi method drastically reduces the number of experiments which have to be carried out by providing a framework for design and also a simplified analysis of results which makes the Factorial design accessible to non-statisticians. In many situations full factorial analysis will involve many experiments. Three factors each with two possible values, or levels, would involve only 2^3, or eight, experiments but fifteen two level factors would involve 32,768 experiments. By using fractional factorial experiments, identified through the use of orthogonal arrays, the number of experiments can be drastically reduced. In the case of fifteen two level factors only sixteen experiments would be necessary. Through statistical analysis techniques the optimum situation (any one of the 32,768 options) could be determined. Full details of the Taguchi process can be found elsewhere (Taguchi, 1986) but we may summarize the standard Taguchi procedure as follows:

2.1 Design and Conduct Experiments

Taguchi experiments are designed according to strict rules. The basic concept is for the design team to agree on the quality characteristic which would be a yardstick for measuring the performance of the product or process under study. The team then identifies the input factors in the development of the product which are considered to influence the quality characteristic of the output. The design of the experiments will be based on the selection of an appropriate orthogonal array. Experiments are then conducted to determine values of the quality characteristic associated with the factor levels determined from the orthogonal array.

Orthogonal arrays are a set of tables devised by Taguchi and are used to determine the minimum number of experiments (in our case prototype interfaces) and their input conditions. The term orthogonal is used in the sense that the arrays are both balanced and ensure independence. Orthogonal arrays are the foundation of the experimental design and are essential to the Taguchi technique. The orthogonal arrays are efficient at obtaining small amounts of data which can then be translated into meaningful and verifiable conclusions.

Firstly the design team has to identify the number of key input factors and the settings or levels of these factors which they want to test. For example it could be decided to investigate an input factor at high, medium and low settings, representing three levels. Frequently just two levels, high and low would be used. When the factors and levels are agreed the orthogonal array can be selected, assigning the factors to columns and determining the conditions for individual experiments. Figure 1 illustrates the first two orthogonal arrays, the L_4 array which would deal with up to

Column / Condition	$L_4(2^3)$ 1	2	3
1	1	1	1
2	1	2	1
3	2	1	2
4	2	2	1

Column / Condition	$L_8(2^7)$ 1	2	3	4	5	6	7
1	1	1	1	1	1	1	1
2	1	1	1	2	2	2	2
3	1	2	2	1	1	2	2
4	1	2	2	2	2	1	1
5	2	1	2	1	2	1	2
6	2	1	2	2	1	2	1
7	2	2	1	1	2	2	1
8	2	2	1	2	1	1	2

Figure 1: Orthogonal arrays.

three factors and the L_8 array which can cope with up to 7 factors. The orthogonal arrays are systematically named as $L_A(B^C)$ where A is the maximum number of experiments, B is the number of levels and C is the number of factors or columns.

Some factors in the design can influence each other and may not be independent. The Taguchi method enables the design study to investigate both the input factors and the suspected interactions between the factors. Taguchi provides a number of tools for dealing with interactions. The interaction between two factors is assigned a column in the orthogonal array. This means that every interaction which is included in the study takes up column space and may mean a larger orthogonal array will be required with an increased number of experiments. The correct columns must be assigned to the interactions, otherwise the results will not be reliable. The orthogonal arrays are independent — every column covers one factor and has the same number of occurrences of each level as every other column. This ensures that any differences in the results are only due to the change of factors. Orthogonal arrays are balanced because there are always an equal number of occurrences of each level in every column. The number of columns dictates the number of single factors or interactions which can be investigated. An $L_8(2^7)$ can deal with seven factors or four factors and three interactions

2.2 *Analyse the Results Using ANOVA to Determine Optimum Conditions*

The main effects are evaluated and their influence determined quantitatively. This gives the optimum condition and the factorial effects as shown below in the pilot study. ANOVA is performed on the results to identify the relative strengths of the factors. Multiple runs can be carried out and the results analysed and the signal to noise ratios (S/N) calculated. The S/N ratio represents a concept developed by Taguchi as an estimate of the relative strengths of the effects of the system factors vs. the noise in the environment.

2.3 *Run a Confirmatory Test Using the Optimum Conditions*

A further test of the optimum conditions must be made to confirm the performance.

3 Applying Taguchi Methods to Interface Design

Taguchi techniques have not previously been applied to the development of information systems although they have been applied to the solution of specific software problems, for example by Turton (1994) to genetic algorithms and by Khaw et al. (1993) to optimize the design of neural nets. The Taguchi Method for interface design offers:

1. A disciplined way of developing a user interface.
2. A way of investigating development problems.
3. A cost effective way of investigating alternative interface designs.

In commercial prototyping approaches there is a tendency to develop a prototype interface which may not have all the functionality required, so that the software developer adjusts aspects of the design, usually one at a time, until an apparently acceptable design is achieved. The decision to stop prototyping may be based not only on the design itself, but also on project cost and budget pressures. The rationale behind the proposed method outlined here is to develop a more systematic and rigorous procedure for developing and optimizing user interfaces. The Taguchi approach to interface design is an evolutionary technique which emphasizes the design rather than the iterative testing of the interface. It should produce robust interfaces with inherent reliability characteristics. The Taguchi method is an evolutionary approach because the factors and levels selected can be adjusted after testing / trialling and the system tuned and re-tested. The analysis of the results should provide the following information:

What is the optimum interface design?
What factors and associated levels give the optimum design?
What is the expected quality characteristic (usability metric) for the optimum interface?

In terms of the terminology used in Taguchi techniques it is necessary for us to discuss the role of both the factors and quality characteristics. Central to the approach we adopt here is the fact that within interface design there are an extremely large number of design factors. Indeed at the start of the design process there is an infinite space of design options. However, at particular stages within a prototyping process the design space, although still large, will be restricted. At this stage it will be possible to determine a range of factors, with their respective levels, for example the choice of interaction object (radio button or push button), colour of screen and nesting level of menus. In terms of the quality characteristic the interface designer again has a far wider choice. In production control applications the quality characteristics are limited in number and far more obvious to identify (e.g. strength). The quality characteristics for a user interface can be far more numerous and less clear. They will, however, relate to usability metrics and quantitative user satisfaction levels. This paper presents the results of a preliminary investigation of the application of the Taguchi method to interface prototyping

4 Taguchi Pilot Study

4.1 Overview of the Study

The experimental study of the development of an interface was conducted using a Taguchi factorial design system. In general a thorough knowledge of both the application area and the process of interface design is required in order to identify the factors which affect the usability of the interface in development. The task set was to develop an interface for a specified case study. The system was to be developed using industry standard software, ORACLE 6 DBMS with SQL Forms 2.3 which provided a limited range of user interface design options. In order to keep the number of factors to a sensible minimum three design factors were included in the pilot study; these were screen layout, colour and help provision. These factors were considered to be independent (i.e. no interaction was expected between the factors in determining the performance characteristics of the design). The design method will, however, cater for the situation where there is thought to be interaction between the key factors. In that case additional experiments have to be undertaken to investigate the strength of the interaction and a different orthogonal array would be selected. Each factor was investigated at two levels as follows:

1. Screen design — single or multi-screen layout.
2. Screen colour — blue / yellow or green / black.
3. Help provision — help by menu or through screen field.

4.2 The Experiments

In order to conduct the pilot, students enrolled on undergraduate degree courses in Information Systems and Computer Science were asked to implement and evaluate each of the required factorial experiments. The experimental study was carried out as part of a second level module in IT Systems Building and the students who were involved as developers were strongly motivated and had completed graduate level courses in systems analysis and design, and user issues. The 36 second level students were randomly assigned to 9 development groups (identified as Group 1 to Group 9) which acted as teams of designers / developers of the individual interfaces. First year students from the same degree courses acted as users for the purpose of the usability tests. Every group was provided with the same relational table designs, integrity constraints and test data. In addition each group was given different specific requirements for the interface design corresponding to the design factors set out in the Taguchi orthogonal arrays described below.

4.3 Procedure

The subject groups developed the interfaces over a period of approximately 10 hours. An example interface is provided in Figure 2. At the end of the development time the interfaces were demonstrated to the authors to verify compliance with the general and specific requirements. When the requirements were acceptable the group was assigned a randomly selected group of users. The users were all IT literate and had previous experience of using applications based upon ORACLE SQL Forms.

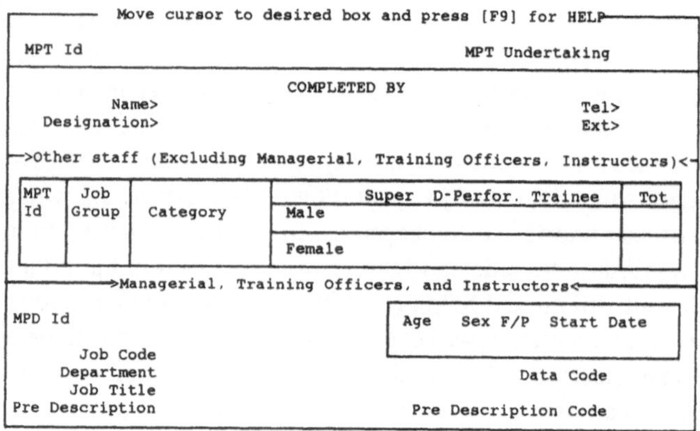

Figure 2: Example ORACLE interface.

Variables/Factors	Level 1	Level 2
A Screen Layout	A_1 - single	A_2 - multi
B Screen Colour	B_1 - green/black	B_2 - yellow/blue
C Help Provision	C_1 - by field	C_2 - by menu

Table 1: Interface design factors and levels.

The results of the experiments were based on the measurement of a quality characteristic. In general this can be a single criterion or a combination of multiple criteria. Although a number of measures of user satisfaction and user performance were considered it was decided for the purposes of the pilot study to adopt a single criterion 'Percentage of Useful Time' (PUT) which possessed a 'bigger the better' characteristic. The PUT was defined as the percentage of time the user was engaged in activities which would lead to successful completion of the specified task. All student groups calculated this metric. The task scenarios took a maximum of 15 minutes to complete so that noise factors such as user fatigue were minimized.

4.4 Analysis of Results

The analysis is based on a special adaptation of ANOVA. For the pilot study the three factors are shown in Table 1. Since there are three factors at two levels Taguchi shows that the study corresponds to an L_4 orthogonal array. From this it can be seen that four trials are required to identify the optimum interface. In the study, however, all eight possible combinations were trialled in order to explore the sensitivity of the

Design Group	Variables	PUT
1	$A_1B_1C_1$	56.8
8	$A_1B_2C_2$	61.9
4	$A_2B_1C_2$	67.5
6	$A_2B_2C_1$	75.2
Total		261.4

Table 2: Experimental layout for interface design.

Factor/ Level	Average Performance	Total of Factor	Sum of Squares	Variance of Factor
A_1	59.36	118.71	143.60	143.60
A_2	71.34	142.67	143.60	143.60
B_1	62.15	124.31	40.75	40.75
B_2	68.53	137.07	40.75	40.75
C_1	65.98	131.97	1.65	1.65
C_2	64.70	129.40	1.65	1.65

Table 3: Average effects and total variance.

results. The results of the four necessary trials are given in Table 2 and suggest that the optimum conditions for the interface could be $A_2B_2C_1$. The results are analysed in detail by determining the average performance of each factor and the significance of the results is checked by a variation of ANOVA. Table 3 gives the average effects of each factor and the variance. This shows that the best performance (PUT) would indeed be expected from an interface using $A_2B_2C_1$, a combination included in this array.

The calculation of the variance of each factor is the sum of the squares of the results of the trials involving the factor, minus the correction factor (CF) where:

$$\begin{aligned}
&T && = \text{Total of all results} && = 264.1 \\
&N && = \text{Total number of results} && = 4 \\
&CF && = T_2/N = (261.4)^2/4 && = 17081.13
\end{aligned}$$

and for Factor A, Sum of Squares S_A:

$$\begin{aligned}
S_A &= A_1{}^2/N_{A_1} + A_2{}^2/N_{A_2} - CF \\
&= (59.36)^2/2 + (71.34)^2/2 - 17081.13 \\
&= 143.60
\end{aligned}$$

where N_{A_i} represents the number of results with factor A at level i.

The results from Table 3 give the average performance (PUT) of all factor / levels as 65.34 and confirms the optimum design as $A_2B_2C_1$ a design produced by Group 6. The predicted performance of the optimum design is calculated from the

Factor	DF	Sum Sq.	Percentage
A	1	143.60	77.20
B	1	40.75	21.90
C	1	1.65	0.90
Error	0		
Total	3	185.99	

Table 4: ANOVA.

Group		Trial Result			Average
1		67.5	52.9	50.0	56.8
8		64.7	61.6	59.4	61.9
4		75.0	67.5	60.0	67.5
6		71.4	87.5	66.6	75.2
Factor	DF	Sum Sq.	Var.	F	Percentage Ratio
A	1	431.16	431.16	6.36	39.17
B	1	122.43	122.43	1.81	11.12
C	1	4.97	4.97	0.08	0.45
Error	8	542.08	67.76		49.25
Total	11	1100.65			100.00

Table 5: ANOVA summary of repetitions.

average performance of each factor and the contribution of $A_2B_2C_1$ above average performance:

$$\begin{aligned} Y_{opt} &= T/N + (A_2\text{-}T/N) + (B_1\text{-}T/N) + (C_2\text{-}T/N) \\ &= 75.17 \end{aligned}$$

The result of this analysis confirms that the optimum interface would be Group 6 corresponding to factors $A_2B_2C_1$ with predicted optimum performance (PUT) of 75.17. In fact the result of Group 6's tests was a performance of 75.2. The total sum of the squares is S_T and is the sum of the squares of each trial minus the correction factor (CF):

$$S_T = 185.99$$

The percentage contribution of each factor is the ratio of the factor sum to the total expressed as a percentage. For example:

$$P_A = S_A \times 100/S_T = 143.60 \times 100/185.99 = 77.20$$

Factor C makes such a small contribution that the optimum interface could correspond to the factors $A_2B_2C_2$. This interface was produced and tested by Group 9 with a performance of 68.9 which tends to confirm the above analysis. However we cannot be confident of the predicted result since the variance ratio could not be calculated because the error degrees of freedom is indeterminate for an L_4 array. This can however be overcome by carrying out a number of repeated trials. In this case three repetitions were carried out for each trial giving the total degrees of freedom as 11. This process is shown in Table 5. $F_{crit(1,8)}$ at 90% confidence is 3.22 and at 95% it is 4.84. Therefore from Table 5 it is clear that the results are statistically significant for factor A, but not for factors B and C. The results with the repetitions give the projected optimum as 75.15.

4.5 Noise

Noise is recognized as emanating from the technical, physical, social and organizational environment. One example would be the errors from metrics for 'trained' and 'untrained' users. In this pilot study the noise factors could include variation in the user ability, variation in the usability tests (conditions and expertise of testers) and other unidentified factors in the interface design.

5 Developing LUCID

Bevan (1995) has suggested that quality of use should be the major design objective for an interactive software product using the criteria "does the product enable the intended users to achieve the intended tasks, rather than does it merely satisfy its specification". Although the Taguchi technique for interface development can be used as a stand alone technique, the authors are currently in the early stages of developing a new interface design methodology called Logical User Centred Interface Design (LUCID) which, by integrating Taguchi and human factor methods will, it is suggested, assist in achieving Bevan's aims.

The discipline of Human–Computer Interaction is maturing rapidly and a wide number of interface design methods such as User Software Engineering (Wasserman et al., 1985), HUFIT Toolkit (Allison et al., 1992), Supportive Evaluation (Robinson & Fitter, 1992) and Method for Usability Engineering (Lim & Long, 1994) have been developed within the last decade. Outside of the specific HCI arena, Dynamic Systems Development Method (Millington & Stapleton, 1995) is being supported as a developing standard for Rapid Application Development. It might at first, therefore, seem unnecessary to propose yet another method.

One of the problems with usability is that it is often evaluated through testing relatively late in the development cycle. As a result only limited changes to the user interface can be achieved. This late usability testing can reveal deeper problems with functionality or basic dialogue design. If usability evaluation is left until just before implementation there will be no chance to make any significant changes in design to correct deficiencies. In prototyping methods evaluation tends to take place much earlier in the development process and may involve a phase of parallel design in which several different designers explore alternative designs before settling on a single approach which is developed further.

LUCID will propose a complete change of direction so that users are involved in establishing factors (and levels) together with quality characteristics and subsequently evaluating a number of prototypes created by designers on a 'design by

	Phase	Activities
1	Functional Analysis and Design	• requirements capture • task analysis etc.
2	Exploratory Investigation	• through brainstorming sessions users and developers identify key factors, associated levels and performance criteria • *exploratory* prototypes tested
3	Taguchi Design	• selection of appropriate orthogonal array • investigate interaction between factors • design of experiments
4	Taguchi Testing	• user *assessment* testing • analysis of results • selection of optimum design
5	Refinement	• confirmatory *validation* testing • further iterative refinement

Figure 3: Stages in the LUCID method.

experiment' basis. The use of brainstorming sessions is seen as vital to produce the necessary level of understanding of the exact context in which the software system will be used to be able to replicate the important aspects of the context for evaluation. The exact determination of the quality characteristic(s) will involve both designer and user. It is not expected that users on their own will determine usability metrics. It is expected however that, in partnership, users and developers can select a range of characteristics including usability metrics, task related performance measures and satisfaction levels. Measures of effectiveness, efficiency, and satisfaction could be combined to produce an overall, system specific, performance indicator.

In proposing a new interface design methodology it is necessary to take account of previously identified requirements. Shackel (1986) has identified five fundamental features of designing for usability. The user centred design process should be *participative*, include *experimental design*, adopt formal *user tests*, be *iterative* and *support the user*. Johnson et al. (1989) have extended the list and state nine attributes of a general method. Smith & Dunckley (1995) describe an approach whereby the user-centredness of the development process can be evaluated. LUCID will be compatible with requirements for interface design whilst providing support for the integration of Taguchi techniques.

LUCID relies considerably on effective usability testing. Rubin (1994) describes four types of testing. The methods are *exploratory* testing performed early in the process, *assessment* tests carried out early to mid way, *validation* tests undertaken late in the process and *comparison tests* (between two types of system) which can be performed at various times within development. LUCID will adopt all types with the main Taguchi test being a combination of an assessment and comparison. The basic stages in the proposed method are outlined in Figure 3 and a diagrammatic comparison between the LUCID approach and parallel design approaches is provided

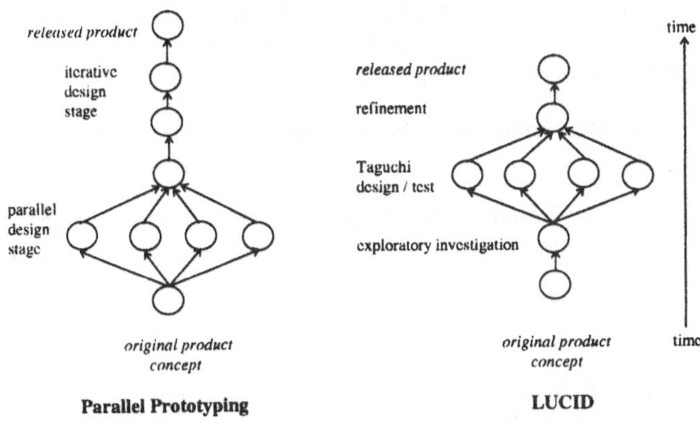

Figure 4: LUCID vs. parallel prototyping.

in Figure 4. From this it can be seen that whilst the parallel prototyping phase is later in the process, the iterative prototyping stage is much shorter and the overall development time could be reduced whilst enhancing quality.

6 Conclusions

The pilot study described suggests that a Taguchi approach to interface design is both feasible and worthwhile. It enables the interface designer to test a limited number of interface designs at an early stage in the development process and determine with a high degree of certainty the major factors within the optimum interface specification. Iterative prototyping can later be used to refine other more minor factors which may not have been included.

Whether the Taguchi approach to user interface design should be considered to be one of 'breakthroughs' that Hartson & Boehm-Davis (1993) seek, it certainly provides significant support for two of the issues which they highlight, as outlined in the introduction. The Taguchi parallel design and testing strategy ensures, subject to early prototype constraints and the identified quality characteristic, the identification of the optimum interface design. In addition the Taguchi variant of ANOVA provides a technique whereby the features most significantly effecting usability (credit and blame) can be determined. LUCID is in the early stages of development. The authors look forward to further developing and testing the approach adopted in the Taguchi design phases by carrying out further investigations.

References

Allison, G., Catterall, B., Dowd, M., Galer, M., Maguire, M. & Taylor, B. (1992), Human Factors Tools for Designers of Information Technology Products, *in* M. Galer, S. Harker & J. Ziegler (eds.), "Methods and Tools in User Centred Design for Information Technology", Elsevier Science, pp.13–28.

Bevan, N. (1995), "Measuring Usability as Quality of Use", *Software Quality Journal* **4**(2), 115–130.

Bias, R. G. (1994), The Pluralistic Usability Walkthrough: Co-ordinated Empathies, *in* J. Nielsen & R. L. Mack (eds.), "Usability Inspection Methods", John Wiley & Sons, pp.65–78.

Dale, B. G. & Plunkett, J. J. (1990), *Managing Quality*, Philip Allan.

Dillon, A., Sweeney, M. T. & Maguire, M. C. (1993), A Survey of Usability Engineering Within the European IT Industry — Current Practice and Needs, *in* J. Alty, D. Diaper & S. Guest (eds.), "People and Computers VIII (Proceedings of HCI'93)", Cambridge University Press, pp.81–94.

Hartson, H. R. & Boehm-Davis, D. (1993), "User Interface Development Processes and Methodologies", *Behaviour & Information Technology* **12**(2), 98–114.

Hewett, T. (1986), Role of Iterative Evaluation, *in* M. D. Harrison & A. Monk (eds.), "People and Computers: Designing for Usability (Proceedings of HCI'86)", Cambridge University Press, pp.197–214.

Johnson, G. I., Clegg, C. W. & Ravden, S. J. (1989), "Towards a Practical Method of User Interface Evaluation", *Applied Ergonomics* **20**(4), 255–260.

Juran, J. M. (1979), *Quality Control Handbook*, 3rd edition, McGraw-Hill.

Khaw, J. F. C., Lim, B. S. & Lim, L. E. N. (1993), Using Taguchi Method for the Optimal Design of Neural Networks, *in* "Proceedings of 5th Workshop on Neural Networks", SCS, pp.307–312.

Lim, K. Y. & Long, J. (1994), *The MUSE Method for Usability Engineering*, Cambridge Series on Human–Computer Interaction, Cambridge University Press.

Mayhew, D. J. (1992), *Principles and Guidelines in Software and User Interface Design*, Prentice–Hall.

McGinley, J. & Hunter, G. (1992), *SCOPE Catalogue of Software Quality Assessment Procedures 3: Usability Section*, Verilog.

Millington, D. & Stapleton, J. (1995), "Developing a RAD Standard", *IEEE Software* **12**(5), 54–55.

Nielsen, J. (1993), *Usability Engineering*, Academic Press.

Nielsen, J. (1995), Getting Usability Used, *in* K. Nordby, P. H. Helmersen, D. J. Gilmore & S. A. Arnessen (eds.), "Human–Computer Interaction — INTERACT'95: Proceedings of the Fifth IFIP Conference on Human–Computer Interaction", Chapman & Hall, pp.3–12.

Robinson, D. & Fitter, M. (1992), "Supportive Evaluation Methodology: A Method to Facilitate System Development", *Behaviour & Information Technology* **11**(3), 151–159.

Rubin, J. (1994), *Handbook of Usability Testing*, John Wiley & Sons.

Shackel, B. (1986), Ergonomics in Designing for Usability, *in* M. D. Harrison & A. Monk (eds.), "People and Computers: Designing for Usability (Proceedings of HCI'86)", Cambridge University Press, pp.44–64.

Smith, A. & Dunckley, L. (1995), Human Factors in Software Development — Current Practice Relating to User Centred Design in the UK, *in* K. Nordby, P. H. Helmersen, D. J. Gilmore & S. A. Arnessen (eds.), "Human–Computer Interaction — INTERACT'95: Proceedings of the Fifth IFIP Conference on Human–Computer Interaction", Chapman & Hall, pp.380–383.

Taguchi, G. (1986), *Introduction to Quality Engineering*, Asian Productivity Organisation.

Turton, B. C. H. (1994), "Optimisation of Genetic Algorithms using the Taguchi Method", *Journal of Systems Engineering* **4**(3), 121–130.

Wasserman, A. I., Pircher, P. A., Shewmake, D. T. & Kersten, M. L. (1985), "Developing Interactive Information Systems with the User Software Engineering Method", *IEEE Transactions on Software Engineering* **12**(2), 326–345.

Wharton, C., Rieman, J., Lewis, C. & Polson, P. (1994), The Cognitive Walkthrough Method: A Practitioners Guide, *in* J. Nielsen & R. L. Mack (eds.), "Usability Inspection Methods", John Wiley & Sons, pp.105–140.

Whiteside, J., Bennett, J. & Holtzblatt, K. (1988), Usability Engineering: Our Experience and Evolution, *in* M. Helander (ed.), "Handbook of Human–Computer Interaction", North-Holland, pp.791–817.

Wixon, D., Jones, S., Tse, L. & Casaday, G. (1994), Inspection and Design Reviews; Frameworks, History and Reflection, *in* J. Nielsen & R. L. Mack (eds.), "Usability Inspection Methods", John Wiley & Sons, pp.79–104.

Games as a Metaphor for Interactive Systems

Kostas Stathis & Marek Sergot

Department of Computing, Imperial College of Science, Technology and Medicine, 180 Queen's Gate, London SW7 2BZ, UK.

Tel: *+44 171 594 8254*
Fax: *+44 171 589 1552*
EMail: *{ks,mjs}@doc.ic.ac.uk*

We present the use of games as a metaphor for constructing and organizing interactive systems, with particular attention to the provision of Knowledge-Based Front-Ends (KBFEs) to software packages. Interaction is viewed as a rule governed activity which may usefully be regarded as a game. Given a specification of the rules, implementation of an interactive system requires construction of an umpire, a component that enforces compliance of the players with the rules and thereby controls the interaction. Advice giving components added to the system are analogous to games played in the presence of an advisor who recommends moves to the participants. Complex interactive systems are constructed as compound games built up from simpler sub-games; coordination of moves chosen from the sub-games is then a key issue. We exemplify these points by showing how the games metaphor is employed in the design of a complex interactive system providing a KBFE to the statistical package GLIM. We also sketch an alternative design in order to illustrate how the games metaphor can impose discipline on the developers of a complex interactive system.

Keywords: games, metaphors, interactive systems, knowledge-based front ends.

1 Introduction

One of the most important goals for designing interactive systems is how to convey the functionality of the system to a user via an easy-to-use human–computer interface.

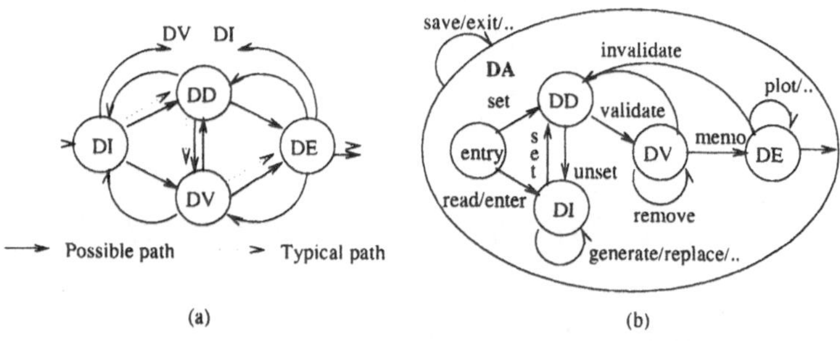

Figure 1: GLIMPSE and FAST activity networks.

Many authors have suggested, for example (Carroll & Mack, 1985; Hammond & Allinson, 1987; Carroll et al., 1988; Wonzy, 1989) and more recently (Erickson, 1990; Laurel, 1990; Anderson et al., 1994), that a very powerful method for achieving this goal is to use familiar metaphors to represent system properties. Catch phrases such as "a text editor is like a typewriter" (Douglas & Moran, 1983) or "the screen is like a table" (Zloof, 1978) often determine the usability of interactive systems. For example, the success of the desktop interface (Kratzer, 1987), originally introduced by Xerox Star and subsequently made popular by Macintosh, is based on the metaphor that "the computer functions like a user's desktop" and on the association of user operation on the computer with familiar objects such as *folders*, *calendars*, and *notepads*.

The metaphor of this paper is that "interactive systems are like games". However, the value of the metaphor is here intended primarily for the system developer, to serve as a conceptual framework for the design and organization of an interactive system with complex functionality. We are developing the use of this metaphor with particular attention to the class of interactive systems that provide Knowledge-Based Front-Ends (KBFEs) to existing software packages. A front-end to a software package is designed principally to make the package easier to use and to extend the facilities provided by it. KBFEs are front-ends that contain explicitly represented knowledge about the package and its domain (Bundy, 1984). In this way, they can offer advice on the system in general and on how to make effective use of its facilities in particular. One feature of KBFEs, however, is that they tend to be complex: a package which merits a front-end is a complicated thing, and its use has to be structured into manageable collections of tasks and commands. In the context of KBFEs, a metaphor is even more valuable because it disciplines the designer to provide a coherent organization of the user interface. To exemplify these points, we present a case study which shows how games are employed in the design of *the LAST system*, a KBFE that provides a graphical user interface to the statistical package GLIM 3.77 (McCullagh & Nelder, 1987).

LAST results from attempts to reconstruct the interactions of *the GLIMPSE system* (Wolstenholme et al., 1988), a first attempt to build a KBFE to GLIM. Expertise in GLIMPSE was encoded in terms of *tasks*. These group one or more GLIM commands into higher-level actions that the designers had identified as useful during the process of a GLIM analysis. In turn, GLIMPSE tasks were grouped into *activities*. For example, the task of entering a new vector or the task of reading a set of vectors from a file both belong to the data input (DI) activity. Similarly, the tasks of typing the values of a vector and relating statistically their values belong to the data definition (DD) activity. Other activities in GLIMPSE include the data validation (DV) activity which must be successfully completed before mathematical models may be investigated by data exploration (DE), model selection (MS) and model checking (MC) activities. The user moves between activities in the course of an analysis. Moves need not be, and usually will not be, linear; loops will occur in any thorough statistical analysis. Figure 1a shows the activity network for DI, DD, DV and DE in GLIMPSE.

Statistical expertise was also encoded explicitly in GLIMPSE allowing the user to invoke *context sensitive* and *strategic* advice within activities. Advice was provided in a non-authoritarian style, formulated as rules executed by the APES (Hammond & Sergot, 1987) system, an interpreter that augments Prolog with a number of facilities including explanations and Query-the-User (QtU) (Sergot, 1983). QtU is a conceptual model of system-user interaction in which the user is regarded as "an extension of the database containing the missing facts of a logic program". The idea is that, in principle, these facts could all be listed in advance, before the interaction begins, though for many pragmatic reasons it is required that they are elicited as execution of the program proceeds. However, QtU, although sufficiently high-level, is inappropriate for the kind of interaction involved in GLIMPSE and KBFEs in general, where changes of state are important and where information cannot all be listed in advance but is dependent on the evolving state. To illustrate the point, consider a game of computer chess. Could one realistically imagine that a user could, even in principle, provide all chosen moves in advance? No: as observed in (Sergot, 1983) the form of interaction here is different from that covered by the QtU model. It is not that one cannot reproduce this kind of interaction in QtU, but that it is unnatural to do so. Although attempts were made to extend APES in GLIMPSE to deal with interactions involving changes of state, most of these extensions fell outside the spirit of the original QtU model. GLIMPSE grew into a complex system that became increasingly difficult to maintain. In our view, many of these problems resulted directly from the attempts to force the required forms of interaction into the wrong conceptual model.

The drawbacks of GLIMPSE were one main motivation for the development of *the FAST system* (Stathis, 1994a). FAST reconstructs parts of GLIMPSE in FOCUS (Hague & Reid, 1993), a programme that developed tools to provide a *graphical user interface* (Edmonds et al., 1992) for KBFEs. FAST organized the interaction around a control panel. In order to simplify the interleaving between activities, FAST further re-structured the activities of GLIMPSE using a new data analysis (DA) activity that included the other activities as sub-activities, as shown in Figure 1b. In FAST user interaction was driven by *state transition* rules. These were suited to the message-based architecture (Edmonds & McDaid, 1990) of FOCUS, and at the initial stages of the development of FAST appeared to be very flexible. However, they were found to be too low level and difficult to maintain later as the system's functionality became more complex.

The games metaphor aims to address these development problems by providing a model of interaction that is higher level than the state transition rules of FAST and applicable to forms of interaction where QtU does not fit. Interaction is viewed as a rule-governed activity which we may think of as a *game*. The emphasis is on the existence of clearly specified legal moves (as in 'dialogue games') rather than on any notion of 'winning'. Construction of an interactive system proceeds by building up a complex game from simpler, easily implementable ones.

The rest of the paper is organized as follows. In Section 2, we identify the components of the games metaphor in more detail, and in Section 3 illustrate how it can be applied to the design of the LAST system. Section 4 focuses on coordination issues in the specification of complex games. In Section 5, we outline an alternative structure for LAST to raise the possibility of design principles for the organization of a system interface. Games are related with other forms of specification in HCI in Section 6. We summarize the discussion in Section 7, where we also discuss the potential of applying games more generally to the development of other types of interactive systems.

2 The Games Metaphor

In this paper we interpret the rules governing an interactive system as the rules specifying a game. Under this metaphor, interactions made by the participants of an interactive system are interpreted as moves selected by the players of a game. Specifying the legal moves of a game corresponds to defining the preconditions of actions in the interactive system. The effects of a move on the state of the game correspond to the effects of an action on the state of the interactive system. Games with more than one player correspond to interactive systems with more than one interactive participant. In order to implement an interactive system we construct an *umpire*. This is a component that displays the current state of the game in some appropriate fashion, provides means by which users can select their moves, enforces compliance of the players with the rules of the game and thereby controls the interaction.

An important characteristic of the umpire is that it allows variations of play. For example, through the umpire players may play the game from physically distant locations over a network as in networked-games. This resembles interactive systems whose participants interact from physically distant places (Sasse et al., 1993). The analogy between an interactive system spread in a network and a networked game is depicted in Figure 2.

What is to be gained from thinking in these terms? The idea is that specifying a simple game and implementing it by means of an umpire is easy. Complex interactive systems can then be built up as *compound games* composed from simpler sub-games. As an example of a compound game consider a *master's game* of Chess, where a Chess master plays several Chess games with different student players simultaneously, as shown in Figure 3. This game has many similarities with interactive systems: the Chess master is like the user of the system; the Chess games that are in progress are like the components of an interactive system that the user can invoke; the totality of all the legal Chess moves in all of the currently active games corresponds

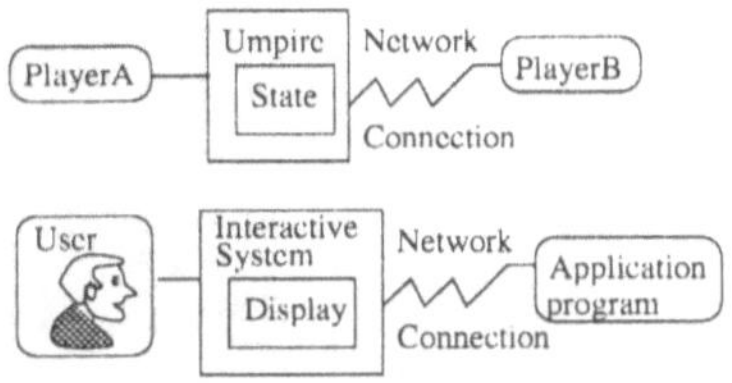

Figure 2: Playing a game vs. interacting with an interactive system.

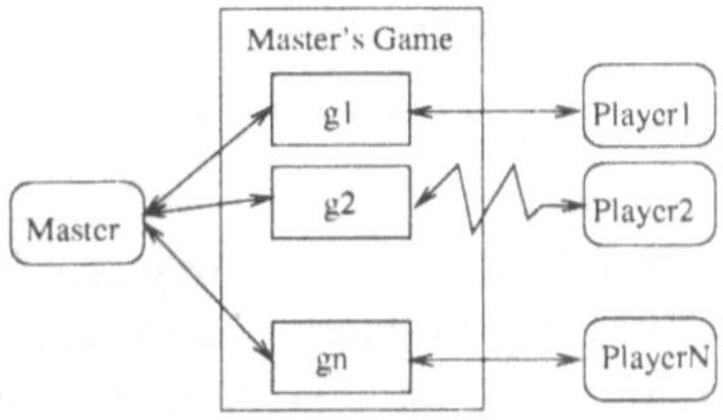

Figure 3: The master's game.

to the collection of system operations from which the user is able to select. Of course in an interactive system the component sub-games are not normally all instances of a single game as in master's Chess; they would normally correspond to different application programs (Edmonds et al., 1992), but the system as whole may be viewed as a compound game nevertheless.

A further benefit of the games metaphor is that the addition of advice-giving components to the interactive system (Wolstenholme et al., 1988) can be done in a structured and natural way, by providing an advisor for the corresponding game (Van Emden, 1980). Both context sensitive and strategic advice can be formulated in terms of best moves as determined by some expert strategy. More than one advisor can be present in a game in the same way that different types of advice may be available in an interactive system. It is important to note that the advisor itself does not necessarily need to incorporate the rules of the game in order to make recommendations. A winning strategy for the game of Nim, for instance, can be formulated as a simple arithmetic test without reference to the rules of the game. A Chess-playing program will calculate the relative strengths of various positions and moves without using an explicit representation of the legal moves of Chess. This point is important because it allows the advice-giving components of an interactive system to be separated and developed independently of the other parts. The advisors can be added or replaced in a modular way as they become available.

It should be noted that in some cases the advisor itself may have to interact with the user. In GLIMPSE, for example, the advisor sometimes needed to be told whether a given displayed graph was linear, or nearly linear, since this was something that the user could determine more easily than the system. Similarly, advisors sometimes

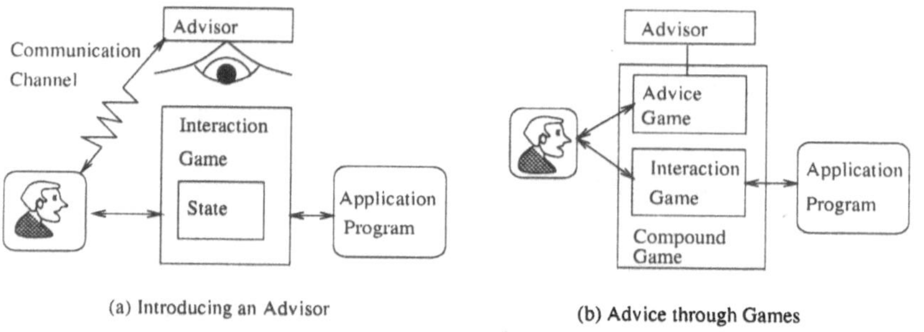

(a) Introducing an Advisor

(b) Advice through Games

Figure 4: Adding an advisor to an interactive system game.

need to ask users about their intentions before they are able to offer advice on recommended moves. The conceptual structure of an interactive system incorporating an advisor is depicted in Figure 4a. Note that communication between the user and the advisor can also be regarded as a game, the *advice game*. In this new game, the advisor is a player containing an explicit representation of how various user goals can be achieved at different stages of the interaction. Note also that the advice game is a sub-game of the interactive system that is now seen as a compound game, as shown in Figure 4b. Furthermore, in the process of providing advice, the provision of explanations from the advisor can be seen as a sub-game of the advice game. In particular, the request for an explanation by the user can sometimes be seen by the system as a challenge that has to be met, as in a dialogue game (Bench-Capon et al., 1992). It may even be helpful to interpret the successful provision of explanation from the system as the system winning and the user losing an argument (Bench-Capon et al., 1991b). These are not points on which we wish to dwell here, however, and further consideration of these suggestions is beyond the scope of this paper.

3 The Design of LAST using Games

LAST is designed as a compound game called the *mediation game* with players a user, the back-end GLIM and the advisor. The user makes moves in the mediation game via the control panel shown in Figure 5.

Like the master in the master's game of Chess, the user interleaves sub-games of the mediation game selecting them via items of the panel and their moves from the corresponding menus. The legal moves that are exclusive to the mediation game are accessed from the **special** item of the panel. The rest of the legal moves in the mediation game are legal moves that can be made by the user in the sub-games. Some of the sub-games of the mediation game are outlined next.

3.1 The Facilitation Game

The *facilitation game* is a compound game consisting of four *task facilitation games* corresponding to the panel items **file**, **vector**, **data-matrix** and **graph**. The umpire of the facilitation game acts as a *facilitator* between the user and the back-end GLIM, the only two players of this game.

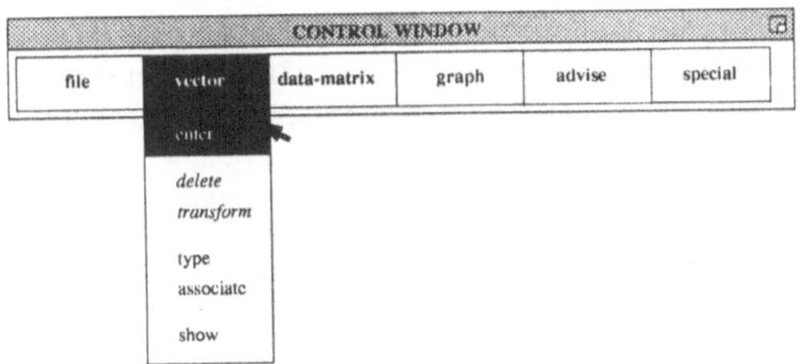

Figure 5: The main window of LAST.

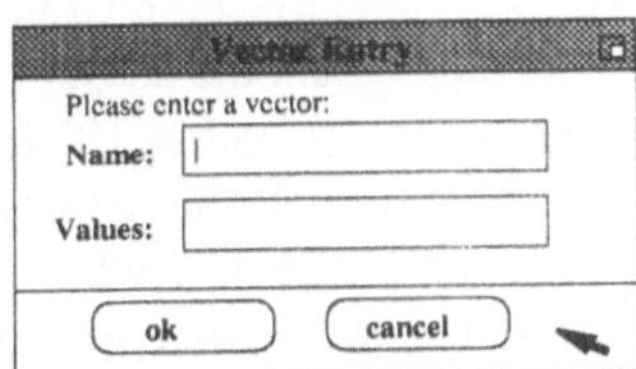

Figure 6: The *vector entry* task game in LAST.

3.1.1 Task Facilitation Games

Task facilitation games are also compound games where the user and GLIM are the players. In these games, moves of the user select items from menus accessed via panel items (see for example Figure 5). These moves enable the user to start new tasks by starting new sub-games; these allow the specification and execution of tasks. In general, depending on how many moves a task facilitation game has, menus can be structured in sub-menus. Different organizations are possible in this case; for instance, items in sub-menus may be regarded either as a set of moves of the task facilitation game or moves that belong to sub-games of the task facilitation game. In other words, games provide a flexible device supporting different interface organizations of an interactive system.

3.1.2 Task Games

Moves in task facilitation games start *tasks*, that is, sub-games normally played between the user and GLIM. Moves of the user specify the parameters of the task while moves of GLIM execute the task. In Figure 6 we present an example task game showing how the system interacts with the user for the entry of vectors. This game is a sub-game of the **vector** game and is started as a result of applying the effects of the move made in Figure 5.

Figure 6 shows the initial state of the task game where the task parameters for the name and the values of the vector are undefined. The game has three further moves for the user: edit a task parameter (one of **Name:** and **Values:**), submit the task for execution (by pressing the **ok** button) and cancel the task (by pressing the

cancel button). Execution of the task is a move made by the GLIM player. As in FAST, we use the notion of a Back-End Manager (BEM) (Prat et al., 1990) to allow the GLIM package to communicate in the same language with the rest of the system components.

3.2 The Advice Game

The *advice game* allows the user to obtain recommendations and suggestions from the advisor components. Moves of this game are accessed via the **advise** panel item. The advice game shares the state of the task facilitation game, thus enabling the advisor to observe the most recent development of the interaction. Some moves made in the advice game allow the user to request information about the area of the statistical domain where advice is needed. These moves initiate advice sub-games which further provide context for giving advice; in GLIMPSE and FAST context was provided through the use of activities. Also, the advice game and its sub-games are based on *interactive procedures* as in FAST (Stathis, 1994b). An interactive procedure is part of the knowledge representing how the advisor player has to play the advice game. Using these procedures the advisor decides which tasks to recommend next at the various stages of the advice game. Interactive procedures will also be discussed in the next section because they are relevant to the issue of coordinating sub-games.

4 Coordination of Sub-games

The main issue in specifying compound games is controlling interleaving of moves between sub-games. Interleaving provides a means of coordinating sub-games in compound games. It is defined by specifying under which conditions a sub-game is *active* in a compound game. The legal moves of a compound game are then defined to include the legal moves exclusive to that game plus all the moves in the active component sub-games. Different forms of coordination are possible and given by suitable definition of what is an active game. We distinguish two main classes of interleaving: *free interleaving* where moves from the sub-games can be selected freely by players and *constrained interleaving* where there are restrictions on selections of sub-games determined by domain specific constraints.

In LAST, we use free interleaving to support multi-tasking in the task facilitation game. In this case, any task facilitation game can be played by the user concurrently. Constraint interleaving, on the other hand, is used to define single-tasking in LAST. In this mode of interaction, a task sub-game of the facilitation game is active if in a task facilitation game there is a task sub-game that has not been completed. Otherwise, if there is no pending task game, any task facilitation game can be selected from the facilitation game as in free interleaving.

One requirement of LAST is to retain the non-authoritarian structure of the GLIMPSE advice. To provide this we need additional coordination primitives supported in the form of moves. For example, in the case of advice, the mediation game supports as a move the *suspension* of the advice game. Once the advice game is suspended, the user can make another move in the facilitation game, so avoiding the advice recommended by the advisor. The advice game can be subsequently *resumed*; this too is formulated as a move at the higher-level mediation game.

Other types of coordination primitives can be defined for compound games. In *sequenced games*, a sub-game must be terminated before the next sub-game is played. There are two types of sequenced games that we find useful. One is where all games that need to be sequenced are started in advance. In this case, sequencing can be achieved via constraint interleaving — constraints always select the first active game. The other form of sequencing requires that games are started dynamically by moves of a player. In this case, sequences are achieved by players that follow *interactive procedures*. An example of this form of sequencing in LAST is defined in the advice game. In particular, suitable definitions of the selection strategy of the advisor simulate *conditional statements*, *loops* and *procedures* as part of sequenced games. In this way, the designers can control domain strategies specifying what are the best task games that must be played next.

5 An Alternative Design for LAST

In constructing complex systems out of simpler components (sub-games), the main complication is dealing with the inter-dependence of sub-games. The easiest organization to specify and implement is one where dependence of sub-games is reduced to a minimum. The version of LAST presented in the previous section is more or less a reconstruction of the earlier FAST system in the game-playing framework. In this section we present some drawbacks of this design and we sketch an alternative. The two designs are then compared in terms of implementation ease and issues such as multi-tasking support.

5.1 Dependent Games

As an example of dependent sub-games in a game, consider the task facilitation game and its sub-games, specifically, the **data-matrix** sub-game. Here the user tries to set up the matrix of the relevant input vectors needed for the rest of the analysis. In this game, the user needs to use names of vectors recorded in the state of a different sub-game, the task facilitation game **vector**. In other words, the state of one sub-game depends on the state of another sub-game in that to start playing one we need to access the state of the other.

State dependencies complicate the specification of LAST. Consider as an example the situation where the user is playing the task game for validating the data in the **data-matrix** panel game. Once the user has submitted this task, the umpire forces GLIM to play next in order to execute the task. However, the validation requires a lot of checking to be performed by GLIM. When the system is in multi-tasking mode, the user will typically want to do something else instead of waiting for the validation process to finish, for instance 'delete a vector'. In this case, the umpire enabling this task ought to make sure that the vector does not belong to the matrix that is currently being validated by GLIM. An alternative to checking for conflicts of this kind is to leave the responsibility to the user. (Version 3.1 of the UNIX editor `vi` allows a user to invoke the editor twice on the same file, further permitting saved changes made in one invocation to be lost by the most recent changes saved in the other.) But if conflicts are to be avoided by the system, the designer is forced to make the compound game more complicated.

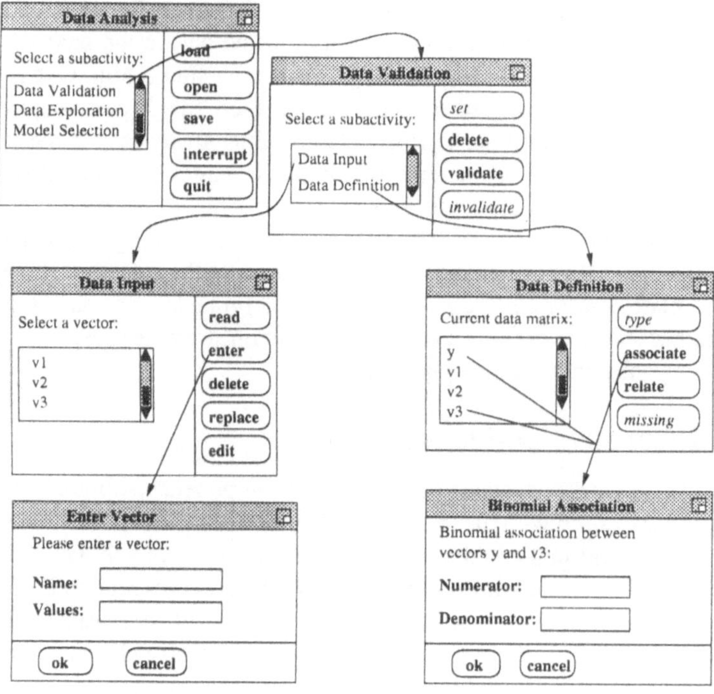

Figure 7: An alternative design for LAST.

5.2 *Independent Games*

We now consider an alternative organization of LAST where operations on interface objects are not grouped according to classes of objects, as with the current design of LAST, but grouped orthogonally according to their functionalities. For example, in the current design of LAST the tasks of 'enter a vector' and 'transform a vector' belong to the same group as they both manipulate vector objects. In the new design, 'enter vector' and 'read file' belong to the same group as they both manipulate input data. This new organization is closer to the original organization of the GLIMPSE system, where tasks were components of specific activities. In terms of games, this organization requires the introduction of new *activity games* composed from sub-activity games. This organization for LAST is shown in Figure 7.

In this alternative organization the top-level of the mediation game corresponds to a data analysis activity, as in FAST. The mediation game still contains the advice and task facilitation games as sub-games but the structure of the facilitation game is changed. In this new sub-game of the mediation game, different interface activities correspond to independent activity games. The user's selection of a sub-activity implies that a sub-game is created. The sub-game will either have more structure, that is, contain more sub-games representing sub-activities, or consist of a number of moves that initiate task games.

Figure 7 illustrates how tasks are selected in the new interface by depicting two possible branches. The first branch shows how the task game for entering a vector can be selected in the context of the data input game, which is part of the data validation game in the larger context of the data analysis, mediation game. The second branch shows which active sub-games must be followed in order to 'binomially associate' two vectors. Note that task games can be interrupted at any time. Interruption is a move in the data analysis game. Notice also that disabled moves in the higher-level activity games will be enabled after moves made in the lower-level sub-games; the user has a global view of the main compound game as it develops.

5.3 Comparison of the Two Designs

Compound games can support designs where sub-games are both dependent and independent. In the organization of LAST where games are dependent, the games metaphor does not appear to capture naturally the multi-tasking interactions. For instance, in the master's game different Chess games do not depend on each other and so they can be played simultaneously without problems. In general, in the multi-tasking mode, games as a metaphor favours the new organization of LAST where sub-games are independent of each other.

Let us therefore take *independence of sub-games* as a design principle for interactive systems viewed as compound games. What are the advantages? One advantage is that designs where games are independent allow interactions from different sub-games to be explored concurrently. For example, in Figure 7 both branches can be explored in parallel. Moreover, the new organization is cheaper in that the number of rules required to formulate the interaction between sub-games is reduced, since we do not have to check for dependencies and conflicts. These advantages, however, need to be weighed against the main disadvantage of the new interface organization, which is that it requires a less natural presentation at the level of the graphical user interface. On this point we should add that as a general principle we try to keep separate the internal organization of sub-games on the one hand and the way they are displayed at the user level on the other. However, it is obviously easier if there is a clear relationship between sub-game structure and features of the actual interface; a poor mismatch here is also indicative of a flowed interface design.

6 Relations with Work in HCI

There are similarities between the games metaphor described here and the earlier proposals of, amongst others, Bench-Capon et al. (1991a; 1992) and Finkelstein & Fuks (1989) to base interface construction on 'dialogue games'. The similarity is that these proposals also view interaction as a form of rule governed activity. The difference is that those proposals place no emphasis on compound games and coordination of moves in sub-games. It is also not clear to us exactly how, e.g. Bench-Capon et al., intend the dialogue games to be used and which game specifically they have in mind.

The games metaphor provides a conceptual device for understanding a variety of other dialogue models often applied in *User Interface Management Systems*. We mention briefly the three dialogue models surveyed in Green (1986): *transitions networks*, *context-free grammars* and *events*. In its simplest form a transition network is a finite state automaton expressing allowable sequences of input by associating input tokens with transitions between states. In the games metaphor transitions of the state automaton correspond to game transitions resulting from player moves, giving rise to a network of possible game states. Context-free grammars are used to express the hierarchical breakdown of tasks from higher-level descriptions to terminal ones. In the games framework, higher-level descriptions correspond to complex games defined from sub-games that eventually reduce to basic games. Complex games composed from sub-games can also capture *Augmented Transition Networks* consisting of sub-networks. Finally, games can support multi-threaded dialogues, traditionally based on the event model. Events are like moves made by players and *event handlers* are like programs defining how moves are received and displayed by the umpire; these are triggered from moves made in active games.

Games also relate naturally to interactive systems based on the *multi-agent* model (Coutaz, 1989) or metaphor (Laurel, 1990). In this model agents may be regarded either as players or as umpires, further structuring the *process-oriented* languages that these systems are normally specified and implemented (McCabe & Clark, 1994). Here games can be employed as a useful device for organizing user interfaces in terms of software agents built from sub-agents (Nigay & Coutaz, 1991), where umpires of complex games use the rules to coordinate the umpires of their sub-games. In fact the organization of roles that agents play in the interaction (Skarmeas, 1995) are similar to players in a role-playing game. In this case, games offer also a means of communication between players by sharing a set of common rules.

7 Conclusions

The outline of the LAST front-end is intended to demonstrate that games can support interactions that are highly structured, allow the addition of advice components in a natural way, and support interactions where sub-games of compound games are dependent. We have also shown that a more thorough examination of the interface in terms of games favours interface organizations where user sub-games are independent. In this way, the games metaphor can act as a design principle that disciplines the designer of the interactive system. Organizations based on independent sub-games have the added advantage of being more flexible, in that for example, they can easily support concurrent specifications of tasks, at the expense of perhaps requiring a less natural organization of objects at the interface.

The games metaphor may further improve the design of interactive systems to include new features taken directly from games. An example of this is the accommodation of feedback in terms of success measure mechanisms during interaction. Normally, users of interactive systems develop ways of measuring the accomplishment of a task or the achievement of a goal, although this feature is not explicitly supported in most systems. Consequently, users frequently have little sense of whether they are making progress, or how well they have performed. One feature that can improve this situation is to include scoring mechanisms as with playing a game, so enabling users to find out how well they have used the system perhaps in terms of the interactive facilities used during the interaction. In addition to a number of predefined scoring mechanisms which are likely to be relevant to users, users could further find out how other users have performed and even define their own specification of what user-defined measures are (Neal, 1990).

In the same way that games can make suggestions for the design of a complex interactive system, they can also be applied to define and improve the structure of manuals describing these systems. It is often the case, for instance, that manuals of interactive systems describe interactions only in terms of the possible instantiations of an action and its effects. Using games, however, a manual can be organized as explaining the rules of a compound game, in terms not only of legal moves and their effects but also of the context and structure provided by the game. In this way the manual can also describe why certain moves are not possible or which moves follow a specific user move and further describe their effects. Error handling can be grouped according to specific games rather than being long-listed in the end of a manual. More structured manuals improve user acceptance and form an essential part of the system's life cycle: from requirements and design to usability (Addison & Thimbleby, 1994).

As a final remark we should add that although the LAST applications described here are implemented, no user evaluation has been undertaken yet. Empirical studies are needed to evaluate interactive systems as games and see what users have to say about the value of the metaphor. From the programmer's/designer's point of view the best organization is that which minimizes inter-dependence between (concurrent) sub-games. Is this organization best for the user too? The answer to this question we leave for future research.

Acknowledgements

Thanks to the anonymous referees and to Francesca Toni for their comments on a previous version of this paper.

References

Addison, M. & Thimbleby, H. (1994), Manuals as Structured Programs, *in* G. Cockton, S. Draper & G. Wier (eds.), "People and Computers IX (Proceedings of HCI'94)", Cambridge University Press, pp.67–79.

Anderson, B., Smyth, M., Knott, R. P., Bergan, M., Bergan, J. & Alty, J. L. (1994), Minimising Conceptual Baggage: Making Choices about Metaphor, *in* G. Cockton, S. Draper & G. Wier (eds.), "People and Computers IX (Proceedings of HCI'94)", Cambridge University Press, pp.179–194.

Bench-Capon, T. J. M., Dunne, P. E. S. & Leng, P. H. (1991a), Interacting with KBS through Dialogue Games, *in* "Proceedings of the 11th Annual Conference on Expert Systems and their Applications, Avignon", EC2, pp.123–130.

Bench-Capon, T. J. M., Dunne, P. E. S. & Leng, P. H. (1992), A Dialogue Game for Dialectical Interaction with Expert Systems, *in* "Proceedings of 12th Annual Conference on Expert Systems and their Applications", EC2, pp.105–113.

Bench-Capon, T. J. M., Lowes, D. & McEnery, A. M. (1991b), "Using Toulmin's Argument Schema to Explain Logic Programs", *Knowledge-based Systems* **4**(3), 177–183.

Bundy, A. (1984), *Intelligent Front Ends*, Research Paper No.227, Department of Artificial Intelligence, University of Edinburgh, UK.

Carroll, J. M. & Mack, R. L. (1985), "Metaphor, Computing Systems, and Active Learning", *International Journal of Man–Machine Studies* **22**(1), 39–57.

Carroll, J. M., Mack, R. L. & Kellog, W. A. (1988), Interface Metaphors and User Interface Design, *in* M. Helander (ed.), "Handbook of Human–Computer Interaction", North-Holland, pp.67–86.

Coutaz, J. (1989), UIMS: Promises, Failures and Trends, *in* A. Sutcliffe & L. Macaulay (eds.), "People and Computers V (Proceedings of HCI'89)", Cambridge University Press, pp.71–84.

Douglas, S. A. & Moran, T. P. (1983), Learning Text Editor Semantics by Analogy, *in* A. Janda (ed.), "Proceedings of CHI'83: Human Factors in Computing Systems", ACM Press, pp.207–211.

Edmonds, E. A. & McDaid, E. (1990), "An Architecture for Knowledge-Based Front-Ends", *Knowledge-based Systems* **3**(4), 221–224.

Edmonds, E. A., Murray, B. S., Ghazikhanian, J. & Heggie, S. P. (1992), The Re-use and Integration of Existing Software: A Central Role for the Intelligent User Interface, *in* A. Monk, D. Diaper & M. Harrison (eds.), "People and Computers VII (Proceedings of HCI'92)", Cambridge University Press, pp.415–427.

Erickson, T. D. (1990), Working with Interface Metaphors, *in* B. Laurel (ed.), "The Art of Human–Computer Interface Design", Addison–Wesley, pp.65–73.

Finkelstein, A. & Fuks, Y. (1989), Multi-party Specification, *in* "Proceedings of the 5th International Workshop on Software Specification and Design", *ACM SIGSOFT Software Engineering Notes* **14**(3), ACM Press, pp.185–195.

Green, M. (1986), "A Survey of Three Dialogue Models", *ACM Transactions on Graphics* **5**(3), 244–275.

Hague, S. & Reid, I. (1993), FOCUS: Fourth Annual Report, Technical Report FOCUS/NAG/16/23.3-P, NAG Ltd, Oxford, UK.

Hammond, N. & Allinson, L. (1987), The Travel Metaphor as a Design Principle and Training Aid for Navigating around Complex Systems, *in* D. Diaper & R. Winder (eds.), "People and Computers III (Proceedings of HCI'87)", Cambridge University Press, pp.75–90.

Hammond, P. & Sergot, M. J. (1987), *APES: Augmented Prolog for Expert Systems, Programmer's Manual*, Logic Based Systems Ltd, London, UK.

Kratzer, K. (1987), The Desktop Metaphor: Visualisation of Office Applications on a Desktop, *in* "Proceedings of a Symposium on Office Automation", IEEE Computer Society Press.

Laurel, B. (1990), Interface Agents: Metaphors with Character, *in* B. Laurel (ed.), "The Art of Human–Computer Interface Design", Addison–Wesley, pp.355–365.

McCabe, F. & Clark, K. L. (1994), APRIL — Agent Process Interaction Language, *in* M. J. Wooldridge & N. R. Jennings (eds.), "Proceedings ECAI'94 Workshop on Agent, Theories, Architectures and Languages", Springer-Verlag, pp.324–340.

McCullagh, P. & Nelder, J. A. (1987), *Generalized Linear Models*, Chapman & Hall.

Neal, L. (1990), Implications of Computer Games for System Design, *in* D. Diaper, D. Gilmore, G. Cockton & B. Shackel (eds.), "Proceedings of INTERACT'90 — Third IFIP Conference on Human–Computer Interaction", Elsevier Science, pp.93–99.

Nigay, J. & Coutaz, J. (1991), Building User Interfaces: Organising Software Agents, *in* "Proceedings of ESPRIT'91", Elsevier Science, pp.707–719.

Prat, A., Lores, J., Fletcher, P. & Catot, J. M. (1990), "The Back-End Manager: An Interface between a Knowledge-Based Front-End and its Application Subsystems", *Knowledge-based Systems* **3**(4), 225–229.

Sasse, M. A., Handley, M. J. & Chuang, S. C. (1993), Support for Collaborative Authoring via Email: The MESSIE Environment, *in* G. de Michelis, C. Simone & K. Schmidt (eds.), "Proceedings of ECSCW'93, the 3rd European Conference on Computer-Supported Cooperative Work", Kluwer (Academic Press), pp.249–264.

Sergot, M. J. (1983), A Query-the-User Facility of Logic Programming, *in* P. Degano & E. Sandewall (eds.), "Integrated Interactive Computer Systems", North-Holland, pp.27–41.

Skarmeas, N. (1995), Modelling Organizations through Roles and Agents, *in* S. Katsikas (ed.), "Proceedings of 5th Hellenic Conference on Informatics", EPY, pp.521–531. Earlier version published as "Organizations through Roles and Agents" in Proceedings of COOP'95: International Workshop on the Design of Cooperative Systems, pp.385–404.

Stathis, K. (1994a), A FAST Front End Application, *in* L. Sterling (ed.), "Proceedings of the 2nd International Conference on the Practical Applications of Prolog", REN Associates Inc, pp.537–548.

Stathis, K. (1994b), How to Give FAST Advice, *in* "Proceedings of the 7th Symposium and Exhibition on Industrial Applications of Prolog, INAP'94", REN Associates Inc, pp.59–67.

Van Emden, M. H. (1980), Chess-Endgame Advice: A Case Study in Computer Utilisation of Knowledge, Research Report CS-80-05, Computer Science Department, University of Waterloo, Canada.

Wolstenholme, D. E., O'Brien, C. M. & Nelder, J. A. (1988), "GLIMPSE: a Knowledge-Based Front-End for Statistical Analysis", *Knowledge-based Systems* **1**(3), 173–178.

Wonzy, L. A. (1989), "The Application of Metaphor, Analogy and Conceptual Models in Computer Systems", *Interacting with Computers* **1**(3), 273–283.

Zloof, M. M. (1978), Design aspects of the Query-by-Example data base management language, *in* B. Shneiderman (ed.), "Databases: Improving Usability and Responsiveness", Academic Press.

Cultural Bases of Interface Acceptance: Foundations

Donald L Day

School of Information Systems, The University of New South Wales, Sydney, NSW 2052, Australia.

Tel: *+61 2 385 4760*

Fax: *+61 2 662 4061*

EMail: *Donald_Day.chi@xerox.com*

This paper introduces an ongoing research project which seeks to contrast the cultural expectations of ethnically diverse users with the styles of interface implemented in globally marketed software packages. A modified Technology Acceptance Model is applied, focusing upon culturally specific user expectations and system design features. The paper includes discussion of two supporting research streams, drawn from science and technology studies, psychology, information studies, sociology, HCI and anthropology. It also introduces methods being used to calibrate instruments, validate procedures and identify variables for later direct observation of user behaviour.

Keywords: cognitive style, appropriate technology, knowledge representation, adaptation, globalization, technology transfer.

1 Introduction

Historically, one of the goals of technology has been "to enable people to survive and adapt to the natural environment, later controlling it to enhance their quality of life" (Segal, 1994). Unfortunately, the encounter between people and technology often has been frustrating rather than enabling. Too frequently, people must adapt to technology rather than adapting it to their needs.

The attempt to construct a *one size fits all* interface for software products is no exception. Efforts to *globalize* interfaces developed originally for national cultures have proven difficult, in part because of an inadequate understanding of how cultural factors impact user acceptance. People in many cultures struggle with what are to them awkward interfaces — systems that degrade effectiveness, efficiency, productivity and satisfaction.

The project introduced in this paper seeks to identify aspects of culture that may impact the applicability of findings in several areas of HCI research. The project's first tasks (begun during early 1996) are to identify system design features that frustrate users, to calibrate data collection instruments, and to validate procedures for later direct observation. The goal of this work is not to dispute the applicability of existing findings in HCI, but instead to qualify them in the context of cultural factors which have practical importance to the global marketing of computerized information systems.

To date, much HCI research has accepted implicitly what are known in the cross-cultural literature as *Northern* biases — perspectives identified with European and American thinking (more commonly described as *Western*). Importantly, these include what Weizenbaum (1976) termed "the imperialism of instrumental reason" or of technological inevitability — the conviction that any problem can and should be solved using technology. Because new systems often result in social change (Szlichcinski, 1983), the implications of such biases for non-conforming cultures can be profound. Research conducted with Northern biases is not necessarily bad or wrong, but it does represent a special (limited) case of far ranging cultural perspectives.

It is true that inter-cultural perspectives in HCI have not been ignored totally. In particular, Fernandes (1994) emphasizes the need to examine biased concepts, metaphors, and icons in globalized software, Teasley et al. (1994) criticize intuitive inter-cultural design, and Russo & Boor (1993) discuss inter-cultural aspects of imagery, flow of control and functionality. However, the majority of inter-cultural HCI research is conducted in proprietary efforts to improve the marketability of software products overseas. Some findings and guidelines are available, e.g. (Apple Computer Inc, 1990), but only at commercial prices and not as part of the academic literature. Therefore, their potential to inform open, non-proprietary research is severely limited.

2 Conceptual Framework

Two research streams figure prominently in the cultural bases of interface acceptance (Figure 1). The first of these includes consideration of cultural context in the *appropriate technology* literature — which this project extends to include technology assessment and related areas such as cognitive decision-making style, knowledge representation and social control. The second stream, *change management and adaptation*, includes software globalization or nationalization, technology transfer and user acceptance, and existing interface design techniques for cross-cultural applications.

The project proposes:

- that any technology should be assessed to determine its appropriateness for a given culture; and

3.1 appropriate technology

- 3.1.1 cognitive decision-making style
- 3.1.2 knowledge representation (semiotics and iconography)
- 3.1.3 social control (mechanisms and impact)

3.2 change management and adaptation

- 3.2.1 globalization, nationalization, standards
- 3.2.2 technology transfer, diffusion of innovation, user acceptance
- 3.2.3 existing interface design techniques for cross-cultural applications

Figure 1: Primary research streams.

- that the goal of information system technologies is to help users manage change by providing enabling tools.

It also assumes that extending HCI research to include cultural context is important to understanding user acceptance.

Change management may be appropriate to varying degrees, depending upon techniques applied, mechanisms in place and cultural context. Techniques are addressed in the second stream; mechanisms and context are concerns of the first. Some elements in this framework are addressed within existing HCI literature. Others are drawn from science and technology studies, psychology, sociology, information studies, and anthropology.

3 Previous Research

Previous research was the basis for items included in the questionnaire for the project pretest. Although little of this literature specifically addresses the cultural bases of interface acceptance, collectively it identifies concerns that may be important to the generation of culturally sensitive products.

3.1 Appropriate Technology

The substantial literature in appropriate technology primarily addresses concerns about sustainable development and human ecology. It is critical of insensitively applied technology. Representative work includes Papenek (1972), de Moll (1977), Carr (1985) and Riedijk (1989). Of particular interest is Willoughby (1990), which counters several critiques of the appropriate technology perspective.

The project introduced in this paper applies a form of technology assessment — an adjunct of appropriate technology which evaluates the social impacts of technology (Porter et al., 1980). For example, Tepper (1993) examines the use of paradigms and metaphors during research and development to forecast a technology's impact before new products are released. It is fundamental to this work that all technology functions within a web of cultural values — addressed as part of Samovar & Porter's (1991) review of inter-cultural communication research, and in Schwartz & Sagiv's (1995) survey of cultures in 40 countries.

3.1.1 Cognitive Decision-making Style

The mediation by an interface between human cognition and task is important to system effectiveness (Allen, 1992), to user problem solving capabilities (Day, 1995a), and to the creation of cognitive schemata that people use to interact with social and institutional structures (Blackler, 1992). Interfaces that are at odds with users' cognitive styles may cause shallow, inefficient learning of system operation. Dillon (1987) suggests that this is because users who are confronted with an intuitively difficult interface learn by stressful memorization of action-response associations. This 'shallow' knowledge is ineffective if new situations are encountered — situations that require understanding of the system's underlying principles.

3.1.2 Knowledge Representation (Semiotics and Iconography)

Semiotics is the study of significance or meaning; iconography is the art of representing signs in ways that are recognizable to users in the context of their experience.

Rochberg-Halton (1982) notes a classic problem of semiotics addressed in this project: the degree to which user understanding relies upon situational context. Semiotic symbols associate referents (system features) to cognition — and symbols are far from transparent (they introduce noise to the communication, refracting and distorting meaning). Users understand symbols in interfaces only in terms of what they already know, knowledge which 'comes into focus' only in the context of culture (Watt, 1987). Apple Computer Inc (1992) note that symbols and colloquial language often are culturally dependent. When symbols fail to communicate effectively because they are culturally inappropriate, they create a condition of information scarcity — in which the user, struggling to find salient cues, tends to rely on culturally conditioned habitual responses (Nicholson et al., 1992).

Several properties which determine the *success* of an icon have been identified — in particular, guessability. It has been said that a successful icon is "one which can, given its *context* of use, communicate its intended meaning to the user" (Moyes & Jordan, 1993, emphasis added). Yet, little work has identified culture as a key part of context. One goal of the project introduced here is to qualify icon recognition research by determining whether culture is a significant variable.

3.1.3 Social Control

The means with which control is exercised in a computerized tool can impact significantly the attitudes, perceptions, satisfaction and behaviour of users (Day, 1995b). Cultural constraints may be the most effective controls implemented in *globalized* interfaces, precisely because they are implicit (to interface designers, if not to those who use their products). This is particularly important because typically such constraints are unintentional. Cultural constraints in computerized tools act not only as they are projected from the culture of origin to the culture of use (via the tools), but also as applied by users within the context of application, from the users' own perspectives.

One key social referent is *field dependence*, the degree to which a user defers to significant others in society for decisions about appropriate behaviour (Gudykunst & Kim, 1992). Users in field dependent (e.g. East Asian) cultures are more sensitive to cues and tend to take integrative, holistic, intuitive approaches — and generally are more attuned to environment than are users in field independent (e.g. EuroAmerican) cultures. The constituents of field dependence are discussed as dimensions of cultural values in Gannon (1994). In practical terms, field dependent users can be expected to accept constraints in interfaces more readily than would their field independent counterparts. (Users from field dependent cultures are less likely to resist or even recognize strictly applied constraints.)

In a sense, the HCI literature addresses contextual impact in its discussion of organizational culture (which may be taken as analogous in some ways to social culture). This work examines user learning and adaptation (Eason, 1982), the need for contextual data about task and the organization of work (Hellman, 1989), and the interactions between use of information technology and organizational culture (Morieux & Sutherland, 1988).

3.2 Change Management and Adaptation

The discussion thus far has concentrated on characterizing appropriate technology and its cultural context. The study introduced here also builds upon existing attempts to design and market interfaces across cultures, with particular attention to their impact in technology transfer and the diffusion of innovation.

International standardization has become a key facet of globalization, on the premise that globally marketed software must be uniform in order to offend as few potential users as possible. The base concept of standardization, however, is sameness. If interfaces are to be sensitive to cultural differences in user populations, their *standardization* must be at most functional — not presentational. But, much of the literature in interface standardization addresses presentational issues. Although such work stresses the need to accommodate user characteristics, a concern for indigenous language sensitivity is about as close as most work gets to cultural issues. (The cross-cultural literature suggests that *language* is a subset of *culture*.)

Change management is the process of ensuring a relatively seamless transition from one situation to another — of ensuring that stress is as low as possible at the intersection of contrasting systems. As a factor in change management, the definition and implementation of standards can be important to users' acceptance of the technology that the standards define (Morell, 1994).

Whenever users encounter an unfamiliar interface, the effectiveness of man-machine interaction relies upon adaptation. Commonly, man must adapt to machine. However, Paetau (1993) supports machine adaptation to man in calling for 'socially acceptable technology' — i.e. implementations that support flexibility, adaptability and 'configurativity'. Kim & Gudykunst (1987) discuss characteristics of user adaptation behaviour relevant to the project introduced here.

3.2.1 Globalization, Nationalization, Standards

Several major firms that market computer products internationally have attempted to adapt their wares for overseas use. Rafii & Perkins (1995) report, for example, that in Summer 1993 Lotus released a new version of 1-2-3 in 23 languages. The authors describe concurrent engineering practices which seek to speed the modification of base systems to incorporate differences in language, culture and user preferences in overseas markets.

Approaches by such international software firms range from mere *globalization* (applying an allegedly culture-less international standard for use in all markets) to *internationalization* (designing base structure with the intent of later customizing the interface) to *localization* (developing packages specific to a particular market).

The project introduced here proposes that globalization forces *all* users to adapt to a partially unfamiliar interface. It also proposes that the mere translation of interfaces into a multitude of languages is insufficient and may lead to confusion, as users in Southern cultures encounter familiar languages grafted onto alien semiotic, iconographic and procedural conventions. Regardless of these concerns, multilinguality continues to be considered sufficient for marketing overseas (Information Age, 1995). The language translation approach may appear to be more adequate than it in fact is because graphics changes must be made in several cultures to accommodate ideographic character manipulation (Morisaki et al., 1991). However, mere graphics changes in support of language display are only an extension of translation.

The project introduced here will suggest guidelines for the development of software with high modularity, such that base functionality can remain standard even if appropriate semiotic, iconographic and procedural features are customized for a user culture. This technique may be viewed as somewhat like a camera whose film-pack (back) can be interchangeable while keeping the same optics, transport, etc.

3.2.2 Technology Transfer, Diffusion of Innovation, User Acceptance

User acceptance (the transfer of technology and its diffusion within a target culture) is the essential goal in all international marketing. The seminal work in diffusion of innovation is Rogers (1962), which establishes that shared norms are crucial to the adoption (first, acceptance) of innovations. Later work emphasizing the role of human factors in technology transfer includes Baumgartel (1983), Heller (1985) and Stewart & Nihei (1987). Baumgartel notes that problems of 'slow' development stem largely from psychological factors that limit the diffusion and the rate of adoption of new technology. Heller addresses socio-cultural barriers and the appropriateness of technology. Stewart & Nihei examine local environments in terms of technology transfer in Indonesia and Thailand, by contrasting approaches fielded by the US vs. Japan.

Post-adoption IT implementation behaviour is examined by Saga & Zmud (1994), training reactions to new technology are reported by Breslawski & Bankowski (1993), and the impact of enculturation upon acceptability within organizations is discussed by Becker (1988). Davis (1993) reports that attitude (driven by perceived usefulness) has a significant effect on technology usage and proposes a Technology Acceptance Model (see Figure 2). Lee (1993) also discusses the importance of perceived usefulness, suggesting that users will adapt to interface resources and will circumvent interface problems in order to satisfy the demands of a task. A specifically cross-cultural note is added by Sensales & Greenfield (1995), who report that socio-cultural factors produce significant differences in attitude toward computer technology.

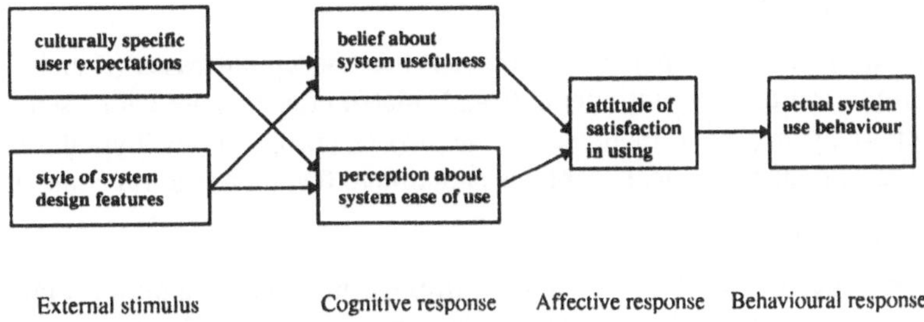

Figure 2: Modified technology acceptance model, based upon (Davis, 1993).

3.2.3 Existing Interface Design Techniques for Cross-cultural Applications

To date, there have been some attempts to address inter-cultural HCI outside of commercial venues. However, there also has been a substantial amount of work that could benefit by including cultural factors in the mix of variables studied.

One of the few works that focuses upon inter-cultural HCI is the collection of papers edited by Jakob Nielsen from a panel he chaired at the 1990 SIGCHI meeting (Nielsen, 1990). This work includes a paper that directly addresses socio-cultural and perceptual variables within interfaces intended for Asia (Sukaviriya & Moran, 1990). Also notable is Teasley et al. (1994), which takes to task a *Communications of the ACM* article (Marcus, 1993) that proposes graphically adaptive interfaces for 'culturally diverse users' (European males, American women and English speakers with an international orientation). The project introduced in this paper examines a broader range of cultural diversity, as does Russo & Boor (1993). One of the few papers to address the expectations of Southern users directly, this article goes beyond language concerns to note image recognition and acceptability, intended eye movement patterns, symbols, and the sub-text communicated by colour selection. Other work which concentrates more on language but nevertheless is useful to the project is that by Stone (1984), Becker (1984; 1985; 1987), Hsu (1991), Kataoka et al. (1992).

Several areas of HCI research could benefit from cross-cultural perspectives. These include work about the coupling of metaphors to system (Anderson et al., 1994), about the characteristics of natural language vs. direct manipulation (Agou et al., 1993), about the impact of array shape on users' visual search patterns (Scott, 1993), and about the deliberate use of sound as a key part of the interface (Nielsen & Schaefer, 1993).

Finally, there is a considerable body of work in HCI related to adaptive interfaces, which could be implemented in localized products to modify systems as they are used, effectively customizing their original other-culture designs. Examples include Mo & Witten (1992) and Hassell & Harrison (1994).

4 Methodology

Because the goal of this paper is to present the conceptual bases (foundations) of the inter-cultural HCI project, methods and related concerns are addressed in detail elsewhere (Day, in press). Included are the project's propositions (hypotheses) and a discussion of methodological problems endemic to the inter-cultural context.

4.1 Subjects

However, it may be said that the pretest currently underway is a pilot for more comprehensive future research. This pretest includes individuals from varying cultural backgrounds who are enrolled as first year students at The University of New South Wales. Most subjects are recent immigrants, to reduce the likelihood that they will be acculturated substantially to their new environment. A smaller control group is drawn from the locally predominant Northern culture. Co-operation in subject recruitment and data collection is being provided by the university's Foundation Studies Program (FSP) and by an institute of languages, which manages the teaching of English as a second language. (Participation in the FSP is required of newly arrived international students.)

In the main study, subjects will consist of a stratified international sample of ethnically diverse individuals, many participating from within their native cultures. Collaborators for that effort include Jane Carey at Arizona State University West (US) and Alvin Yeo at the University of Waikato (New Zealand). Several co-operating researchers have agreed to distribute a questionnaire to subjects in East and Southeast Asia, and in Russia.

4.2 Instruments

All subjects will be asked to complete a four-page questionnaire. The English edition of this instrument will be qualified in advance as semantically neutral by the university's institute of languages. Topics addressed will include attitudes toward and perceptions of information technology, culture of origin, experience applying tools to typical problems, characteristics that make technology appropriate to context, recognition of common GUI icons, feelings about the importance of significant others as behavioural referents, and willingness to accept products shaped in other cultures for indigenous culture applications.

4.3 Procedures

A selected subsample will be asked to complete a scripted training module for two computer applications. The module will be designed to test perceptions and attitudes similar to those addressed in the questionnaire. (Later, questionnaire responses will be compared to actual behaviour.) Both the main (Southern) group and the control (Northern) group will train on two computer applications. The first will be a *globalized* application developed originally within the EuroAmerican context. The second will be a *localized* product targeted for ethnically diverse users. Subjects will train individually, to minimize peer effects, although initial questionnaires may be completed in small groups.

While subjects are completing their training modules, they will be encouraged to vocalize their reactions using think-aloud techniques. Transcripts will be scored

	Globalized Software Package	Localized Software Package
Predominant Culture Control Group	*relatively high fit of GUI to expectation*	*relatively low fit of GUI to expectation*
Ethnically Diverse Experimental Group	*relatively low fit of GUI to expectation*	*relatively high fit of GUI to expectation*

Table 1: Experimental design.

using content analysis (Weber, 1985) and will be annotated to indicate which features of the interface were being addressed at the time of each utterance (to provide an association between interface characteristics and user responses). A 2×2 factorial model (Table 1) will be applied, to evaluate the effects of culture specificity upon user beliefs, perceptions, satisfaction and behaviour.

5 Conclusion

By itself, this project will not be able to establish techniques for generating ethnically sensitive interfaces. However, its findings may make possible further study toward appropriate standards. This work at least will contribute to an improved understanding of the information needs of Southern cultures. A better understanding of the techniques used and conventions expected by users from differing cultures may lead to more efficient and effective human-computer interfaces. Given the anticipated global market for software products during the next few decades, the benefits of culturally sensitive interfaces may be substantial in terms of financial profit as well as user satisfaction.

Acknowledgements

The author is indebted to Alvin Yeo (University of Waikato) and to referees of the HCI'96 conference for their critiques of an earlier version of this paper.

References

Agou, S., Raskin, V. & Salvendy, G. (1993), "Combining Natural Language with Direct Manipulation: The Conceptual Framework for a Hybrid Human–Computer Interface", *Behaviour & Information Technology* **12**(1), 48–53.

Allen, R. (1992), "Cognitive Factors in Human Interaction With Computers", *Behaviour & Information Technology* **11**(3), 257–278.

Anderson, B., Smyth, M., Knott, R. P., Bergan, M., Bergan, J. & Alty, J. L. (1994), Minimising Conceptual Baggage: Making Choices about Metaphor, *in* G. Cockton, S. Draper & G. Wier (eds.), "People and Computers IX (Proceedings of HCI'94)", Cambridge University Press, pp.179–194.

Apple Computer Inc (1990), *International Design Guidelines*, Apple Developer Group.

Apple Computer Inc (1992), *Human Computer Interface Guidelines*.

Baumgartel, H. (1983), "Human Factors, Technology Diffusion, and National Development", *Journal of Applied Behavioral Science* **19**(3), 337–348.

Becker, F. (1988), Technological Innovation and Organizational Ecology, *in* M. Helander (ed.), "Handbook of Human–Computer Interaction", North-Holland, pp.1107–1117.

Becker, J. (1984), "Multilingual Word Processing", *Scientific American* **251**(1), 96–107.

Becker, J. (1985), "Typing Chinese, Japanese and Korean", *IEEE Computer* **18**(1), 27–34.

Becker, J. (1987), "Arabic Word Processing", *Communications of the ACM* **30**(7), 600–610.

Blackler, F. (1992), "Information Systems Design and Planned Organization Change: Applying Unger's Theory of Social Reconstruction", *Behaviour & Information Technology* **11**(3), 175–183.

Breslawski, S. T. & Bankowski, H. K. (1993), The Impact of Interface Mode and Training on the Determinants of Behavioral Intentions for Acceptance of CASE Software, *in* D. Khosrowpour (ed.), "Proceedings of 1993 Information Resources Management Association International Conference", Idea Group Publishing, pp.478–484.

Carr, M. (ed.) (1985), *The AT Reader*, Intermediate Technology Publications.

Davis, F. (1993), "User Acceptance of Information Technology: System Characteristics, User Perceptions and Behavioral Impacts", *International Journal of Man–Machine Studies* **38**(3), 475–487.

Day, D. (1995a), Adaptive Discovery and Least Commitment: An Extension of Cognitive Fit, *in* H. Hasan & C. Nicastri (eds.), "HCI: A Light into the Future — Proceedings of OZCHI'95", Ergonomics Society of Australia (Downer, ACT), pp.256–261.

Day, D. (1995b), User Responses to Constraints in Computerized Design Tools, PhD thesis, School of Information Studies, Syracuse University. University Microfilms International (95-44905).

Day, D. (in press), Cultural Bases of User Acceptance: Methods, *in* J. Carey (ed.), "Proceedings of 2nd Americas Conference on Information Systems", Association for Information Systems.

de Moll, L. (1977), *RAINBOOK: Resources for Appropriate Technology*, Schocken Books.

Dillon, A. (1987), Knowledge Acquisition and Conceptual Models: A Cognitive Analysis of the Interface, *in* D. Diaper & R. Winder (eds.), "People and Computers III (Proceedings of HCI'87)", Cambridge University Press, pp.371–379.

Eason, K. D. (1982), "The Process of Introducing Information Technology", *Behaviour & Information Technology* **1**(2), 197–213.

Fernandes, T. (1994), "Global Interface Design". Tutorial notes of Tuorial 12, CHI'94 Conference: Human Factors in Computing Systems.

Gannon, M. J. (1994), *Understanding Global Cultures: Metaphorical Journeys through 17 Countries*, Sage Publications.

Gudykunst, W. & Kim, Y. (1992), *Communicating with Strangers: An Approach to Intercultural Communication*, 2nd edition, McGraw-Hill.

Hassell, J. & Harrison, M. (1994), Generalisation and the Adaptive Interface, *in* G. Cockton, S. Draper & G. Wier (eds.), "People and Computers IX (Proceedings of HCI'94)", Cambridge University Press, pp.223–238.

Heller, P. (1985), *Technology Transfer and Human Values: Concepts, Applications, Cases*, University Press of America.

Hellman, R. (1989), "User Support: Revealing Structure Instead of Surface", *Behaviour & Information Technology* **8**(6), 417–435.

Hsu, S. C. (1991), A Flexible Chinese Character Input Scheme, *in* "Proceedings of the ACM Symposium on User Interface Software and Technology, UIST'91", ACM Press, pp.195–200.

Information Age (1995), *Fluxus: Global or Bust*, Vol. 8 of *Information Age*, Australian Computer Society. (Ref. "Globalisation: Creating New Markets with Translation Technology", by Ovum London.).

Kataoka, Y., Morisaki, M., Kuribayashi, H. & Ohara, H. (1992), "A Model for Input and Output of Multilingual Text in a Windowing Environment", *ACM Transactions on Office Information Systems* **10**(4), 438–451.

Kim, Y. Y. & Gudykunst, W. B. (eds.) (1987), *Cross-Cultural Adaptation: Current Approaches*, Sage Publications.

Lee, W. (1993), Adapting to Interface Resources and Circumventing Interface Problems: Knowledge Development in a Menu Search Task, *in* J. Alty, D. Diaper & S. Guest (eds.), "People and Computers VIII (Proceedings of HCI'93)", Cambridge University Press, pp.61–77.

Marcus, A. (1993), "Human Communications Issues in Advanced UIs", *Communications of the ACM* **25**(4), 101–109.

Mo, D. & Witten, I. (1992), "Learning Text Editing Tasks from Examples: A Procedural Approach", *Behaviour & Information Technology* **11**(1), 32–45.

Morell, J. A. (1994), "Standards and the Market Acceptance of Information Technology: An Exploration of Relationships", *Computer Standards and Interfaces* **16**(4), 321–329.

Morieux, Y. & Sutherland, E. (1988), "The Interaction Between the Use of Information Technology and Organizational and Culture", *Behaviour & Information Technology* **7**(2), 205–213.

Morisaki, M., Kawada, E., Kuribayashi, H., Kuwari, S. & Narita, M. (1991), XJp System: An Internationalized Language Interface for the X Window System, *in* "Proceedings of the ACM Symposium on User Interface Software and Technology, UIST'91", ACM Press, pp.185–193.

Moyes, J. & Jordan, P. (1993), Icon Design and its Effect on Guessability, Learnability, and Experienced User Performance, *in* J. Alty, D. Diaper & S. Guest (eds.), "People and Computers VIII (Proceedings of HCI'93)", Cambridge University Press, pp.49–59.

Nicholson, J., Maddox, N., Anthony, W. & Wheatley, W. (1992), "Imaginal Technology and Management Information Processing: A Review of the Applied Literature", *Behaviour & Information Technology* **11**(6), 309–318.

Nielsen, J. & Schaefer, L. (1993), "Sound Effects as an Interface Element for Older Users", *Behaviour & Information Technology* **12**(4), 208–215.

Nielsen, J. (ed.) (1990), *Designing User Interfaces for International Use*, Elsevier Science.

Paetau, M. (1993), System-Adaptation and Reality's Own Dynamism, *in* T. Grechenig & M. Tscheligi (eds.), "Proceedings of the Human Computer Interaction Vienna Conference VCHCI'93", Springer-Verlag, pp.364–376.

Papenek, V. (1972), *Design for the Real World*, Random House.

Porter, A., Rossini, F., Carpenter, S. & Roper, A. T. (1980), *A Guidebook for Technology Assessment and Impact Analysis*, Elsevier Science.

Rafii, F. & Perkins, S. (1995), "Internationalizing Software with Concurrent Engineering", *IEEE Software* **12**(5), 39–46.

Riedijk, W. (ed.) (1989), *Appropriate Technology in Industrialized Countries*, Delft University Press.

Rochberg-Halton, E. (1982), "Situation, Structure, and the Context of Meaning", *The Sociological Quarterly* **23**(3), 455–476.

Rogers, E. (1962), *Diffusion of Innovations*, Free Press.

Russo, P. & Boor, S. (1993), How Fluent Is Your Interface? Designing for International Users, *in* S. Ashlund, K. Mullet, A. Henderson, E. Hollnagel & T. White (eds.), "Proceedings of INTERCHI'93", ACM Press, pp.342–347.

Saga, V. L. & Zmud, R. W. (1994), "The Nature and Determinants of IT Acceptance, Routinization, and Infusion", *IFIP Transactions A: Computer Science and Technology* **A-45**, 67–86. Proceedings of IFIP TC8 Working Conference on Diffusion, Transfer and Implementation of Information Technology, 11-13 Oct 1993, Pittsburgh.

Samovar, L. & Porter, R. (eds.) (1991), *Intercultural Communication*, 6th edition, Wadsworth Publishing.

Schwartz, S. & Sagiv, L. (1995), "Identifying Culture-Specifics in the Content and Structure of Values", *Journal of Cross-Cultural Psychology* **26**(1), 92–116.

Scott, D. (1993), "Visual Search in Modern Human–Computer Interfaces", *Behaviour & Information Technology* **12**(3), 174–189.

Segal, H. P. (1994), *Future Imperfect: The Mixed Blessings of Technology in America*, University of Massachusetts Press.

Sensales, G. & Greenfield, P. (1995), "Attitudes Toward Computers, Science, and Technology: A Cross-Cultural Comparison Between Students in Rome and Los Angeles", *Journal of Cross-Cultural Psychology* **26**(3), 229–242.

Stewart, C. & Nihei, Y. (1987), *Technology Transfer and Human Factors*, Lexington Books.

Stone, H. (1984), "Computer Research in Japan", *IEEE Computer* **17**(3), 26–32.

Sukaviriya, P. & Moran, L. (1990), User Interface for Asia, *in* Nielsen (1990), pp.189–218.

Szlichcinski, K. P. (1983), "Designing for the Day After Tomorrow: The Interaction Between Communications Systems Design and Social Change", *Behaviour & Information Technology* **2**(3), 253–261.

Teasley, B., Leventhal, L., Blumenthal, B., Instone, K. & Stone, D. (1994), "Cultural Diversity in User Interface Design: Are Intuitions Enough?", *ACMSIGCHIB* **26**(1), 36–40.

Tepper, A. (1993), "Future Assessment by Metaphors", *Behaviour & Information Technology* **12**(6), 336–345.

Watt, W. C. (1987), "Semiotic Mediation: Sociocultural and Psychological Perspectives", *American Ethnologist* **14**(4), 805–806. (Review of 1985 Academic Press book edited by E Mertz & R Parmentier).

Weber, R. (1985), *Basic Content Analysis*, Sage Publications.

Weizenbaum, J. (1976), *Computer Power and Human Reason: From Judgment to Calculation*, Freeman.

Willoughby, K. (1990), *Technology Choice: A Critique of the Appropriate Technology Movement*, Intermediate Technology Publications.

A Unified Concept of Style and its Place in User Interface Design

Philip Gray & Stephen Draper

GIST (Glasgow Interactive Systems cenTre), University of Glasgow, Glasgow G12 8QQ, UK.

Tel: *+44 141 339 8855*
Fax: *+44 141 330 4913*
EMail: *pdg@dcs.gla.ac.uk, steve@psy.gla.ac.uk*

The term 'style' is used with great regularity in user interface design literature, yet it appears to refer to widely disparate phenomena. We present a notion of style which unifies these various uses. We then demonstrate how the notion may form the basis of a representation of style that can provide design assistance.

Keywords: user interface styles, UIDEs, user interface design.

1 Introduction

Many word processors and text editors offer their users the facility to specify and apply sets of text properties to separated blocks of text, thus avoiding the tedious repetitive setting of these properties line by line or paragraph by paragraph. Such groups of settings are typically called styles. For example, in the text style facility of Microsoft Word, it is possible to define a set of hierarchic heading styles, such that each lower-level style uses a smaller font than its parent heading. Such styles, once defined, may be re-used in other documents. Often, however, one would like to be able to change some feature, such as text size, globally. For example, heading styles for conference papers might be appropriate for a memo, but only if the styles are globally reduced in size. Unfortunately, this is not possible. A number of other text editors and formatting systems (Andrew, LaTeX) offer the facility to define one font size relative to another, but it is rare to find the ability to define a heading style in this relative way. What is offered in the way of style definition and application varies widely from system to system and, in general, matches user requirements in an ad hoc way. There is an apparent absence of any common understanding of text style from which required and desirable features might be derived.

Corporate identity is often represented by a similarity of appearance of documents, products, images, etc. Typically, such similarity is based on style rules which are applied to corporate artifacts. Often these rules are complex and interrelated. This can cause difficulties for a designer who is trying to determine their applicability. This is especially the case for conditional rules which may only be relevant in certain circumstances. Consider a rule that states that, for WWW pages, the name of the institution must appear immediately below the institution logo unless the institution name appears in the page title. It is quite likely that a user may forget the conditionality of the rule, especially if the institution name appears in the title as a result of a late modification, after the rest of the page has been designed.

Sometimes we apply the term 'style' to system properties which are more abstract than either text properties or corporate logos. In Macintosh™ applications, the **File** and **View** menus appear in the same relative position in the menu bar, possess a subset of choices which are always present, and associate these choices with similar functions in each application. Sometimes this style of menu representation is violated, usually resulting in disorientation of experienced users. A trivial example is the puzzle application found on early Macintosh computers. The **Clear** option in the **Edit** menu for this puzzle causes the puzzle pieces to toggle between a pictorial and a numeric representation, which is not the conventional semantics of the **Clear** option as found in most other applications. Consistency, in the sense of maintaining the command name semantics of the Macintosh menu style, would have prevented this problem.

Each of these three examples, widely different though they are, capture ordinary uses of the notion of style. In this paper we will argue that they all represent variations of a single concept, a concept which is central to the process of design. We will present a general theory of style which explicates the advantages of the use of style, such as in our examples above, and we will suggest ways in which a proper understanding of style may lead to better assistance to the designers and users of interactive systems.

2 Notions of Style

References to style are encountered with great regularity in the literature of user interface design, in textbooks, (Shneiderman, 1992), user interface guidelines (Smith & Mosier, 1986), and style guides (AT&T, 1990). However, the phenomena referred to by the term appear to be widely disparate. Consider the following iconic representation of a file, taken from the Macintosh Finder:

The icon exhibits, or belongs to, a number of styles:

- A visual representation style.
  This representation of a file is primarily pictorial rather than textual, and more specifically, is the Finder's 'icon' as opposed to its 'small icon' view.

- A graphical style — one particular type of representational relationship.
  The appearance of a piece of paper with a turned-over corner is using pictographic similarity, rather than an arbitrary symbol (cf. the international radioactivity symbol), to suggest meaning.

- A direct manipulation style.
  That is, in its home context you can click on the icon to operate on the object it refers to.

- A metaphorical style.
  The icon's depiction of a piece of paper is prompting you to think of the computer file in terms of the printed paper it can be used to produce, which is one, but only one, of the functions and properties of the file.

- A 'house' style for Macintosh applications.
  We use 'house style' to refer to a set of standards enforced within an organization for functional reasons rather than to promote recognizability. Apple's user interface guidelines (Apple Computer Inc, 1986) are in part an attempt to export a house style.

- A 'corporate' style for Microsoft.
  Corporate styles are designed for recognizability rather than functionality.

- A style of file naming.
  A personal practice to make file names more meaningful to the individual.

In addition, there are some types of style not obviously exemplified by this icon. These include:

- Architectural style, e.g. the Gothic style, in which various and seemingly unrelated decorative features can be demonstrated to derive from a unified design-generating strategy or set of principles.

- Fashion styles in clothing, e.g. haute couture.

- Style as the visual resemblance created by expert typographers, allowing one to recognize similarity between otherwise quite different glyphs, e.g. 'o' and 't', as belonging to the same font family.

The most obvious common thread amongst all these varieties of style is the fact that the categories they form are used by designers, and indeed, by users. 'Style' is a central element in both the language and practice of user interface design. However, how is it used? Is there some common thread of meaning which ties these uses together? Or are the stylistic ascriptions to the icon above ambiguous, having meanings in each of its occurrences so different from one another that only the use of an informal English word 'style' binds them together? If, on the other hand again, there is such a common semantic core, is it something of value to designers?

We propose that style is any set of decisions or constraints fixed before a particular stage of the design process, e.g. dictated to a designer as part of her brief. Furthermore, a family of designs sharing the same set of constraints are likely to look similar to observers — styles are often recognizable. We argue that there is such a common property, that it is relevant, indeed central, to design, and that it may be used as the basis for a representation of style in computerized design support tools.

3 A Definition of Style

3.1 Style as Categories of Fixed Design Decisions

We suggest that style refers to the fixedness of a collection of design choices or decisions. This notion of fixedness, the degree to which the choice is available for change (or the degree to which the designer is committed to the decision), is related to a number of aspects of the design decisions. Thus, one decision may lead to, or limit, other choices which may be made, i.e. a logical ordering. Often, the choices are viewed in terms of the temporal ordering of the acts of decision-making.*

Design has both a search space and a sequence, or at least a partial time ordering, of decisions. Design methods and interactive system architectures both have features intended to enforce or allow for the separability of design and specification decisions, but there are actually two aspects of this. One is being able to take decisions independently in any order; the other is being able to take later ones with no backtracking i.e. no interaction or repercussion on ones already taken.

Traditional top down design methods in computing are only viable if in fact there is an order that allows the latter: taking decisions with no backtracking; and that this order is from top to bottom, from high level specifications to low-level code. This actually seems plausible because or when:

1. Programming is seen as converting functional specifications to code.
2. Computers are Turing equivalent.

Thus there will always be an implementation of any function or component function found in the specification or derived during design.

However in real life, whether in commercial programming or in undergraduate Pascal exercises, the actual specification (i.e. including the implicit specifications as well as the written ones) almost always includes non-functional requirements. Principal among these is a specified machine, language, and often support software (e.g. the X window system and its widget toolkits). This latter type of specification means that most design is not building out from a single fixed point at the top (the function to be computed) but from two fixed points — the function and the implementation platform (top and bottom). In general there may be any number of fixed points, as becomes clear in cases where re-use of code is emphasized and programming is explicitly a matter of gluing together old code for new uses, e.g. using Rexx.

*These two forms of ordering form the basis of two views of design reasoning: justificatory and historical (MacLean et al., 1991).

Reflecting on this draws attention to the temporal dimension in design. Some decisions are taken early on, e.g. in the requirements, and may not then be changed (more accurately, the costs of changing them are hugely greater than for changing other decisions). A given designer, then, is usually operating with what for her are fixed points that have been decided earlier. Even within an individual's design activity, there may be a more or less full ordering of decisions: top down methodologies imply a full ordering, while successes at separation, e.g. in UIMS and CAL authoring, allow a substantial degree of parallelism or independence in decision making (e.g. in deciding separately on screen appearance and on underlying functionality).

3.2 *Application to UI style*

The essence of the idea proposed here is that this early fixing or pre-empting of design decisions has in practice many varied forms. The word 'style' may without straining it be applied to all of these. It is a general phenomenon: to decide in advance either particular decisions, or particular conditional decisions (e.g. if there is an error message then it will have the following format). The key feature to note is that this restriction is not necessarily concerned with the functionality (the function to be computed); it may be function-neutral (always use insertion sort, always use one font style in menus — where the item chosen performs a vital function but is only one of a number of equivalent solutions), or function irrelevant (put the same logo on the screen, the casing, the shipping boxes, and the documentation — where the item chosen in no way supports the overt, overall function).

Styles, then, are sets of predetermined design solutions. As a result designers are working within a reduced, simplified, constrained design space. They have fewer alternatives to choose from, although possibly this may make it harder to achieve their goals, e.g. optimal performance. Furthermore, the space is additionally structured in that the types of choices available once the style is fixed are (partially) ordered. Thus, having chosen to use menus, the designer is forced to decide upon how the menu will appear, how items will be selected, how selection will be indicated; these choices are highlighted as important, indeed, necessary, within the context of the style. Other choices are relegated to the background, although they may be organized with respect to other style choices.

Designs produced with the same style often have a family resemblance — they 'look' or 'feel' the same to people. They are recognizable. They have something in common that other designs, from a wider design space, do not have. This recognizability decouples style identification from a knowledge of its development history or its design-oriented justification. Styles not only serve designers, but their recognizability can also be used by users; this identifiability gives users cues as to the meaning or expected behaviour of artefacts which exhibit a style they know.

A style apparently cannot be defined without a tacit contrast set: a larger set of alternatives of which it is one, from which it is chosen. But how then can we recognize a style bottom up? Only because, or when, we have seen other solutions to the same larger design space. It is of course possible to be familiar with a style, but not be aware of it as a style until one sees a contrasting example. For instance, pie menus are called 'pie menus' while vertical menus are just 'menus' and tiled windows are called 'tiled windows' while overlapping windows are just 'windows'.

The term 'style' as used here is neutral with respect to the particular type of design space structuring which it provides. That is, it may refer to choices which flow from a coherent principle or principles, like metaphorical representation, or it may refer to choices which are simply related due to common practice or convention, like visual style for menu items.

3.3 Style and Design Rationale

Newman (1988) has argued that what is important in the analysis of a style is the design rationale which underlies it. That is, the important aspect of style is its role as a structuring of the design space around which to organize design reasoning. There are some cases in which all the properties of a style are justified by a common design rationale, e.g. the features of a corporate image are justifiable solely with respect to making the corporate identity recognizable. However, there are other styles for which this is not the case, e.g. the style of UNIX command naming, which has arisen through practice rather than as the result of a conscious and well-defined design process.

Furthermore, concentrating on the relationship between design rationale and style obscures the other ways in which the concept of style influences design. Menus are devices for making choices from a set of items, just those where the choices are presented to user at the time the choice is to be made. Central questions then become:

1. how the choices are presented; and

2. how the choice is made.

Peripheral, though still important, are decisions about the length of time to display the choices, how to indicate selection, how to handle nested structures of choices. Equally, we may identify the 'near neighbours' of menus: command languages, data-entry forms and scrollable lists but not video sequences or icon images. Scroll bars and editable text fields perhaps lie somewhere between forms and images in their relation to menus. The important point here is that the concept of a menu adds a structure onto the features of a design, a structure which partially orders those features with respect to potential design decisions. Such structuring, which may be captured via style definitions, need not include the reasons for the decisions. Although important for software engineering reasons, the justification is separate from, or rather exists on top of, the structures offered by styles.

The grouping of choices as a style coexists with, but is distinct from, design reasoning. The work of justifying the set of choices may be carried out independently of the rest of the design and indeed, prior to the particular design enterprise. Style guides and uses of style in guidelines capture this pre-justification by giving conditions in which the selection of a style is appropriate; the justification is often absent and assumed (or its existence flagged by references to relevant studies). In fact, the absence of facilities to incorporate styles by grouping named, and perhaps parameterized, design rationales for selected sets of choices is a notable failing of current work on design rationale notations.

We thus reject Newman's assertion. Design rationales relate to one important part of design reasoning, but 'styles' refer to a distinct and broader class of structures that are important in design independently of whether their justification is recorded and used.

4 Current Tools and the Design Space

4.1 Implications for UIDEs

Support tools for designers should help them. If they are working in a restricted design space, then the tool should capture that. If it does not, in effect they will have to repeat work unnecessarily: (re-) specify to the tool decisions that are not real cognitive decisions because they are already in the brief dictated to the designer. Thus 'styles', that is predetermined decisions, should be reflected in the tool once made. However since there is a very wide range of styles, as the above argument shows, this building-in is not something to be done in the factory, but more like defaults set at the site or per project. The appropriate tool to build therefore is one with a language for defining styles, which are then reflected in the design space presented to the actual designer.

Since changing a style is done much less often than other design decisions, it can be harder work. On the other hand since, as argued earlier, a given human designer may well have some time-ordering constraints on their design work; in this case a given individual may design a style and then work with it as part of a project. Thus the interface to design specification must be usable by the designers / programmers, not only by special experts.

4.2 Inadequacy of Widgets

Current user interface prototyping and construction tools are not particularly good at assisting a designer in discriminating among styles, largely because they use too simple a model, if any at all, of the specification as a collection of design choices. The standard X toolkits offer widgets, highly parameterized interaction objects. A designer's choices with widgets consist of:

1. choosing a widget class (which determines the widget's parameters); and

2. setting the parameters.

The class structure among widgets reflects an inheritance hierarchy and does not correspond, except by chance, to any other categorization of interaction objects according to style or use. For example, MenuShell and ScrollingList, two of the widget classes in the Open Look™widget set which support selection (a characterization in terms of rationale) do not have a common parent class; their common class ancestor is the Composite widget class. Thus, the fact that they are both instances of a style of selection device is not reflected in the hierarchy.

Second, the widget's parameter space is entirely flat. There is nothing to indicate that setting one parameter is more or less important, from a design point of view, than another. As a convenience, most widget parameters have a default setting, so that a designer may safely ignore most of a widget's parameters. But which ones? There is no differentiation among the parameters to help.

The resource mechanism provided by X and similar window systems (Davison et al., 1992) enables the values of some attributes of a widget to be determined, leaving other attributes to be set by default or by other resource specifications. Other systems take a similar approach to style, like HUMANOID's templates (Szekely et al.,

1992). Thus, styles which can be expressed as default parameter values to widgets are supported, but others are not, e.g. metaphorical styles and many aspects of house styles designed for usability. Also missing is any way of representing differences in degree of fixedness of choices.

4.3 Design Assistance

Several user interface management systems, such as Olsen's (1992), Georgia Tech's UIDE (Foley et al., 1989) and MASTERMIND (Szekely et al., 1996) make a distinction between fixing the high-level decisions about an interactive system in a specification of its conceptual model, leaving decisions until later about the appearance and behaviour of the interaction objects to which the components of the conceptual model are related. Such systems employ sets of rules which putatively capture user interface styles and, when applied to the conceptual model, generate the user interface automatically.

Two types of fixed design decision can be identified in these systems. First, the conceptual model constitutes a set of fixed choices and, in terms of our definition of style, forms a style. This seems reasonable, since systems belong to recognizable categories with respect to the objects and operations which make up their conceptual model. However, this suffers from the problem identified in Section 3.1, viz., that decisions about the conceptualization of the application are fixed before, and independently of, decisions about the user interface's appearance and behaviour. This does not take into account the way decisions about the hardware / system software / basic interaction style may restrict choices about the application's conceptual structure.

Second, the rules by which the user interface are generated are a fixed set of design choices, albeit ones (usually) without alternatives. This approach has been demonstrated to produce acceptable results when applied to limited domains of design choices, but its assistance fades as the range of design choices increases in scope; it is unlikely that, given current models of application, interface and style, the same technique will work for more sophisticated styles and application domains, such as metaphorical representation of a wide range of types of data and input techniques. Furthermore, the rule-based approach has so far focused solely on the generation of presentations based on the specification of the application and has ignored other types, such as 'corporate' style.

5 Design-time Constraints on Interface Specifications

5.1 Style as Design-time Constraints

A style is any set of decisions taken before subsequent design proceeds, which will appear as constraints on or structuring of the remaining design space. A system supporting the general approach to styles which we have argued is actually required, must offer a language for specifying styles. This language will be, in effect, a language on the design specification; expressions in such a language specify the remaining design space and hence the allowed designs.

The solution which we propose to the problem of style-based support for design is to model design-time constraints on interface specifications: this is information about design significant properties which fixes the choices which a designer may make, and indeed sometimes forces additional design decisions to be made. The role of such constraints is to impose a structure, or indeed a variety of structures, on the various attributes which make up the interaction object's definition, ordering them with respect to the design considerations in terms of which the interaction object properties are specified. Facilities can then be included in design tools for defining and resolving these constraints.

Consider the Macintosh Finder icon discussed earlier. Design-time constraints one might place on such an object include:

- It must represent (i.e. carry information about) objects in the underlying file system, such as discs, directories and files.
- It must be one of a collection of such icons.
- It must possess a label which corresponds to the name of the represented object.
- It must be selectable.
- It should have an image which corresponds to the type of the represented object.

Some constraints, such as the choice of representational image, may have strong weightings, although they may be relaxed. The weighting of the choice is intended to make a decision regarding use of such an image a central decision in the context of icon design. That is, the designer should be forced to consider it early on in the design of the icon. Its absence may be compensated for by modifying other features, but if the decision is left too late, these other features may not have been modified appropriately.

Additionally, one may wish to include annotations to the constraints, such as the rationale for them. The constraint that the image be representational might include an annotation asserting that this property enables inferences about the type of the underlying object to be drawn from the nature of the image.

A corporate house style might be based on the incorporation of some features of the company's logo in the artefact being designed (Mahony & Gower, 1991). Which features may depend upon a number of other design considerations. What is important here is to include a constraint on the properties of the object such that they satisfy the logo incorporation requirement. The means of doing so is not part of the constraint. It may be satisfied, perhaps, by using company colours, or by including the logo in the widget's area, or by including the logo in a component part of the object. Such a constraint is likely to be satisfiable only as the result of the activity of designers trying out alternatives, comparing them for adequacy against a variety of criteria and, finally, asserting a solution by including its specification in the design. In cases of this sort, the relationship of design rationale to style application becomes central.

5.2 The Role of Design-time Constraints

Design-time constraints have a number of roles in the design process. First, they restrict, perhaps conditionally, the choices which a designer may make. Thus, given the choice to present information via a map, that information must be presented via a collection of appropriately located visual elements. This restriction is equivalent to the structure imposed by interaction object (e.g. widget) type or class as found in most user interface construction tools. Second, styles organize consequent choices, indicating the importance of specifying certain features of the chosen alternative interaction object type or class. Third, since styles are properties of specifications, they may be stored and retrieved for reuse in analogous situations (i.e. applied to new specifications).

Finally, as illustrated in the corporate logo example, some design constraints may force the designer to assert that certain design conditions or requirements are met. A central feature of these design constraints is that their satisfaction may require the intervention of a human designer. We cannot assume that:

1. we can produce a constraint satisfaction engine sufficiently sophisticated to resolve constraints without such intervention; and

2. we can represent the knowledge to resolve the constraints in a design knowledge base.

More importantly, the resolution of the constraints may be essentially unresolvable until a designer decision is taken, perhaps as the result of further reasoning or empirical investigation.

As the previous section suggested, sets of design-time constraints may be definitive of a set of solutions to a design problem. Thus, the notion of a map defines a class of solutions to the problem of displaying multi-dimensional data. A corporate 'style' is a family of solutions to the problem of making artefacts identifiable as representing an institution. A representational or interaction object may satisfy more than one set of constraints at the same time and thus may belong to more than style.

5.3 Constraint Satisfaction

Constraints typically are defined as relationships among entities (Leler, 1988); in a dynamic system these must be maintained true via a constraint satisfaction mechanism. Typically, constraint mechanisms have been employed to model dynamic systems specified declaratively.

This may appear an unlikely method of modelling style in a user interface design tool. However, if we conceive of a style as placing restrictions upon the degree of freedom which with certain features of a specification may be modified interactively by a designer, then the concept of a constraint appears more appropriate. A style, then, consists of a set of relationships, each a tuple of system property and conditions on that property, perhaps modified by a degree of fixedness (here represented by 'must' or 'should', cf. 'glue' in Knuth's TEX box and glue model). In the Macintosh icon example, its style consists of:

Mac icon style =

1. Source must be element of a collection.
2. Representation must be element of a collection.
3. Source must be filing system objects.

4. Representation must have a label representing the name of the source object.
5. Representation must be selectable.
6. Representation should have an image which pictorially represents the source object type.

The first five constraints are easily satisfied if:

1. collection is one of the legal values for the domain type;
2. collection is one of the legal types or classes of representation (e.g. widget);
3. the type of the source objects can be determined;
4. the properties of the objects are known to the system; and
5. selectability is one of the potential behaviours of interaction objects.

Determining if the sixth constraint is satisfied is more difficult. First, the constraint specifies a 'should have' relationship between the attribute and its value. Second, it may be impossible, in the absence of a knowledge-base which holds information about the representational properties of images, for the system to tell if a given image is representative of a given file object type. Thus, the satisfaction of this constraint may well require input from a designer in the form of an assertion that the constraint has or has not been satisfied. This forces the designer to consider whether other factors influencing the design make necessary the inclusion of pictorial representation of type. The purpose of the constraint is to guarantee that the decision is made.

Constraint satisfaction occurs at different points in the process of specification. Thus, the constraint on representation type (i.e. element of a collection) will require satisfaction when an attempt is made to change the type of the representation, typically by restricting the choices available to the designer. The constraint on the label attribute of iconic elements must be satisfied when an instance of the specification is linked to a source domain and the name of source domain entities is mapped onto iconic elements.

The degree of fixedness of a style is modelled in the notion of style application permissions. When a designer applies a style to a specification, she may state whether that style may be removed from the specification or relaxed (temporarily made inactive). Styles which can be neither removed nor relaxed constitute the 'givens' of a design, beyond the control of the designer to modify, perhaps because of project requirements which cannot be negotiated. Relaxable constraints represent those which are a central feature of the design, but may be 'traded off' against other features. Removable constraints are those which are part of the current design hypothesis, available for retraction if evaluation shows they are not desirable.

5.4 The Structures of Styles and Constraint Satisfaction

Styles may be placed in an inheritance hierarchy, such that styles inherit and possibly override the constraints of their parent. While useful in providing a structure for styles themselves, there are problems with this approach.

As demonstrated earlier, one specification may exhibit, or possess, a number of different styles. If styles were structured in a single hierarchy, this would result in redundant constraints being applied. The constraint satisfaction mechanism must be able to remove such redundancies. More seriously, it is possible that inconsistent or mutually unsatisfiable constraints be applied to a specification. The constraint satisfaction mechanism must be able to handle such cases. Alternative techniques include disallowing more than one constraint applicable to the same attribute for the same relationship type (pre-emptive) or determining constraint conflicts and asking the designer to 'relax' constraints until satisfaction is possible (interactive).

5.5 Assistance with Style Application

We suggested at the beginning of this paper that the application of styles to a computer-based artifact or design can be difficult. Without assistance, making document headings follow a consistent style requires wasteful repetition. Complex sets of style rules, such as in corporate styles, can be difficult to apply without inconsistencies and oversights. Finally, some styles are abstract and thus likely to be overlooked, as with the semantic consistency style of Macintosh menus.

There are three types of style-oriented assistance which can be offered by a computer based tool:

Automatic style application: The style facilities in word processors provide automatic style application. Some UIMSs have automatic style application systems, such as DON in the UIDE (Kim & Foley, 1990), and some automated visualization systems (Mackinlay, 1986; Casner, 1991) use rules analogous to style rules. In all of these systems, the rules which can be specified are limited in terms of domain and in what can be specified within those domains. For example, none allow for applications or their component structures to exhibit different styles. Also, the style rules which can be expressed are only those which can be dealt with automatically. There is no provision for style rules which go beyond computer-based semantics to include design constraints which require some designer intervention.

Critiquing: If styles exist as a set of assertions expressed in a well-formed language, it is possible for a system to examine them for consistency and completeness. Although design critiquing systems currently exist (Malinowski & Nakakoji, 1995), their rules do not incorporate the notion of style as elaborated here.

Design space management: A tool which supports style as we have defined it would be able to hold design-significant information about those styles. For example, it would be possible to link styles which are related to one another by history (they have been used together in the past), design rationale (they share a design justification), domain of application (e.g. they have been previously applied to model geographic information). Furthermore, such a system could maintain a record of the design constraints which require designer input for resolution, reminding the designer of any such constraints not yet dealt with. No existing system offers such services.

6 Conclusions

This paper has analysed the apparently disparate uses of the word 'style', and combined this with considering the varying degrees of fixedness of design decisions to arrive at proposed requirements for a design support tool. Such a tool would be a general style definition facility, allowing designers to make and record decisions early on (as styles) that have a high degree of fixedness given the requirements (including implicit and general requirements such as 'implement in X Windows', 'make the corporate identity visible', 'obey house style guidelines'). These decisions may be implemented early or late in existing design environments (e.g. corporate logos fitted in late on), but in fact are logically fixed from the outset and so should be dealt with early to avoid wasteful backtracking (e.g. having to redesign the page layout to make room for a logo whose presence was in fact predictable).

These requirements suggest significant limitations in what is currently available. Current facilities mainly revolve around what is easy to implement (e.g. word processor styles) or fixed UIDE architectures (e.g. X widgets) or support for design justifications. They do not, we have argued, correspond to the decisions designers actually have to fix, and therefore wish to record, at the early stage corresponding to designing a 'style'. However, by drawing on the mechanisms for constraint resolution including prompting the designer through structured judgements where these cannot be automated, a much more advanced facility could be implemented.

Such a design tool must benefit the designer by allowing and supporting a better ordering of design decisions that corresponds more nearly to the order of fixedness of decisions given the requirements, however heterogeneous those decisions are. Benefits to the end user will be limited inevitably by our understanding of what really matters to users. Styles for designers correspond to consistency for users; both refer to the issue of similarity across different designs, but not all similarities turn out to benefit user performance. While the work on Task Action Grammar (Payne & Green, 1986) has demonstrated some of the issues that matter to users, Grudin (1989) shows that not all kinds of 'consistency' do benefit users. However, as we learn more about the relationship of consistency to user performance, we will have an even greater need for tools such as we propose with which designers can directly and re-usably express these as constraints on design.

Acknowledgements

We wish to thank Dr David England and Dr Kevin Waite, who offered useful comments on an earlier draft of this paper.

References

Apple Computer Inc (1986), *Human Interface Guidelines: The Apple Desktop Interface.*

AT&T (1990), *AT&T Open Look Graphical User Interface Style Guide.*

Casner, S. M. (1991), "A Task Analytic Approach to the Automated Design of Graphic Presentations", *ACM Transactions on Graphics* **10**(2), 111–151.

Davison, A., Drake, K., Roberts, W. & Slater, M. (1992), *Distributed Window Systems*, Addison–Wesley.

Foley, J., Kim, W. C., Kovacevic, S. & Murray, K. (1989), "Defining Interfaces at a High Level of Abstraction", *IEEE Software* **6**(1), 25–32.

Grudin, J. (1989), "The Case Against User Interface Consistency", *Communications of the ACM* **32**(10), 1164–1173.

Kim, W. C. & Foley, J. (1990), DON: User Interface Presentation Design Assistant, *in* "Proceedings of the ACM Symposium on User Interface Software and Technology, UIST'90", ACM Press, pp.10–20.

Leler, W. (1988), *Constraint Programming Languages: Their Specification and Generation*, Addison–Wesley.

Mackinlay, J. (1986), "Automating the Design of Graphical Presentations of Relational Information", *ACM Transactions on Graphics* **5**(2), 110–141.

MacLean, A., Young, R. M., Bellotti, V. M. E. & Moran, T. P. (1991), "Questions, Options and Criteria: Elements of Design Space Analysis", *Human–Computer Interaction* **6**(3–4), 201–250.

Mahony, K. & Gower, A. (1991), The Development of a Visual Style for a BT X Window System Toolkit, *in* D. Diaper & N. Hammond (eds.), "People and Computers VI: Usability Now! (Proceedings of HCI'91)", Cambridge University Press, pp.265–279.

Malinowski, U. & Nakakoji, K. (1995), Using Computational Critics to Facilitate Long-term Collaboration in User Interface Design, *in* I. Katz, R. Mack, L. Marks, M. B. Rosson & J. Nielsen (eds.), "Proceedings of CHI'95: Human Factors in Computing Systems", ACM Press, pp.385–392.

Newman, W. (1988), The Representation of User Interface Style, *in* D. M. Jones & R. Winder (eds.), "People and Computers IV (Proceedings of HCI'88)", Cambridge University Press, pp.123–137.

Olsen, Jr, D. R. (1992), *User Interface Management Systems: Models and Algorithms*, Morgan-Kaufmann.

Payne, S. & Green, T. (1986), "Task Action Grammars: A Model of the Mental Representation of Task Languages", *Human–Computer Interaction* **2**(2), 93–133.

Shneiderman, B. (1992), *Designing the User Interface*, 2nd edition, Addison–Wesley.

Smith, S. L. & Mosier, J. N. (1986), Guidelines for Designing User Interface Software, Technical Report MTR-10090, EDS-TR-86-278, The Mitre Corporation.

Szekely, P., Ping, L. & Neches, R. (1992), Facilitating the Exploration of Interface Design Alternatives: The HUMANOID Model of Interface Design, *in* P. Bauersfeld, J. Bennett & G. Lynch (eds.), "Proceedings of CHI'92: Human Factors in Computing Systems", ACM Press, pp.507–515.

Szekely, P., Sukaviriya, P., Castells, P., Muthukumarasamy, J. & Salcher, E. (1996), Declarative Interface Models for User Interface Construction Tools: The MASTERMIND Approach, *in* L. Bass & C. Unger (eds.), "Engineering for Human–Computer Interaction: Proceedings of the IFIP TC2/WG2.7 Working Conference on Engineering for Human–Computer Interaction", Chapman & Hall, pp.120–150.

Developing University Courses to Enable Students to Specify and Solve Human–Computer Interaction Design Problems

M Andrew Life & John Long

Ergonomics and HCI Unit, University College London, 26 Bedford Way, London WC1H 0AP, UK

Tel: *+44 171 380 7777 ext.5318*

Fax: *+44 171 580 1100*

EMail: *a.life@ucl.ac.uk*

Aspiring practitioners must be taught to specify and to solve discipline problems. We begin by considering the gap between HCI research and system development, but particularly as it relates to teaching. The gap manifests itself through the dissatisfaction many system developers express with the adequacy of HCI teaching. We next suggest that one reason for the gap lies in the current tendency to teach HCI as a multidisciplinary applied science subject. This tendency results in incomplete and incoherent coverage, not well-suited to the needs of system development. We suggest that a top-down approach to the subject and stronger design orientation should ameliorate some of the weaknesses. We utilize a conception of HCI as a framework for specifying more effective HCI courses. We report the development of a course in the Human Factors of HCI which has exploited the conception, and we informally evaluate the conception as a partial solution to current inadequacies in HCI teaching.

Keywords: education, design problems, syllabi, HCI curricula.

1 Introduction

Disciplines, including Human–Computer Interaction (HCI), consist of knowledge supporting practices which solve general problems (Long & Dowell, 1989). A discipline thus requires knowledge to be acquired which can be applied by practitioners to solve problems within the scope of the discipline. In the case of HCI, such knowledge is being acquired through research and, less formally, through the description of successful system development practice. Some have argued that knowledge is further embodied in the artefacts.

HCI knowledge is applied to solve user interface design problems. Such application is facilitated if the knowledge is expressed in a conception which makes explicit the design problems of practitioners. A conception has been proposed by Dowell & Long (1989). The conception provides a framework within which to reason about the implications of designs for system performance. The framework is concordant with the trend towards design, discernible in recent HCI research. It is further compatible with notions of top-down design, fundamental to software engineering practice.

2 Teaching and the HCI Research and Development Gap

2.1 An Assessment of Current HCI Education

Teaching is one means by which practitioners learn to specify discipline problems. It is also a means by which they acquire knowledge to enable the problems to be solved. Teaching must meet the needs of practitioners with respect to research (i.e. to ensure dissemination of new knowledge and to teach research methods); and of practitioners who are directly concerned with the solution of discipline problems (i.e. to teach them to solve design problems).

These needs have been recognized by HCI. Government and other initiatives, both in the UK and abroad, have long accepted the importance of training programmes to educate HCI professionals. For example, the UK government, under the Alvey Initiative, predicted a progressive increase in industry's requirements for specialists in user interface development and recommended support for its inclusion in university courses (Alpar, 1986). Some funding for training was forthcoming under the initiative of the UK joint research councils in Cognitive Science and HCI (Pollitzer, 1994). In the USA, the Special Interest Group in Computer-Human Interaction of the Association for Computing Machinery (ACM) established a curriculum working group to identify HCI teaching needs and to propose curricula to meet those needs — published by ACM (1991). The British Computer Society established a similar working group to address the equivalent issue in the UK (Preece, 1991). More recently, the US. National Science Foundation recommended support for a closer relationship between academia and industry in the training of graduates, specifically with respect to user interface development (Strong, 1994).

The need for training in HCI dates back almost a decade. However, the re-expression of the same needs suggests that those engaged in such training are failing in its delivery. This failure is increasingly voiced by the system development community; e.g. at a 1994 CHI Conference panel; and at industrial workshops organized by the BCS HCI Curriculum Working Group (Life et al., 1995). A common complaint is that new graduates in software engineering and HCI lack the knowledge and skills which enable them to engage in user interface development early in their careers. It is suggested that graduates' knowledge is too academic and not oriented to practical problem solving.

One interpretation of the dissatisfaction of employers of HCI professionals is that it is a manifestation of a research and development gap. Just as researchers are now recognizing a need to orient towards design, so teachers of HCI similarly need to enable students to engage explicitly with design problems. In the next section, we explore the proposition that HCI teaching is currently not well-suited to the solution of user interface design problems and identify possible reasons why this should be so.

2.2 Reasons for the R&D Gap

HCI is accepted as being multidisciplinary; see, for example, (Long, 1987). Long & Dowell (1989) have further distinguished three conceptions of HCI — *craft, applied science* and *engineering* — arguing that current practice bears the characteristics of a craft, with some recruitment from applied behavioural sciences. Most current undergraduate and postgraduate textbooks – e.g. (Booth, 1989; Dix et al., 1993; Johnson, 1992; Preece et al., 1994) project HCI as a multidisciplinary subject with a strong applied science orientation. For example, all include introductory chapters on human experimental psychology for subsequent reference.

The multidisciplinary applied science model is evident in conceptualizations of HCI intended to support the planning of educational courses; for example, the frequently cited ACM SIGCHI framework (ACM, 1991). In this framework, knowledge of HCI is partitioned into six topic areas:

- The nature of HCI.
- Use and context of computers.
- Human characteristics.
- Computer system and interface architecture.
- Development process.
- Project presentations and case studies.

Each of these areas is decomposed into sub-topics, e.g. *Human characteristics*:

- Human information processing.
- Language, communication, interaction.
- Ergonomics.

Decomposition of these sub-topics enables the scoping of individual lectures.

The framework is intended to specify courses for a variety of needs. Courses may be specified for computer science undergraduates; for psychologists wishing to specialize in human interaction with computers; and for non-technical professionals (e.g. managers) whose work may involve user interface development. The objectives of each course are reflected in weightings of the topics and sub-topics in the framework. Thus, a course for computer scientists will have a smaller weighting on *human characteristics* and more on *computer system and interface architecture* than the course for psychologists.

The multidisciplinary applied science model of HCI is not an unreasonable one — it is a reflection of the way that HCI has emerged from the conjoint interests of software engineers and ergonomists / human factors engineers. Applied science provides one framework for the processes of validation and generalization of knowledge. The ACM framework, in particular, has proved a useful organizer for those planning HCI courses or writing textbooks for courses — e.g. (Preece et al., 1994), and non-USA educationalists have adapted it to suit their local conditions — e.g. in Sweden — (Löwgren & Holmberg, 1993).

However, an applied science conception encourages a view of the discipline as one concerned with analysis and understanding of systems, rather than with their design. For example, the ACM framework tends to emphasize the individual elements of human-computer systems, but it seems to leave implicit the critical interaction between them. Furthermore, while its coverage of the development process includes *example systems and case studies*, there is no address of the domains in which systems operate. Hence, there is no foundation for reasoning about the implications of alternative designs for task performance. Of course, in using the ACM framework, course organizers will bridge the gap to design. However, the absence of reference to such topics leaves open the possibility that students will be taught about the components of interactive systems, but not about designing them as a whole.

The centrality of applied science in HCI teaching, in the absence of a complete and coherent view of human computer interactions, may give rise to some of the shortcomings in education and training. The applied science conception risks being incomplete. It provides no basis for reasoning about the effectiveness of alternative system design solutions. It risks being incoherent, because applied science disciplines do not share the same terminology and conceptualization of their concerns (e.g. notions of performance in course components of organizational behaviour, applied experimental psychology, physiology and biomechanics). Finally, the applied science conception risks being unfit for purpose, being oriented to the (scientific) explanation and prediction of human behaviour rather than to diagnosis and prescription of effective user interface designs.

3 Requirements for HCI Courses which Bridge the R&D Gap

Earlier, we identified a gap between research in HCI and system development. We suggested that a trend was emerging towards design as a means of bridging the gap. The analogous gap between the knowledge taught to students in HCI and the needs of system developers might similarly be bridged by teaching students to specify and solve design problems with the support of HCI knowledge. In effect, this bridging means moving the focus from the teaching of applied science knowledge to design. A further interpretation of the failure of HCI education to meet the needs of system developers might lie in the incompatibility of the current bottom-up emphasis in the teaching of HCI with software engineering design practices, which are essentially top-down. New graduates may be unable to apply the HCI knowledge they have acquired, because it is poorly suited for application in the context of software design methods. A top-down conception of human factors should enhance the uptake of human factors knowledge in system development.

Although not oriented towards teaching courses, various conceptualizations of HCI have been advanced with claims of completeness, coherence and design-orientation — e.g. (Storrs, 1989; Dowell & Long, 1989; Gaines & Shaw, 1986). We selected the conceptualization of Dowell & Long on the grounds of its apparent adequate scope and coherence. Further, the conception is compatible with a top-down approach to design.

The next section shows how the conception has been adapted to the needs of HCI course design. We then describe the specification of a course using the conception, and its implementation as a teaching programme.

4 Using the Conception to Design HCI Courses

4.1 The Conception as a Framework for Syllabus Design

Dowell & Long (1989) express the problem of human-computer system development as to design the interacting behaviours of computers and users such that they support desired performance. The user and computer are conceptualized as an *interactive work-system* (IWS) which conducts work in a domain. The objective of the IWS is to transform the attributes of objects in the *domain*. Performance is an expression of the extent to which the desired changes in the domain are achieved (*task quality*) and of the resource costs incurred by the IWS in so doing (*computer costs* and *user costs*). The *behaviours* of the user and computer are conceptualized as being supported by their respective *structures*.

Dowell & Long (1989) distinguish two sub-disciplines of HCI. Human factors (HF) seeks to solve the design problem with respect to the user. Human factors may be contrasted with computer factors — more usually termed software engineering — which solves the design problem with respect to the computer. In practice, the two sub-disciplines of HCI are not independent. However, the distinction reflects the activities and knowledge of different HCI practitioners.

The solution of discipline problems is supported by discipline *practice*. This procedure recruits: *declarative knowledge* of IWS behaviour and of its optimization (the 'what' of good design); and *methodological knowledge* of techniques for solving the problem in line with declarative knowledge (the 'how' of good design). A course in HCI should provide students with such knowledge to solve HCI design problems or to carry out research to extend knowledge.

4.2 Use of the Conception to Develop the UL HF/HCI Syllabus

4.2.1 Specifying the Syllabus

The University of London has offered an intercollegiate Masters course in Ergonomics since the 1960s. During the 1980s it became evident that:

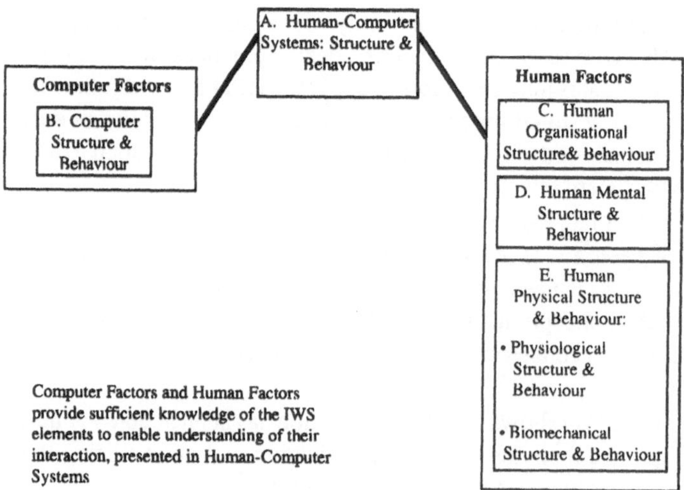

Figure 1: University of London MSc course in Human Factors of HCI.

1. many students were subsequently pursuing careers in HCI; and
2. the knowledge of HCI was growing rapidly and could no longer be adequately covered in a general ergonomics course.

We therefore decided to offer alternative options to students: a *General Ergonomics* option or a new *HCI* option. The HCI option extends only to the HF subdiscipline of HCI (hence, HF/HCI).

The course attempts to provide students with knowledge enabling them to address general problems of HCI, in careers in which they practise either research (i.e. acquiring knowledge); or application (i.e. using knowledge to solve design problems). The course has three major components: *Human–Computer Systems: Structure and Behaviour; Human Factors; and Computer Factors*. Their relationships are shown in Figure 1.

Central is the component *Human–Computer Systems: Structure and Behaviour*. Students are taught a systems approach to the analysis of the interaction between people and computers to perform work effectively and to the design of such systems. However, knowledge is required of the separate system elements (i.e. humans and computers). The course provides this knowledge.

Although the orientation is HF, students require sufficient knowledge of computer behaviour and of software engineering methods to enable them to understand technological constraints on design and to co-operate with engineers in product development. This knowledge is offered in *Computer Structure and Behaviour*.

The technological component is complemented by *human factors* concerned with human structure and behaviour, both physical and mental. It contains three subcomponents. *Human Physical Structure and Behaviour* includes both *Biomechanical* and *Physiological Structure and Behaviour*. The constitution and operation of work organizations is covered in *Human Organizational Structure and Behaviour*. *Human Mental Structure and Behaviour* lies in the domain of human experimental psychology.

Each component provides the student with three types of knowledge with which to address the design problems:

1. Declarative design knowledge of the structure and behaviour of human–machine systems and their elements;

2. Knowledge of techniques and methods supporting the practice of HF/HCI (methodological knowledge);

3. Knowledge of the application of (1) and (2) in HF/HCI research and product (system) development.

The content of each component of the course is summarized in the Appendix.

4.2.2 Implementing the Course

The HF/HCI option consists of a year of full-time study. Thirty weeks are spent on a taught programme (including written examinations) and 12 weeks on an individual project.

Although the conception maintains a design orientation, students only acquire the ability to solve design problems if they practise the application of the knowledge taught. To this end, *Human-Computer Systems: Structure and Behaviour*, in particular, has been designed so that knowledge is supported either by live demonstrations or by video examples of user interface design problems. In each lecture, students undertake exercises in which they analyse problems (e.g. of a user in a video extract of an interaction); or attempt to solve them using the methods taught (e.g. a task analysis to support design of a computerized route-finder).

The top-down approach to design predominates in the teaching. However, much current HCI practice has the characteristics of craft and applied science. The techniques taught therefore range from the application of user interface guidelines and design heuristics through human factors structured analysis and design methods, to semi-formal approaches to the analysis and design of interaction behaviour.

The classroom-based lectures are supplemented by visits to industrial and governmental organizations engaged in user interface research and/or development, ranging from nuclear power station control rooms, through aircraft cockpit systems, to office and home-based systems. Visits have associated with them fieldwork exercises, so helping to maintain a problem-solving focus. Where industrial visits are not feasible, practitioners are invited to describe their work in case studies.

A criticism of HCI teaching by system developers — e.g. (Strong, 1994) is that students are not exposed to problems of the complexity encountered in the commercial world. Limited time and resources makes such exposure difficult. However, the HF/HCI course culminates in a design exercise in which students undertake a 5-day role playing exercise in which, under simulated commercial conditions, they develop a user interface from the requirements specification, through design, prototype implementation, evaluation, redesign and presentation of their work. Examples of projects include interfaces for: video and compact disc programming; portable computerized street navigation; home energy management; and computerized rail travel planning. Students are free to recruit the methods they see fit, although lecturer supervision is provided. Most students employ top-down techniques prior to the implementation of their prototypes, recruiting notations such as structured diagrams and data flow diagrams.

At the end of their course (standard in UK Masters programmes), students undertake a 3 month project. They demonstrate either the generation of HCI knowledge through research, or its application in system development. While the project is unlikely to reproduce commercial system development, application-oriented projects expose students to realistic design problems. They force them to deal with pragmatic constraints which they will encounter in their careers. Such a project is the specification of generic user requirements for interactive public information systems (May, 1993), which used an analytic model to reason about compatibility between computer and user representations of the domain. Some students undertake their projects under joint supervision of commercial software developers; for example, specifying, implementing and testing prototype software to support health and safety professionals in assessing manual handling problems in the workplace (Ralph & Life, 1994). This student employed a structured evaluation method to specify prototypes. Both these examples illustrate the orientation to design and a strategy of top-down development.

Although the design focus is most evident in application projects, it is also reflected in research projects. For example, a study of formal software specification languages (in this case, CSP) to describe the behaviour of human–computer systems (Stork, 1992); and a method to enable software designers to select appropriate user interface prototyping tools (Middlemass, 1993). In these cases, the work is seeking to enhance software development, with emphasis on the design process.

5 Evaluation of the Conception as a Basis for Course Development

5.1 Adequacy of the Conception for Course Specification

The use of the conception for HCI course specification was rationalized on the grounds of coherence, completeness and fitness for purpose in teaching. Coherence has been achieved at a high level by the relations between the device (computer or other machine) and the user in the work-system, and by interaction prescription through knowledge of the structure and behaviour of the components individually. At a lower level, coherence is maintained through the technical properties of the conception. For example, evaluation criteria such as usability, ease of use, fatigue etc. may all be re-expressed in terms of the fundamental concepts of task quality and user resource costs. The generality of the notions of IWS and domain, and of performance, meets the criterion of completeness in the conception. Few significant concepts of HCI cannot be accommodated.

The conception has oriented the syllabus towards teaching students to address design problems. Although the applied sciences continue to be taught (particularly as concerns human structure and behaviour) coverage is better oriented to HCI, and students better appreciate their relevance. In summary, the experience of the University of London HF/HCI option course suggests that the programme has not only benefited from the completeness and coherence of the conception, but it has also achieved an enhanced fitness for purpose, as evidenced by students' success in addressing design problems.

Although generally successful, some problems remain. The conception fails to accommodate directly a small number of topics which are becoming recognized as important for students. The conception is primarily oriented towards IWSs comprising single users, but computer supported co-operative work, involving networked machines, is of increasing interest. Although multi-machine and multi-user IWSs can be expressed within the conception, that expression requires refinement.

The conception is further restricted to the technical knowledge of HCI. With user interface tools reducing technical obstacles to development, knowledge of aesthetic aspects of design may become important (Card, 1993). Universities are also placing increasing emphasis on the teaching of *transferable* skills, such as verbal communication; presentation and project management. Such topics are implicit in the conception, being pre-requisites to the students successfully undertaking and presenting their practical work. These limitations of the conception are insufficient to warrant changes at this time; although some might be necessary in the longer term.

5.2 Adequacy of the Course Implementation

The practical orientation of the course appears to go some way towards addressing the complaint from employers that new graduates are not equipped with knowledge and experience to meet the demands of system development at the outset of their careers. It must be acknowledged that the relatively large proportion of practical work inevitably increases the need for teacher supervision and assessment. Where possible, practical exercises are undertaken in small groups, the members of which present their work to the rest of the class. In this way, students develop their critical skills and learn from each other, while incidentally reducing the demand for marking by teachers. However, some students have indicated that they would prefer a still greater opportunity to practise techniques (particularly more advanced prototyping and structured user interface development methods). At present, the main limitations remain those of time and teaching resources. An increased practical component might require a reduction of the breadth of the course, although such reduction is currently felt to be undesirable.

Adherence to the conception at the lower levels of teaching implementation varies across course components, partly because of the distribution of teaching across several University schools. At present, the main application of the conception appears in *Human-Computer Systems: Structure and Behaviour*, where it helps students integrate the broad coverage of the course. There is no compulsion on component organizers to use the conception, and some do so selectively.

The course continues to be monitored in the light of the requirements of students (and employers) and developments in the fields of HCI. The conception has since been exploited in the specification of short commercial courses in HCI and of HCI modules for undergraduate and postgraduate computer scientists. It is now becoming evident that the extent to which the underlying conception is made evident to students tends to vary: at least some HCI masters students appear to find an explicit structure an aid to understanding, whereas non-specialists (e.g. undergraduate computer scientists) seem to find the structure unnecessarily abstract for their needs. Courses for the latter students may benefit from the underlying structure remaining transparent to the students. Nevertheless, the use of the conception in course design is judged to have been successful, suggesting potential for further development.

Appendix: Content of the HF/HCI Option Curriculum

A more detailed version of the curriculum is available from the first author on request.

A. Human–Computer Systems: Structure and Behaviour (HCSSB)

i. Foundations of Human Factors

- History.
- Framework.
- General systems theory.
- HCI knowledge as: craft-based heuristics; applied science guidelines; engineering principles.
- Discipline practice as supported by tools, techniques and methods to solve the design problem.
- Domains of work, to illustrate the acquisition of knowledge to support system development and the application of knowledge in practice.
- Future trends and development.

ii. Human–Machine Systems

Human–Machine Systems — General Principles

- Analysing human-machine system behaviour.
- Complex control tasks.

Human–Computer Systems — Structure and Behaviour

- Input–Output behaviour:
  - I/O level models of interaction.
  - Constraints on I/O device selection.
- Dialogue styles and communication styles:
  - Options for dialogue implementation.
  - Models of interaction.
  - Constraints on choice of dialogue style (e.g. task and user factors).

Task Determinants of Behaviour

- Models of Computer-based Tasks:
  - Structural models.
  - Behavioural models.
  - Models of computer users.
  - Computer support for complex tasks.

Organizational Constraints on System Behaviour

- Impact of alternative system implementations.
- Current developments.

iii. HCI Methods

System Representation Methods

- Analytic models (including the strengths and limitations of analytic approaches).
- Simulation models/prototypes.
- Simulation theory as it relates to HCI.

Methods For User Interface Development

- Types of development methods:
  - Formal methods.
  - Structured methods.

  - Prototyping.
- Task analytic methods:
  - Task analysis for specifying user requirements.
  - Task analysis for design.
  - Task analysis for evaluation.
- Empirical methods:
  - Field observation, including video protocol analysis.
  - Empirical evaluation methods, including walkthroughs, experiments and interview and questionnaire techniques.

iv. Practical exercises

Students participate in short class exercises in the use of analytic and empirical HCI methods in design and evaluation. Use of these methods is further practised in broader exercises requiring students to undertake the development (i.e. performance setting, design, implementation and evaluation) of user interfaces for small-scale human-computer systems.

B. Computer Structure and Behaviour (CSB)

i. Computer Structure and Behaviour

Basic principles of computing:

- Background:
  - Data and knowledge structures.
  - Basic data processing.
  - Programming languages.
- Application:
  - Principles of computer architecture.
  - Illustrations of the distinctions between: applications programs; operating systems; database systems; communication systems.

User Interface Technology

- I/O devices:
  - Character-based data entry.
  - Graphical interaction.
  - Speech interaction.
- Implementations of user-computer dialogue.
  - Commands, menus, object-oriented interfaces, window-based interfaces.
  - Graphics.
  - Interface metaphors/workspace models.
  - Window management systems.
  - UIMS; toolkits.
  - Hypermedia.

ii. Software Engineering Methods

Alternative Strategies in System Development

- Requirements for a discipline of software engineering.
- Waterfall model of development.
- Evolutionary model.

Methods for System Development

- Formal methods.
- Structured methods.
- Object-oriented system development.

Programming

- Prototyping tools.

Software evaluation

- Quality assurance.
- Software validation.
- Software verification.

iii. Practical exercises

Students undertake small-scale exercises in user requirements specification and design using SE methods. Students are also taught to use a high level programming language (HyperTalk), enabling them to implement simple user interface prototypes. Methods taught in the CSB course are also exploited in practical work for the HCSSB course.

C. Human Organizational Structure and Behaviour (HOSB)

i. Organizational Structure and Behaviour

Organizations as systems

Organizational sub-systems

- The individual within the organization.
- Working groups: structure, behaviour and performance.
- Human computer sub-systems:
  - Impacts of IT on system/sub-system performance:
    - Political impacts.
    - Accidents/human error.

ii. Methods Addressing Organizational Factors

Methods for Organizational Analysis

- e.g. Soft Systems Method — Checkland.

Methods for Organizational Evaluation

- e.g. role of management consultants; client–consultant relationship.

Methods for Organizational Design

- Including change (e.g. job design; personnel selection and training methods; management of change.

iii. Practical Exercises

Students undertake small-scale exercises (either investigating local organizational issues or by role playing exercises). These issues would also be expected to arise in system design exercises conducted within other courses (e.g. in HCSSB).

D. Human Mental Structure and Behaviour (HMSB)

i. Mental Structure and Behaviour

Systemic Factors and Processes

- Vigilance.
- Fatigue.
- Mental workload.
- Circadian rhythms.
- Stress.
- Life span development processes.
- Individual differences.

Mental Processes

- Input processes (vision, hearing, other sensory processes).
- Output processes (manual, vocal, other effector processes).
- Central processes (memory, communication, decision-making).
- Human knowledge representation (classes of knowledge, mental models).

Task Related Behaviour

- Motor behaviour.
- Representations of task knowledge (users' models, expert knowledge).
- Planning.
- Problem solving.
- Communication (textual, graphical, interpersonal, human-computer).

ii. Psychological Research Methods Applicable to HCI

- Video analysis.
- Questionnaire design.
- Human performance measurement.

iii. Empirical Research: Design and Interpretation

Research Design

- Methods for empirical research (e.g. observation; survey; experimentation).
- Process and product of experimental design (including ethical considerations).

Statistical Interpretation

- Descriptive statistics
- Inferential statistics
- Correlation

Interpretation in Complex Experimental Designs

- ANOVA.
- A priori and post hoc means comparisons.
- Non parametric techniques.

Survey Methods

iv. Practical Application of Psychological Knowledge

Students gain an insight into practical issues by means of demonstrations (e.g. of video analysis) and practical exercises based on visits (e.g. Air Traffic Control). Methods taught in HMSB are further exploited in practical work for the HCSSB course and in the practical research project.

E. Human Physical Structure and Behaviour (HPSB)

i. Human physical structure and behaviour

Human Physical Structure

- Musculo-skeletal structure.
- Anthropometrics.

Human Physical Behaviour

- Systemic behaviour (i.e. behaviours of the whole body):
  - Physical work.
  - Physiological issues.
  - Biomechanical issues.
  - Musculo-skeletal disorders.
  - Sleep.
  - Circadian rhythms.
  - Stress.
  - Thermo-regulation.
- Sub-systemic behaviour:
  - Upper limb structure and function.
  - Seated posture.

ii. Methods for the Design of the Physical Workspace

Requirements specification:

- Use of anthropometric data.

Design

- Anthropometric data as a basis for computer hardware design.
- Standards/guidelines for design of the physical working environment.

Evaluation

- Postural comfort assessment.
- Environmental measurement techniques.

iii. Practical Design and Evaluation of the Physical Workspace

Students undertake practical exercises in the design of the workspaces using anthropometric and biomechanical data, and in the measurement of the environmental conditions of the workplace. Students are taught to identify situations requiring the involvement of specialists in biomechanics and applied human physiology.

HF/HCI Practice

The course offers students substantive and methodological knowledge to support the practice of HCI research or of user-interface development. It is therefore necessary for students to be:

- exposed to examples of practice; and
- engaged in practice themselves.

All components of the course include illustrative examples drawn from practice and also practical exercises. However, students are given opportunities to integrate the knowledge acquired in the other components and to apply it in practical situations.

Coursework

Visits and Fieldwork

Group visits to industrial and research centres take place throughout the course, as do fieldwork exercises. The visits and field exercises are followed up by discussions, class presentations or written reports.

Case studies

The case study represents an important part of the teaching, by which the practice of HCI is illustrated and the use of HF/HCI techniques demonstrated. Speakers are invited from outside centres (industrial, research and academic) to discuss work in which they have been involved, or to review an area of interest.

Evaluation exercises

Students conduct HCI evaluations of implemented software.

Development exercise

Students undertake a 5-day exercise in groups of three, involving the development of a user interface from requirements capture, through implementation in HyperTalk, to final evaluation.

Project

Each student is required to undertake a practical project under the general supervision of University staff.

References

ACM (1991), "ACM SIGCHI Curricula for Human Computer Interaction". Report of the Association of Computing Machinery.

Alpar, S. A. (1986), "Human Interface Aspects of Man–Machine Interaction in Higher Education". The Alvey Directorate.

Booth, P. (1989), *An Introduction to Human–Computer Interaction*, Lawrence Erlbaum Associates.

Card, S. K. (1993), Presentation at INTERCHI'93 Workshop on HCI Teaching.

Dix, A., Finlay, J., Abowd, G. & Beale, R. (1993), *Human–Computer Interaction*, Prentice-Hall International.

Dowell, J. & Long, J. (1989), "Towards a Conception for an Engineering Discipline of Human Factors", *Ergonomics* **32**(11), 1513–1535.

Gaines, B. R. & Shaw, M. L. G. (1986), "Foundations of Dialog Engineering: The Development of Human–Computer Interaction, Part II", *International Journal of Man-Machine Studies* **24**(2), 101–123.

Johnson, P. (1992), *Human–Computer Interaction: Psychology, Task Analysis and Software Engineering*, McGraw-Hill.

Life, M. A., Kirby, M., Istance, H., Hole, L., Crombie, A., Scown, P. & McManus, B. (1995), "HCI Teaching in our Universities: Getting it on the Computer Science Map", *Interfaces* **28**, 3–8.

Long, J. (1987), Cognitive Ergonomics and Human–Computer Interaction, *in* P. Warr (ed.), "Psychology at Work", Harmondsworth (Penguin), pp.73–95.

Long, J. & Dowell, J. (1989), Conceptions of the Discipline of HCI: Craft, Applied Science and Engineering, *in* A. Sutcliffe & L. Macaulay (eds.), "People and Computers V (Proceedings of HCI'89)", Cambridge University Press, pp.9–34.

Löwgren, J. & Holmberg, L. (1993), "Customizing the SIGCHI Curriculum for use in Sweden", *ACM SIGCHI Bulletin* **25**(4), 8–11.

May, A. J. (1993), Development of Generic User Requirements for Interactive Public Information Systems, Master's thesis, Ergonomics and HCI Unit, University of London.

Middlemass, J. R. (1993), Towards a Method to Guide the Production of Specifications to Support User Interface Prototyping Tool Selection, Master's thesis, Ergonomics and HCI Unit, University of London.

Pollitzer, E. (1994), Presentation to workshop on Cognitive Science and HCI, Osaka, Japan.

Preece, J. (1991), "Human–Computer Interaction: What about Teaching and Training?", *Computer Bulletin* **3**(6), 16–17.

Preece, J., Rogers, Y., Sharp, H., Benyon, D., Holland, S. & Carey, T. (1994), *Human–Computer Interaction*, Addison–Wesley.

Ralph, G. & Life, M. A. (1994), Rolling the DiCE: Towards a Manual Handling Assessment System for Non-specialists, *in* N. Adams, N. Coleman & M. Stevenson (eds.), "Proceedings of 30th Annual Conference of the Ergonomics Society of Australia", Ergonomics Society of Australia, pp.4–12.

Stork, J. A. J. (1992), A Formal Description of Worksystem Behaviours and Interactions, Master's thesis, Ergonomics and HCI Unit, University of London.

Storrs, G. (1989), "A Conceptual Model of Human–Computer Interaction?", *Behaviour & Information Technology* **8**(5), 323–334.

Strong, G. W. (1994), "New Directions in Human–Computer Interaction Education, Research and Practice". Report of US National Science Foundation (Planning Grant No.IRI-9322659).

3D or not 3D: Is it Nobler in the Mind?

Alistair Sutcliffe & Uma Patel

Centre for HCI Design, School of Informatics, City University, Northampton Square, London EC1V OHB, UK.

Tel: *+44 171 477 8411*
Fax: *+44 171 477 8859*
EMail: {*A.G.Sutcliffe,U.Patel*}*@city.ac.uk*

A design method for complex visual interfaces in information systems applications is proposed and tested by developing prototype applications using Text, 2D and 3D representations. The 3 prototypes are evaluated in empirical studies to investigate performance differences and patterns of user-system interaction. 3D designs and graphics show some performance advantages but individual differences are important. Systematic design seems to improve the effect of all representational modalities.

Keywords: 3D visualization, visual interfaces, design guidelines, usability.

1 Introduction

Three dimensional visualization has attracted considerable interest for design of complex information displays. A number of innovative 2D and 3D designs have been produced, e.g. Cam Cones (Robertson et al., 1993), Perspective Walls (Mackinlay et al., 1991), Table Lens (Rao & Card, 1994), Starfields (Ahlberg & Shneiderman, 1994) to cite but a few; however, apart from metric based evaluation (Card et al., 1994) and a preliminary report of usability of Semnet in which disorientation problems were found (Fairchild et al., 1988), little is known about the cognitive functioning of these interfaces. Indeed, there is little data and few criteria for assessing the effectiveness and usability of 3D interfaces over 2D designs. With the growth in virtual reality, understanding the usability of 3D representations will be critical for design.

Another problem is the lack of methodology or rationale for designing complex visualization of information spaces. Semnet used metrics of semantic relatedness to determine node clustering (Fairchild et al., 1988); other design approaches imply mapping to category hierarchies e.g. Information Visualizer designs (Robertson et al., 1993); or layouts driven from attribute values for 2D scatter plots in Starfield displays (Ahlberg & Shneiderman, 1994); or sort order in the Table Lens (Rao & Card, 1994), and hierarchy with connectivity in 3D butterfly displays (Mackinlay et al., 1995). However the designer's rationale is hidden in these exemplars giving practitioners no guidance for matching their information space to these template designs. A systematic method is necessary to map information requirements to visualization design. This paper reports a preliminary method for developing visual interfaces for information retrieval/browsing applications. The focus is primarily on representation of the information space to help users browse complex information and remember its structure. The method is applied to design of prototype interfaces for a photography information system in 3 representation paradigms, 3D, 2D graphics and formatted text.

The method is validated in an empirical study comparing 3D vs. 2D and text representations. We were interested in investigating how different representation paradigms support learning and comprehension of information spaces i.e. formation of the user's mental model of the information categories and their relationships. Another motivation was to test the hypothesis that graphical representations may be more effective in promoting memory of an image organization and the corresponding underlying information structure (Sutcliffe & Patel, 1993). While image details are not well remembered (Mayes et al., 1988) we hypothesized that well designed visualizations should promote gist memory. If this is so then users should be able to home-in on their required information using spatial cues.

The paper is organized in five sections. First, the design method is described followed by the prototypes and the experimental approach. The next section deals with the experimental results, followed by conclusions and future work.

2 Design Method

The design method followed for all three implementations had five steps:

1. an information model was constructed;
2. this was calibrated with further analysis of task and task related information;
3. design heuristics were used to map the information task model to components of a morphology to create a visualization;
4. structure of the image along side task requirements were used to design manipulation and animation functionality; and
5. presentation of dense connectivity between information instances was visually simplified with views and pre-formulated queries.

These steps will now be described in detail:

1. Construct a data model of information categories using entity-relationship techniques, but extending these to model information groups, e.g. task related instances of attributes and entities for browsing purposes. Hierarchical organization of information is analysed so the resulting data model shows classes as

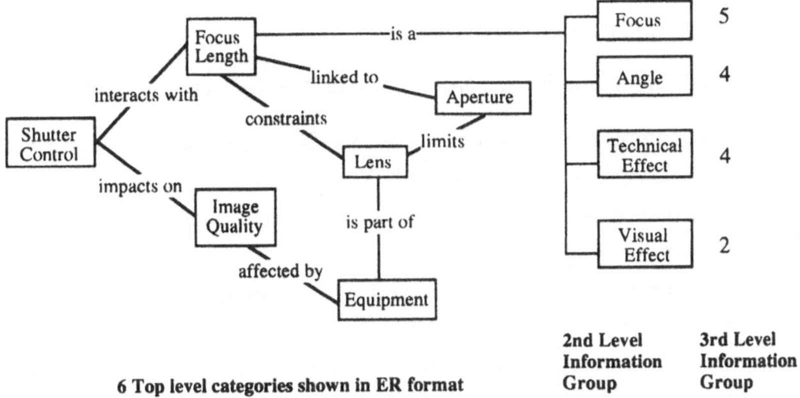

Figure 1: Extended ER model for the Camera domain. Information sub-classes are only shown for the focus entity.

well as entity-relationships. The users' view of information clusters is acquired by asking them to group information related to task goals; e.g. in photography, selecting equipment, analysing lighting conditions, composing shots, etc. Modelling task related entities from the users' viewpoint often results in a different data model than may be created from traditional techniques, as functional clusters of information are identified. For instance in the Camera domain this resulted in identification of an entity 'Image quality' as a cluster of attributes describing an image rather than more traditional entities such as 'film' or 'picture'. This created the data model illustrated in Figure 1.

2. Analyse information paths by taking task related scenarios of information usage. This involved asking questions about information necessary to carry out a task, and produced specifications either of pre-formed queries or hypertext pathways connecting related information. In our case study domain of photography, an example question was "what would you need to know for photographing flowers in close up". This created links between angle of view, zoom lens, depth of field and aperture control. Pre-formed queries were designed for finding all information related to a topic, e.g. getting started, focusing shots, lighting conditions, etc. The results of information path analysis influence relationships within the data model, but placing all paths in the model can create a confusing diagram. This dilemma has to be addressed in the visualization design. Placing more relationships in the image helps the user but adding too many makes the image over complex. Three design options have to be balanced:

   - Using relationship links as explicit paths on the visualization.
   - Making links implicit as hypertext anchors, or providing user-configurable views, i.e. the user can change the visualization so that only links of a specific type are displayed.

- Providing pre-formed queries.

The following heuristics are proposed to help designers assess their options:

- For complex information needs, when several entities have to be accessed, design a pre-formed query.
- When the databases are volatile use pre-formed queries, as hypertext links will be difficult to maintain.
- Select relationships rated by users as being important and essential to the task, for explicit visualization.
- Use hypertext for optional links, paths to additional information which is rated as useful but not essential.
- When different tasks require access to the same database, or different viewpoints can be established, sort relationships into separate sets. These can be implemented as user-selectable views.

The output from this step is a list of information paths and design options.

3. Map information categories to components of a morphology. Morphologies are sets of shapes associated with one or more organization metaphor. Design templates are chosen from a morphology library organized by a top level metaphor, e.g. star system, and containing components following the metaphor, (nodes and arc shapes representing galaxies, stars, planets, orbits) with a representational rationale for the visualization. For instance, a hierarchy is expressed by solar system/star cluster/galaxy dimension; semantic relatedness within hierarchical levels is expressed by spatial proximity, while sequential dependencies are expressed by placing information nodes on the same orbit path. Similar rationales are proposed for other visualizations. Mapping heuristics help the designer to select the appropriate visualization and then tailor it to the data model. The first choice is between hierarchical oriented visualizations for class/category information spaces (maps to star systems and many other metaphors), or networks (map to hypertext oriented designs), or list structures (map to Starfields (Ahlberg & Shneiderman, 1994), Table Lens (Rao & Card, 1994), and others). The second choice is to select low level components to represent database items, higher order components for categories, and arcs for paths between information items. The third selection is to mark categories/items which the user considers to be important or good memory cues with salient shapes. For the photography domain we chose carousels with hexagon shapes to visualize the hierarchy of information categories, with a fishing line metaphor to illustrate lower level information groups. The text design was by necessity limited to formatted blocks.

4. Attach manipulations and animations to morphology components. To supplement standard functions provided by the graphics environment, e.g. zoom/pan, manipulations are advisable so users can inspect specific components by 'pull out', 'local magnify' etc. commands. Some manipulations will be provided by

the software environment (e.g. pan, zoom, etc.); however to encourage user exploration and prevent disorientation it is advisable to design manipulations tailored to the chosen morphology. Suggestions for such manipulations are held in the design template library. Manipulations support the user with interactive functionality for exploring and inspecting detail, while more complex implementations may provide decision support. The current set of manipulations within our design library are:

Inspect label: Pointing at a node or link causes a text label to be displayed.

Local explode: Selecting a node causes it to be displayed in magnified form within the perspective of the background image. This is used for browsing higher level components which can be inspected at random without having to change the visualization by zooming.

Local expand: Selecting a node causes the nearest neighbour nodes to be displaced away from it, while the relationships arcs stretch. This manipulation is useful for inspecting complex parts of an image.

Stretch arcs: In this cases a node is selected and may be moved. The arcs follow the node by rubber band effect but each arc may break if it stretched beyond a preset parameter value. This is used for decision support when relationships have a strength weighting, e.g. for finding all the items related to query according to a keyword matching value.

Show views: Different sets of arcs are displayed on a user command.

For the CameraWise design we selected 'inspect label' and 'local explode' manipulations and attached them to composite (information categories) nodes. This is important for encouraging user exploration.

5. Design hypertext anchors and explicit links where necessary. This implements pathways as additional views of the information space, complementing the visualization metaphor. Increased connectivity rapidly impairs readability so subsets of links are organized into views and presented as pre-formed queries. Dynamic links connect answers with pre-formed questions depicting the information and query in context. We employed a 'bird cage' visualization to show this effect in 3D.

3 Prototypes

Three interfaces were developed representing the same information in Text, 2D or 3D graphics for the CameraWise information system on practical photography. The database comprised 121 text and image items, and 96 classifying concepts, organized in three hierarchical levels. At the top level, the information was partitioned into six categories; equipment, lens, image quality, focal length, aperture, and shutter control, each divided into 18 sub-categories. The lowest level consisted of text information. Upper level categories had text based explanations of each term and pre-formed queries were provided, e.g. 'How to get started', also divided into sub-queries.

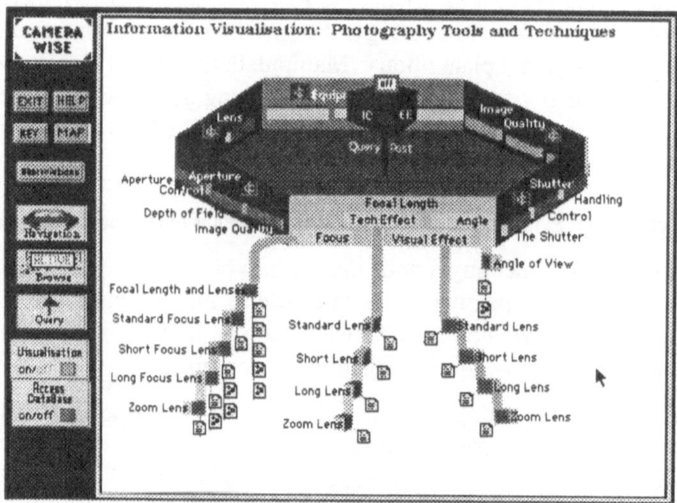

Figure 2: CameraWise-3D browse screen.

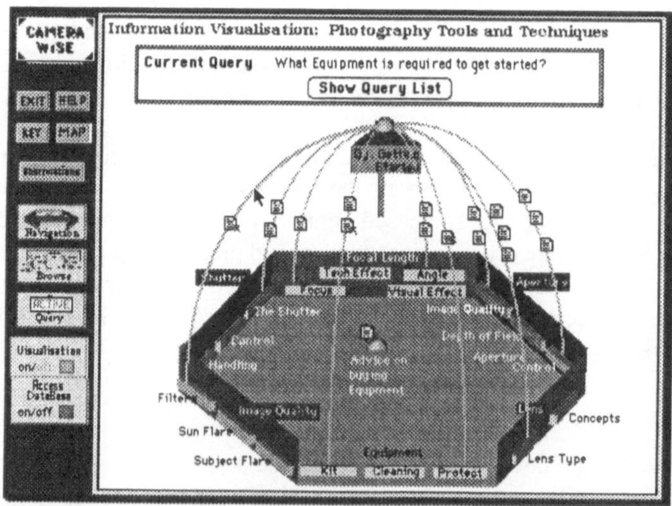

Figure 3: 3D Visualization showing the bird cage metaphor for connecting queries with answers.

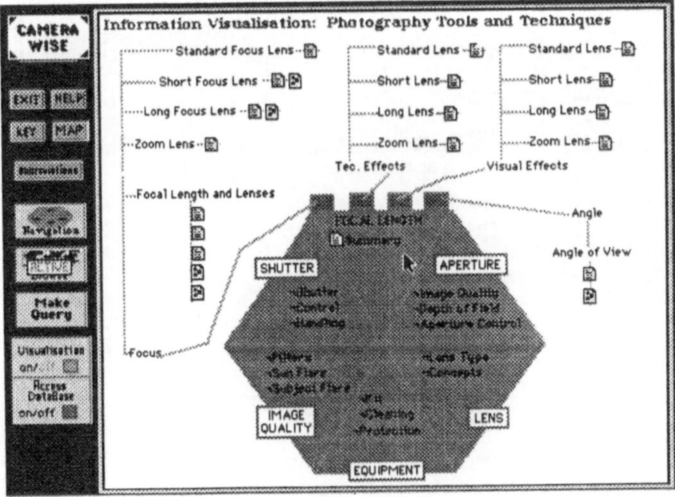

Figure 4: CameraWise-2D browse screen.

Navigation was supported by visible arcs or hypertext links between the six main and 18 sub-categories of information. The three designs were balanced with the same functionality, interface look and feel, and response time. The user interfaces differed in the style of information representation and in image specific manipulations. Visibility and readability were standardized as far as possible across the three conditions by using the same number of windows to represent the information. The three designs were developed on the Macintosh Quadra 900 using MacroMind Director, Swivel-3D and Colour HyperCard. The prototypes were evaluated against usability heuristics (Nielsen, 1993) to ensure that each prototype reached equivalent standard. In the 3D design the top level categories were represented by solid hexagon with sub-category on the hexagon sides. The hexagon could be rotated or tilted and sub-category trees expanding with the fishing line metaphor to show 3rd level data for browsing style inspection (see Figure 2). Buttons on each category node accessed explanatory text. Pre-formed queries were made by selecting the 'query post' in the centre of the hexagon. This connects to the appropriate information categories with a 'bird cage' morphology providing display of results within the context of the overall information structure (see Figure 3). Queries by pointing to level 3 nodes allowed access to the database information.

In the 2D design the six main categories of domain information are represented by a flat hexagon (see Figure 4). Font size and shape cues differentiate 1st and 2nd level categories. Sub-category trees can be displayed, again following the fishing line metaphor, by clicking the appropriate text button. The hexagon could be shifted in an animated sequence for browsing. Queries were made by selecting the centre of the hexagon or the make query button which displayed sub-query options. Results were displayed in context by spider links showing connections to higher level categories.

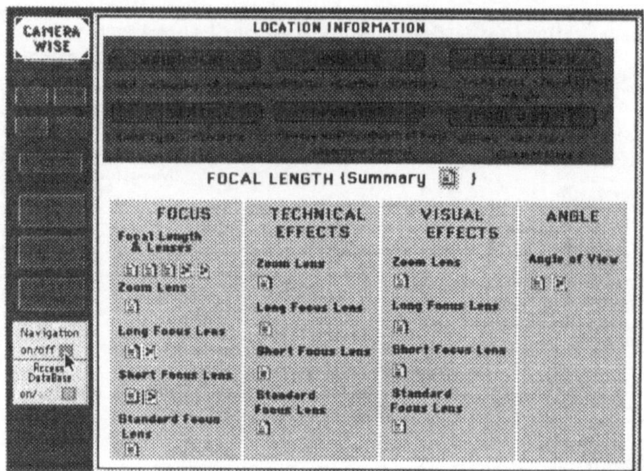

Figure 5: CameraWise formatted text design.

The formatted text design (see Figure 5) used a columnar format to organize first and second level categories. Sub-category trees were displayed by selecting hypertext buttons on main categories. A non-interactive information map provided a structure overview and location information similar to the other designs. Shifting to a lower level was cued by a screen wipe as an equivalent motion cue to the animation used in the 2D and 3D graphical designs. Pre-formed queries were effected by selecting buttons positioned after the category 'blocks'.

4 Methods

Thirty subjects were randomly allocated to the three conditions: Text, 2D and 3D, in a between groups design. The subjects were undergraduates in computer science and staff employed at the City University who were not experienced in the CameraWise domain, i.e. photography, but were familiar with GUIs.

The experimental session was divided into six stages: training, exploration, inspection/query task approximately 40 minutes in duration, distracter task, memory test, questionnaire and debriefing. Training consisted of a scripted verbal explanation and a short demonstration. The subjects were then asked to systematically explore the database. For the experimental task the subjects had to find out as much information as they could about the topic of Focal Length, containing 35 items, and were asked to use the query facility at least once. After the experimental task the subjects were given a short, paper-based distracter task, i.e. a spot the difference visual/verbal matching task, to clear working memory before they completed a memory test. The session concluded with an attitude rating questionnaire and debriefing interview.

A pre-test questionnaire captured the subjects' computer and domain experience. During the exploration and experimental phases recordings were taken of user actions, interface features interacted with, timing of user actions and screen display

Level	3D	2D	Text
Top level node visits	36	22	15
2nd level	74	86	34
3rd level	82	87	94
Total actions visits & manipulations	282	223	156

Table 1: Average patterns of activity/subject in the exploration task.

changes. Session logs were analysed for patterns of user action and nodes visited in information structure hierarchy. After the experimental and distracter tasks, five memory tests were carried out:

1. Spatial memory: Subjects were supplied with a screen dump of the level 1 and 2 categories with the concept labels concealed, and a list of the labels. They were asked to match labels to their corresponding location.
2. Cued recall of higher order categories: Subjects were given a list of categories at the 2nd level and asked to recall the superordinate each one belonged to.
3. Cued recall of lower order categories: subjects were given a list of categories at the top and middle levels and asked to recall all the 3rd level items.
4. Un-cued recall of detail: Subjects were asked to recall as much information as possible about focal length.
5. Reasoning test: The subjects were required to recall information located in different parts of the database and use it in a reasoning task. This test used multiple choice questions and two open-ended questions e.g. "Which lens would you use to photograph a wedding and why". This section was scored and cross marked by a second researcher.

A post test questionnaire gathered data on subjects' subjective rating of the UI designs on a 1–7 scale.

5 Results

5.1 *Exploration Task*

Exploration activity was measured as average number of user actions (mouse selections) reflecting the frequency of interaction and node visits.

Exploration was not significantly different between the three conditions; however, graphical designs had higher scores with 3D in the lead (see Table 1). Interactions with the 2nd level were more frequent in 2D, while inspect (3rd level) interactions were more frequent in Text. However, there were more manipulations overall and more shifts between sub-trees in 3D (use of 'go to' commands) compared to 2D and Text.

The 3D design may stimulate more user interaction because of the affordances for interaction suggested by the image. This was investigated further by looking at

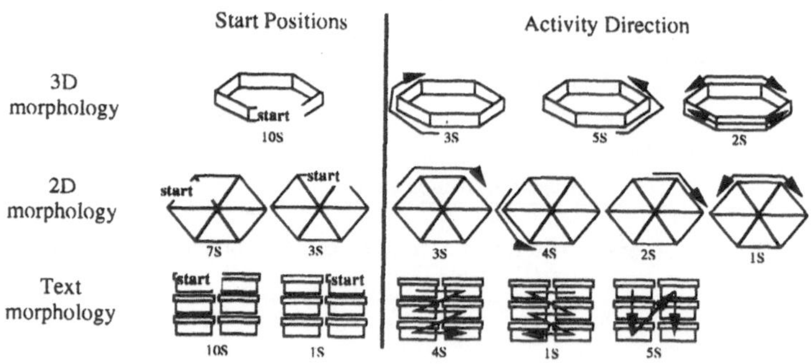

Figure 6: An illustration of start positions and activity direction in the 3 conditions.

traces of nodes visited by the subjects. The Text subjects tended to serially inspect the database, while the 2D and 3D subjects browsed using the different patterns. 2D and 3D subjects tended to inspect the category explanation texts, while Text subjects serially inspected the titles. An explanation may lie in the design morphology as the Text design is closer to a list structure than the 2D and 3D hexagons, and hence encourages serial search.

In the Text condition, nine subjects began with the top left category and explored serially from left to right, while one subject followed the inverse pattern. In the 2D condition, seven subjects began on the left face of the hexagon and three on the top face of the hexagon. There were a variety of paths through the information space but all followed features of the 2D hexagon metaphor. In the 3D condition all subjects began exploration on the front face of the 3D hexagon, but there were a variety of paths related to the image structure, as users either rotated it to view sides or tilted it to change their angle of view. Changing viewpoint (e.g. view side commands) was not used. User exploration in the graphical conditions appears to be cued by the structure of the image metaphor, with manipulations acting on image components being used frequently, while more generic view commands (e.g. pan, zoom, change viewpoint) were not. In the text design serial reading of text blocks was the dominant pattern. (See Figure 6)

5.2 *Experiment Task*

The subjects' experience from the pretest questionnaire was categorized as maximum, moderate or minimal. There were no statistically significant differences according to the users' experience in memory or reasoning task scores (ANOVA). The efficiency of the subjects' searching was assessed by counting the information nodes visited by each subject and expressing this as a percentage of a 'gold standard' of the minimum number of nodes which had to be visited to correctly answer the focal length question. No significant differences were found between the three designs, means 57.2 (3D), 47.7 (2D), 54.0 (Text), but individual differences were noticeable. Analysis of variance for memory of the three design conditions (see Table 2) yielded a significant difference in the reasoning task (Test 5) for 3D over other designs ($p > 0.013$).

	Text vs. 2D vs. 3Ds Graphics			Graphics	
	Text	2D	3D	p>	p>
Spatial memory	5.3	5.4	4.6	0.875	0.258
Cued recall higher order category	13.3	16.0	15.7	0.128	* 0.042
Cued recall lower order category	6.1	6.6	5.5	0.351	0.770
Un-cued detailed recall	12.4	11.1	7.9	0.224	0.404
Reasoning test	11.9	12.6	13.8	* 0.013	* 0.030

* significant differences in scores between conditions.

Table 2: Summary of findings — usage outcome.

	Text		2D		3D	
	Explore	Exp	Explore	Exp	Explore	Exp
Serial	5	3	4	4	3	3
Category inspect	5	5	4	4	2	0
Category sample	0	0	2	3	3	2
Content search	0	0	0	0	1	4
Other	0	2	0	0	1	1

Table 3: Subjects' search strategies in exploration and experimental tasks.

There were no significant differences in other memory test scores, although when scores for the two (2D and 3D) graphics conditions were grouped, the graphical designs were better than text for cued recall of higher order categories, ($p = 0.042$). Graphical designs overall appear to improve recall of higher order categories, and 3D graphics, in particular, help recall when information is used in a reasoning task.

When the search scores verses the gold standard were correlated with recall task scores for the focal length question a significant association was found for the text and 3D conditions (Spearman correlation coefficient $p \leq 0.05$). This suggests that subjects' search strategies for information may be important in influencing their memory. The subjects' pattern of activity was analysed following the same practice as with the exploration task. Four main search strategies were observed from traces of node visits:

Serial search by visiting all instances in selected categories. Category inspect when subjects visited one or two items from each level 2 category. Category sample when they visited categories and serially searched within them but not for all nodes. Content strategies when selection was guided by the content of previously visited node.

Absolute frequencies (see Table 3) showed no differences between exploration and experimental tasks. Serial exploration appears to be a more dominant strategy in the text design, whereas category strategies were more noticeable in graphics, especially 3D. Most subjects (8 Text and 7 2D) were consistent in their searching

	3D	2D	Text
Navigating information space	+15	+2	-9
Interacting with screen image	+18	+17	+8
Accessing database information	+7	+6	+5
Support to understand information structure	+7	+3	-3
Support to understand database content	+17	+16	+11
Help functionality	+19	+16	+8
Overall interface design	+21	+19	+15

Table 4: NPV user satisfaction scores. Net positive values from Likert scales aggregated for all users in each condition.

strategies in both exploration and experimental conditions; however, in 3D only three serial searchers remained consistent while the others shifted to content or category sample strategies. This shift may be because the 3D image provides better cues for goal directed searching in the focal length task. In retrospective interviews subjects commented on the usefulness of the 3D design in facilitating exploration of information categories, and the bird cage connectivity between information related to pre-formed questions. Text designs received neutral or adverse comments, while the 2D design was considered to be helpful. All subjects inspected the advice text after making a query, and the summary text for the topic of focal length. 2D and 3D subjects also showed a 'maintain context' pattern by quickly revisiting top level categories already explored before continuing lower level searching.

From post test questionnaire data, the 3D design appears to be preferred marginally over the 2D design; however, the main difference between the two graphical conditions was the users' preference for interacting and navigating in 3D (see Table 4). Text received poor scores for supporting navigation and understanding the information structure. Graphical designs received a favourable rating for the overall interface design and helping understanding of the database contents. Overall users preferred graphical representations and 3D appears to have an additional advantage for navigation.

5.3 Individual Differences

To follow up on the possible effects of searching patterns, the two best and worst subjects in each condition were investigated. Subjects who performed worst in all conditions had low scores in search efficiency against the gold standard but their exploration activity scores in task one were no different from the better performers (see Table 5).

All poor performing subjects had serial type search strategies, whereas all the better subjects had category inspect/sample style so it seems that the style of search rather than overall exploration activity influenced performance. This was particularly noticeable for 3D subject 2 who had a high exploration activity but this reflected serial manipulation of the image rather than systematic exploration. Hence, even though 3D does promote exploration, in some cases this may not be effective as users are attracted by the animation and play with the image rather than exploring

	Memory Test % 1–4	Search % vs. Gold std.	Recall focal length/35	Search activity task 1
Best				
3D_s6	49	78	15	164
3D_s7	48	80	14	189
2D_s19	46	77	15	149
2D_s20	47	78	15	151
T_s23	47	80	14	132
T_s29	43	72	15	144
Worst				
3D_s2	27	20	10	200
3D_s8	29	18	5	156
2D-s11	22	10	5	178
2D-s15	29	20	10	156
T_s25	31	18	10	116
T_s26	26	15	5	137

Table 5: Comparison of best and worst performances with analysis of patterns of activity and exploration strategies.

the information categories. Although memory test and experimental search scores correlated, both concerned focal length subject matter and no effect was found for the reasoning test, nor is there any relationship with the activity scores.

6 Conclusions

It appears there is no great advantage in 3D visualization based on the limited study we have reported, but several caveats are necessary. First, our emphasis of basing visualization design on user models of the information space may demonstrate that systematic design is more important than the representation modality, even in text. Secondly, the database used was small and 3D advantages may become more apparent with larger information spaces. Nevertheless, we have shown that graphical visualizations do have an advantage over text in promoting gist memory of high order information structures, and 3D seems to have a performance advantage for information retrieval. In reasoning tasks we suggest that this arises from the richer affordances for interaction and exploration in 3D. For example, users had to do more work with the 3D design to view the 2nd level categories by rotating the hexagon, compared with the other designs, and the bird cage query-answer links gave clearer connectivity than is possible in 2D or Text. However, clearly 3D is no panacea, as some subjects performed poorly. One tentative explanation is that their serial search strategies and ineffective use of the visual structure may indicate a mismatch with cognitive style. Graphics, and 3D in particular, may not help more verbally inclined people, whereas the visualizers will benefit. In our future work we will investigate cognitive style differences.

The graphical paradigms we propose embed an organizational metaphor that should be easy to memorize in two ways. First the morphology suggests a coherent organization, e.g. the solar system morphology prompts the user's memory. Secondly, the method encourages a close mapping between the underlying information structure and the physical organization of the graphical morphology. This should provide additional cues for memorization of the information structure which can be reused during retrieval. Which metaphors are more effective for a range of information spaces, and indeed task, awaits further experimentation. Furthermore, how comprehensible the metaphors are when implemented in different designs is another interesting question which could be tackled by assessing our template library against visualization design criteria proposed by Green (1990).

The design method proposes a mapping between conceptual entities in a data model and a set of morphology templates. A similar distinction between conceptual and physical entities is made in the ERMIA method (Green & Benyon, 1995) which extends data modelling for user interface design. The design templates we propose are a set of predefined structure maps in ERMIA terms, however, we go beyond the restrictions of the entity relationship models to include classes of information categories which are necessary when modelling bibliographic databases and large information spaces.

The study raises many questions. Usability of the graphical and text interfaces may have been influenced by a variety of factors ranging from the role of the metaphor, manipulations, and presentation layout. Even though we controlled the inter-design variation as far as possible by usability testing each variant and based the design on a common data model, we cannot be sure which factors were key determinants of user performance as found by other studies of this kind (Wright & Lickorish, 1994). Unfortunately, there are no easy answers with complex artefacts, as controlled experimentation is not feasible with complex multi-variate products. The small inter-design effects we found probably illustrate the point that structured visualization design improves usability in both text and graphical modalities. Our future work will involve iterative development of the diagram paradigms we have proposed with usability testing, combined with empirical studies using protocol analysis techniques to gain further understanding about how design features support or hinder user interaction. We see our work following in the claims analysis task artefact tradition (Carroll & Rosson, 1992), by a combination of performance measures and empirical analysis of interaction. Linking users interaction patterns with how well they perform provides some explanation for how designs function in cognitive terms. This can be integrated with metric based analysis (Furnas & Bederson, 1995).

The design method we have described applies to the representation of any set of categorizable information. The information structures we currently account for are hierarchies (e.g. class structures) and networks (e.g. entity relationships) as well as combinations of two. In our future work we will extend the method to deal with explicit expression of time varying data (Plaisant et al., 1996) and more detailed guidelines for visual encoding of attributes (Tweedie et al., 1996). The method and our experimental results, however, do not extend to concrete 3D/2D images, for instance in scientific visualization, where recognition of familiar images may have different connotations for interaction. On the other hand our findings may well generalize to a wide range of abstract images which have to be learned. We argue that structured design based on the users' task model will improve the process of memorization, recall and hence enhance usability. However, further research is required to establish the relative contribution made by interactive functionality and visual structure of such interfaces.

Given the expense of experimental tests, visibility cost-effectiveness metrics following (Card et al., 1994) may be a promising way to evaluate candidate designs. However, we believe that empirical studies are necessary to understand how users search strategies can be efficiently supported by complex visualizations for different information seeking needs.

Acknowledgements

Many thanks to Ann Doubleday and Michele Ryan for their significant contributions. Jennifer Sam is thanked for her assistance with data collection.

References

Ahlberg, C. & Shneiderman, B. (1994), Visual Information Seeking: Tight Coupling of Dynamic Query Filters with Starfield Displays, *in* B. Adelson, S. Dumais & J. Olson (eds.), "Proceedings of CHI'94: Human Factors in Computing Systems", ACM Press, pp.313–317.

Card, S. K., Pirolli, P. & Mackinlay, J. D. (1994), The Cost-of-Knowledge Characteristic Function: Display Evaluation for Direct-Walk Dynamics in Information Visualization, *in* B. Adelson, S. Dumais & J. Olson (eds.), "Proceedings of CHI'94: Human Factors in Computing Systems", ACM Press, pp.238–244.

Carroll, J. M. & Rosson, M. B. (1992), "Getting Around the Task Artefact Cycle: How to Make Claims and Design by Scenario", *ACM Transactions on Office Information Systems* **10**, 181–212.

Fairchild, M. K., Poltrock, S. E. & Furnas, G. W. (1988), SemNet: Three Dimensional Graphic Representations of Large Knowledge Bases, *in* R. Guindon (ed.), "Cognitive Science and its Applications for Human Computer Interaction", Lawrence Erlbaum Associates.

Furnas, G. W. & Bederson, B. B. (1995), Space-scale Diagrams Understanding Multiscale Diagrams, *in* I. Katz, R. Mack, L. Marks, M. B. Rosson & J. Nielsen (eds.), "Proceedings of CHI'95: Human Factors in Computing Systems", ACM Press, pp.234–241.

Green, T. & Benyon, D. (1995), Displays as Data Structures: Entity–Relationship Models of Information Artifacts, *in* K. Nordby, P. H. Helmersen, D. J. Gilmore & S. A. Arnessen (eds.), "Human–Computer Interaction — INTERACT'95: Proceedings of the Fifth IFIP Conference on Human–Computer Interaction", Chapman & Hall, pp.55–60.

Green, T. R. G. (1990), The Cognitive Dimension of Viscosity: A Sticky Problem for HCI, *in* D. Diaper, D. Gilmore, G. Cockton & B. Shackel (eds.), "Proceedings of INTERACT'90 — Third IFIP Conference on Human–Computer Interaction", Elsevier Science, pp.79–86.

Mackinlay, J. D., Rao, R. & Card, S. K. (1995), An Organic User Interface for Searching Citation Links, *in* I. Katz, R. Mack, L. Marks, M. B. Rosson & J. Nielsen (eds.), "Proceedings of CHI'95: Human Factors in Computing Systems", ACM Press, pp.67–73.

Mackinlay, J. D., Robertson, G. G. & Card, S. K. (1991), The Perspective Wall: Details and Context Smoothly Integrated, *in* S. P. Robertson, G. M. Olson & J. S. Olson (eds.), "Proceedings of CHI'91: Human Factors in Computing Systems (Reaching through Technology)", ACM Press, pp.173–179.

Mayes, J. T., Draper, S. W., MacGregor, A. & Oatley, K. (1988), Information Flow in a User Interface: The Effect of Experience and Context on the Recall of MacWrite Screens, *in* D. M. Jones & R. Winder (eds.), "People and Computers IV (Proceedings of HCI'88)", Cambridge University Press, pp.275–289.

Nielsen, J. (1993), *Usability Engineering*, Academic Press.

Plaisant, C., Milash, B., Rose, A., Widoff, S. & Shneiderman, B. (1996), Lifelines: Visualizing Personal Histories, *in* G. van der Veer & B. Nardi (eds.), "Proceedings of CHI'96: Human Factors in Computing Systems", ACM Press.

Rao, R. & Card, S. K. (1994), The Table Lens: Merging Graphical and Symbolic Representations in an Interactive Focus and Context Visualization for Tabular Information, *in* B. Adelson, S. Dumais & J. Olson (eds.), "Proceedings of CHI'94: Human Factors in Computing Systems", ACM Press, pp.318–322.

Robertson, G. G., Card, S. K. & Mackinlay, J. D. (1993), "Information Visualisation Using 3D Interactive Animation", *Communications of the ACM* **36**(4), 56–71.

Sutcliffe, A. G. & Patel, U. (1993), The Three Dimensional Graphical User Interface: Evaluation for Design Evolution, *in* J. Alty, D. Diaper & S. Guest (eds.), "People and Computers VIII (Proceedings of HCI'93)", Cambridge University Press, pp.311–334.

Tweedie, L., Spence, R., Dawkes, H. & Su, H. (1996), Externalisaing Abstract Mathematical Models, *in* G. van der Veer & B. Nardi (eds.), "Proceedings of CHI'96: Human Factors in Computing Systems", ACM Press.

Wright, P. & Lickorish, A. (1994), "Menues and Memory Load: Navigation Stratagies in Interactive Search Tasks", *International Journal of Human–Computer Studies* **40**(6), 965–1008.

Specific Design Issues

Can Design Choices for Language-Based Editors be Analysed with Keystroke-Level Models?

Mark A Toleman[†] **& Jim Welsh**[‡]

[†] *Department of Mathematics and Computing, The University of Southern Queensland, Toowoomba, Qld 4350, Australia.*

Tel: *+61 76 31 2533*
Fax: *+61 76 31 2721*
EMail: *markt@usq.edu.au*

[‡] *Software Verification Research Centre, Department of Computer Science, The University of Queensland, Qld 4072, Australia.*

Tel: *+61 7 3365 2787*
Fax: *+61 7 3365 1533*
EMail: *jim@cs.uq.edu.au*

We have been concerned for some time with the lack of rigorous experimental evaluation of design options chosen for tools used by software engineers. In a series of studies using various evaluation techniques we built Keystroke-Level Models (KLM) and conducted an empirical usability study of a design issue (choice of editing paradigm for language-based editors) that has reached a 'subjective stalemate' in the research community. The KLM analysis enabled us to predict usage differences and while this was useful we also noticed several problems, in particular we were concerned about the estimated value and placement of the memory operator. By utilizing the same tasks in the usability study as in the KLM analysis, we were able to compare results from both evaluations and effectively validate the overall KLM estimates and the specific operator values involved.

Keywords: keystroke-level model, model validation, language-based editors.

1 Introduction

Two basic paradigms for editing are commonly associated with language-based editors: tree-building and text-recognition. Briefly, with the tree-building paradigm the user is only allowed operations that ensure the structural correctness of the program tree at all times. To extend a program the user selects a template from a menu of templates allowable at that point in the program. With text-recognition the user manipulates the displayed representation in textual terms, and the editor parses any changes to deduce the program tree required.

The debate about the choice between tree-building and text-recognition as language-based editing paradigms continues (Welsh et al., 1991; Minör, 1992; Khwaja & Urban, 1993; Whittle et al., 1994). For example, Khwaja & Urban (1993) suggested that the strict discipline imposed by the tree-building approach was appropriate for novices but not for experienced software developers. Thus a decision could be based on the type of user expected to utilize the product. An alternative they suggested was to consider user preferences and base a decision on a majority of user views, but where no clear majority prevailed provide both. No single solution was proposed by Whittle et al. (1994) where it was suggested that a 'subjective stalemate' had been reached between advocates of one or the other of these approaches to language-based editing.

From our perspective, the key word above is *subjective* since to the best of our knowledge no systematic attempt to demonstrate the advantage of one paradigm or the other, either by application of relevant theories or by empirical investigation, has been attempted. In a previous study Toleman & Welsh (1994a) examined the use of predictive modelling (GOMS/KLM) as a tool to evaluate editing paradigms. Using this approach a model is built that can be used to help evaluate various issues before prototyping commences. GOMS/KLM is the one 'real' engineering approach to user interface evaluation that is currently available to software engineers but, compared to other engineering disciplines, GOMS/KLM is immature and our understanding of its application in many design situations is at an early stage of development. Our previous study noted a number of problems with the Keystroke-Level Model KLM including its assumption of error-free expert behaviour but, in particular, the technical difficulty of allocating memory operators and a concern about the estimate of the memory operator of 1.35sec. To convince ourselves that the technique was worthwhile to apply in our design domain we believed that experimentation and validation of the KLM was required.

Thus, in a second study Toleman & Welsh (1995) compared the two editing paradigms using a laboratory-style experiment. As in the predictive modelling exercise we were interested in the relative efficiency of the two paradigms, that is, finding which paradigm was most efficient for use by software engineers engaged in typical software development tasks. However, by utilizing the same program development tasks as the predictive modelling study, we were able to collect data to validate the predictive models involved. The results of this comparative validation form the primary content of this paper. Firstly, though, we briefly describe the use of the KLM and then the experiment that generated our validation data.

2 The Keystroke-Level Model

The Keystroke-Level Model (KLM) (Card et al., 1980) enables a designer to predict the time taken by experienced-expert users in carrying out a given task using a given tool or paradigm. In our case the tasks involved source code development and maintenance, and a range of typical tasks were devised. The KLM was then used to model each task for each editing paradigm, thus enabling comparison of execution time estimates for the paradigms.

Time to execute a task can be described using four physical parameters, **K** (keystroking), **P** (pointing), **H** (homing) and **D** (drawing), one mental operator **M** and a system response operator **R**. The execution time for a task is the sum of the times for each of these operators (expressed as $T_{parameter}$) and is given by

$$T_{execute} = T_K + T_P + T_H + T_D + T_M + T_R.$$

Estimates of these various parameters have been determined (Card et al., 1980). Total time spent in keystroking and button pressing is given by T_K and is based on the number of keys pressed (keys not characters, so an upper case A is two keystrokes — `SHIFT a`) and average typing speed, (40wpm) for the typical non-secretarial typist of 0.28sec per keystroke.

The **P** operator represents pointing to a target using a mouse, an average 1.1sec. With multiple input devices, the user must shift hands between these devices. The homing **H** operator accounts for this movement with an average 0.4sec between devices.

The **D** operator represents using the mouse to draw straight line segments. Originally this was included by Card et al. (1980) to indicate the wide scope of tasks that could be covered by the KLM (for example computer-aided drafting, graphics and painting) but we adapted it to indicate text highlighting tasks that were effectively drawing tasks (point–button down–draw–button up). The **D** operator has two parameters, the number of lines drawn and the length of those lines. The time taken to draw a single line of length $l_D$cm is $0.9 + 0.16 l_D$sec.

Time spent 'mentally preparing' to carry out a physical operator is covered by the **M** operator which is an average time of 1.35sec. Heuristic rules describe the placement of **M** operators in an analysis of a task (Card et al., 1983, p.265).

The **R** operator represents the system response time. It is only relevant when the user has to wait before execution of one of the four physical operators and may be partially or totally subsumed by an **M** operator.

The 'physical encoding' for the KLM operators is relatively simple — it follows typical use of a system by an experienced-expert user. However the 'cognitive encoding' (use of the **M** operator) is more difficult although the heuristic rules act as a guide to their placement. These rules have an underlying psychological principle that users cognitively organize methods according to sub-method 'chunks'. The time estimate for the **M** operator represents the time to retrieve a chunk of information from long-term memory into working memory.

In Figure 1 we present a simple example of a development task — a Pascal procedure. The software engineer would have little difficulty in entering this code

```
PROCEDURE Check;
  BEGIN
    IF Flag THEN count := count + 1
  END;
```

Figure 1: An example program input task.

Operation	Physical Operators	Include Ms	Remove Ms
Select `procedure` from menu	P [`procedure`]	MP	MP
	K [left button]	MK	K
Select <name> of `procedure`	P [<name>]	P	P
	K [left button]	K	K
Reach for keyboard	H [keyboard]	H	H
Enter `Check`	6K [`Check`]	6K	6K
Reach for mouse	H [mouse]	H	H
Select `<statement>` (in procedure)	P [`<statement>`]	P	P
	K [left button]	K	K
Select `ifthen` from menu	P [`ifthen`]	MP	MP
	K [left button]	MK	K
Reach for keyboard	H [keyboard]	H	H
Enter `Flag`	5K [`Flag`]	5K	5K
Select **forward-with-optionals** (move to `<statement>`)	K [`RETURN`]	MK	MK
Enter `count:=count+1`	16K [`count:=count+1`]	16K	16K
Select **pointer-down** (finish text input)	K [↓]	MK	MK

Table 1: KLM analysis for program code input for tree-building paradigm with mouse-based menu selection (CSG-TB).

using any program editing paradigm. A KLM analysis provides an estimate of the time taken to input the code.

Table 1 shows the KLM analysis for this program development example for the Cornell tree-building editor. The first column in the table presents the method used for each part of the task (for example, Select `procedure` from menu) while the second gives the physical operator encoding as set out in the KLM (for example, P [`procedure`]). Column three represents the application of 'Rule 0' for inserting the memory operator, **M**, while column four shows the application of the other heuristic rules for the removal of **M** operators (Card et al., 1983, p.265). It is this last column that provides the list of parameters for the execution time estimate.

In the next section we describe the usability experiment that generated data for validating the KLM time estimates for individual tasks and paradigms, and KLM parameter estimates.

3 Experimental Design

3.1 *Subjects*

The type of user in which we were interested was special. Software tools are required by and used by experienced and expert users — software engineers. General computer users are usually interested in tools with built-in knowledge in domains other than computing, whereas software engineers use tools that incorporate specialized knowledge about software and software development. The interfaces between the user and the computer required for these different purposes are likely to be as different as the tasks themselves. In addition, the expertise of individual software engineers varies over time, with engineers becoming more proficient in the use of a tool as experience with the tool grows. Since software engineers are likely to spend much of their time at this higher level of expertise, designing user interfaces for software tools should emphasize the need to optimize the physical and intellectual ergonomics involved, rather than ensuring comprehensibility for users unfamiliar with the tool. Thus, we needed users who were familiar with the 'look and feel' of the editors, familiar with their use and familiar with the programming language and tasks to be performed. This group was small since the editors were experimental research tools primarily used to test conceptual ideas of various researchers. We used five final year honours students who participated in the experiment as part of their course.

3.2 *Apparatus*

For this experiment we used a Labtam X-terminal (48cm monitor, 16Mb memory) connected to a Sun SPARCstation 20. We used two editors; an existing text-recognition editor, UQ1 (Welsh et al., 1986), and a Pascal editor provided with the Cornell Synthesizer Generator (Reps & Teitelbaum, 1984; Reps & Teitelbaum, 1989a; Reps & Teitelbaum, 1989b). The particular UQ1 editor had been enhanced to allow the editor to simulate template-based input (that is, menu selection of language components) without the need to compromise its basic text-recognition editing paradigm. By using the one UQ editor for experimenting with both paradigms, we potentially avoided confounding effects of different physical interface presentation that prevail when two different editors were compared. The program input and maintenance tasks to be performed were the same as those used in the predictive modelling study and were detailed in Toleman & Welsh (1994b). Input tasks included input of simple Pascal procedures, procedure and function stubs, and various language construct types. Maintenance tasks ranged from trivial alterations such as changing a variable's name within a procedure to significant structural changes to a program. They represented a cross-section of the types of tasks in which programmers might engage.

3.3 *Procedure*

Before the experiment, all subjects were given a document that explained the aims and objectives of the experiment as well as some detail of the procedures to be followed. The experiment was conducted on the same equipment in the same room for each subject. This arrangement necessitated individual testing of subjects with each subject allocated up to one hour to complete the required tasks for the designated editor/paradigm. As far as possible, the time of day that subjects participated in the experiment was the most convenient time for the subject.

There were three treatments:

- program input using text-recognition (UQ1-TR);
- program input using tree-building via the UQ1 editor (UQ1-TB); and
- program input using tree-building via the Cornell editor (CSG-TB).

For each of the five subjects there were 20 tasks to be completed on each of three days. These tasks included nine program input tasks and eleven program maintenance tasks as outlined in Toleman & Welsh (1994b). Of the program input tasks the first and the last were almost identical. Subjects completed all program input tasks and then all maintenance tasks.

Treatment sequence was randomly assigned for each subject. Subjects undertook the software development tasks for one paradigm on one day, another paradigm on the next day and the remaining paradigm on the following day. This randomization decreased any carry-over (or residual) effect. We reasoned that there might be some settling-in effect or even a learning effect so all subjects completed the tasks in the same order to minimize variation between tasks. Two tasks, tasks 1 and 9 for input, were essentially identical so we were able to note any learning effect by comparing these tasks.

Before beginning with a particular editor or paradigm, subjects were given an opportunity to relax and become familiar with the experimental setup. This involved physical adjustments of chair, screen, mouse, and so on, as well as preliminary experimentation with a set of programs and tasks not included in the experiment proper.

During the experiment two computer-based logs were automatically kept. The first monitored the load on the computer while each user was carrying out the allotted tasks. All mouse and keyboard events were monitored using a second log. The programs, collectively called `xmon`, and including `xmonui` and `xmond` (McFarlane, 1991), were used for this data collection and monitoring function. Use of this program was relatively straightforward. The user interface allowed selection from a wide range of possible **X** events for capture but for this experiment we restricted the data collection to `ButtonPress`, `ButtonRelease` and `KeyPress` events. Even with such a restricted set of events the log files ranged in size up to 1Mb.

All experimental sessions were video-taped* with the video camera placed to the left of the subject and pointing at the terminal screen. Audio recording was also enabled to obtain comments made by subjects during a session. Subject reactions were monitored but intervention during a session was only undertaken when clarification of a task was required or when system functions needed attention. Between the computer-based log, the video-taping and the observation, all errors, the time required for all tasks and individual mouse and keyboard activity were recorded.

*Initially we had thought that the computer-based log would be sufficient but the video was essential for deciphering editing tasks and useful for recording user opinions about various issues.

Input Task	UQ1-TR	UQ1-TB	CSG-TB
Check–PROCEDURE	23.60	35.90	29.52
AddNumbers–PROCEDURE	17.24	21.95	24.56
AddNumbers–FOR	28.81	36.60	31.75
StoreCount–CASE	56.44	59.90	56.59
Random–FUNCTION	14.38	15.38	29.19
ComputeChange–IF-THEN-ELSE	14.17	19.75	23.18
CheckInput–REPEAT-UNTIL	41.67	44.56	42.06
IterativeSum–WHILE-DO	32.38	36.76	26.60
Count–PROCEDURE	18.66	30.11	18.15
Maintenance Task	**UQ1-TR**	**UQ1-TB**	**CSG-TB**
WHILE-DO change	13.15	17.44	31.07
IF-THEN change	13.97	13.36	1.39
AddNumbers–insert statement	20.94	17.28	19.51
AddNumbers–remove statement	4.64	3.08	5.82
AddNumbers–reverse loop	14.23	18.82	14.46
AddNumbers–alter variable name	19.11	18.95	26.34
ComputeChange–remove IF	13.84	13.61	27.17
ComputeChange–insert IF	15.20	24.09	35.16
ComputeChange–alter IF	7.35	5.15	6.29
IterativeSum–remove WHILE	17.27	11.42	19.58
IterativeSum–insert WHILE	26.33	36.18	24.67

Table 2: Empirically measured times for program input and maintenance tasks used in KLM study.

4 Validation of Keystroke-Level Model

The structure and conduct of this experiment meant that we were able to examine not only usability issues related to the editors and editing paradigms (Toleman & Welsh, 1995) but also to perform a validation of theoretical models proposed in Toleman & Welsh (1994a). In Table 2 we present data generated by differencing overall task completion times and task error times and averaging for the subjects. These data are comparable to the KLM data from Toleman & Welsh (1994a), summarized in Table 3.

Several methods were available to compare predicted and empirical results. The two used were *percentage absolute error* and *correlation/regression*. The figures in parenthesis in Table 3 represent percentage absolute errors for each task and editor. Each of these values was calculated as:

$$\frac{100 \mid \text{predicted} - \text{empirical} \mid}{\text{empirical}}$$

Averages for these errors were calculated for each editor: UQ1-TR 17.7%, UQ1-TB 23.4%, CSG-TB 26.8% (CSG-TB 17.9%, if the large value for IF-THEN change was omitted).

Input Task	UQ1-TR		UQ1-TB		CSG-TB	
Check–PROCEDURE	17.49	(25.9)	20.51	(42.9)	20.24	(31.4)
AddNumbers–PROCEDURE	17.36	(0.7)	17.69	(19.4)	21.21	(13.6)
AddNumbers–FOR	23.98	(16.8)	29.70	(18.9)	29.59	(6.8)
StoreCount–CASE	40.22	(28.7)	50.05	(16.4)	50.77	(10.3)
Random–FUNCTION	12.60	(12.4)	13.21	(14.1)	18.36	(37.1)
ComputeChange–IF-THEN-ELSE	12.83	(9.5)	15.63	(20.9)	16.70	(28.0)
CheckInput–REPEAT-UNTIL	33.55	(19.5)	34.72	(22.1)	37.70	(10.4)
IterativeSum–WHILE-DO	25.66	(20.8)	28.96	(21.2)	30.03	(12.9)
Count–PROCEDURE	17.49	(6.3)	20.51	(31.9)	20.24	(11.5)
Maintenance Task	**UQ1-TR**		**UQ1-TB**		**CSG-TB**	
WHILE-DO change	14.36	(9.2)	16.53	(5.2)	32.39	(4.2)
IF-THEN change	14.64	(4.8)	15.97	(19.5)	4.11	(195.7)
AddNumbers–insert statement	15.15	(27.7)	15.15	(12.3)	15.12	(22.5)
AddNumbers–remove statement	4.11	(11.4)	4.11	(33.4)	5.05	(13.2)
AddNumbers–reverse loop	11.84	(16.8)	11.84	(37.1)	19.00	(31.4)
AddNumbers–alter variable name	21.78	(14.0)	21.78	(14.9)	18.87	(28.4)
ComputeChange–remove IF	10.28	(25.7)	10.28	(24.5)	29.03	(6.8)
ComputeChange–insert IF	19.63	(29.1)	22.85	(5.1)	29.54	(16.0)
ComputeChange–alter IF	7.96	(8.3)	7.96	(54.6)	4.69	(25.4)
IterativeSum–remove WHILE	9.32	(46.0)	9.32	(18.4)	18.28	(6.6)
IterativeSum–insert WHILE	21.03	(20.1)	23.81	(34.2)	19.04	(22.8)

Table 3: KLM analysis time estimates and, in parenthesis, percentage absolute error of these compared with empirical data for program input and maintenance tasks.

Editor	Correlation	Linear Regression		
	Coefficient (r)	Intercept	Slope	SE Slope
UQ1-TR	0.819	7.05	0.509	0.036
UQ1-TB	0.890	4.63	0.602	0.035
CSG-TB	0.845	5.02	0.691	0.047

Table 4: Correlation and regression results for comparing KLM predicted and actual times.

Correlation analyses between predicted and empirical times for individual subjects produced highly related results. For each editor there was a highly significant correlation ($P < 0.01$) between predicted execution times (KLM) and actual execution times. Linear regression relationships also reflected this high correlation with a linear relationship between predicted times (dependent variable) and actual times (independent variable) accounting for between 67.1% and 79.2% of the overall variation (Table 4). Figure 2 displays the linear relationships between predicted and actual execution times for all three editors.

The three regression equations indicate that actual execution times are marginally greater than predicted values. This result is not as obvious from the other analysis,

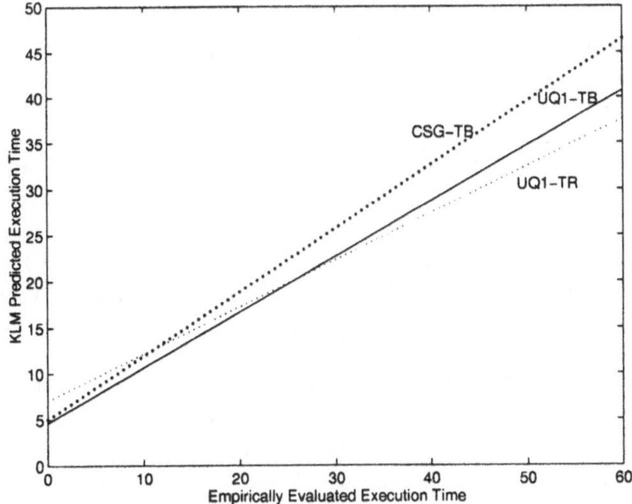

Figure 2: Linear relationships between KLM predicted and actual execution times for three editors.

percentage absolute error, since there the direction of any error is not available. Thus, although there is a reasonable correlation between empirical data and KLM predicted data, there appears to be a systematic difference as well. For example, for an actual execution time of 20sec, the KLM predicted times for each editor are: UQ1-TR 17.23, UQ1-TB 16.67, CSG-TB 18.84.

Both analyses, average percentage absolute error, and correlation and regression, indicate that model-predicted values represent close to 80% of empirical data values. This accords with other literature (Card et al., 1980; Olson & Olson, 1990; Peck & John, 1992; Gray et al., 1993).

4.1 Data Collection for Parameter Estimation

All key press, mouse button press and release events and timings were recorded for each subject and for each editor. The KLM predicted equivalent actions in each of the tasks analysed so timings for model predictions were compared with actual timings.

As already indicated, the principle concern with the KLM was with the estimate of time for the memory operator, **M**. For all instances with the KLM this parameter was predicted to be 1.35sec. With each task and editor there were events that were predicted to include this memory operator. There were four instances of such events.

1. For the editors UQ1-TR and UQ1-TB an **M** operator was assumed to precede acceptance of downstream symbols using the two keystroke sequence, `CTRL a`. Such events were modelled as **M2K** and all were extracted from the computer-based log of events for each editor and subject.

2. Single keystroke sequences that were predicted to be preceded by an **M** operator were evident in all three editors. In both UQ editors the `ESC` key was

used to exit from insertion mode and return to navigation mode. The CSG-TB editor implemented the `ENTER` or `RETURN` key to finalize statements input by the subject and provide template holes for filling by the user. Such events were modelled by **MK**.

3. All three editors included event sequences that required subjects to use the mouse to point to items for selection purposes. Items included editing commands, such as insert, delete and change for the UQ editors, and language command menu items, such as `ifthen` and `while` for the UQ1-TB and CSG-TB editors. The KLM placed **M**s in front of all such events that were modelled as **MPK**.

4. Editing operations involving one editor, CSG-TB, required subjects to use a pull-down menu to select editing operations, cut, copy and paste. Each event here involved pointing to a menu bar, holding down the left mouse button and *drawing* to the required editing operation (cut, copy or paste) and releasing the mouse button. This was modelled as **MPD** (**D** for draw). An alternative would have been to model this event as **MPK** ***press*** **PK** ***release*** since it was possible to use the menu in this way. However, actual use of the editor by subjects indicated that this was not the preferred method and **MPD** more closely simulated their actions.

To estimate memory operator times for these event types we also needed estimates of times for **K**, **PK** and **PD**. Estimates for **K** may be found by using the computer-based log of all keystrokes not involving or biased by memory operators. Unfortunately, estimates for the other two parameter combinations were more problematic. It was possible to estimate the values of **P** and **D** by counting video frames but the main difficulty was in knowing when to start the times for each parameter, that is, when had the **M** effect stopped and the other parameter started. We chose, therefore, to consider the events *in toto* rather than attempt to split them into component parts.

4.2 Hypotheses Related to KLM Validation

There were three principal aims for this analysis. Two related to hypotheses relevant to the types of event already listed. The third involved obtaining estimates of timings for the events.

Thus for each event there were up to two null hypotheses concerning the timing measurements associated with those events, namely:

1. There are no differences between editors.

2. There are no differences between subjects.

The second hypothesis related to the variability of performance of the subjects, a commonly cited problem (Koester & Levine, 1994).

When null hypotheses were rejected estimates of timings needed to be calculated for the individual treatments or subjects. If an hypothesis was not rejected then an estimate was based on all available data across treatments, subjects or both.

Source of Variation	Degrees of Freedom	Sums of Squares	Mean Squares	F Test	Significance
Treatments	1	9.403	9.403	2.06	$P > 0.05$
Subjects	4	5.374	1.343	0.29	$P > 0.05$
Error	2	9.133	4.567		
Sampling	140	147.6			
Total	147	168.7			

Table 5: Analysis of variance table for M2K events.

Subject	M2K		MK	MPD	Typing Speed
	UQ1-TR	UQ1-TB			
1	1.971	–	0.882	–	0.161
2	1.307	2.581	1.261	3.051	0.189
3	–	1.691	1.174	3.404	0.216
4	1.948	2.213	1.555	2.323	0.319
5	1.736	1.784	0.835	2.826	0.273

Table 6: Mean times for subjects for M2K, MK and MPD events and typing speed.

4.3 *Statistical Analysis*

The data were analysed by analysis of variance. There were one, two or three treatments (editors) depending on the type of event (**M2K, MK, MPK, MPD**) with up to five subjects and a variable number of instances of events (samples) within each combination of treatment × subject. In experimental designs with unequal subclass numbers (samples) the method of analysis involves the fitting of general linear models using statistical software such as GLIM (Nelder, 1985). Fitting these models is an iterative process and although there is no technical difficulty in fitting them, their interpretation is complex.

4.4 *Results for M2K*

Table 5 shows the analysis of variance for the timing data pertaining to **M2K** events. Similar analyses were conducted for the other event types.

The analysis indicated no significant ($P > 0.05$) effects of either editors or subjects. It was worthy of note however, that for one subject there was no data available (through an accident of data collection) and for another subject there was no data for this event type. Table 6 shows the mean times for **M2K** events for each editor and subject. Subject 2 was the only subject recording an appreciable time difference between editors.

The overall mean time for **M2K** events of 1.971 sec compared very favourably with the KLM predicted value of 1.91 sec.

Editor	MK	MPK
UQ1-TR	1.372	2.592
UQ1-TB	1.317	2.868
CSG-TB	0.976	4.320

Table 7: Mean times for MK and MPK events for editors.

4.5 Results for MK

The analysis indicated significant ($P < 0.05$) differences between editors and between subjects. Table 7 shows the mean times for **MK** events for each editor while Table 6 gives the means for subjects.

For each editor the mean time for an **MK** event was less than the KLM predicted value of 1.63sec. The timing for CSG-TB events of this type was significantly less ($P < 0.05$) than for events from either of the UQ editors. Timings for the UQ editors were similar. There was variability between subjects also.

In the CSG-TB editor the event related to use of the RETURN key which was a relatively large key compared to the ESC key — the UQ1 key represented by this event type. Proximity of the RETURN key, compared with the ESC key, to all of the other keys may have been a factor.

There was a positive correlation ($r = 0.479$) between the time subjects took for the event and their average typing speed but this was not significant ($P > 0.05$). An alternative explanation was that some subject variability was a factor for this event type for all editors.

4.6 Results for MPK

The analysis indicated a significant ($P < 0.05$) difference between editors but not between subjects. Table 7 shows the mean times for **MPK** events for each editor.

For each UQ editor the mean time for an **MPK** event was comparable with the KLM predicted value of 2.73sec. The timing for CSG-TB events of this type was significantly greater ($P < 0.01$) than for events from either of the UQ editors. The two UQ editors were similar. The longer time for CSG-TB events may have been related to the structure of the menu from which users selected items. It was essentially horizontal and, depending on the context, there were potentially many choices from which to select. The UQ1-TB menu for similar contexts was a vertical layout (but the same number of choices would have been evident).

4.7 Results for MPD

Table 6 shows the mean times for **MPD** events for each subject for which events were recorded. There is an indication of a difference between subjects. In all cases, subjects recorded times less than the KLM predicted value of 3.67sec (assuming an average 2cm distance traversal for the mouse cursor before lifting the left mouse button).

KLM Event	Actual			Predicted
	UQ1-TR	UQ1-TB	CSG-TB	KLM
M2K	1.971	1.971	–	1.91
MK	1.372	1.317	0.976	1.63
MPK	2.592	2.868	4.320	2.73
MPD	–	–	2.774	3.67

Table 8: Comparison of actual and predicted times (sec) for KLM events including M2K, MK, MPK, MPD.

5 Conclusions for the KLM Validation

This analysis indicates that, overall, KLM estimates of time to execute tasks are reasonably accurate. KLM predicted execution times account for about 80% of actual empirically measured execution times. However, we did find some differences between predicted and empirically measured values for some events involving memory operators. Table 8 shows a summary of the predicted and empirically determined timings for the KLM events analysed here.

These values could be used as alternatives to those supplied by Card et al. (1980) when comparing design options for software development tools of the type described here. Using these empirically determined time estimates of KLM events we predicted a new set of KLM time estimates for our tasks. Table 9 shows these new predictions and the corresponding calculations of absolute percentage error.

Average errors for the individual editors are now: UQ1-TR 17.1%, UQ1-TB 22.8%, CSG-TB 34.4% (CSG-TB 19.9%, if the large value for IF-THEN change is omitted). These figures are almost identical with those from the averages calculated from Table 3.

In Table 10 we show the new correlation coefficients and regression equations obtained after re-estimating KLM data for our tasks and comparing with actual times. While no significant improvement in overall correlation is noticed there has not been any reduction in association between predicted and actual times either. On this basis the original KLM estimates from Card et al. (1980) appear to be reasonable. Further improvements to the predictions might be obtained by considering alternative estimates of **P** based on Fitt's Law calculations, since screen layout of each of the editors is known. Improvements might also be noticed if actual rather than estimated values of typing speed of users were included. Neither of these has been considered at this stage since our principal concern was with estimates and placement of **M** parameters, though this may be considered in future work.

The KLM assumes that users perform their tasks in as efficient a manner as possible including the selection of optimal methods where there are alternatives. Users invariably use or select methods with which they are familiar or they think are best (in some context) or are part of their minimal set of methods. It is in situations such as this that other models such as GOMS (Card et al., 1983) and CCT (Kieras & Polson, 1985) may be useful but even these cannot handle error scenarios

Input Task	UQ1-TR		UQ1-TB		CSG-TB	
Check–PROCEDURE	17.67	(25.1)	20.97	(41.6)	22.11	(25.1)
AddNumbers–PROCEDURE	17.36	(0.7)	17.83	(18.8)	21.49	(12.5)
AddNumbers–FOR	24.10	(16.3)	30.22	(17.4)	29.44	(7.3)
StoreCount–CASE	40.34	(28.5)	50.25	(16.1)	52.36	(7.5)
Random–FUNCTION	12.60	(12.4)	13.35	(13.2)	17.33	(40.6)
ComputeChange–IF-THEN-ELSE	12.89	(9.0)	15.89	(19.5)	16.33	(29.6)
CheckInput–REPEAT-UNTIL	33.61	(19.3)	34.92	(21.6)	37.33	(11.2)
IterativeSum–WHILE-DO	25.78	(20.4)	29.36	(20.1)	31.90	(19.9)
Count–PROCEDURE	17.67	(5.3)	20.97	(30.4)	22.11	(21.8)
Maintenance Task	**UQ1-TR**		**UQ1-TB**		**CSG-TB**	
WHILE-DO change	13.57	(3.2)	16.32	(6.4)	37.67	(21.2)
IF-THEN change	14.17	(1.4)	15.76	(18.0)	5.70	(310.1)
AddNumbers–insert statement	15.01	(28.3)	15.29	(11.5)	13.81	(29.2)
AddNumbers–remove statement	3.97	(14.4)	4.25	(38.0)	5.53	(5.0)
AddNumbers–reverse loop	11.44	(19.6)	11.67	(38.0)	19.58	(34.4)
AddNumbers–alter variable name	21.38	(11.9)	21.61	(14.0)	18.33	(39.9)
ComputeChange–remove IF	10.00	(27.7)	10.56	(22.4)	29.82	(9.8)
ComputeChange–insert IF	18.90	(24.3)	22.84	(5.2)	32.09	(8.7)
ComputeChange–alter IF	7.56	(2.9)	7.92	(53.8)	4.04	(35.8)
IterativeSum–remove WHILE	9.04	(47.7)	9.60	(15.9)	19.98	(2.0)
IterativeSum–insert WHILE	20.30	(22.9)	23.80	(34.2)	20.78	(15.8)

Table 9: KLM estimates using empirically determined values of M2K, MK, MPK, MPD and, in parenthesis, percentage absolute error of these compared with empirical data for program input and maintenance tasks.

Editor	Correlation	Linear Regression		
	Coefficient (r)	Intercept	Slope	SE Slope
UQ1-TR	0.823	6.69	0.517	0.036
UQ1-TB	0.894	4.63	0.608	0.035
CSG-TB	0.828	5.45	0.707	0.052

Table 10: Correlation and regression results for comparing new KLM predicted and actual times.

adequately and so experimentation and usability studies are still needed to compare design options where errors are a significant concern.

The validation of the KLM predictions shows that even simple models can be useful in providing evidence to assist design choices. We applied the KLM analysis to a complex tool in a domain where such evaluation is rare and, although we had reservations about some aspects, our validation shows that the technique (KLM) is as accurate in this domain as many others. Thus, models play a useful role in user interface design for software development tools and provide a reasonable basis for decisions on design choices.

References

Card, S. K., Moran, T. P. & Newell, A. (1980), "The Keystroke-level Model for User Performance Time with Interactive Systems", *Communications of the ACM* **23**(7), 396–410.

Card, S. K., Moran, T. P. & Newell, A. (1983), *The Psychology of Human–Computer Interaction*, Lawrence Erlbaum Associates.

Gray, W. D., John, B. E. & Atwood, M. E. (1993), "Project Ernestine: Validating a GOMS Analysis for Predicting and Explaining Real-world Performance", *Human–Computer Interaction* **8**(3), 237–309.

Khwaja, A. A. & Urban, J. E. (1993), Syntax-directed Editing Environments: Issues and Features, *in* E. Deaton, G. H. Berghel & G. Hedrick (eds.), "Applied Computing: States of the Art and Practice — 1993", ACM Press, pp.230–237. Also in Proceedings of the 1993 ACM SIGAPP Symposium, Indianapolis, USA, 14–16th February.

Kieras, D. E. & Polson, P. G. (1985), "An approach to the formal analysis of user complexity", *International Journal of Man–Machine Studies* **22**(4), 365–394.

Koester, H. H. & Levine, S. P. (1994), Validation of a Keystroke-level Model for a Text Entry System used by People with Disabilities, *in* E. P. Glinert (ed.), "ASSETS'94: Proceedings of The First Annual International ACM/SIGCAPH Conference on Assistive Technologies". 31st October–1st November, Los Angles.

McFarlane, G. (1991), "Xmon UNIX Manual page".

Minör, S. (1992), "Interacting with Structure-oriented Editors", *International Journal of Man–Machine Studies* **37**(4), 399–418.

Nelder, J. A. (1985), "Glim77 Reference Manual", Royal Statistical Society.

Olson, J. R. & Olson, G. M. (1990), "The Growth of Cognitive Modeling in Human–Computer Interaction since GOMS", *Human–Computer Interaction* **5**(2-3), 221–265.

Peck, V. A. & John, B. E. (1992), Browser-Soar: A Computational Model of a Highly Interactive Task, *in* P. Bauersfeld, J. Bennett & G. Lynch (eds.), "Proceedings of CHI'92: Human Factors in Computing Systems", ACM Press, pp.165–172.

Reps, T. W. & Teitelbaum, T. (1984), "The Synthesizer Generator", *ACM SIGPLAN Notices* **19**(5), 42–48. Also in P Henderson, editor, Proceedings of ACM SIGSOFT/SIGPLAN Software Engineering Symposium on Practical Software Development Environments, Pittsburg, USA, May 1984.

Reps, T. W. & Teitelbaum, T. (1989a), *The Synthesizer Generator: A System for Constructing Language-Based Editors*, Springer-Verlag.

Reps, T. W. & Teitelbaum, T. (1989b), *The Synthesizer Generator Reference Manual*, 3rd edition, Springer-Verlag.

Toleman, M. A. & Welsh, J. (1994a), An Evaluation of Editing Paradigms, *in* S. Howard & Y. K. Leung (eds.), "Harmony Through Working Together — Proceedings of OZCHI'94", Ergonomics Society of Australia (Downer, ACT), pp.73–78.

Toleman, M. A. & Welsh, J. (1994b), A Keystroke Analysis of Language-based Editing Paradigms, Technical Report 94-5, Software Verification Research Centre, Department of Computer Science, The University of Queensland, Brisbane, Australia.

Toleman, M. A. & Welsh, J. (1995), An Empirical Investigation of Language-based Editing Paradigms, *in* H. Hasan & C. Nicastri (eds.), "HCI: A Light into the Future — Proceedings of OZCHI'95", Ergonomics Society of Australia (Downer, ACT), pp.163–168.

Welsh, J., Broom, B. & Kiong, D. (1991), "A Design Rationale for a Language-based Editor", *Software — Practice and Experience* **21**(9), 923–948.

Welsh, J., Rose, G. A. & Lloyd, M. (1986), "An Adaptive Program Editor", *The Australian Computer Journal* **18**(2), 67–74.

Whittle, B. R., Gautier, R. J. & Ratcliffe, M. (1994), "Trends in Structure-oriented Environments", *International Journal of Software Engineering and Knowledge Engineering* **4**(1), 123–157.

Deriving Information Requirement in the Design of a Mathematics Workstation for Visually Impaired Students

Carol Linehan & John McCarthy

Department of Applied Psychology, University College Cork, Ireland.

Tel: *+353 21 902878*
EMail: *clineham@ucc.ie*

Mathematics presents particular access problems for students who are visually impaired. Although multi-media, computer technologies provide opportunities for creative solutions, a lack of empirical analyses of people who are visually impaired doing mathematics remains an obstacle for designers. We demonstrate the use of task analysis, and particularly the 'Wizard of Oz' technique, for eliciting user requirements in this context. The analysis highlights requirements relevant to the units of information used, the strategies employed for gaining and manipulating information, initiative in the interaction, and memory constraints when doing mathematics.

Keywords: requirements analysis, system design, Wizard of Oz, visual impairment, mathematics.

1 Introduction

The ability to understand and apply mathematics is a necessary element in education for life, for critical thinking, and not least for jobs:

> "The value of the subject [mathematics] must not be underestimated in terms not only of developing logical thinking and problem solving, but also in terms of opening up vocational possibilities and forming an essential skill in many areas of daily life. … The need for pupils to be able to manage their own money, to plan ahead in terms of cause and effect, to budget and keep simple accounts is self evident." (Chapman, 1978)

It is therefore essential that all students benefit from a thorough mathematical education. However, most mathematical notation is presented in a visual, two-dimensional, non-linear form, which provides access problems for students who are visually impaired. The term visual impairment refers to all forms of visual impairment from partial sight to total blindness.

The emergence of multi-media, computer technologies provides opportunities for creative solutions to this access problem. A number of research projects are engaged in this endeavour. MathTalk (Stevens & Edwards, 1994) uses earcons, based on non-verbal prosodic cues, to facilitate access to mathematical expressions. Non-speech audio presentation has also been used by Raman (1992). In contrast, Gardner's DotsPlus employs a mix of braille for numbers and variables and raised print for symbols (Monaghan, 1993). The technical problems in developing computer-based solutions are not trivial, and as a consequence most of these projects have been primarily concerned with establishing the technical feasibility of proposed solutions — a necessary first step. In the longer term a satisfactory solution requires a systematic, user-centred approach. The MATHS project takes just such an approach.

Mathematical Access to Technology and Science (MATHS) is a European Community funded project, the immediate aim of which is to develop a multi-media interactive computer workstation which enables blind and partially sighted users to read, write, and manipulate algebraic expressions. The MATHS system is primarily intended as a performance assistant rather than as a teaching system. A central focus of this project is a concern for usability at all stages in design and evaluation. As a first step in ensuring usability, the requirements analysis process was user centred. Surveys and interviews with visually impaired students were used to define broad problems of accessibility to mathematics and to computer technology from the perspective of the user (Cahill & McCarthy, 1994). A common element in most theoretical approaches to doing mathematics is a concern with the knowledge requirements that underlie performance. Lewis (Anderson, 1981, Ch.3) discusses the types of knowledge required to solve equations. The application of strategic knowledge during task performance involves both:

- A knowledge of operators or mathematical procedures, which are most likely built up from school based learning

- A decision making or executive function which decides for example what operators to apply and at what juncture. It also has a monitoring function for example if the expression is deemed too complex then the decision may be referred to the executive function whether to proceed or not.

The knowledge requirements discussed above are in some sense internal structures brought to the problem solution situation by the user. However before any operations or rules are applied there is an initial phase which is concerned with making sense of the maths problem. Ernest (1987) focuses on the mental representation of the meaning of the linguistic expressions of mathematics. He presents an information-processing model for the construction of mental representations. The first phase involves meaning extraction, during which students form a representation of the surface structure of an expression and then construct a more detailed representation through the analysis of sub-expressions. Related to the process of meaning representation is the manner in which the task is framed. Ernest claims that the routine presentation of mathematical expressions in the classroom is not usually a comprehension exercise contributing to the construction of a larger meaning context. Routinely maths are presented as the initial state of a task. Both Ernest and Lewis' account of knowledge requirements and problem representation focus on visually based mathematical problem solving.

However, in the absence of empirical analyses of visually impaired people doing mathematics, a comprehensive task analysis was carried out in order to better understand how visually impaired people go about reading and manipulating mathematical expressions. The objective of the analysis was to provide designers with user centred recommendations for the input and manipulation languages of the MATHS workstation. This paper is concerned with the results of one aspect of that analysis, the analysis of information requirements.

Task analysis in the context of capturing and analysing requirements is methodologically challenging. Diaper (1989, p.64) has argued that:

> "current practice in a task is frequently tied to the existing technology employed in the task and it is therefore difficult to produce a creative novel solution to system design based on such methods."

In an attempt to overcome this "paradox of change" the Wizard of Oz technique was employed in the current study. This technique allows the experimenter to simulate the expected behaviour of the new system. Previous applications of the technique include for example, Hill & Miller' (1988) investigation of the complexities of intelligent on-line help through an observation of the interaction between users of a statistical package and a human playing the role of help system. Maulsby et al. (1993) used the Wizard of Oz technique to test a new design for an intelligent agent. The present study demonstrates how Wizard of Oz can be used to elicit user requirements for system design in the absence of a functional prototype.

2 The Study

The Wizard of Oz technique attempts to simulate a basic MATHS workstation. This is achieved by the experimenter behaving as if she were a computer. The functionality of this human 'computer' was limited to giving (reading out) and storing (writing down) information according to subjects requests. The technique is structured in such a way that participants have to continually elicit information from the experimenter in order to complete seven mathematical problems. The goal in using this methodology is to determine the information requirements, cognitive strategies and labels used by people when doing mathematics. Eight visually impaired participants took part in this study. Their education ranged from early second level to third level (from 15 to 22 years of age). Participants were asked to work on seven mathematics problems, which consisted of solving equations and factorizing, for example:

- $5y^2 + 3(10 + 2(6y - 4) - 5)$. Solve when $y = 2$.
- Factorize $x^2 + 19x + 48$.

The instructions subjects received are given below:

> "The purpose of this session is to determine exactly how people go about doing maths. I'll read out a number of maths problems one at a time which I would like you to work on. It really doesn't matter if you get them right or wrong. When you are trying to work out the maths problems imagine that I am a computer which can store information for you, if you ask me to store, and read back anything to you, if you give the read command. As you solve the problems please do your best to think aloud. Don't worry if you are not sure about how to do a problem most people would not remember how to do all of them. Telling me what you are doing is far more important than getting the problem right"

Subjects could ask the experimenter to store (write down) and retrieve (read out) any details of the expression, or their manipulations of it. The face to face interaction was audio recorded. Transcriptions were then produced from the tapes.

A comprehensive quantitative analysis of all transcripts was undertaken, during which the type and frequency of each information request, action and error was recorded. Systematic qualitative analysis of the transcripts has also been carried out in order to identify relevant sequences of interaction. This allows an understanding of the types of strategies subjects use and the changes in strategy that occur during the solution of a problem because it explores sequences of interaction not just interactional events. Winograd & Flores (1986) have suggested that interaction regularities are best observed at that level. The complete results of both analyses are available in Linehan & McCarthy (1995). What follows is intended to exemplify the kind of data collected and information requirements derived from our analyses.

3 Information Requirements

Results of the task analysis highlighted requirements which are discussed here under the following headings: the units of information used, the strategies employed for gaining and manipulating information, initiative in the interaction, and memory constraints when doing mathematics.

3.1 Units of Information Used

Figure 1 is an extract from interaction between the experimenter (E) and a subject (S) which illustrates requirements for different units of information to be considered in the design of the workstation.

This task was quite complex and it is interesting to note the various information requests made by the subject. The subject begins in line 2 to ask for a chunk of information (i.e. more than one term but less than the whole expression) "the middle bracket" and then proceeds in line 4 to refer back to an earlier term. The subject then inputs this and asks for "the next bit" similar to a next term strategy. So here we see

1	E	5y squared plus 3 open bracket 10 plus 2 open bracket 6y minus 4 close bracket minus 5 close bracket. Solve when y equals 2 and I can write down or read back.
2	S	the middle bracket
3	E	6y minus 4
4	S	what's the first one y squared
5	E	5y squared
6	S	5y squared okay write it down and what's the next bit
7	E	plus 3 open bracket 10

Figure 1: An extract from interaction between the experimenter (E) and a subject (S) which illustrates requirements for different units of information.

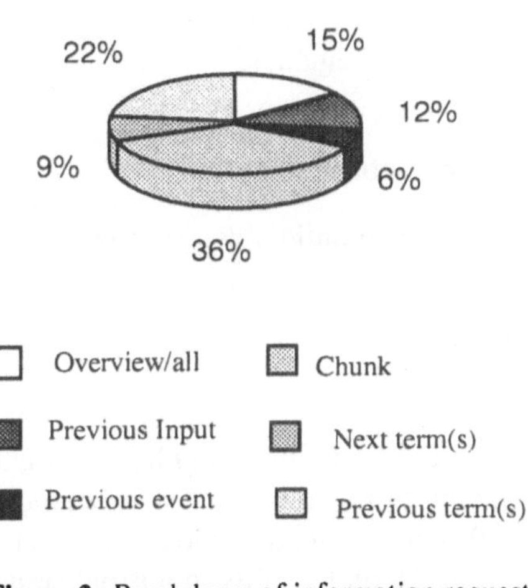

Figure 2: Breakdown of information requests.

in just 7 lines of interaction the subject asking for 3 different types of information and this was by no means uncommon among subjects.

People employed a variety of conceptual units when requesting information, as can be seen in Figure 2.

Looking at Figure 2 it can be seen that:

- 36% of all information requests were for chunks.
- 31% were for terms, of those 22% were for previous terms and 9% for next term.
- 15% of requests were for an overview of the original expression; "the question", "the equation", "the whole thing".
- 12% for the S previous input; "Give me what I've given you there to write down".
- 6% for the previous event:

E ... on the left hand side is $5x + 10 - 1 + 4x + 6 + x$

S ... \4\ repeat it again please

(\...\ indicates a pause of ... duration, measured in seconds. This / symbol denotes an interruption.)

Chunks were the most frequently requested unit of information, followed closely by terms both 'next' and 'previous'. The system will therefore need to be capable of presenting/retrieving information in a variety of units; chunks, terms, overviews etc. Designers should also bear in mind the individual differences observed, which suggest that some functions will not be used at all or less by some subjects while others will use these functions very frequently. Thus flexibility in command construction is essential. Subjects often wished to 'refer back' to an earlier term/chunk of information therefore some kind of 'search' facility may be more useful than simply scrolling up through reams of mathematics.

3.2 Strategies

Subjects demonstrated a number of strategies to:

- gain information in order to build a deeper representation of the expression; and
- carry out manipulations.

3.2.1 Gaining Information

Figure 3 is an extract of interaction which highlights an interesting strategy used for gaining and manipulating information. In this interaction the subject begins by asking for a chunk of information "there's another bracket isn't there can I have that one now", but from line 16 on he shifts to a serial strategy of asking for next number, next number etc. What is particularly interesting about this excerpt is that it shows the subject inputting and requesting information almost simultaneously (see lines 18 to 26). Having dealt with a string of terms the subject, in line 26, then requests the problem to be read out as it stands following his manipulations. There is an expectation that the results of the computations are being automatically stored. S has close control on the flow of information being presented however inputting is assumed by S to be done automatically. Having assumed the input of a number of terms over a number of lines the S then asks for a combined output of these terms. This requires a combination of the original problem and the parts the subject has worked on. Requests such as these highlight the importance of being able to combine input, manipulation and output in a 'seamless' manner.

Another common action was frequently to refer back in order to check information while inputting/manipulating the current expression, see Figure 1 line 4. The MATHS workstation should have no preference for one sequence of actions/type of strategy over another. The system should be directed at enabling users to make full use of their natural solution strategies for example for accessing, retrieving and manipulating information.

An alternative information gathering strategy is demonstrated by a different subject in the extract represented in Figure 5. Here the subject's strategy involved

14	S	then there is another bracket isn't there can I have that one now
15	E	sure 3 open bracket 10 plus 12y minus 8 minus 5 close bracket
16	S	the number outside the bracket
17	E	3
18	S	and the first number is
19	E	10
20	S	30 the next number
21	E	12y
22	S	36y the next number
23	E	minus 4 or sorry minus 8
24	S	minus 24 next number
25	E	minus 5
26	S	minus 15 \7\ and so what does the sum read again

Figure 3: An extract of interaction which illustrates strategies used for gaining and manipulating information.

---

trying to gain an overview of the expression, see line 3, followed by her interruption at line 4 to alter her request to that of "just read the 1st half". This is a sample of a very common strategy exhibited by many subjects, that of beginning by getting an overview of the expression followed by attempts to build up a deeper representation of the problem through analysing sub-expressions.

In the absence of a visual modality subjects could not easily gain a comprehensive overview of an expression. Therefore they seemed to undergo a longer preamble to meaning extraction. This was often followed by the subject checking to see if the structure of the expression was familiar and if the procedure for working it out was retrievable. If the subject encountered difficulties at this stage common responses were to withdraw from the interaction or ask for help. However if subjects felt relatively familiar with the structure of the expression and the procedure needed to work it out then they began to construct a more detailed representation of the expression. The system needs to support subjects gaining an overview of the initial expression in an efficient manner, particularly as this seems to be a common starting point for many in their attempts to build up a representation of the expression.

3.2.2 Manipulating Information

Two common action strategies used were input and move. In Lewis' account of problem solving (Anderson, 1981), he mentioned a number of operations such as transpose and collect. These operations were also demonstrated by subjects in this study that is moving and grouping like terms. With regard to explicit actions subjects will want to input both terms and chunks of information and move terms and chunks around. These types of activity must be supported. Commands such as 'move <specified> term' and 'move <specified> chunk' to <specified> location would be useful manipulation tools for potential users.

There were individual differences in the use of input and move actions, therefore there will have to be flexibility in command construction. There was an assumption

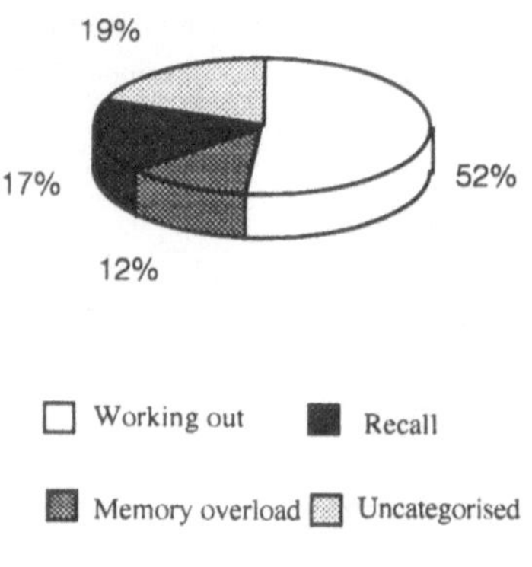

Figure 4: Breakdown of pauses.

---

of automatic input by some subjects that is they issued no explicit command to input (see Figure 3), consequently there may have to be some kind of cautionary signal issued by the workstation to guard against manipulations being lost. MATHS will have to take account of some users model of the system which involves automatic input and compilation of their verbalized manipulations. It was found that some subjects withdrew from the interaction if their efforts at problem solution were not successful. This would imply that following a lengthy pause the system may need to deliver a 'help option' sound or written message to re-orient the S to the task.

3.3 Initiative

Looking at Figure 4 it can be seen that the most frequently occurring pause was for working out at 52%. Limitations in working memory accounted for 29%, which breaks down into 17% for recall and 12% for memory overload pauses. And finally 19% of pauses could not be adequately categorized. The user not the system must have the initiative in the interaction as much of the mental work is being carried out in the user's head, as evidenced by the large amount of working out pauses.

E x squared plus 19x plus 48

S \8\ so ahm open up two sets of brackets first of all where there is room for 2 pieces within each (example of a pause to work out the mathematical procedure to be used)

The above example of a 'working out' pause highlights the importance of the user and not the system deciding how much time is required to formulate actions. Figure 5 is an extract of interaction which highlights the necessity for the interaction to be user driven.

In line 8 the experimenter reads the chunk of information the subject asked for, but the pause and the statement by the subject in line 9 "you'll have to say it again I'm sorry I can't I can't" clearly indicates problems of information overload. In line 12 the subject appears to be making some progress by focusing on the numbers alone

1	E	5x plus 10 minus 1 plus 4x plus 6 plus x equals 2x minus 3 minus x
	(Note S looked startled)	
2	E	take your time
3	S	could you repeat it so please
4	E	5x /
5	S	/can you read just the first half
6	E	yes so you want me to read everything on the left-hand side
7	S	yes
8	E	5x plus 10 minus 1 plus 4x plus 6 plus x
9	S	\6\...you'll have to say it again I'm sorry I can't I can't
10	E	that's fine I'll read it again
11	E	5x plus 10 minus 1 plus 4x plus 6 plus x
12	S	okay 15 write down 15 \4\ plus \4\ what was the very first x?
13	E	5x
14	S	\3\ 9x minus 1x 8x sorry now

Figure 5: An extract which highlights the issue of user initiative in the interaction.

and working those out, however once this has been done the subject can no longer remember the x terms and so asks "what was the very first x?".

The interaction must be user driven not just temporally but also in terms of the amount of information the user takes on, and when such information is presented, for example it is quite likely that the user will wish to access information in chunks/terms at various points in the interaction rather than just receiving the whole equation by default. On the issue of control there may be a need for an interrupt facility, to enable a re-issuing of commands by the subject (see Figure 5 line 5). If the user lacks such control over the flow of information, overload is likely to result. It is vital that users be given control of the interaction so that their natural strategies are not overly constrained by the system. However it is possible that if the user becomes frustrated in their attempts at problem solution they will relinquish control of the interaction to the system.

3.4 *Memory*

Figure 6 details the breakdown of errors made by subject:

- 27% were due to errors with signs;
- 22% were as a result of faulty recall;
- 16% of errors were procedural;
- 14% resulted from memory overload;
- 13% were accounted for by miscalculations;and
- 8% could not be categorized.

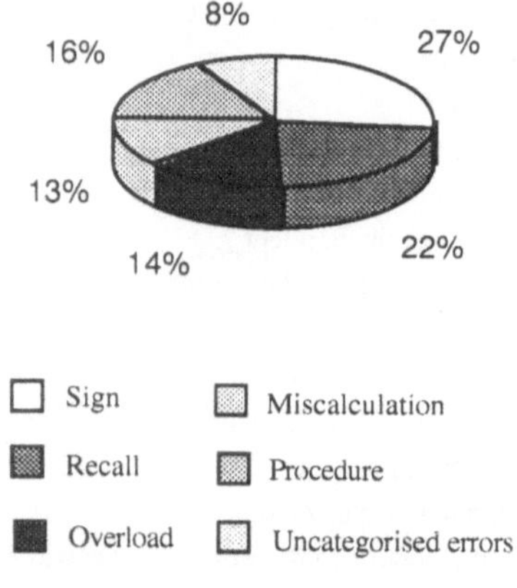

Figure 6: Breakdown of errors made.

The error categories of faulty recall, the special case of faulty recall of a terms sign and memory overload which together account for 63% of errors made all involve limited memory capability.

Problems of overload appeared to be quite common among subjects, for example:

E now $5x + 10 - 1 + 4x + 6 + x$ equals $2x - 3 - x$ and solve for x

S $5x - 4x$ is x is there another x equals $2x$ is it

In this interactional event E presents information and S attempts to give details of/a verbatim recall of the information presented but does so incorrectly. With 64% of information requests involving terms or chunks (see Figure 2), this would seem to suggest that the whole expression seemed too much to handle for many subjects, who lacked an external memory source. By requesting smaller units of information it could be inferred that subjects were trying to reduce the burden on working memory by breaking up the problem into more manageable units, for example chunks, in order to form a mental representation of the expression. However by breaking up or dealing with expressions term by term or in chunks it is likely that blind students may miss out on the type of information conveyed by scanning the whole expression. Problems such as parsing errors, forgetting or missing out part of the expression or manipulations done may arise because the blind student is restricted to looking at discrete sections of the expression. Perhaps, ideally, blind students as with their sighted counterparts could gain an overview of the expression followed by a more detailed analysis of various sub expressions.

An analysis of the pauses made by subjects during task performance highlighted some interesting issues (see Figure 4). Pauses due to limitations in working memory occurred quite frequently and consistently across subjects. For example:

"15 \4\ plus \4\ what was the very first x"; or

"\6\ you'll have to go through it again I'm sorry I can't I can't".

The consistency in the occurrence of pauses due to memory overload and recall suggests that these problems are common among subjects. This reinforces the finding in an earlier user survey by Cahill et al. (in press) that visually impaired students difficulties with algebraic expressions are mainly due to memory overload and accuracy and speed of manipulation.

Most errors were due to memory limitations and/or information overload, therefore the role of the system as an efficient external source of memory is quite important. The majority of subjects difficulties seemed to lie in failing to remember material or remembering it incorrectly. Limitations materialized as:

- Difficulties forming an adequate representation of the structure of an expression.
- Problems remembering terms in the expression.
- Keeping track of the manipulation process.

There is a need for the system to act as an efficient external memory source to relieve the burden on users working memory and to make their problem solving more economical both in terms of length of manipulations and time taken. There should be little cost for interruptions to a task. If task performance is interrupted you may lose some internal information for example an idea forming of what you are about to do next. However the manipulation process to date should be easily re-accessed by the user and the display should facilitate recovery. MATHS should provide the same type of cues for blind students as an external visual display does for sighted students. Such cues aid users in choosing a solution strategy and perhaps reduce the likelihood of parsing errors occurring. Display based problem solving is resistant to many errors because the display makes the process largely independent of internal memory failures.

It should be noted that some subjects needed to hear the problem a number of times before they could begin to work it out whereas others solved the same problem having heard it only twice. A possible reason for this is that subjects who had had more recent experiences with algebra were familiar with the procedures for working out the problems, therefore less of their running memory capacity would be taken up with trying to remember how to do the problem, leaving them freer to concentrate on remembering the terms and doing the necessary calculations. A possible implication for the system is that it will have to take account of differing levels of ability/experience and so it needs to be flexible in its presentation of material.

4 Discussion

The aim of this study was to understand better the processes by which visually impaired students read and manipulate mathematical expressions. To that end a systematic task analysis of visually impaired and sighted students working on seven algebraic expressions was carried out. Using the Wizard of Oz technique the experimenter simulated the behaviour of the eventual workstation.

The process of solving equations is subject to some constraints for example the rules of mathematics. However within the confines of these constraints people solve equations in many orders. From the results of this task analysis it should be clear that people use a variety of strategies to tackle algebraic problems. MATHS should not impose any further constraints on peoples natural solution strategies. The frame of the task for many subjects appeared to be as Ernest proposed — the initial state of a mathematical task rather than contributing to the construction of a larger meaning context. Many subjects seemed to focus on completing the task and producing an acceptable response rather than gaining a better understanding of mathematics. However in contrast others viewed the task as a co-operative activity. Their focus was on the interaction itself rather than the task at hand. In terms of the system such users will probably want a great deal of interaction during the solution process. Subjects with a 'co-operative' model of the system were seen to externalize everything, the subject put it all 'out there' for the experimenter (or system) to pick up, store or check. The interaction process is not driven by a need for information but rather to elicit co-operation.

There appeared to be no shared systematic use of labels with regard to mathematics by this group of subjects. Words such as plus, minus, multiply and divide are quite commonly used but beyond these the labels used were quite vague. For example the maths tasks were referred to as questions, problems, the original thing, etc. The individual terms were referred to as x's, numbers, the next bit, what other y numbers do we have, etc. The way that subjects labelled terms was quite vague but this could be in part attributed to the interpersonal context of the task that is they were interacting with another person rather than a computer.

4.1 Design Recommendations

The analysis also resulted in some specific design principles/recommendations.

- It is vital that the user have control over the flow of the interaction to avoid problems of overload. An obvious solution to part of this problem is to allow the reader to control which part of an expression is presented at any one time by using browsing. The default browsing style in MATHS speaks one term, or complex item (such as a fraction), each time the user presses the space bar. Free style browsing is also allowed. A set of commands, referred to as the algebra browsing language (ABL), allows the reader to move to any part of the expression, by either using a single simple command or combining a set of commands to achieve a goal. The commands are a combination of an action and target word for example, next term or show expression. As well as browsing, the notion of using place holders to hide complex information is used. Place holders are a mechanism by which the amount of information presented to the user at any one time may be controlled. Within a document, text and algebra notation are available in separate views. The mathematical expression appears as a place-holder within the text for example as a tag that links to the expression displayed visually in a separate window on the screen.

As the user moves through the text he or she will meet an object that simply says 'an expression' or appears as a braille place-holder with the same message. The reader can ask for a full utterance by issuing the command 'show expression' from the keyboard or by using speech input, thus giving the user greater control over information flow.

- It was found that many errors occurred due to memory limitations therefore the system needs to provide an efficient external memory source. One method to reduce the load on internal memory is given with the ABL. The ABL offers the user a means of gaining access to any part of an expression therefore the user may not have to rely on remembering the whole of an expression during a task.

- The system needs to support subjects gaining an overview of the initial expression in an efficient manner, particularly as this seems to be a common starting point for many in their attempts to build up a representation of the expression. An important module in the MATHS workstation is the document editor which presents maths in a 'What you see is what you get' (WYSIWYG) manner while working according to an internal representation. A main feature of the editor is its capability to open several views on the same document, for every view a new window is opened showing the text in a different way for example as a table of contents or a mathematics view. In terms of gaining an overview, the view with the table of contents can be available permanently in a separate window. By simply selecting this window a quick overview can be gained. These views can be rendered for a student who is visually impaired through a speech synthesizer or braille display.

  A user can also ask for a non-speech audio 'glance' at an expression. A glance at the structure of an expression was designed for MATHS, these were called algebra earcons. In an algebra earcon each object within an expression is replaced by a musical tone. Earcons share the same parameters of rhythm, pitch, amplitude, timbre, tempo as speech. A glance can give the listener a preview of the structure of an expression so that he or she can judge the complexity and decide how to tackle the reading of that expression.

- People employ a variety of conceptual units when doing mathematics. Therefore it is proposed that the MATHS workstation should support interaction with objects at the following levels:

  Chunks.
  Terms, both next and previous.
  An overview of the expression.
  Access to Previous input.
  Access to Previous event.

- Individual differences were observed in the use of functions; consequently there will have to be flexibility in command construction. The requirement for flexibility arose from the observation of the number of strategies used by subjects to access and manipulate information. The system should provide support for the variety of input and manipulation actions that subjects engaged in. The patterns of interaction observed underline the importance of being able to combine input, manipulation and output in a seamless manner.

In conclusion, we would argue that early attention to the context of use and the specific requirements of the user are central to designing systems which will solve the mathematical access problem for those who are visually impaired. The analysis and recommendations outlined in this paper demonstrate the value of task analysis, particularly the Wizard of Oz technique, in eliciting requirements before any usable prototype is available.

Acknowledgements

The MATHS project is being carried out as part of the Commission of European Communities TIDE(Technology Initiative for Disabled and Elderly People) programme. The MATHS project consortium consists of researchers from University College Cork (Ireland), Katholieke Universiteit Leuven (Belgium), University of York (UK), University of Bradford (UK), F H Papenmeier (Germany), GRIF SA (France) and Electric Brain Company (UK). We would like to thank all of the MATHS partners for their comments on this work.

References

Anderson, J. R. (1981), *Cognitive Skills and their Acquisition*, Lawrence Erlbaum Associates.

Cahill, H. & McCarthy, J. (1994), "Ensuring Usability in Interface Design: A Workstation to provide Usable Access to Mathematics for Visually Disabled Users", *Information and Technology for the Disabled Journal.* (electronic journal).

Cahill, H., Linehan, C., McCarthy, J., Bormans, G. & Engelen, J. (in press), "A Survey of Blind and Partially Sighted Students' Mathematical Access Difficulties and Experience of Computer Technology in Ireland and Belgium", *Journal of Visual Impairment and Blindness.*

Chapman, E. K. (1978), *Visually Handicapped Children and Young People*, Routledge and Kegan Paul.

Diaper, D. (ed.) (1989), *Task Analysis for Human–Computer Interaction*, Ellis Horwood.

Ernest, P. (1987), "A Model of the Cognitive Meaning of Mathematical Expressions", *British Journal of Educational Psychology* **57**, 343–370.

Hill, W. C. & Miller, J. R. (1988), Justified Advice: A Semi-naturalistic Study of Advisory Strategies, *in* E. Soloway, D. Frye & S. B. Sheppard (eds.), "Proceedings of CHI'88: Human Factors in Computing Systems", ACM Press, pp.185–190.

Linehan, C. & McCarthy, J. (1995), A Task Analysis of Students doing Mathematics: Contributing to the Design of the Input and Manipulation Languages, EC TIDE Project 1033: MATHS Internal Report 15.3, University College Cork.

Maulsby, D., Greenberg, S. & Mander, R. (1993), Prototyping an Intelligent Agent through Wizard of Oz, *in* S. Ashlund, K. Mullet, A. Henderson, E. Hollnagel & T. White (eds.), "Proceedings of INTERCHI'93", ACM Press, pp.277–284.

Monaghan, P. (1993), "Gaining Inspiration from Catastrophe", *The Chronicle of Higher Education.* 27th October.

Raman, T. V. (1992), "An Audio View of LaTeX Documents", *Tugboat* **13**(3), 372–377.

Stevens, R. & Edwards, A. (1994), Analysis of Audio Approaches, MATHS Project, Internal Report 6, Department of Computer Science, University of York, UK.

Winograd, T. & Flores, F. (1986), *Understanding Computers and Cognition: A New Foundation for Design*, Addison–Wesley.

Second-Language Help for Windows Applications

George R S Weir[†], Giorgos Lepouras[‡] & Ulysses Sakellaridis[§]

[†] *Department of Computer Science, University of Strathclyde, Glasgow G11 XH, UK.*

Tel: *+44 141 552 4400*
EMail: *gw@cs.strath.ac.uk*

[‡] *Department of Informatics, University of Athens, Athens 157 71, Greece.*

Tel: *+30 1 729 1885*
EMail: *glepoura@di.uoa.gr*

[§] *Business Administration Department, University of the Aegean, Chios 821 00, Greece.*

Tel: *+30 271 43689*
EMail: *osak@aegean.gr*

This paper describes an approach to the second-language problem for user-support in the context of existing MS-Windows applications. We outline a methodology for deriving foci for support, and present guidelines for the addition of second-language enhancements. Finally, we detail our procedure for implementing such help facilities with examples of enhanced Chinese and Greek second-language support.

Keywords: user support, help re-engineering, second-language help.

1 Introduction

In a context in which non-native speakers of English are increasingly obliged to operate with English-based computerized information systems, problems in user interaction are inevitable. Language itself will introduce particular scope for difficulties and misunderstanding in the use of such systems. This situation and attempts to alleviate its adversity characterize the 'second-language problem' for human–computer interaction. The present paper outlines a methodology for addressing the second-language problem and details our guidelines and procedures for enhancing user support in existing MS-Windows applications.

1.1 The Second-language Problem

In recent years some attention has focused on the issue of 'internationalization' (Russo & Boor, 1993) while the development of Unicode (van Camp, 1994) has addressed support for diverse font families. According to Uren et al. (1993, p.5):

> "The purpose of Internationalization is to enable a software product, that is, to provide the features so that Localizers may conveniently and easily choose the appropriate form of the feature for their particular language."

Through such internationalized software, the cost of producing localized versions of the product decreases, but full language localization of software also faces obstacles. The main drawback of this solution is its likely cost in terms of time and effort. This increases radically in cases of software products that have not been designed on internationalized principles, which is often the case with existing applications. In such cases, complete re-implementation may be the only adequate solution. But this strategy is usually reserved for cases where the user community (and the market potential) can justify the cost.

One might expect that a fully language-localized software product would solve all problems of language misunderstanding for the end user. Experience suggests otherwise, that is, instead of full amelioration, it adds or replaces problems with new ones. One reason for this is the absence of standardized terminology.

1.2 Terminological Difficulties

In a cross-language comparison between three well known and widely used, localized word processors (Greek Word 6.0 for Windows, Greek Lotus Ami Pro 3.0 for Windows, Greek WordPerfect for Windows, and their English counterparts), we found that all of the English word processor versions used the same core set of terminology, but this was not true for their Greek versions (Lepouras & Weir, in preparation).

For example, the term 'header' may be familiar to native speakers of English and is used across each of the English-based word processors, but the choice of Greek equivalent is problematic.

Microsoft has replaced 'header' with 'κεφαλίδα'. Although this is the accurate translation of the English term, it is an uncommon expression in Greek with no familiar connotation. In contrast, Lotus has replaced 'header' with 'υπέρτιτλος'. This Greek term means 'super-title'. Finally, in Greek WordPerfect we find that the term 'header' has been replaced with 'τίτλος σελίδας'. This Greek phrase literally means 'page title'.

There can be little doubt that Greek speakers face confusion over this range of terminology, particularly since the header bears no obvious connection to the title of a document.

Further illustrations can be drawn from this comparison of localized word processors. For example, the Greek equivalent of the English term 'bullets' appears in Microsoft Word as 'κουκκίδες'. The commonest interpretation of this Greek term corresponds to the meaning of 'bullets' (as found in a document format).

WordPerfect, in contrast, uses a literal translation of 'bullets' ('σφαίρες') which usually refers to bullets as found in a gun (or more generally to 'spheres'). Finally, Lotus Ami Pro substitutes 'bullet' with 'σύμβολο' which means 'symbol'. Again, the lack of standard terminology promises scope for misunderstanding.

Of course, the subtlety of the Greek language was not simply ignored during design of these systems. There are difficulties inherent in the translation process which impose a burden of interpretation on native Greek users.

1.3 Mixed Environments

Further problems can arise when the user has to work in a 'mixed' environment (i.e. an environment where both localized and non-localized applications exist). In this situation the advantage of uniformity and consistency is lost. In all windowing interfaces, applications are expected to be, amongst other things, linguistically consistent within themselves and with other applications. This is a problem illustrated in the above examples, but it also stands true for applications that convey their messages, text, help, etc. in different languages.

Consider the case of a user who is obliged to work both with a localized word processor and a non-localized designer application. Here, the advantage of using a localized application becomes a drawback, since the user is compelled to interact in two different languages. Inevitably, the need for proficiency in any second-language (even English) can lead to confusion.

1.4 Cross-language Confusion

Boulton describes several causes of cross-language misunderstanding and identifies four common characteristics (Boulton, 1973):

- Malapropism.
- Differences in definition.
- Differences of association.
- Misunderstanding of the context.

Each of these scenarios describes a basis for miscomprehension. In the first case, the second-language user confuses one term with another that is morphologically similar but semantically dissimilar. For example, the English word 'routing' might be confused with 'routine' which looks similar but means something quite different. Malapropisms are likely to be common among second-language readers since such users characteristically attend to 'surface' features of the lesser known language.

Misunderstanding may also arise through differences in the definition of words. This may occur in cases where one term has frequent use but diverse applications. For example, the word 'server' as applied to X Windows applications may readily be misconstrued by someone who is acquainted solely with distributed file systems.

Differences in association relate to the connotation of words. A native language speaker may be aware of connotative aspects that are lost on the second-language user, though the latter may be familiar with the foreign word or expression in question (e.g. linguistic metaphors). Finally, influence from the cultural context in which terms are familiarly encountered may influence the interpretation of second-language expressions.

Beyond these potential comprehension failures, a number of general factors are likely to cause difficulties for non-native users of English. These include 'special use' expressions, (e.g. jargon, slang, or idioms) which are likely to prove unfamiliar or elusive for second-language users. Likewise, acronyms depend upon the readers familiarity with their expansion. Such abbreviations are a compressed form of language but for non-native speakers of English acronyms are a compressed foreign language.

Even between American and British English there are instances of apparently identical words bearing different meanings or cases of what is acceptable in one language being vulgar in the other. This is a case of 'interference' in which the reader's interpretation of the second-language is influenced (and often corrupted) by the native language.

Naturally, we colour our interpretation according to our own background and experience. In the context of second-language interpretation such background can become interference and lead to error. Indeed, the scope for such interference in user-computer interaction should not be underestimated.

For example, in a survey of twenty Greek subjects at a Word for Windows seminar for novice users, there were cases of people being confused by the term 'font'. Several thought this equivalent to 'φόντο' ('fonto') which means 'background'. This typifies interference from a native language on the interpretation of English.

In the face of such problems, one may adopt a charitable view and regard such terminological and linguistic turmoil as an inevitable consequence of misfit in system conversion from English to native language (rather akin to inherent difficulties in translation from one cultural and linguistic context to another). Perhaps the aim of complete localization is misguided or destined for problems.

1.5 Second-language Support

With respect to support for information exchange between user and computer system, a more realistic approach may seek to provide partial duplication of an English-language original. This holds the prospect of facilitating comprehension where the perceived need is greatest whilst minimizing the effort of implementing the native language component.

'Second-language explication' is a subtle approach to the application of local language supplements. This alternative focuses on 'key' areas of interaction where the greatest need for native language support is anticipated. In some cases, the needs of the computer user may be adequately met through equivalent translation of existing English information. In other cases, e.g. problematic points in user interaction, the best support may lie not in providing a translation of English help, but through a first-language *elucidation* of the original English material. This approach promises a number of significant benefits over full software localization. These include:

- Low cost and low implementation effort.
- Easy targeting of different user expertise levels.
- Opportunity to remedy existing shortcomings in original application help.
- Focus on specific linguistic needs in delivered information.

At the same time, the second-language explication approach raises a number of vital issues, including:

- How to identify the most likely problematic areas of user interaction.
- How to categorize the possible user interaction so as to provide the most suitable type of user support, for example, explication, annotation, summary, example, tutorial (Weir & Ni, 1993).
- How to integrate this type of user support within existing applications.

In the following, we briefly outline a methodological approach to these issues before describing in detail our principles and procedures for enhancing existing applications with second-language user support.

2 Methodology

Since our purpose in this paper is to elucidate guidelines and techniques for second-language enhancement in user support we do not present the methodology for enhanced user support in detail. However, the proposed alternative to full language localization requires two major stages:

1. Determine foci for support.
2. Implement enhanced support in user's native language.

Clearly, the first stage in this methodology is crucial. In order to provide lean and efficient second-language support one must identify those aspects of the application which are most likely to generate user difficulties. This is the classical component of the re-engineering problem. The second aspect in determining focus is the extra requirement to locate likely sources of language-based user problems. The process of determining the focus for second-language enhancements includes the following:

- User monitoring.
- Help system analysis.
- Feature checklist.
- Native speaker informants.

An on-line user monitoring facility assists in the detection of problematic areas of user interaction for specific target applications. This information is coupled with several analyses of any existing on-line documentation. This aims principally to determine the adequacy of present help coverage.

Subsequently, a systematic content analysis is used to produce an application feature checklist. In turn, this checklist is used in collaboration with a native-language informant to classify the likely benefit of second-language enhancements. The final step in this sequence is use of the annotated checklist to support selection of native language supplements. This leads directly to the implementation phase of the enhanced user support. Such help re-engineering aims to have low overheads, be application independent, and also native language independent.

3 Guidelines for Second-language Enhancement

In the course of developing the above methodology we have formulated a number of guidelines to assist in the design of second-language enhancements. These guidelines are derived from our experience in working with second-language computer users and the use of localized systems. While not presented as a comprehensive list, the following guidelines apply specifically to applications with existing English-language on-line help:

- Provide 2nd language for section headings.
- Avoid literal translations where alternative local terms are available.
- Identify 'key terms' in existing help and provide 2nd language equivalents in situ.
- Illustrate potentially 'obscure concepts' with examples in 2nd language.
- Summarize verbose but significant aspects of help.
- Explain any existing acronyms in local terms.
- Clarify any jargon, idioms, or aphorisms.
- Where 'accurate' translation is difficult, employ explication to avoid confusion.

As with all guidelines, these recommendations require a degree of interpretation in the context of any specific computer application. Additionally, these principles presuppose insights derived from the application analysis, the feature checklist and native language informant, in order to identify the most significant information components and the points at which English language usage may give rise to problems in comprehension.

In what follows, we illustrate the results of applying this re-engineering process to existing help in MS-Windows applications.

4 Enhancing Windows Help Applications

Microsoft Windows 3.1 provides a standard help system that supports the presentation of context sensitive help across all Windows applications. This employs a 'help engine' (WinHelp) which operates on application specific help files (files with the *.hlp* suffix). These help files are created using a Microsoft help compiler on original data files. Help files are structured hypertext with keyword search and support for multimedia.

Context sensitive 'hooks' tie help files to the application that they support. Significantly, this approach entails a separation between any Windows application and its associated help files. When combined with the inherent separation between the Windows help engine and its data files, this renders Windows an ideal environment for help re-engineering. By decompiling the original data files from the compiled *.hlp* file, adding selected information (specifically second-language support) and then recompiling, the result is an enhanced help file that retains all its context sensitive links from the original application.

4.1 Adding Second-language Support

After the design phase for addition of second-language support, the software re-engineering process begins with de-compilation of the original application help files. For this purpose, a help decompiler has been developed at the Department of Informatics, University of Athens. This program re-creates the initial data files from the compiled *.hlp* files. (For background on the structure of *.hlp* files (Davis, 1993a; 1993b).

Step two entails modification of these data files to include the desired additional support. These supplements take the form of second-language translations, examples, explanations and summaries. (Of course, further information in English can be added if required.) To maintain the integrity of the original application help system, changes are not normally made to its initial content or layout.

Some languages, including Chinese, Greek. Arabic, Thai and Japanese, require extended facilities to support the input and display of non-Latin characters. In our examples, for Chinese text processing we employed Microsoft Windows 3.1, Chinese version, while Greek character handling was achieved through use of Microsoft Windows 3.1 with Greek support.

The final step in the mechanics of help re-engineering for Windows is re-compilation of help files. For this purpose, any of a range of help compilers can be used. Such a compiler is standardly provided with Microsoft programming environments, such as Visual C++, Visual Basic. In addition, Microsoft recently released their compiler into the public domain.

When recompiled, the newly enhanced help file appropriates the name of the original application's *.hlp* file which it replaces. All context sensitive links from the application to its help topics are undisturbed.

4.2 Examples

For evaluation of the second-language enhancement methodology, a Windows application was selected (an arcade-style game called Gravity Well). Although the help

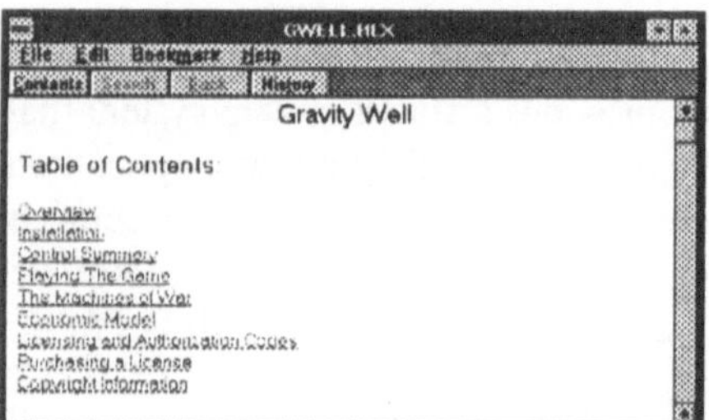

Figure 1: Original Gravity Well help screen.

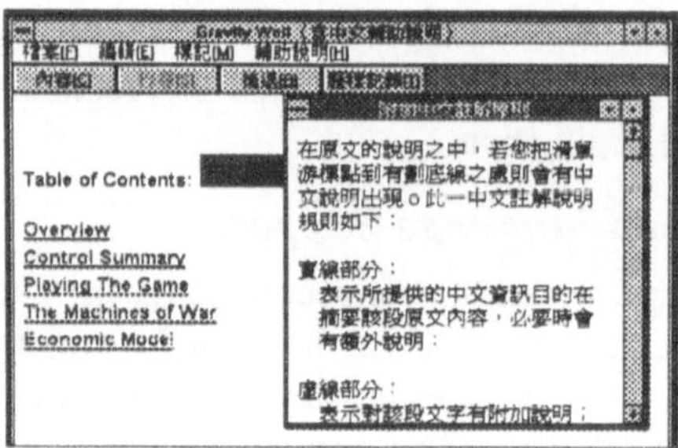

Figure 2: Chinese enhanced help screen.

---

files for this game were relatively small, the complexity of the game itself meant that there was enough depth for evaluation purposes.

A new version of the application help system was created containing Chinese text and audio enhancements. Figure 1 shows a screen from the original Gravity Well help file.

In the enhanced Chinese help system for Gravity Well, three techniques are used to convey the availability of Chinese language enhancements to the user. Underlining indicates a summary for the following paragraph, if appropriate, additional Chinese explanation is also be attached. Dotted underlining signifies the presence of Chinese explanation for the underlined text. Finally, buttons with Chinese labels explicitly identify the information that can be invoked through their selection.

Figure 2 shows a screen from the Chinese support for Gravity Well with an introduction to the enhancements already opened. As a simplification for the purposes of evaluation, three topics from the original help system have been omitted. Since these items concerned product licensing, purchasing and copyright, they were regarded as superfluous to the needs of the experiment.

A similar approach has been adopted in developing Greek-enhanced help systems. Figure 3 shows an initial screen from the Greek-support version of the Gravity Well help system.

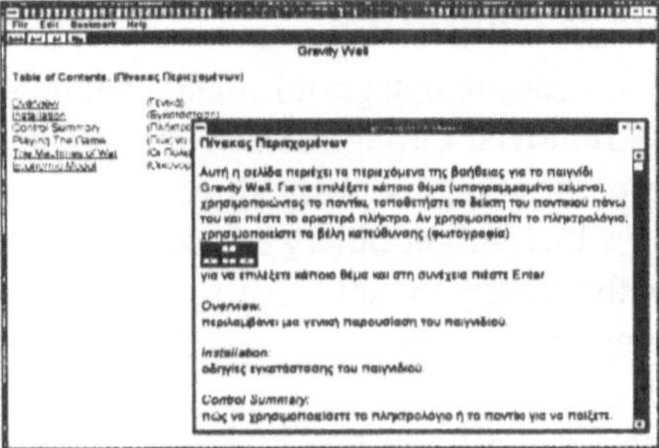

Figure 3: Greek enhanced help screen.

Note that, in keeping with our guidelines, in the Greek and Chinese systems the section headings also appear as translated second-language.

5 Conclusions

The methodology presented in this paper is advocated as an alternative to full language translation of software and has two objectives:

- To enhance the effectiveness of existing application help.
- To avoid problems that might arise during the full translation process.

The first objective is addressed by identifying potential shortcomings in the original help and providing suitable remedial support. This is preferable to a full translation approach, which, by retaining the information content of the original, would maintain any inadequacies of that version. The second objective is addressed by alleviating problems that might otherwise beset the full translation process. To substantiate this claim, we might consider how the advocated 'selective' second-language approach fairs against the difficulties cited earlier for the full translation strategy.

5.1 Terminological Difficulties

Any risks to comprehension caused by non-standard terminology are met through use of annotations and examples rather than simple direct translations. While there is never any fail-safe in translation, this strategy should minimize the causes of terminological difficulty.

5.2 Mixed Environment

On our selective second-language approach we aim to leave the user interface unaltered by the second-language supplements. Thereby, the consistency of the environment is not violated. The use of native language is restricted to user support and does not replace the original help. Rather, it strengthens the user support by providing information redundancy in the form of native language support.

5.3 *Cross-Language Confusion*

The probable causes of cross-language misunderstandings are minimized and in some cases completely removed through selective support in the user's native language. The guidelines described previously, directly address any obscure concepts, acronyms, jargon, etc., which might otherwise cause linguistic confusion. In summary, the proposed methodology for selective second-language support tackles the key failings of the complete translation approach whilst yielding significant additional enhancements in user support.

As well as having low cost and low effort in implementation, this approach offers easy targeting of different user needs both in terms of application expertise and linguistic competence. Furthermore, the presented examples endorse the practicality of this approach for the MS-Windows environment.

We are presently conducting evaluations on Chinese and Greek examples of such support under Microsoft Windows 3.1 and preliminary indications vindicate the recommended approach. Full details of these findings will be presented in the near future.

Acknowledgements

We are grateful to Paoli Kuo (University of Strathclyde), Eleni Koutrouli, and Marianna Papavasiliou (University of Athens) for their project work on Chinese and Greek support. Our collaboration is supported by the British Council and the University of Athens under project #70/4/1755 and by the EU within the Robust Human–Machine Interaction (RoHMI) project.

References

Boulton, M. (1973), *The Anatomy of Language: Saying What We Mean*, Routledge and Kegan Paul.

Davis, P. (1993a), "Documenting Documentation — Part I", *Dr Dobbs Journal* **120**, 23–40.

Davis, P. (1993b), "Documenting Documentation — Part II", *Dr Dobbs Journal* **120**, 116–121.

Lepouras, G. & Weir, G. R. S. (in preparation), "Its not Greek to Me: A Cross Language Study of Three Word Processors".

Russo, P. & Boor, S. (1993), How Fluent Is Your Interface? Designing for International Users, *in* S. Ashlund, K. Mullet, A. Henderson, E. Hollnagel & T. White (eds.), "Proceedings of INTERCHI'93", ACM Press, pp.342–347.

Uren, E., Howard, R. & Tiziana, P. (1993), *Software Internationalization and Localization*, Van Nostrand Reinhold.

van Camp, D. (1994), "Unicode and Software Globalisation", *Dr Dobbs Journal* **121**, 46–50.

Weir, G. R. S. & Ni, X. Q. (1993), Second-language User Support, Research Report HCI-03–93, Department of Computer Science, University of Strathclyde, Glasgow, UK. This document is available at ftp://ftp.cs.strath.ac.uk/research-reports/.

Extending GUIs

Eye-based Control of Standard GUI Software

Howell Istance†, Christian Spinner† & Peter Alan Howarth‡

† *Department of Computer Science, De Montfort University, The Gateway, Leicester, Leicestershire LE1 9BH, UK.*

EMail: *hoi@dmu.ac.uk*

‡ *Department of Human Sciences, Loughborough University, Loughborough, Leicestershire LE11 3TU, UK.*

EMail: *P.A.Howarth@lboro.ac.uk*

This paper discusses the design and initial evaluation of a visual on-screen keyboard, operated by eye-gaze, intended for use by motor-impaired users. The idea of an on-screen keyboard controlled by eye or by other modalities is not new. However, the keyboard presented here is different in two important respects. First, it enables interaction with unmodified standard Graphical User Interface (GUI) software written for able-bodied users, and provides eye-based control over menus, dialogue boxes, and scrollers; it is not solely designed around the need to enter text. Second, the software architecture enables the keyboard to respond to events generated in the windows environment by the application it is controlling. This allows the keyboard to adapt automatically to the application context by, for example, loading a specific set of keys designed for use with particular menus whenever a menu is displayed in the target application. Results of initial evaluation trials are presented and the implications for improvements in design are discussed.

Keywords: eye-control, visual keyboard, physically-challenged, disability, handicapped.

1 Introduction

An important element in enabling people with various forms of motor impairment to work in office environments is to provide the means whereby they can use the same software tools at the workplace as their able-bodied colleagues. This requires building interaction devices which not only enable effective interaction with a single application but are sufficiently flexible to allow the user to switch quickly between different software applications without the need to reconfigure the device. Eye-based interaction is attractive for a number of reasons. First, it offers the prospect of reducing learning time by providing a 'natural' means of pointing at a displayed object on-screen. Second, moving the eye is fast and positioning a pointer on a required object can be done quickly, even if other interaction components may be relatively time-consuming compared with normal usage of keyboard and mouse. Third, users with severe degrees of motor impairment often retain good ocular motor control, and so devices based on eye-movement may be used by a larger range of users with motor impairments than devices relying on other muscle groups.

The advantages have, however, to be offset against the known problems of eye-based interaction. These include the level of accuracy with which eye position can be measured, the degree of fine control that the user can exercise over eye movement and the need to be able to disengage eye-control whenever the user wishes to look at the screen without issuing commands. To overcome these problems, eye-based control may be combined with other input modalities, such as speech, so that eye-gaze is used for pointer positioning only and other modes of input are used to make selection actions (equivalent to those normally made by the mouse button). However, at this stage we have restricted ourselves to the use of the eyes alone for both cursor control and selection, rather than investigating such combinations. Previous work (Istance & Howarth, 1994) investigated the use of eye-gaze for emulation of a mouse to interact directly with standard Graphical User Interface (GUI) applications, and it was concluded then that an indirect 'soft' control device, such as an on-screen keyboard,* offered a means of overcoming many of the problems associated with the direct eye-based interaction approach. If these problems are overcome, then one has no need to invoke additional input modalities, and one does not then have to rely upon the user having any form of motor control other than over their eyes alone.

The idea of a visual keyboard displayed on a screen and operated by some external device is certainly not new. Indeed, visual keyboards have been developed in the past for use with a variety of interaction devices, such as joysticks and mice, as well as eye-gaze control. Some of these have emulated normal keyboards, but in doing so have been restricted almost entirely to text entry. These have not allowed control over the variety of objects, such as those contained in menus and dialogue boxes, found in modern direct manipulation GUI software. There are many applications, such as Web browsers, which have very limited requirements for text entry but instead require interaction with displayed documents, such as scrolling or clicking on links, as well as

*In this paper, '*virtual keyboard*' is used as a general term to describe alternative keyboards (which do not necessarily have a visual presentation on the screen), whereas the terms *visual keyboard* and *on-screen keyboard* (used interchangeably) always refer to a keyboard displayed on a screen. A keyboard can be made up of a number of different key configurations, each of which is termed a *keypad*.

interaction with menu items. Other visual keyboards have been developed to control specific software applications only, for example communication and control systems, and can not be used as general purpose input devices.

2 Functions and Design of Existing Virtual Keyboards

2.1 Single Application Keyboards

An example of an eye-controlled text-entry system is ERICA, an application for PC-DOS systems with a menu-based interface (Hutchinson et al., 1989; White et al., 1993). The interface of ERICA was limited in that it could not display the complete screen-based keyboard within one window (Frey et al., 1990). This is a recurrent problem with applications designed for eye-based interaction, in which interface objects like buttons and menus need to be made sufficiently large to overcome the limitations of pointing accuracy inherent in eye-control systems. EyeScan (Eulenberg et al., 1985), BlinkWriter (Murphy & Basili, 1993) and EyeTracker (Friedman et al., 1981) were further examples of applications which supported eye-gaze controlled text entry, but which similarly could not be used as a general input device for standard software.

2.1.1 Keyboard Layouts

Several studies have examined the respective efficiencies of alphabetical or QWERTY arrangements of keys — e.g. (Roussos, 1992; Quill & Biers, 1993; Douglas & Happ, 1993; Mackenzie et al., 1994). The recommendations for key arrangements vary from study to study and depend heavily on assumptions about the user and the pointing device to be used. The studies have generally neglected the flexibility available in presenting on-screen keyboards in comparison with the normal hardware keyboard. Effective and successful keyboard emulation requires more than simply duplicating the key arrangements of conventional keyboards on-screen. The screen representation of the WiViK visual keyboard of Nantais et al. (1994) matches, more or less, a conventional keyboard with QWERTY layout. Their design has the advantage that all keys are selectable with a single step. However, WiViK is intended to be operated by a head motion input device which permits a higher spatial resolution of the key matrix than in the case of an eyetracker. A single interface which accommodates *all* the keys of a conventional keyboard remains problematic for an eye-controlled on-screen keyboard.

2.1.2 Techniques for Alphanumeric Text Input

Early text entry devices for physically-challenged users arranged letters according to their frequency of occurrence in text and allowed indirect selection by stepping through a matrix (e.g. MAVIS system in Schofield (1981); HandiWriter in Ten Kate et al. (1980). This technique has the advantage of accommodating a large set of characters and other symbols within a single template. Demasco & McKoy (1992) proposed a virtual keyboard model which, besides scanning single characters, also supports scanning of words. This technique is unnecessarily restrictive for eye-based pointing and it is better suited to devices reliant on more limited forms of motor control. Nevertheless, laying out character keys on the basis of frequency of use is an important design consideration. As selecting larger targets is easier than selecting smaller targets when using an eyetracker, frequently used keys can also be within the keypad (static sizing) or they can be expanded temporarily when the pointer moves within the key (dynamic sizing), as well as being positioned appropriately.

Operating a visual keyboard by eye is comparable to the one-finger approach of a novice user who also delays each keystroke after the position of a desired key has been recognised. It is a highly sequential task as text must be entered character-by-character with forced delays between the 'eyestrokes'. Consequently, text entry becomes tedious and keystroke savings through a word prediction system not only have the potential to improve speed but also to reduce errors and user fatigue.

The study of Koester & Levine (1994) examined user performance in text entry tasks with word prediction by considering the trade-off between the number of keystrokes and the additional cognitive and perceptual loads imposed by having to select from the presented word choices. They concluded that the cognitive cost of presenting a set of word choices, and explicitly selecting one, largely eliminated the performance advantage of keystroke savings. However, their results depended very much on the degree of disability and the chosen method of controlling the keyboard. For instance, there may be a different trade-off when using a mouthstick for typing on conventional keyboard than in the case of a visual keyboard, where the input and output channel is the same. Indeed, the absence of the need to switch between external keyboard and screen suggest that there will be a lower cognitive load when a visual keyboard is in use.

Swiffin (1988) reported keystroke savings of between 30% and 60% through the use of a *Predictive Adaptive Lexicon* (PAL). This is based on prediction of words which have been entered so far in a document and is therefore useful when word redundancy occurs. This approach is probably a good choice for programming tasks. Demasco & McKoy (1992) used a technique in their keyboard model which took a compressed message and expanded it into a sentence.

With the exception of PAL, word prediction as well as word selection techniques have the advantage of helping to avoid typing errors. In the context of the visual keyboard, where text input is a laborious task, any additional correction aid becomes an important consideration because of the laborious nature of the correcting task. If the visual keyboard is used to control a state-of-the-art word processor which incorporates a spell checker, then the performance lost as a consequence of inputting incorrect text is greatly reduced.

2.2 General Purpose Keyboard Emulators

EyeTyper, developed by Friedman et al. (1985) was an eye-gaze controlled keyboard which could be used in place of the standard keyboard of an IBM-PC. Hence, it was transparent to the host computer's software but its architecture was based on a single keypad template which did not allow more than a very simplistic keyboard emulation.

More recently, the visual keyboard developed by Bishop & Myers (1993) at the University of Iowa supports control by an eyetracker device. The arrangement of character keys is advantageous and groups frequently-used characters towards the centre of the screen. In our experience, a discrepancy between visible cursor position and actual eye position is more likely in the screen corners, and the keys and button sizes of their visual keyboard are arranged to take this into account. However, the

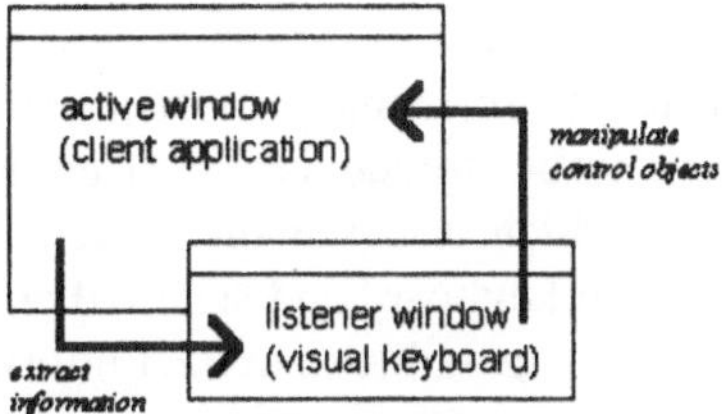

Figure 1: Active window/listener window architecture.

support for editing text is quite limited. Key combinations to highlight text, such as *<Ctrl+Shift+Right>* are not possible, and whereas characters are available for text input, they are not available for command selection (e.g. *<Alt+F>*). Thus it is not possible to make use of the rich functionality of a word processor like MS-Word, thereby loosing the advantage of services such as spell-checking.

As a general purpose device for use with a text processor, a visual keyboard has to be able to satisfy the following requirements:

- Text entry.
- Command selection.
- Error correction.
- Controlling the visibility of text document.
- Key combination support.
- Precise caret location with the text.

However, when used with other client applications, the priorities for support can be different. For instance, browsing through hypertext documents requires point-and-click actions on links in documents, selection of menu items and scrolling through documents. Editing text, for example, is far less important with this application, and a visual keyboard primarily designed for text entry tasks would no longer be optimal. Furthermore, space limitation makes it impossible to display all keys within a single window if they are to be of adequate size for eye control.

3 Issues in Designing the Visual Keyboard

3.1 Communication Between the Client Application and the Visual Keyboard

Virtual keyboards which were primarily designed to provide an alternative form of text entry and control of a character-based user interface typically lack support for effective interaction with GUI objects. Shein et al. (1991) discussed the development of virtual keyboards for GUI environments and identified functional text entry and manipulation of GUI objects as the two main problem areas.

Jacob (1993) presented a number of eye-based interaction techniques for components of the WIMP interface. Unfortunately, most design features of the underlying user interface are not transferable to standard GUI environments. However, the architecture of that system, which is based on an *active* and *listener* window is suitable for transfer. The visual keyboard and standard client applications can enter into the same relationship as it is possible to extract information from the client applications (Figure 1). Multitasking GUI environments and client-server architectures offer this possibility through their event-driven communication. Events associated with the target application (active window) can be inspected by the visual keyboard application (listener window).

Jacob's (1993) concept of active and listener window requires separating *object selection* from continuous display of that object's *attributes*. For instance, if a menu is displayed by the client application (such as a word-processor) in the active window, information about the currently-highlighted menu item can be extracted and displayed in the listener window as part of the keyboard.

The listener window, in addition to displaying attributes, must also support the need for manipulation of the selected control object in the active window. This can be done by presenting the attributes in a form which is more appropriate for eye-controlled interaction. One example based on this concept is to present a part of the active window as an enlarged view in the listener window. A similar zoom-in interaction technique was proposed by Starker & Bolt (1990) for use with an eyetracker system and is also used for overcoming device inaccuracies for pixel operations within bitmap editors.

3.2 Supporting Current Task Context

Graphical User Interface objects such as menus, buttons, list boxes and dialogue boxes occur in nearly all applications. These objects are controlled in the same way regardless of the tasks for which they are used. Most objects can be manipulated with a small subset of keys. For example, when interacting with a menu, the:

<Alt>, *<Left>*, *<Right>*, *<Up>*, *<Down>*, *<Esc>* and *<Enter>*

keys are sufficient. This characteristic allows the provision of keypads which are best suited to a particular group of interface objects. If the visual keyboard can detect when the client application has a dialogue box displayed over its main window, then the visual keyboard can automatically load and display the appropriate 'dialogue box keypad'. Similarly, if the keyboard can detect the currently highlighted item in a client application menu, then the text of that menu item can be used within the visual keyboard itself.

3.3 Supporting Different Interaction Methods

Typically, interface objects can be controlled with a variety of combinations of input devices. For instance, a single menu command can be selected through:

- Selecting menu item through a mouse-click.
- Selecting menu item through a sequence of key-based shortcuts.

- Mouse-click at smarticon of toolbar.
- Keyboard accelerator (e.g. CTRL-S to save).

The preferred interaction method depends very much on the experience and preference of the user, and ideally the visual keyboard should support all interaction methods in order to address the needs and preferences of different *types* of user. Smarticons, tool- and colour-palettes however are frequently restricted to mouse input.

3.4 Emulating Command Actions by Dwelling

Using this technique, the user has to fixate, or dwell, on a key for some specified time in order to select a key. The duration used has a major impact both on performance and on user errors in cases of unintentional command execution. In previous studies the dwell time has varied from 100ms (Istance & Howarth, 1994) over the more common 500ms (Cleveland & Cleveland, 1992; Shaw et al., 1990) up to 1000ms for menu commands (Jacob, 1993). Nevertheless, even long dwell times cannot eliminate the risk of unintentional commands.

The performance loss caused by long dwell times settings has recently been addressed by Nantais et al. (1994). They developed a visual keyboard for MS-Windows which was controlled by head motions in conjunction with the dwell time protocol. Instead of assigning an overall dwell time for all the keys, a key selection probability model was introduced with very short dwell times for those keys which are likely to be chosen next, based on lexical probability calculations from the previous input. Dwell times were reduced by between 20% and 60% while the error rate increased not more than 3%. This technique is therefore potentially of interest for eye-based text entry. We can conclude that different *types* of keys can also be assigned different dwell times depending on whether speed or preventing unintentional operation is important. In addition, we can assign different dwell times depending upon the size of the keys.

3.5 Adjusting the Size and Position of Client Window and Keyboard Window

In order to make best use of the workspace available, the visual keyboard should not be of a fixed size. The arrangement of the listener keyboard window and the size of client application windows are likely to change during interaction. As part of the screen will be occupied by the visual keyboard window, it is necessary to provide some functionality to facilitate easy rearrangement of the relative size and position of these windows. Some applications benefit from the use of a maximised window whereas other applications require only a small part of the screen (e.g. calculator, character table). This will also accommodate differences in the user's pointing ability as enlarging the keyboard window will increase the size of the keys contained within it.

3.6 Customizing the Keyboard

The requirements discussed so far indicate the importance of end-user customisation, however it is necessary to limit the amount of customisation necessary during normal interaction to prevent the keyboard becoming overloaded with customisation functionality. The problem can be minimised through:

- Providing suitable configurable defaults for the keyboard (e.g. dwell time settings).
- Providing an off-line keypad editor to enable new keypads to be created which are suited to different applications.
- Providing the option to create keys which invoke macros. For example, a keypad intended for use with Netscape might contain a key to display a particular page, and this would invoke a macro with the keystrokes necessary to display the URL prompt and enter the characters defining the data.
- Self-adaptation of visual keyboard to the current application context (e.g. automatically loading a menu keypad).
- Configuration of client application to enhance access (e.g. enlarge font, show toolbar).

3.7 *Summary of Design Requirements*

In summary, there are a number of requirements that a visual keyboard controlled by eye needs to satisfy:

- It should support both keyboard and mouse emulation.
- It should support effective interaction with GUI components such as the scrollable lists, text fields and buttons found with dialogue boxes and not be solely designed around the need for text entry.
- It should provide mechanisms to compensate for the inaccuracy inherent in eye-based control.
- It should enable the individual to customise the device to suit individual preferences concerning tasks within specific applications, but should allow the user to switch between different applications without the need for device reconfiguration.

4 Design and Operation of the Visual Keyboard

4.1 *System Architecture*

The eyetracker provides raw data on the positions of the left and right eye to the host machine (Istance & Howarth, 1994). This data is processed completely separately from the visual keyboard. The software responsible for this uses the current gaze position to move the mouse pointer. The visual keyboard runs as an application, and is sensitive to the position of the mouse pointer. Its window is overlaid on top of the active client window. If the mouse pointer remains within the area of the key for a specified time (dwell time), a Windows event corresponding to the key is generated. In this way, it is possible to set different dwell times for different types of key. The

Figure 2: Visual keyboard interface (text keypad).

---

visual keyboard is thus completely separate from the eyetracker system providing the data, and although we have concentrated on eye-control, the keyboard could perfectly well be used with other types of driver device, such as a joystick or mouse.

4.2 Overall Design of the Visual Keyboard

The keyboard itself can be considered to be made up of a number of distinct sections, the centre section of which is referred to here as a keypad. The design of each keypad is based around the need to support different types of command, and each keypad can be selected from a keypad menu. As an example, Figure 2 shows the keyboard with the text keypad loaded, and the three sections of the keyboard are:

1. General keyboard system commands menu (left).

2. Text keypad (centre).

3. Keypad selection menu (right).

Of the general system commands, *<pause>* engages and disengages eye control of the pointer, *<assign>* selects a keypad (Section 4.4) *<paging>* moves a client application window (Section 4.6) and *<return>* closes the keyboard and displays the keypad editor.

In the keypad selection menu and the system command menu, each key expands when the pointer first moves into it and reverts to its original size when the pointer moves over another key. When the cursor moves off either menu, the last key expanded remains enlarged. In Figure 2, the user has just loaded the text pad. This makes dwelling with the eye within the key area easier without the penalty of taking up window space for keys which are not being used (the same principle as a pull-down menu). Additional keypads may be created in the keypad editor and added to the menu of standard keypads or may replace them in the menu.

4.3 Keypad Design

4.3.1 Text Keypad

The current text keypad (shown in Figure 2) incorporates two important design decisions. First, it is based on an alphabetical arrangement of characters (although this could be replaced by a Dvorak or QWERTY arrangement. Quill & Biers (1993) recommend a QWERTY arrangement, but this is rejected for this prototype because

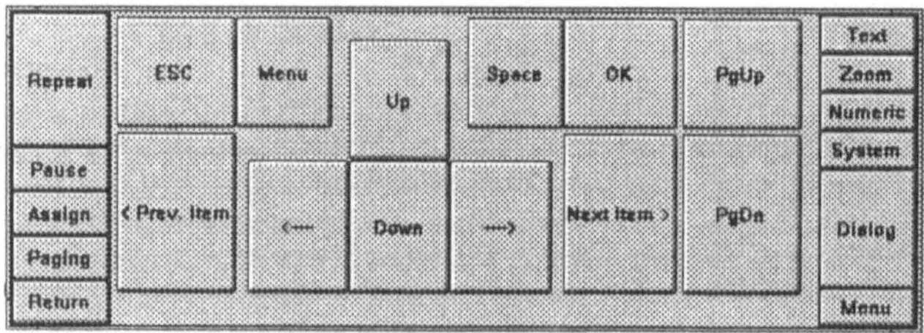

Figure 3: Dialogue keypad.

---

the physically-challenged user is not likely to be familiar with it. Second, the key arrangement gives prominence to the *<cursor>* keys due to their relative importance not only during text entry, see also (Gould et al., 1985), but also during text editing.

4.3.2 Dialogue Keypad

The dialogue keypad shown in Figure 3 contains the keys necessary to control dialogue boxes. There are fewer keys here than in the text keypad and therefore the individual keys are larger. The main keys are the *<cursor control>* keys, the *<next item>* and the *<previous item>* keys (corresponding to *<tab>* and *<shift-tab>* respectively) and the *<escape>* key.

4.3.3 Menu Keypad

The *menu keypad* (not shown) is another context-sensitive keypad for interaction with the menu system. The main keys here are the *<cursor control>* keys, the *<menu>* key (corresponding to the *<alt>* key), the *<escape>* key and a key which contains the text of the currently highlighted menu item. Selecting this key selects the menu item (and is equivalent to pressing the *<carriage return>* key).

4.3.4 Zoompad

Many users may have difficulty in precisely positioning the cursor, and so a zoompad has been incorporated (Figure 4). The zoompad shown here emulates mouse commands. It incorporates the equivalent mouse command selection by means of radio buttons. The user looks at a region of the client window and after a brief dwell interval has expired, the region is copied and enlarged into the keypad. The user effects a click action within the zoom area and the event is sent to the corresponding part of the client window.

4.4 Overriding Automatic Keypad Selection

The visual keyboard automatically loads and displays keypads appropriate to the current task context as, for example, when the user accesses the menu-system in the client application or when a dialogue box is displayed. However, this self-adaptation mechanism is not always desirable. For instance, if the first control object in the dialogue box is a text element, the user may prefer the text keypad for the initial activation. In such cases, the user can make explicit assignments using the *<Assign>* button in the left hand part of the keyboard system command menu. Subsequently,

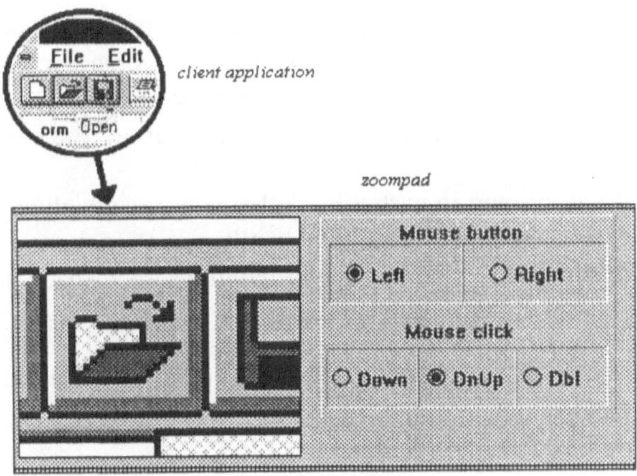

Figure 4: Zoompad.

Dwell object	Dwell time (ms)
<Cursor control> keys	1000
<Enter> key (menu keypad only)	2500
System command menu	1000
Keypad selection menu	500
Target selection (zoompad)	2000
Any other key	1500

Table 1: Dwell time settings.

the assigned keypad will be loaded automatically when the client application context is the same.

4.5 Object Dwell Time

Dwell times for different types of keys can be set individually and these can be altered by the user to reflect personal preference. The values in Table 1 show the different settings used as initial values in the evaluation trials (described in Section 5). The user is warned about expiration of the dwell time by a change in the cursor. The mouse pointer is represented by a circular cursor within the keyboard and this changes to show a black spot in its centre just prior to the end of the dwell interval. If the user does not wish to select the key, they may look away at this point and selection is then inhibited.

4.6 Window Arrangement

The window arrangement of the client application and visual keyboard is supported by three different approaches. In combination, these attempt to compensate for the fact that the on-screen keyboard has to take up a finite part of the available screen area, thereby reducing the area available for the application.

- *Paging*: In the case that the window of a client application is partially overlapped by the visual keyboard or even requires the whole screen, the *<paging>* command moves the client application window so that either its top half or bottom half is displayed in the area of the screen above the keyboard window.

- *Heading*: Windows and in particular dialogue boxes which appear initially in the centre of the screen will be automatically moved to the top of the screen if there is overlap. In the case that the remaining screen space is too small, the *<paging>* command will be selected.

- *Bounding*: Re-sizing the visual keyboard will automatically re-size the client application window.

5 Outcomes of Initial Evaluation Trials

This section reports results from initial evaluation trials with a modern word processor (MS-Word 6.0). More evaluation work remains to be done, both with this application and with other types of application. The trials do, however, give a good indication of the success, or otherwise, of some of the design ideas that have been included in the keyboard. The input device was the eye-control system described previously (Istance & Howarth, 1994).

5.1 Selection of Tasks

A set of five tasks, which constituted an integrated exercise, was completed by each subject:

1. Run application and open text document.

2. Enter a few lines of text (an address).

3. Save the file.

4. Edit the existing text.

5. Require help about a specific problem.

The tasks, and keystroke level actions required to execute them, are transferable to most word processors. Some tasks, such as loading a file via a 'file open' dialogue box or saving a file, are standard across many applications. The means of completing all tasks (except the last) were prescribed to the subjects to ensure that alternative input styles were used. Collectively, the tasks incorporated several forms of command selections requiring the usage of the menu system, toolbar and accelerators and consequently resulting in the use of different keypads. Usage of the help system was included as a task for two reasons. First, many MS-Windows applications have associated help systems. Second, the help system is based on the hypertext concept, and so allows some assessment of the usability of the visual keyboard for hypertext systems.

5.2 Usability Issues

One objective of the evaluation trials was to judge whether the visual keyboard was effective enough to perform the specified tasks. Task completion, and the support of the visual keyboard to enable users to recover from errors, were considered to be major indicators of keyboard efficiency, and keyboard effectiveness could thus be measured by the number of tasks completed and by the number of uncorrected errors made. Measuring effectiveness makes it possible to determine whether eye-based visual keyboard interaction with off-the-shelf GUI software is feasible, even if improvements in efficiency are needed.

In addition, in order to evaluate the efficiency with which the tasks were performed the effort required for the user to correct errors, or to edit text, serves as a useful performance indicator. Comparisons could be made between (virtual) key-based interactions (e.g. navigation with cursor control keys) and the mouse emulation supported by the keyboard in the form of the zoompad. Subjective data was collected in a post-trial interview on issues such as error handling and satisfaction with the functionality provided through different keypads.

5.3 Subjects

Five able-bodied users, recruited from academic staff and students, acted as subjects. It was felt that, at this initial stage, the evaluation trials did not require physically-challenged users as subjects. One subject used spectacles and another subject normally used contact lenses, and all subjects had either normal or corrected-to-normal vision. All subjects reported having previous experience with the GUI of MS-Windows and all were familiar with MS-Word. Two subjects had already had practice in using an eyetracker but none had previously operated an eye-controlled visual keyboard.

5.4 Results and Discussion

All subjects were able to complete the tasks which were given to them. Moreover, all subjects were able to recover from errors and consequently the usability objective of an effective visual keyboard was met in this context. The mean time spent on the completion of all tasks was 19 minutes per subject whereas the total time, including recalibration and repetition of tasks due to eyetracker problems, required on average 38 minutes. The task completion time of the whole task sequence did not vary across subjects by more than three minutes either side of the mean.

5.4.1 Text Entry and Feedback

On average, subjects were able to enter their address in about seven minutes (task 2) which corresponds to a text entry rate of only one word per minute. This is very inefficient and it was observed that most errors occurred during this task. Subjects frequently unintentionally entered a character twice and consequently the time spent on correcting those errors had a major impact on text entry efficiency. The reasons for this lay partly in the techniques used by subjects to get feedback, partly due to a lack of training, partly due to the dwell time being too short, and partly due to a delay in updating cursor position.

Two subjects looked for feedback in the text document after each character was entered whereas the other subjects entered a sequence of characters before checking. When the subject's task completion times were compared, the first approach was found to be more efficient. This was because errors were recognised earlier and consequently the subjects required less cursor control keystrokes to return to the site of the error. However, one might expect reductions in key location and selection times in the second approach as the user's attention remained on the keyboard for longer periods of time. There is clearly room for improvement in the rate of text entry, however even the present rate may be acceptable if text entry is limited to a few letters, such as when entering a file name or a help item to search for.

5.4.2 Interacting with Dialogue Boxes

During tasks 1 and 5, (see Section 5.1) navigation problems occurred when interacting with dialogue boxes. In some cases, subjects mistook the control object with the input focus and so manipulated interface elements by keystrokes which were actually designated for a different object. The visual feedback showing the current input focus was not always clear. These problems are caused by a lack of feedback when moving the input focus from one control to another. When an ordinary keyboard is used, it is possible to press a key and observe changes in the visual appearance of a control simultaneously. Using the eyes to 'press' a virtual key prevents the user from observing the effects of the command as it is taking place. However, during these tasks, unintentional key presses occurred far less frequently than with the text entry task, as one might expect given that the dialogue keypad had fewer, and therefore larger, keys.

5.4.3 Combinations of Keystrokes

The fourth task incorporated the use of shortcut keys for stepping from one word to the next in order to select and highlight text. Most subjects had no difficulties in combining two or three keys and hence were able to move the caret with shortcut keys rather than by a series of cursor control keystrokes.

5.4.4 Dwell as a Means of Activating Commands

Problems associated with interference between mouse events generated directly by the eyetracker software and similar events generated by the visual keyboard were apparent. These arose on occasions when subjects were reading a document or browsing a dialogue box. While subjects were aware that there is some form of response when dwelling too long within the visual keyboard area, the possibility of an event happening inside the client window was not apparent. Whilst it would be possible to disable all event generation in the client window by the eyetracking software, there is a case for letting the user interact directly with the client application (by the eyetracking software sending events directly to it) as well as by using the visual keyboard. The advantage lies in greater flexibility and not always having to use the keyboard on-screen. The disadvantage lies in the possibility of generating unwanted events in the client window. The feedback provided by the change in the cursor, which was intended to warn that dwell time was about to expire, was generally misinterpreted by subjects who thought that the change signified that the key had been pressed.

5.4.5 *Feedback on Modifier Key States*

All subjects were observed to have difficulties in remembering the current state of the modifier keys, for example, forgetting that the <*Shift*> key was locked, and this issue needs addressing. If another keypad was selected after locking the modifier key, then feedback indicating that a subsequent keystroke would lead to a key combination was lost. Errors were also made even though the keypad remained visible, but the effect of the locked key was not obvious. For example, moving the carat with the cursor control keys to correct a typing error with the <*Shift*> key still locked resulted in the text becoming highlighted rather than the carat simply being moved. A strategy such as altering the colour of the keypad during the time the shift key was enabled would provide the user with feedback about its status.

5.4.6 *Mechanisms for Changing Keypads*

All subjects were able to operate the menu-based keypad selection mechanism, although frequently this required more than one attempt. This is acceptable because the keypad selection is based on a short dwell time (500ms). Once the desired keypad button had been 'acquired' subjects could easily keep the pointer within that button because of its large size. The use of expanding, 'fish-eye' buttons has been shown to be particularly successful for this type of eye-based interaction. Furthermore, the self-adaptation by the visual keyboard by loading the appropriate keypad automatically was also successful in reducing user input.

5.4.7 *User Preferences for Interaction Styles with the Visual Keyboard*

In general, the most preferred means of command selection was the use of the zoompad to select the smart icons of the toolbar, followed by menu item selection. The least preferred option was using shortcut keys and accelerators. Preferences appeared to depend on the expertise with MS-Word. For instance, one subject reported frequently using shortcut keys for text editing and preferred to use the keypad supporting use of the shortcut keys. A follow-up trial where all tasks, excepting the text entry task, were performed using the zoompad showed considerable increases in speed.

5.5 *Additional Trials using a Web Browser*

Following the trials with the word processor, trials using Mosiac™ to browse documents located on the Internet were carried out using the same version of the visual keyboard without any modifications. Subjects were required to go to the home page of a computer science department, to find the home page of a particular person, to find a link to a paper from the page and finally to find the conclusions section of the paper. There was no prescribed means of completing the task.

Subjects were able to complete the task without difficulty. In this case, navigating through the document was an important issue and subjects used either the <*page-up*> and <*page-down*> keys or used the zoompad to zoom in on the scroll-bar at the side of the client window. These informal trials demonstrated the utility of the keyboard with a completely different piece of software and the benefits of supporting different ways of completing tasks using the keyboard.

6 Conclusions

This work has demonstrated how a visual keyboard controlled by eye can be used to interact with standard software produced for the able-bodied user and thus allow the physically-challenged user to benefit from the wealth of software produced for modern GUI environments. This includes being able to access the Internet using existing browsers without the need for any modification either to the browser or to the keyboard.

Furthermore, many GUI applications require precise pointing ability which is often lacking in eye-controlled systems (Istance & Howarth, 1994) and the visual keyboard is capable of assisting with these tasks. Adequate solutions for non-keyboard sensitive GUI objects have been considered problematic in the past (Shein et al., 1991; 1992). The zoompad has been shown to provide an effective solution here.

Further work is required to improve the text entry rate achievable with this keyboard. Part of the problem here lies with the eyetracking system and its associated data processing software, rather than with the keyboard itself. A major problem was the need to correct unintentional keystrokes rather than the time required to locate and press an individual key. The next phase in the development will look closely at the causes of this and will examine means of improving text input rates. In addition, means of editing and interacting with existing text using the visual keyboard will be studied more closely. At the workplace, the visual keyboard is perhaps more likely to used for editing existing documents than for original document creation.

Future work with the visual keyboard will focus on the issue of feedback and examine ways of overcoming the visual separation between the keyboard and the region of client window providing feedback on the effects of commands. Additionally, it is intended to examine how direct eye-based interaction with the client application could be integrated with the use of the visual keyboard.

The major conclusion of this project is that the visual keyboard can be considered as a valuable low-cost enhancement to the eyetracker with the capability to compensate for its limitations as a pointing device. It has demonstrated that effective interaction with standard modern software applications using eye-based interaction techniques is entirely possible. This will greatly enhance the possibilities for physically-challenged users to work with the same software products and on a more equitable basis with their able-bodied colleagues.

References

Bishop, J. B. & Myers, G. A. (1993), "Development of an Effective Computer Interface for Persons with Mobility Impairment", *Proceedings of the Annual Conference on Engineering in Medicine and Biology* **15**(3), 1266–1267.

Cleveland, D. & Cleveland, N. (1992), Eyegaze Eyetracking System, *in* "Imagina: Images Beyond Imagination, Proceedings of the 11th Monte-Carlo International Forum on New Images", pp.1–7.

Demasco, P. W. & McKoy, K. F. (1992), "Generating Text From Compressed Input: An Intelligent Interface for People with Severe Motor Impairments", *Communications of the ACM* **35**(5), 68–77.

Douglas, S. D. & Happ, A. J. (1993), Evaluating Performance, Discomfort, and Subjective Preference between Computer Keyboard Designs, *in* G. Salvendy & M. J. Smith (eds.), "Proceedings of the 5th International Conference on Human–Computer Interaction (HCI International '93)", Elsevier Science, pp.1064–1072.

Eulenberg, J. B., King, M. T. & Patterson, H. (1985), Eye-Controlled Communication, *in* "Proceedings of Speech Technology '85 — Voice Input and Output Applications", pp.210–211.

Frey, L. A., White, K. P. & Hutchinson, T. E. (1990), "Eye-Gaze Word Processing", *IEEE Transactions in Systems, Man and Cybernetics* **20**(4), 944–950.

Friedman, M. B., Kiliany, G. & Dzmura, M. (1985), An Eye Gaze Controlled Keyboard, *in* "Proceedings of the 2nd International Conference on Rehabilitation Engineering", pp.446–447.

Friedman, M. B., Kiliany, G., Dzmura, M. & Anderson, D. (1981), The Eyetracker Communication System, *in* "1st National Search for Applications to Aid the Handicapped", John Hopkins University, pp.183–185.

Gould, J. D., Lewis, C. & Barnes, V. (1985), Effects of Cursor Speed on Text-Editing, *in* "Proceedings of CHI'85: Human Factors in Computing Systems", ACM Press, pp.7–10.

Hutchinson, T. E., White, K. P., Martin, W. N., Reichert, K. C. & Frey, L. A. (1989), "Human–Computer Interaction Using Eye-Gaze Input", *IEEE Transactions in Systems, Man and Cybernetics* **19**(6), 1527–1534.

Istance, H. O. & Howarth, P. A. (1994), Keeping an Eye on your Interface: The Potential for Eye-based Control of Graphical User Interfaces (GUI's), *in* G. Cockton, S. Draper & G. Wier (eds.), "People and Computers IX (Proceedings of HCI'94)", Cambridge University Press, pp.195–209.

Jacob, R. J. K. (1993), Eye Movement-based Human–Computer Interaction Techniques: Toward Non-command Interfaces, *in* R. Hartson & D. Hix (eds.), "Advances in Human–Computer Interaction", Vol. 4, Ablex, pp.151–190.

Koester, H. H. & Levine, S. P. (1994), "Modeling the Speed of Text Entry with a Word Prediction Interface", *IEEE Transactions on Rehabilitation Engineering* **2**(3), 177–187.

Mackenzie, S., Nonnecke, B., Riddersma, S., McQueen, C. & Meltz, M. (1994), "Alphanumeric Entry on Pen-based Computers", *International Journal of Human–Computer Studies* **41**(5), 775–792.

Murphy, R. A. & Basili, A. (1993), Developing the User–System Interface for a Communications System for ALS Patients and Others with Severe Neurological Impairments, *in* "Designing for Diversity; Proceedings of the Human Factors and Ergonomics Society", Vol. 2, Human Factors and Ergonomics Society, pp.854–858.

Nantais, T., Shein, F. & Treviranus, J. (1994), "A Predictive Selection Technique for Single-digit Typing With a Visual Keyboard", *IEEE Transactions on Rehabilitation Engineering* **2**(3), 130–134.

Quill, L. L. & Biers, D. W. (1993), On-screen Keyboards: Which Arrangements Should Be Used?, *in* "Designing for Diversity; Proceedings of the Human Factors and Ergonomics Society", Vol. 2, Human Factors and Ergonomics Society, pp.1142–1146.

Roussos, P. (1992), Effects of Keyboard Layout on Children's Performance and Interaction with Computers, Master's thesis, University of Leeds.

Schofield, J. M. (1981), Chapter ?, *in* P. A. Samet (ed.), "Microcomputer-based Aids for the Disabled", Heyden.

Shaw, R., Crisman, E., Loomis, A. & Laszewski, Z. (1990), The Eye-Wink Control Interface: Using the Computer to Provide the Severely Disabled with Increased Flexibility and Comfort, *in* "Proceedings of the 3rd Annual IEEE Symposium on Computer-Based Medical Systems (CBMS'90)", IEEE Computer Society Press, pp.105–111.

Shein, F., Hamann, G., Brownlow, N., Treviranus, J., Milner, M. & Parnes, P. (1991), WIVIK: A Visual Keyboard for Windows 3.0, *in* "Proceedings of the 14th Annual Conference of the Rehabilitation Engineering Society of North America (RESNA)", pp.160–162.

Shein, F., Treviranus, J., Hamann, G., Galvin, R., Parnes, P. & Milner, M. (1992), New Directions in Visual Keyboards for Graphical User Interfaces, *in* H. J. Murphy (ed.), "Proceedings of the 7th Annual Conference on Technology and Persons with Disabilities", California State University, pp.465–469.

Starker, I. & Bolt, R. A. (1990), A Gaze-Responsive Self-Disclosing Display, *in* J. C. Chew & J. Whiteside (eds.), "Proceedings of CHI'90: Human Factors in Computing Systems", ACM Press, pp.3–9.

Swiffin, A. L. (1988), A Predictive and Adaptive Communication System for the Handicapped, Master's thesis, University of Dundee.

Ten Kate, J. H., Frietman, E. E. E., Stoel, F. J. M. L. & Willems, W. (1980), "Eye-Controlled Communication Aids", *Medical Progress through Technology* **8**, 1–21.

White, K. P., Hutchinson, T. E. & Carley, J. M. (1993), "Spatially Dynamic Calibration of an Eye-Tracking System", *IEEE Transactions in Systems, Man and Cybernetics* **3**(4), 1162–1168.

Non-visual Interaction with GUI Objects

Leonard H Poll[†] & Berry H Eggen[‡]

[†] *Philips Research Laboratories, Cross Oak Lane, Redhill, Surrey RH1 5HA, UK.*

Tel: *+44 1293 815327*

Fax: *+44 2193 815500*

EMail: *poll@prl.research.philips.com*

[‡] *Institute for Perception Research, PO Box 513, 5600MB Eindhoven, The Netherlands.*

Tel: *+31 40 2 77 38 32*

Fax: *+31 40 2 77 38 76*

EMail: *eggenjh@natlab.research.philips.com*

Current professional computers are most commonly equipped with Graphical User Interfaces (GUIs) instead of text oriented user interfaces. Today, almost every computer is equipped with a GUI. This poses great problems to blind computer users who were at first given more job opportunities with the advent of character based computers but are now threatened to lose their newly gained employment.

Non-visual access to GUIs requires extraction of information from a GUI and presentation of this information to the blind user by means of a dedicated interaction device. Object oriented methods to extract the information from a GUI are described in (Mynatt & Edwards, 1992) and (Poll & Waterham, 1995). The non-visual GUI objects which have been extracted, can be presented by either tactile or auditory means. The latter option was chosen in our project because of the higher information transfer rate. In our setup the blind user can use an absolute mouse to scan a rectangular area, that is restricted by standing edges, for objects that are presented with help of speech and non-speech sounds. The combination of the absolute

mouse, the restricted area within which the mouse can be positioned and the (non) speech sounds will be referred to as the SoundTablet from now on.

In this paper a description is given of an experiment in which the feasibility of the SoundTablet is explored. The results show that the SoundTablet is suited for use in a non-visual GUI access system. The results indicate also that the addition of an auditory and/or tactile object localization aid is desirable.

Keywords: auditory interfaces, non-visual interaction, GUIs, visually impaired.

1 Introduction

The need of the blind to have access to GUIs mainly stems from the fact that sharing resources in an office environment has gained importance since the introduction of computer networks. The necessity to share soft- and hard-ware resources requires that blind users have access to GUIs.

The fact that blind persons need to have access to GUIs in order to be able to use the same resources as their sighted colleagues defines the environmental requirements for the GUI access system. In practice colleagues will consult and share experiences with each other about the computer resources. For instance, sighted users will, when faced with computer problems, favour consulting another (sighted) colleague rather than a manual (Rettig, 1991). It is expected that blind users will not form an exception to this rule.

The communication between sighted and blind colleagues can be facilitated if the non-visual GUI equivalent gives the blind user the same conceptual 'look' and 'feel' as the GUI of his sighted colleague. As a consequence, the original GUI metaphor, the desktop' has to be maintained in the non-visual GUI equivalent including the direct manipulation techniques. The non-visual equivalent will therefore be object based and will have to include a spatial distribution in order to facilitate common GUI gesture based manipulations.

If a standard relative pointing device like the mouse is used, additional methods are needed in order to present the absolute position of the pointer. This need can be surpassed if an absolute mouse, as used in the SoundTablet, is applied. Research on auditory displays for blind users — e.g. (Edwards, 1989; Martial & Dufresne, 1993; Pitt & Edwards, 1991) gives an indication that the auditory approach is, in general, feasible. However, to determine whether the SoundTablet is suitable for use in a non-visual GUI access system, an experiment was conducted. In this experiment, the non-visual human–machine interaction with objects representing the basic GUI object attributes is tested. The question of how blind users are able to interact with GUI objects of a certain type is not addressed in this paper.

2 SoundTablet

The SoundTablet (see Figure 1) consists of a modified digitizer and audio equipment with which pre-recorded sounds can be made audible. This configuration allows for the interaction with audio objects in a 2D auditory space.

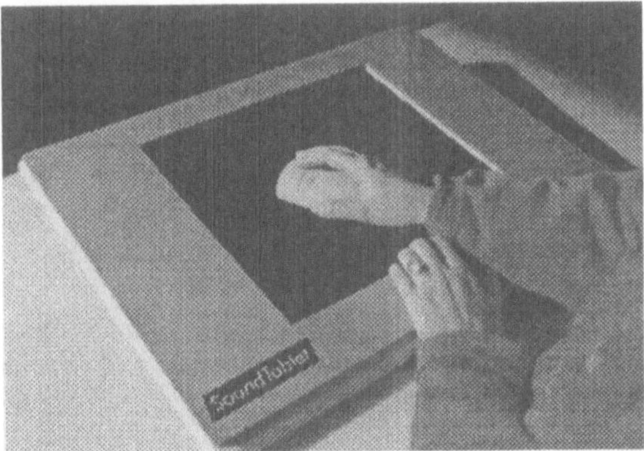

Figure 1: The SoundTablet.

A computer drawing tablet with a cordless puck forms the heart of the SoundTablet. The housing of the original cordless puck is replaced by the housing of a three-button mouse. This mouse can be moved within an area of 31×33 centimetres that is restricted by a physical border of 6 millimetre height. The effective area where objects can be placed measures 21.5×28 centimetre. The height and width ratio of this effective area matches the height and width ratio of a 14″ Visual Display Unit. With the mouse the effective area can be scanned for auditory objects.

Auditory Objects

The presentation of information by means of auditory objects can be divided into two categories:

1. *The presentation of the physical properties:* The borders and occupied space of an object are presented by non-speech sounds. If a user hits an object while he moves the mouse over the SoundTablet, a, so called, impact sound is played. To indicate that the mouse is positioned within the area of an object, coloured noise is used. A steady-state sound like coloured noise is used for this purpose because of the fact that the perceptual system does not remain conscious of the presence of such sounds (Buxton, 1989).

   The physical state changes, appearing, disappearing, resizing and dragging of objects are presented using non-speech sounds. For example, if an object is dragged to another location, the changing of the spatial coordinates is indicated by the sound of someone dragging an object over the floor. Other sound metaphors are used to indicate the appearance and disappearance of objects.

   The sound used to indicate hitting the border starts as soon as the border is hit and is only completed if the mouse stays within the area of the object for a duration that is at least equal to the duration of the sound. If the mouse leaves the object before the impact sound is played completely, the sound is stopped abruptly. In order to support scanning for objects at a relative high speed a hit sound is used with very steep attack and decay rates to increase the chance that the user will perceive the sound even when the mouse is only positioned on top of the object for a short period.

2. *Presentation of the identity:* The identity of an object is formed by two chunks of information; the type of the object and the (textual) label. Pre-Recorded speech is used to present the type and label of an object to the user. The question which of the original GUI-objects have to be presented with what kind of terminology and labels will not be addressed in this paper. A detailed discussion of the non-visual presentation of specific GUI objects can be found in (Poll, 1996).

3 Experiment

The interaction with the basic properties of GUI-objects on the SoundTablet needed to be tested before experiments with a full-fledged non-visual GUI can start. The following research questions needed to be addressed:

- Can the user find the auditory objects?
- Can the user manipulate the auditory objects or, specifically, can the user select, activate or drag the non-visual objects?

Complementary to the questions listed above, the experiment was also conducted to evaluate the general user interface mechanisms for the repetition of an object's label and identity, the retrieval of an object's label in isolation and the general control of identity utterances on the basis of mouse movements.

In order to test the basic properties of the GUI interaction without overwhelming the subject with the information of real GUI objects, we opted for the use of a playing card metaphor instead of the complete desktop metaphor.

3.1 Experimental Setup

During the experiment the subjects were seated in front of a desk on which the SoundTablet was placed. The instructions were automatically generated using pre-recorded speech uttered by a male voice. All user actions were logged on a Personal Computer (PC) for later analysis. The movements of the subjects were recorded on video.

In our experiment objects could be of one of the following types: 'hearts', 'diamonds', 'clubs', 'spades' and 'trashcan'. The label could have all possible card values and 'trashcan'. The object type and label were uttered by a female voice.

User interface mechanisms were designed to give the subject control over the utterances. The type of an object was uttered immediately after playing the hit sound. In order to hear the label of an object, the subject had to press and hold down the right button of the three button mouse. Only while the button was held down the label was uttered once. An early release of the right button abruptly stopped the utterance of the label. Pressing the right button before the utterance of an objects identity was complete abruptly stopped this utterance and started the label utterance.

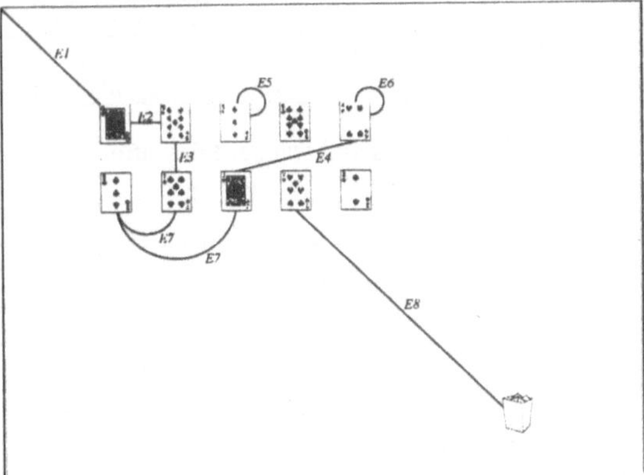

Figure 2: Layout of the screen as used in the experiments. The trashcan was only present when subjects were given drag tasks. The position and number of cards was fixed but the card colours and numbers varied.

3.2 *Subjects*

Two groups of subjects participated in the experiment. The first group consisted of ten visually disabled persons. Three of these subjects were congenitally blind, the others were late blind. The subjects were aged between seventeen and fifty-nine. Four subjects were female. All subjects were legally blind.

The second group consisted of twelve sighted people who were blindfolded before entering the room where the experiment took place. None of the subjects had seen the SoundTablet before. Subject were aged between twenty-four and forty-four. Four subjects were female.

None of the subjects from either group reported hearing deficiencies.

3.3 *Experimental Procedure*

The experiment consisted of two sessions. In each session five training trials and twenty test trials were given. In each trial an auditory screen was used as shown in Figure 2, with the exception that in the first session the trashcan was not displayed. In both sessions the position of the playing cards was fixed but the card colours and values were chosen at random for each trial. Each trial was preceded by the sound of someone dealing cards on a table. The number of cards dealt on the table corresponded with the actual number of auditory objects present on the SoundTablet including the trashcan if present. These sounds were followed by a computer initiated pre-recorded utterance of an instruction. The instruction was however only uttered if subjects had placed the mouse in the upper left corner. If subjects failed to do so within 5 seconds after having heard that the cards were dealt on the table, they were reminded to do so by a pre-recorded message. To support the differentiation between object related utterances and the uttered instructions, a male voice was used for the instructions.

Subject	VD1	VD2	VD3	VD4	VD5	VD6	VD7	VD8	VD9	VD10
Average	14	20	20	25	25	37	24	23	32	67
SD	6	11	13	17	16	28	10	10	24	43

Table 1: Average trial completion times and standard deviations in seconds for the group of blind subjects.

Subject	BF1	BF2	BF3	BF4	BF5	BF6	BF7	BF8	BF9	BF10	BF11	BF12
Average	26	30	36	19	22	15	24	23	47	53	29	17
SD	9	29	28	13	12	8	15	17	33	41	18	9

Table 2: Average trial completion times and standard deviations in seconds for the group of blindfolded subjects.

During the first session subjects were asked to search for a specific card. When found, subjects had to select the card by clicking the left button once. Then the next trial started. This procedure was repeated until the subject completed all the trials.

During the second session subjects were asked to drag a certain card to the trashcan. Once the requested card was found, the subject had to press and hold down the left button of the mouse and move it to the trashcan. If the button was released on top of the trashcan, a successful drop was indicated by the sound of someone crumpling a piece of paper. While dragging, all other auditory objects could still be located.

All subjects were debriefed after having finished the experiment by an informal interview.

3.4 Results

Several quantitative results could be calculated from the log file like the average time spent outside an object, the time spent to drag an object to the trashcan, the number of times the instruction was repeated, etc. Only those quantitative results that are relevant for the discussion in this paper will be described. To give an impression of the average time it took subjects to complete trials, the average trial completion time and standard deviation for the second session are listed in Table 1 and Table 2. The quantitative results of the first session are not used, because video analysis suggests that some subjects still show exploratory behaviour in the first session.

The labelled lines in Figure 2 indicate the several categories of movements. Eighty-eight percent of the movements made by the visually impaired subjects within the rows were either vertical (E3) or horizontal object-to-neighbouring-object movements (E2) or movements the subjects made to return to objects located at the beginning or end of a row (E6). Movements during which the instruction was repeated are not included. Movements of which the duration time does not fit in the 95% interval of a t-distribution of all events in a certain category were considered to be outliers and are not included. These events are added to movement category E7. For blindfolded subjects the average amount of 'structured' movements is eighty-five percent. The remaining percentage of movements within the rows consists of returning movements to objects that are not the first or last object on a row and movements to objects that are not located immediately right, left, above or below the current one.

No statistical differences were found between the quantitative results of the groups of blind and blindfolded subjects. Therefore, in the remaining discussion of the results, the term subject refers to subjects of both groups.

All subjects used the possibility to stop the utterance of an object's label before completion of the utterance. Subjects showed the same type of behaviour when listening to the utterance of the type of an object or to the repeated utterance of an instruction. As soon as the relevant information was perceived, subjects initiated another action like moving, dragging, selecting etc. without waiting for the utterance to finish.

None of the subjects applied a scanning strategy with rapid movements although this kind of behaviour was accounted for in the design of the hit sounds. Most subjects used their free hand as a reference for the other hand that was scanning the auditory space. Some subjects even changed hands as soon as they had to drag the card to the trashcan in the bottom right corner. It was also observed that some subjects used their little finger to locate the trashcan which was for some subjects the length of this finger away from the right edge.

Subjects, in general, were able to drag the cards to the trashcan without dropping it along the way. If a card was accidentally dropped during dragging, all subjects were able to locate it again and finish the drag operation. On average, subjects dropped a card while dragging only once in twenty trials with a maximum of two drops. Subjects were able to notice the drop because of the (sudden) absence of the drag sound.

During the debriefing after the experiment most subjects reported that the cards were located on two rows. There were however subjects that had the impression that the cards were located on three or four rows. Less than two rows was not reported. When asked how many cards were positioned on the SoundTablet most subjects made an estimation of the number which varied from ten to twelve. Only a few subjects reported that they heard eleven cards dealt on the table but mentioned that they could only find ten.

3.5 Discussion

The results show that subjects of both groups were able to find and manipulate the auditory objects. The standard deviation of the trial completion times per subject is however relatively large. This is apart from individual differences between subjects also due to the setup of the experiment. The time needed to find the upper left card compared to the time needed to find the bottom right card differs considerably especially when a sequential scan strategy is applied.

In general subjects applied a sequential scan strategy within and between the two rows which is indicated by the large percentage of structural movements. The remaining percentage of non-structural movements consists of returns to objects that are not the first or last card on a row (E5) and movements to cards that are not located straight above, below or on the left or right of the last card (E4). Returns to objects within a row could be caused by so called shoot-throughs. After moving through a card, the subject realized that the card had the right colour and he/she returned to check out the number of the card. These movements can also be considered to be structural which gives rise to the expectation that the actual number of structural movements is larger than the one reported in 3.4. These returns could also be caused by the level of difficulty to make a straight vertical/ horizontal movement which results in a miss of the next card. The movements from cards to other cards not located straight below, above, on the right or left could be related to the level of difficulty to make vertical/horizontal movements but also to individual differences in search strategies.

Scanning the SoundTablet with use of straight horizontal/vertical lines requires the presence of a reference. Only the free hand could be used as a reference to the hand that was scanning. Complementary to this, scanning horizontally was also difficult due to the fact that most subject scanned while the elbow of the scanning arm remained resting in the same position on the table. This might result in a somewhat curved horizontal movement instead of a straight horizontal line.

From the informal interview carried out after the experiment, it can be derived that most subjects were not able to build a mental model of the screen layout. This is mainly due to the setup of the experiment. During the training trials subjects were made familiar with the tasks but were not given the chance to extensively scan the auditory screen nor were they told that the number and position of the cards was fixed throughout the experiment. This introduced a factor of uncertainty for the subjects which is illustrated by the impression some subjects had that they could easily miss objects without noticing.

In contrast to the position and number of the playing cards, subjects were told in advance where the trashcan was located. In general, subjects made a relatively fast movement to the bottom right corner where they started searching for the trashcan by making slower circling movements. Some subjects used their fingers to measure the distance between the right edge of the screen and the position of the trashcan. The trashcan was approximately one little finger away from the edge.

The feedback indicating that the mouse was positioned in the area of an object or that an object was dragged appeared to be sufficient. Attempts to initiate the utterance of an object's label while the mouse was located outside the area of the object were hardly observed, nor were dragging movements made without actually dragging an object.

None of the subjects had difficulty to select the requested object in the first session by clicking the left mouse button once. It is therefore to be expected that subjects are also able to perform the third standard GUI direct manipulation feature, activation, by clicking the left button twice instead of once.

The hypothesis that only part of the utterance of an object's identity and label suffices to determine whether or not the right object was found is confirmed by the observations. Subjects did, on average, not wait for the utterance of an object's type, label or the repetition of the instruction to complete before initiating another action.

The fact that no significant statistical differences could be found between the quantitative results of the group of blind and blindfolded subjects agrees with the results of an experiment described by Klatzky et al. (1995). In this experiment, no differences were found between the spatial localization abilities of blind and blindfolded subjects. The fact that no differences were found in our experiment can also be partly due to the innovative characteristics of the device. None of the subjects had any early experience in activities requiring hand/ear coordination.

4 Conclusions

The results of the experiment indicates that the SoundTablet can be used as a non-visual interaction device in a non-visual GUI access system. Objects can be located and manipulated using GUI-specific manipulation methods. An auditory and/or tactile localization aid can be added as an optional help for the user to locate objects more accurately. Whenever there is a clear spatial relation between objects, guidance is not necessary which implies that the user has to be able to control the presence of the guidance.

Compared to a GUI the experiments confronted the subjects with a worst-case situation with respect to the spatial layout of the screen. In a GUI more objects are present but the mutual spatial relation of most of those objects is fixed. For instance, menu lines are always located below the title bar of a window, close buttons always have a fixed position within a window etc. In other words the location of one object gives an indication of the location of other objects. This was the case in the experiment as well but this was not mentioned to the subjects which accounts for some uncertainty that resulted. If the structure had been known in advance, subjects could have planned their search strategies in advance.

Objects that can be placed anywhere are, usually, spaced at an equal distance from each other just like the cards used in both experiments, but their location is usually restricted by the larger object within which the smaller objects are placed. For instance, check boxes can be placed within the area occupied by the dialogue box. This implies that the area in which the blind user has to scan in order to find for instance a check box is limited by the area occupied by the dialogue box.

Only the case of the desktop or a full screen window are comparable to the spatial layout used in the experiment. In theory the spatial positions of icons on a desktop or in a full screen window can be positioned anywhere. However, in practice icons present on a desktop are positioned near the border of the screen and are usually spaced at an equal distance from each other. The windows containing a set of icons generally provide options allowing users to organize their spatial positions. Windows can be positioned anywhere but compared to the icons are relatively large and therefore considerably easier to find.

The SoundTablet has to be extended with a speech synthesizer to be able to utter object labels of which the content is not known beforehand as was the case in our experiment. The possibility to abruptly stop the utterance of the label should also be available when a speech synthesizer is used.

Based on the results of the experiments and the consideration mentioned above it is to be expected that a non-visual presentation of the GUI objects with use of the SoundTablet is feasible. This does not however imply that a one to one mapping of the visual objects into auditory objects is the best possible transformation. A trade-off has to be made between combining GUI objects into larger non-visual objects and maintaining the original interface principles to the extent at which the blind users have the impression that they work with the same interface elements as a sighted GUI user.

References

Buxton, W. (1989), "Introduction to this Special Issue on Non-speech Audio", *Human–Computer Interaction* **4**(1), 1–9.

Edwards, A. D. N. (1989), "Soundtrack: An Auditory Interface for Blind Users", *Human–Computer Interaction* **4**(1), 45–56.

Klatzky, R. L., Golledge, R. G., Loomis, J. M., Cicinelli, J. G. & Pellegrino, J. W. (1995), "Performance of Blind and Sighted Persons on Spatial Tasks", *Journal of Visual Impairment and Blindness* **89**(1), 70–82.

Martial, O. & Dufresne, A. (1993), Audicon: Easy Access to Graphical User Interfaces for Blind Persons — Designing for and with People, *in* G. Salvendy & M. J. Smith (eds.), "Proceedings of the 5th International Conference on Human–Computer Interaction (HCI International '93)", Elsevier Science, pp.808–813.

Mynatt, E. D. & Edwards, W. K. (1992), Mapping GUIs to Auditory Interfaces, *in* M. Green (ed.), "Proceedings of the ACM Symposium on User Interface Software and Technology, UIST'92", ACM Press, pp.61–70.

Pitt, I. J. & Edwards, A. D. N. (1991), Navigating the Interface by Sound for Blind Users, *in* D. Diaper & N. Hammond (eds.), "People and Computers VI: Usability Now! (Proceedings of HCI'91)", Cambridge University Press, pp.373–383.

Poll, L. H. D. (1996), Visualising Graphical User Interfaces for Blind Users, PhD thesis, Eindhoven University of Technology.

Poll, L. H. D. & Waterham, R. P. (1995), "Graphical User Interfaces and Visually Disabled Users", *IEEE Transactions on Rehabilitation Engineering* **3**(1), 65–69.

Rettig, M. (1991), "Nobody Reads Documentation", *Communications of the ACM* **34**(7), 19–24.

Earcons as a Method of Providing Navigational Cues in a Menu Hierarchy

Stephen Brewster[†], Veli-Pekka Raty[‡] & Atte Kortekangas[§]

[†] *Department of Computing Science, The University of Glasgow, Glasgow G12 8QQ, UK.*

Tel: *+44 141 330 4932*
EMail: *stephen@dcs.gla.ac.uk*
URL: *http://www.dcs.gla.ac.uk/~stephen/*

[‡] *VTT Information Technology, Kanslerinkatu 12 B, Tampere, FIN-33101, Finland.*

Tel: *+358 31 316 3328*
EMail: *veli-pekka.raty@vtt.fi*

[§] *VTT Information Technology, Tekniikantie 4B, Espoo, FIN-02044 VTT, Finland.*

Tel: *+358 0 456 4311*
EMail: *atte.kortekangas@vtt.fi*

We describe an experiment to discover if structured audio messages, earcons, could provide navigational cues in a menu hierarchy. A hierarchy of 27 nodes and four levels was created with sounds for each node. Participants had to identify their location in the hierarchy by listening to an earcon. Results showed that participants could identify their location with over 80% accuracy, indicating that earcons are a powerful method of communicating hierarchy information. Participants were also tested

to see if they could identify where previously unheard earcons would fit in the hierarchy. The results showed that they could do this with over 90% accuracy. These results show that earcons are a robust and extensible method of communicating hierarchy information in sound.

Keywords: earcons, auditory interfaces, non-speech audio, navigation, menus, phone-based interaction.

1 Introduction

This paper describes an experiment to investigate the ability of non-speech audio to provide navigational cues in a hierarchical menu structure. In some situations graphical feedback cannot be used to provide these cues. In completely auditory interactions, such as telephone-based interfaces or those for visually disabled people, it is impossible to use graphical cues. In other systems where graphical feedback is available, the display may already be completely occupied by information that extra graphical cues would hide. For example, an interface for people with speaking difficulties who need to access a library of pictographic images. The link between these different situations is that a hierarchical structure must be represented without graphics. In this paper we describe an experiment to test sounds to see if they could convey the necessary hierarchy information.

There is a growing body of research which indicates that the addition of non-speech sounds to human-computer interfaces can improve performance and increase usability, for example Blattner et al. (1992), Brewster (1994) and Gaver et al. (1991). Non-speech sound is an important means of communication in the everyday world and the benefits it offers should be taken advantage of at the interface. Such *multi-modal* interfaces allow a greater and more natural communication between the computer and the user. They also allow the user to employ appropriate sensory modalities to solve a problem, rather than just using one modality (usually vision) to solve all problems.

Sound has many advantages. It is omni-directional so the user does not have to concentrate on a particular part of the display to perceive it. In fact, he/she does not even have to be looking at the display. Sound is also attention grabbing and can be effectively used to indicate problems to users. It can work alongside synthetic speech in purely auditory interfaces or be integrated with graphical feedback. Often in graphical interfaces more and more information is displayed on-screen. This can result in overload and important information may be missed. One way to overcome this problem is to use sound. Important information can be displayed on the screen and other information in sound, reducing overload of the visual sense. Brewster (1994) showed that by adding sound to a graphical interface both the time taken to complete certain tasks and the time taken to recover from errors could be reduced.

1.1 Telephone-based Interfaces

One important reason for using non-speech sound is to represent menu structures in interfaces where visual feedback is not possible, for example telephone-based interfaces (phone banking) or interfaces for visually disabled people. In a telephone-based interface a user might call the bank and navigate through a hierarchy of voice menus to find the service required. One problem is that the user can get lost in the hierarchy. As Yankelovich et al. (1995, p.369) say:

> "These interfaces, however, are often characterized by a labyrinth of invisible and tedious hierarchies which result when menu options outnumber telephone keys or when choices overload users' short-term memory".

The communication channel is very limited so little feedback can be given to the user about his/her current location. The more navigation information that is given, the more it obstructs the information the user is trying to access.

Rosson (1985) investigated such a hierarchical phone-based interface to give travel/visitor information. A user could call the system and move through the hierarchy to find information such as addresses and phone numbers of restaurants. She describes one common problem:

> "It is important to note that the information needed to convey position in the hierarchy was implicit in the content of the utterances users heard". (Rosson, 1985, p.251)

Feedback confirming that one had moved from the top to the middle level of the hierarchy was available only by understanding a category/sub-category relationship. After hearing 'Restaurants' and making a 'Down' move, the user might hear 'Chinese' and would have to infer that a move to a lower level of the hierarchy had been made. She suggested that this may have been the source of many of the users problems.

Rosson suggested that one way to solve the problem was to give extra speech feedback. For example "You have moved to the next item in the Chinese Restaurant list. It is ...". She suggested, however, that this would make the interface appear slow and clumsy. This extra feedback might also be longer than the information being retrieved and so obscure it. Such feedback was rejected for this very reason by Stevens (1996) and Stevens et al. (1994) when designing navigation cues in a system to provide non-visual access to mathematics. Rosson (1985, p.251) suggested other methods:

> "More attractive possibilities are to increase the information implicit in the utterance itself, by systematically varying the syntax of the utterances at different levels, or by assigning a different 'voice' to each level".

There are problems with both of these methods. Varying the syntax might result in complex messages that again obscure the information being communicated. The low quality of telephone equipment may also reduce the listener's ability to differentiate many different voices (for example, you do not always recognize acquaintances when they telephone you).

We suggest an alternative solution: Structured non-speech audio messages. These would provide a hierarchical system of sounds that could be used to represent a menu hierarchy. The sounds would play continuously (but quietly) in the background at each level, giving location information. Users could listen to the current sound and from it work out their location in the hierarchy. The sounds would make explicit the differences moving from level to level or across the same level because the sounds would be related in different ways. This is a similar approach to that taken by Stevens (1996) and Stevens et al. (1994) in the MathTalk system. This system displays algebra to blind mathematicians. Non-speech sounds give the listener information about their location in a mathematical structure. They do this without interfering with the synthetic voice presenting the mathematics. The cues are also much shorter than an equivalent voice message. Speech and non-speech sounds are different in the same way as text and graphics. If carefully designed, they can also be used together to provide complementary information.

1.2 Navigation in a Communicator Device

A second reason for investigating the use of sound to represent hierarchies is to present navigational cues in an interface for people speech impairments for the TIDE ACCESS Project 1001. The aim of this project is to create a mobile communication device for people who cannot speak. People will use the device to create messages they want to communicate and then say these messages via synthetic speech. These types of users often use pictographic languages, for example Bliss (Baumgart et al., 1990), to communicate. The pictures represent words or actions and can be combined to create complex messages.

An experienced user with a wide vocabulary may need access to a large number of symbols. It is impossible to display all of the pictures on the screen at the same time. One way around this problem is to use a hierarchy of symbols but this can lead to users getting lost, in the same way as described above.

Graphical feedback could be used to give extra navigational information, for example a map could show the current position in the hierarchy. However, this would take up valuable screen space needed for the pictographic symbols and would also require the user to look at the map when he/she really wanted to look at the symbols. An alternative would be to use different colours to show the different levels. Unfortunately, colour is already used to show other groupings within the symbols such as nouns/verbs/adjectives. We suggest the use of sound; it can be used to give information about one's location in the hierarchy without taking up screen-space. Synthetic speech cannot be used as it would conflict with the message being created. However, non-speech would not suffer from this problem.

Lack of screen space is not only a problem in interfaces for disabled people. Visual displays can only hold so much information. If an interface designer tries to display more and more information then some of it will not fit on the screen without hiding information already there. Blattner et al. (1992) discuss this problem with computerized maps. Only so much information can be displayed before the underlying map is obscured. If additional information must be displayed on a map, space must be allocated for it and eventually a saturation point will be reached. Blattner et al. suggested that sound could be used to avoid these problems.

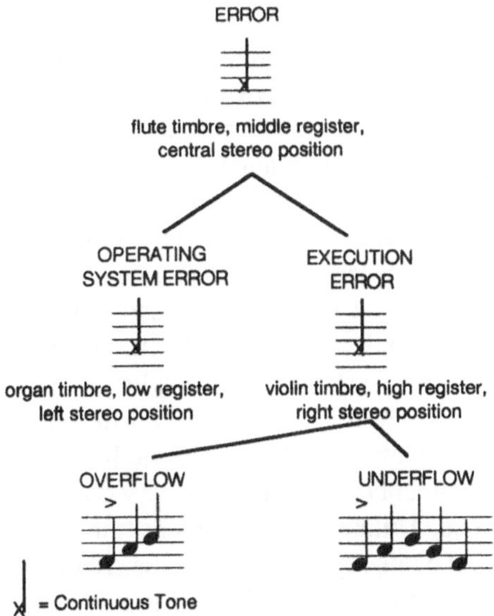

Figure 1: An hierarchy of earcons representing errors — adapted from (Blattner et al., 1989).

2 Earcons

The non-speech sounds used for this investigation are based around structured audio messages called *Earcons* (Blattner et al., 1989; Brewster, 1994). Earcons are abstract, synthetic tones that can be used in structured combinations to create sound messages to represent parts of an interface. Detailed investigations of earcons by Brewster et al. (1993) showed that they are an effective means of communicating information in sound.

Earcons are constructed from motives. These are short rhythmic sequences that can be combined in different ways. The simplest method of combination is concatenation to produce *compound earcons*. By using more complex manipulations of the parameters of sound (such as timbre, register, intensity, pitch and rhythm) *hierarchical earcons* can be created (Blattner et al., 1989) which allow the representation of hierarchical structures.

Figure 1 shows a simple hierarchy of earcons using these types of manipulations. Each earcon is a node on a tree and inherits all the properties of the earcons above it. The different levels are created by manipulating the parameters of earcons (for example, rhythm, pitch, timbre). In the diagram the top level of the tree is a neutral earcon representing a fictitious family of errors. It has a flute timbre (a 'colourless' instrument), a middle register and a central stereo position. The structure of the earcon from level one is inherited by level two and then changed. At level two the sound is still continuous but non-neutral timbres are used (in the figure organ and violin). Register is changed so that it matches a conventional musical layout (low register on the left, high on the right) and stereo position reflects the layout of the hierarchy, for example the node on the left has a left stereo position. At level three a rhythm is added to the earcon from level two to create a sound for a particular error. This rhythm is based on the timbre, register and stereo position from the level above. Other levels can be created by using parameters such as tempo or effects.

Using earcons, this hierarchy is easily extensible. For example, to add another major category of errors all that is needed is a new timbre. This could then be given a middle register and a middle stereo position and be placed between the operating system and execution errors in the diagram. To create a new type of execution error only a new rhythm is needed and it can be added to the existing hierarchy. Therefore earcons provide a very flexible system for creating hierarchies.

An alternative method of presenting information in sound is *Auditory Icons*, for example Gaver (1989) and Gaver (1993). These are based around sounds sampled from the everyday environment (such as metallic or wooden sounds) rather than the musical sounds of earcons. Unlike abstract earcons, these sounds have an intuitive link to the object or action being represented. For the creation of hierarchies earcons have the advantage that the sounds can be varied in a systematic way (as shown in the description above). Auditory icons are based on natural sounds and so cannot be as easily manipulated (if an auditory icon is manipulated too much it may no longer sound like its natural equivalent). Gaver (1993) is working on this problem to allow the controlled variation of auditory icons. However, at the present time it is not possible.

2.1 Previous Attempts to use Earcons to Present Hierarchy Information

Barfield et al. (1991) carried out experiments where they used earcons to aid navigation through a menu hierarchy. The earcons they used were very simple, just decreasing in pitch as a participant moved down the hierarchy. The sounds lasted half a second. They describe them thus:

> "… the tones were played with a harpsichord sound and started in the fifth octave of E corresponding to the main or top level of the menu and descended through B of the fourth octave". (Barfield et al., 1991, p.104)

These sounds did not fully exploit all the advantages offered by earcons (for example, they used neither rhythm nor timbre differences) and did not improve user performance in the experimental task.

Brewster (1994) and Brewster et al. (1993) also tested the ability of earcons to present hierarchical information in sound. In two detailed experiments they showed that, with careful design of the earcons, hierarchy information could be presented effectively. They used earcons to represent a small family of files, folders and applications and manipulated timbre, register, rhythm and pitch to create their hierarchy. Their results showed that 80% recall rates could be achieved for hierarchical earcons even with non-optimal training. This work indicated that earcons could be used to represent hierarchies. However, the hierarchy used was very simple with only nine nodes.

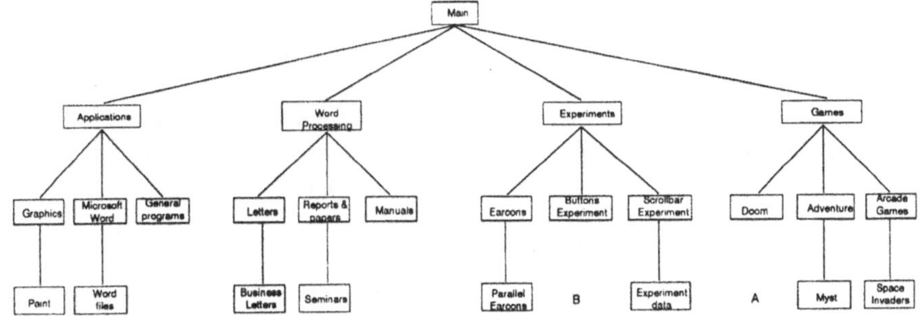

Figure 2: The file-system hierarchy used in the experiment. A and B show the two new earcons presented to participants during testing.

---

3 The Experiment

The aim of the experiment described here was to discover if a larger hierarchy could be represented by earcons. Figure 2 shows the hierarchy used. It had 25 nodes on four levels with four missing nodes on Level four (two of which are marked as A and B). This made a hierarchy of 27 nodes, three times larger than that tried previously. It was loosely based on the structure of the file system on the first author's computer.

3.1 Hypotheses

The main hypothesis was that participants should be able to recall the position of a node in the hierarchy by the information contained in an earcon. If this was correct then high overall rates of recall would be expected.

Participants should also be able to listen to an earcon and position it in the hierarchy even if they have not heard it before by using the rules from which the earcons were constructed. This would be demonstrated by high rates of recognition when participants were presented with new earcons.

3.2 Participants

Twelve volunteer participants were used. They were a mixture of computer science students at Helsinki University of Technology and members of staff at VTT Information Technology. All were familiar with computers and computer file systems.

3.3 Sounds Used

The earcons were designed using the guidelines proposed by Brewster et al. (1995). The sounds were all played by HyperCard on an Apple Macintosh via MIDI using a Yamaha TG100 sound synthesizer and presented to participants via loudspeakers. The sounds used at each level of the hierarchy will now be described:

Level 1: For the top level of the hierarchy ('Main' in Figure 2) a constant sound with a flute timbre was used (see Table 1). It had a central spatial location and a pitch of D_3 (261Hz). A flute timbre was used at it is a pure sound close to a 'timbreless' sine-wave. The earcon was designed to be neutral sounding.

Nodes	Timbre	Stereo position	Register
Main	Flute	Centre	D_3
Applications	Electric organ	Far left	C_4
Word Processing	Violin	Centre left	C_3
Experiments	Drum/synthesizer	Centre right	C_2
Games	Trumpet	Far right	C_1

Table 1: The timbre, spatial location and register for Levels 1 and 2 of the hierarchy.

Level 2: Each family had a separate timbre, register and spatial location. Table 1 shows these. Register was lowest on the left and highest on the right following the conventional musical pattern. The stereo position of the earcons also moved from left to right mirroring their position in the hierarchy.

The continuous sound was inherited from the Level 1 earcon but the instrument, pitch and stereo position were changed. Three parameters were used so that if the listener could not remember which instrument went with which node he/she could still use register or stereo position.

Stereo position was used in the earcons even though it is not available in telephone-based interfaces. We did this because it would be available in interfaces for disabled people based on personal computers, such as the portable communicator device described above or in interfaces for the blind. For these two situations we wanted to use all of the techniques available to maximize usability.

Level 3: At this level rhythm was used to differentiate the nodes. Each left node had one rhythm, each centre node another rhythm and each right node another. Figure 3 shows the rhythms used. From Figure 2 'Graphics', 'Letters', 'Earcons' and 'Doom' all had the left node rhythm, 'Microsoft Word', 'Reports & Papers', 'Buttons Experiment' and 'Adventure' were centre nodes and 'General Programs', 'Manuals', 'Scrollbar Experiment' and 'Arcade Games' were right nodes. Each of these rhythmic groups repeated continuously once every 2.5 seconds. As Figure 3 shows, the first note in each group was accented. The last note of each group was also lengthened slightly. These two help make each group into a complete rhythmic unit (Brewster et al., 1995).

At this level the earcons inherited timbre, spatial location and register from Level 2. This meant, for example, that 'Graphics' used the left node rhythm described in Figure 3 and it was played with an electric organ timbre, on the left side of the stereo space and in the register of C_4. 'Letters' used the same rhythm but, in this case, the timbre was a violin, stereo position was centre left and the register was C_3.

Level 4: A faster tempo was used to differentiate the items. The rhythmic units from Figure 3 now repeated once every second. In addition to this the effects reverb and chorus were applied to all of the earcons. These gave the earcons a

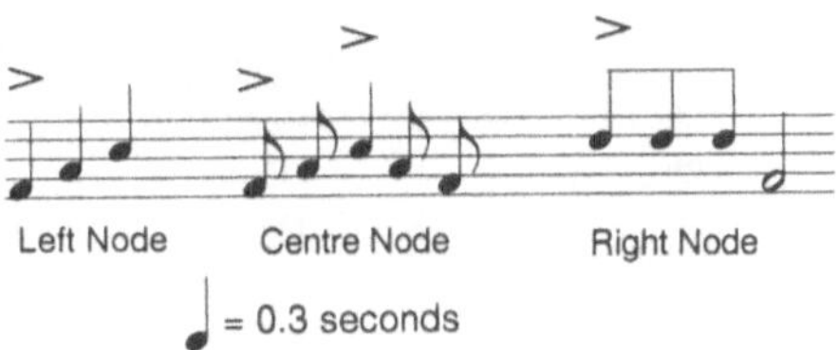

Figure 3: The rhythms used for Levels 3 and 4 of the hierarchy.

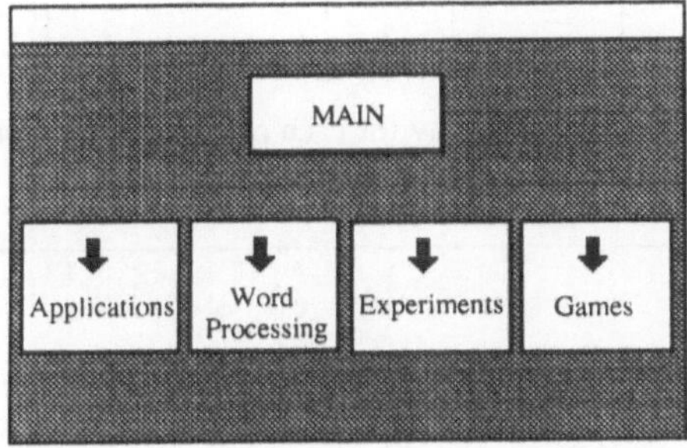

Figure 4: The top level of the hierarchy. The arrows show the direction of movement possible.

much fuller sound. This time rhythm was inherited from Level 3. Each of the nodes in Level 4 used the same rhythm as its parent node but the earcons were repeated more frequently.

3.4 *Experimental Design and Procedure*

As shown in Figure 2, the hierarchy was based on a computer file system. This was an experiment to test the use of earcons to represent a hierarchy and a file system was a convenient hierarchy to use, this paper does not suggest that each directory and sub-directory in a real file system should have a sound.

The hierarchy was constructed in a HyperCard stack. Figure 4 shows the screen of the top level of the hierarchy ('Main'). Each of the boxes in Figure 2 was a card in the stack. Buttons were provided for going up and down levels in the hierarchy and also for going left and right across the same level. As soon as a card was selected its sound started to play and continued until another card was selected.

3.5 *Training*

The training was in two parts. In the first part the experimenter showed the participant each of nodes of the hierarchy in turn and played the associated earcon. This was done once only. The structure of the earcons at each level was fully explained. In the

Question	Level	Node
Q1	2	Word processing
Q2	4	Space invaders
Q3	2	Experiments
Q4	4	Paint
Q5	2	Games
Q6	3	Doom
Q7	4	Word files
Q8	4	Parallel earcons
Q9	3	Graphics
Q10	3	Reports & papers
Q11	4	Business letters
Q12	3	Microsoft word
Q13	4	A
Q14	4	B

Table 2: The node and level in hierarchy for each of the questions. This is the order that the questions were presented to participants.

second part of the training participants were given five minutes to learn the earcons by themselves with no help from the experimenter. The training was short and simple allowing us to see if the rules by which the earcons created were obvious. Users of a communicator device of the type described above might only receive very simple training and have to learn the rest of the system by themselves. Users of a telephone-based system might get a short amount of training when they signed-up for a new telephone service and again have to learn it by themselves. The simple training used here would allow us to test these situations.

During the training participants could look at a map of the hierarchy (similar to Figure 2). The aim of the experiment was not to test the participants' abilities to learn hierarchies but to test their ability to learn the earcons. Instructions were read from a prepared script.

3.6 Testing

The participants heard fourteen earcons during testing. These were randomly selected from all of the sounds in the hierarchy. The same set of earcons was presented to each of the participants. Twelve of the sounds were ones that participants had heard during the training. The last two earcons presented were new ones (marked A and B in Figure 2). These were earcons for gaps in the hierarchy and were constructed using the same rules as the other earcons. Table 2 shows which node represented which question. An earcon was played and the participants then had to choose where the it fitted into the hierarchy. The hierarchy was represented on screen. Again, the aim of the experiment was to test the participants' knowledge of the earcons, not their ability to learn hierarchies. None of the names of the nodes were included in the picture of the hierarchy to avoid any help they might have provided.

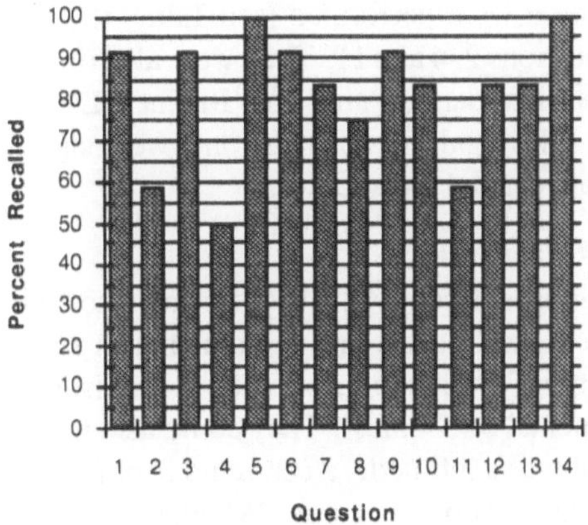

Figure 5: Recall rates for each of the 14 questions.

Questions	Question 4	Questions 2 & 11
q1	Q(154) = 5, p = 0.01	Q(154) = 4, p = 0.01
q2	Q(154) = 1, p = 0.01	—
q3	Q(154) = 5, p = 0.01	Q(154) = 4, p = 0.01
q4	—	—
q5	Q(154) = 6, p = 0.01	Q(154) = 5, p = 0.01
q6	Q(154) = 5, p = 0.01	Q(154) = 4, p = 0.01
q7	Q(154) = 4, p = 0.01	Q(154) = 3, p = 0.01
q8	Q(154) = 3, p = 0.01	Q(154) = 2, p = 0.01
q9	Q(154) = 5, p = 0.01	Q(154) = 4, p = 0.01
q10	Q(154) = 4, p = 0.01	Q(154) = 3, p = 0.01
q11	Q(154) = 1, p = 0.01	—
q12	Q(154) = 4, p = 0.01	Q(154) = 3, p = 0.01
q13	Q(154) = 4, p = 0.01	Q(154) = 3, p = 0.01
q14	Q(154) = 6, p = 0.01	Q(154) = 5, p = 0.01

Table 3: Tukey HSD results comparing the three worst questions. Question 4 was significantly worse than any other question. Questions 2 & 11 were worse than all except Question 4.

4 Results

4.1 Overall

The overall recall rate of the earcons was high: 81.5% of the earcons were correctly recalled. Figure 5 shows the percentage of correct answers for each question. An analysis was undertaken to find out if any of the earcons were less well recalled than any others. A one-factor ANOVA was performed on the scores per question and it showed an effect ($F(13,154) = 2.13$, $p = 0.01$). In order to find out where the effect was (and so which were the worst-recalled earcons) post hoc Tukey HSD tests comparing each question were performed (see Table 3). The three worst recalled earcons were from questions 2, 4 and 11. They were all from Level 4 of the hierarchy. The nodes were: 'Space Invaders', 'Paint' and 'Business Letters'. However, the other Level 4 nodes 'Word Files' and 'Parallel Earcons' were significantly better recalled than these. 'Paint' was recalled worst of all.

4.2 Recall of Components

Each of the participants' answers were broken down to find where the problems occurred. There were three mistakes that could be made. Participants could mistake the *family* of an earcon: For example, whether it was from 'Applications', 'Word Processing', 'Experiments' or 'Games'. They could also mistake the *node* an earcon referred to: Whether it was a left node, a centre node or a right node. Finally, participants could mistake the *level* of an earcon: Whether it was from Level 1, 2, 3 or 4. From the overall data obtained the scores were broken into three. If participants got a question completely right they received three marks, if they got two parts right then two marks were awarded, etc. From this analysis it was possible to see where mistakes occurred.

There were no significant differences between the recall rates of family, level and node. Participants recalled 80% of the family and level components and 76% of the node components. A one-factor ANOVA on the family, level and node scores showed no significant difference between these ($F(2,33) = 1.27$, $p = 0.291$).

4.3 New Earcons

As mentioned above, two new, previously unheard, earcons were presented to the participants during testing. These are marked by the letters A and B in Figure 2. They were both from Level 4 and were constructed using the same rules as the rest of the earcons. By using the rules participants should have been able to identify where in the hierarchy the sounds belonged.

The new earcons were very well recognized (see Questions 13 and 14 in Figure 5): 91.5% were recognized correctly. Ten out of twelve participants recognized the earcon for A in Figure 2 and all the participants recognized the earcon for B. This indicated that the participants were able to use the rules to work out where an unheard earcon belonged.

5 Discussion

5.1 Overall

The overall recall rate of the earcons was good. The participants recalled 81.5% of the earcons after being trained for only a short time. This demonstrates that a listener could use earcons as navigation aids in a menu hierarchy. This was also possible after only a short amount of training. Participants had the sounds described to them once only and then had five minutes to listen to the sounds. This shows that with careful design, earcons can easily be learned. One of the advantages claimed for auditory icons (described above) is that they are easy to learn because they use natural, everyday sounds. The research described here, combined with the earlier work of Brewster (1994) and Brewster et al. (1993), suggests that there may be no significant difference between auditory icons and earcons in this respect.

The results obtained here are approximately the same as the rate of recall in phase I of the second earcon experiment described by Brewster (1994). As mentioned above, the hierarchy used in that experiment was much simpler but the training and testing were less efficient (for example, the earcons were presented in a random order during training). In the experiment described here the training was more structured but the hierarchy was three times larger, leading to the similar recall rates.

The three worst recalled earcons were from Level 4 of the hierarchy. However, the other two earcons from Level 4 were significantly better recalled than these. A detailed analysis of the results gave no clear indication of what might have caused the difficulty. The problem may have been that these earcons were at the bottom of the hierarchy so participants had to remember all of the earcon construction rules to work out their location. This left more opportunity for mistakes than with the recall of earcons higher-up in the hierarchy where less had to be remembered. The manipulations chosen for Level 4 (tempo, chorus and echo) could be further exaggerated to more clearly indicate the differences between items. Further investigation is necessary.

5.2 New Earcons

The ability of the participants to identify the location of previously unheard earcons was very good (91.5%). They were able to use the rules for constructing the earcons to work out where a new earcon belonged. This showed that the listeners had learned the rules well. As discussed above, earcons provide an easily extensible system for adding sound for hierarchies. This research has shown that, if new nodes were added to an existing hierarchy then listeners would not need to be retrained on the sounds, they could use their existing knowledge of the rules to understand the new earcons. This is a very promising result for the use of earcons as hierarchical navigation aids.

The new sounds were from one of each of the main families, or major sub-trees, of the hierarchy so the participants could use all of the earcon creation rules to identify them. There were also only four missing ones so that their choice was reduced. For example, if they could only remember the timbre for the sub-tree they would still be able to identify the new earcon because each new earcon had a different timbre. This test could have been made more difficult by having two missing earcons from the same sub-tree. This would have made it harder to identify the missing one as there would be fewer differences between them. However, the result does show that participants were able to use the rules to locate the new earcons. This indicates that they are a very robust method of communicating hierarchy information in sound.

6 Future Work

These earcons will now be used for the TIDE ACCESS Project (they will be extended where necessary using the techniques described above). The sounds will be played quietly, in the background, when the user is in the hierarchy of pictographic symbols. The sounds will change when he/she moves up, down, left or right to a new node, indicating the new position in the hierarchy. The change in the earcon (plus a small increase in intensity) will capture the listener's attention and indicate the new location. The earcon will then fade back to a lower intensity and recede into the background of the listener's consciousness. The user will only attend to the sound again if he/she gets lost and wants navigation information.

For telephone-based interfaces this work must be extended. In a telephone-based interface the quality of the sounds would be reduced due to the limited bandwidth of telephone equipment. There would also be no stereo effects available. The next stage of the research will be to conduct the experiment again but present the sounds as if they were coming from a telephone. The results would then show what recall would be like under these more difficult conditions. The earcons could then be re-designed if necessary to maximize recall.

7 Conclusions

The aim of the experiment described here was to discover if earcons could provide navigational cues in a system of hierarchical menus. The results have shown that a 27 node hierarchy can easily be represented using earcons. A recall rate of 81.5% was achieved after only a short period of training. This indicates that they are a good way of providing navigational information for hierarchies. Listeners can hear an earcon and tell where it comes from in the hierarchy and hence where their location. Listeners could also recognize new earcons that had not been heard before (with 91.5% accuracy) by using the rules from which the other earcons were constructed. This shows that users could easily learn those rules. Therefore, earcons are a robust and extensible method of communication. This research has shown that earcons are an effective way of providing hierarchy information in interfaces where graphical information cannot easily be used.

Acknowledgements

This research was supported by ERCIM Research Fellowship 94–04. It was undertaken whilst the first author was at VTT Information Technology in Finland. Thanks to Peter Wright at the University of York, UK for helping with the statistical analysis.

References

Barfield, W., Rosenberg, C. & Levasseur, G. (1991), "The Use of Icons, Earcons and Commands in the Design of an Online Hierarchical Menu", *IEEE Transactions on Professional Communication* **34**(2), 101–108.

Baumgart, D., Johnson, J. & Helmstetter, E. (1990), *Augmentative and Alternative Communication Systems for Persons with Moderate and Severe Disabilities*, Paul Brookes Publishing Co.

Blattner, M., Papp, A. & Glinert, E. (1992), Sonic Enhancements of Two-dimensional Graphic Displays, *in* G. Kramer (ed.), "Auditory Display, Sonification, Audification and Auditory Interfaces. The Proceedings of the First International Conference on Auditory Display", Addison–Wesley, pp.447–470.

Blattner, M., Sumikawa, D. & Greenberg, R. (1989), "Earcons and Icons: Their Structure and Common Design Principles", *Human–Computer Interaction* **4**(1), 11–44.

Brewster, S. A. (1994), Providing a Structured Method for Integrating Non-speech Audio into Human–Computer Interfaces, PhD thesis, University of York, UK.

Brewster, S. A., Wright, P. C. & Edwards, A. D. N. (1993), An Evaluation of Earcons for Use in Auditory Human–Computer Interfaces, *in* S. Ashlund, K. Mullet, A. Henderson, E. Hollnagel & T. White (eds.), "Proceedings of INTERCHI'93", ACM Press, pp.222–227.

Brewster, S. A., Wright, P. C. & Edwards, A. D. N. (1995), Experimentally Derived Guidelines for the Creation of Earcons, *in* M. A. R. Kirby, A. J. Dix & J. E. Finlay (eds.), "Adjunct Proceedings of HCI'95", pp.155–159.

Gaver, W. (1989), "The SonicFinder: An Interface that uses Auditory Icons", *Human–Computer Interaction* **4**(1), 67–94.

Gaver, W. (1993), Synthesizing Auditory Icons, *in* S. Ashlund, K. Mullet, A. Henderson, E. Hollnagel & T. White (eds.), "Proceedings of INTERCHI'93", ACM Press, pp.228–235.

Gaver, W., Smith, R. & O'Shea, T. (1991), Effective Sounds in Complex Systems: The ARKola Simulation, *in* S. P. Robertson, G. M. Olson & J. S. Olson (eds.), "Proceedings of CHI'91: Human Factors in Computing Systems (Reaching through Technology)", ACM Press, pp.85–90.

Rosson, M. B. (1985), "Using Synthetic Speech for Remote Access to Information", *Behaviour Research Methods, Instruments and Computers* **17**(2), 250–252.

Stevens, R. (1996), Principles for the Design of Auditory Interfaces to Present Complex Information to Blind Computer Users, PhD thesis, University of York, UK.

Stevens, R. D., Brewster, S. A., Wright, P. C. & Edwards, A. D. N. (1994), Providing an Audio Glance at Algebra for Blind Readers, *in* G. Kramer & S. Smith (eds.), "Proceedings of ICAD'94", Sante Fe Institute, pp.21–30.

Yankelovich, N., Levow, G. & Marx, M. (1995), Designing SpeechActs: Issues in Speech User Interfaces, *in* I. Katz, R. Mack, L. Marks, M. B. Rosson & J. Nielsen (eds.), "Proceedings of CHI'95: Human Factors in Computing Systems", ACM Press, pp.369–376.

User Involvement

Problems for User Involvement: A Human and Organizational Perspective

Carolyn Axtell, Chris Clegg & Patrick Waterson

Institute of Work Psychology, University of Sheffield, Sheffield S10 2TN, UK.

Tel: *+44 114 2756600*
Fax: *+44 114 2727206*
EMail: {*C.M.Axtell,C.Clegg,P.Waterson*}*@sheffield.ac.uk*
URL: *http://www.dcs.gla.ac.uk/~stephen/*

This paper is concerned with problems that can impede the involvement of users in the development process. Several problem areas are highlighted in a case study of an in-house development project, which arise from the organizational context, process of the method and its relationship with other procedures. We discuss the impacts of these problems and the interconnections between them; the key underlying issues being a lack of integrated effort and incomplete knowledge or experience of those involved. We end the paper by suggesting possible ways forward involving work organized in an integrated development cell, greater participation of all parties in the design of the method, one overseeing manager, and a more thorough piloting and evaluation phase.

Keywords: user participation, system development, organizational issues.

1 Introduction

This paper is concerned with the problems that exist within organizations which hamper the involvement of users in system development. This is of interest because a key reason why many investments in new technology fail to realize their objectives, is that human and organizational factors tend to be neglected — e.g. (Kearney, 1990). User participation is widely regarded as an effective strategy for addressing these fundamental issues — e.g. (Mumford, 1983; Eason, 1988).

System development in organizations is typically carried out using highly structured, sequential methods (Clegg et al., in press). However, whilst Structured methods such as Structured System Analysis and Design Method (SSADM) advocate user involvement, users often do not influence key decisions and as a result the final system may fail to adequately reflect human and organizational needs (Damodaran et al., 1988). In addition, the outputs of systems analysis are difficult for users to understand and therefore validate (Browne, 1994). Ratification by users is made easier through the use of prototyping, although this alone without thorough requirements analysis is not adequate (Browne, 1994). Despite wide support for user participation, the extent to which users have real influence in most development projects is still quite low (Clegg et al., 1996).

Users have most commonly been involved at the beginning and end of the process, in requirements analysis and user acceptance testing. However, recommendations for user involvement advocate more than just this. There should be an early focus on users; system design should be iterative and modifiable as a result of testing and evaluation; and finally, all aspects of usability (interface, training etc.) should be integrated under one management and evolve in parallel (Gould & Lewis, 1985; Gould et al., 1991). Involving users early in development is likely to lead to better products because the developers will gain knowledge about users' practice and future use situations — e.g. (Eason, 1988). User involvement is also likely to lead to adjustment of user expectations, making eventual acceptance of the system more likely (Grønbæk et al., 1993).

The notion of participation also exists as a strong tradition within the socio-technical and organizational literature. This advocates the participation of workers in decisions and changes which affect them and has been identified as a means of improving employee satisfaction and productivity — e.g. (Hackman et al., 1975), and of increasing acceptance of change — e.g. (Vroom & Jago, 1988). Also, it is advocated that when managers do not have enough knowledge or information to make a decision themselves, participative decision making should be adopted (Vroom & Jago, 1988). In any planned organizational change, success is considered to be dependent on the quality of the process of implementation — e.g. (Ginzberg, 1979), higher quality denoting greater participation and more of a joint effort between managers and other workers.

Socio-technical theory (Cherns, 1976; 1987) offers insight into how work should be organized and redesigned to be most effective, which can help us analyse and inform the processes of development. The theory advocates highly participative work groups with control over how they conduct their work; the withdrawal of organizational boundaries that impede the sharing of information, learning and knowledge; availability of information for those who need to take action and access and authority over resources. Decision-making should be devolved to the work groups so that their problems can be resolved at source. Other systems supporting the focal group should be congruent in their design and the process of work redesign should be continuous, undergoing constant review and evaluation.

However, there are many problems that exist which can prevent user participation from being practised or being effective. For instance, Grudin (1991) outlines a number of obstacles to user involvement in product development organizations, which he suggests will be less salient for in-house development where contact between users and developers should be easier to manage. Nevertheless, any in-house project is likely to be affected by a variety of problems which will have an impact on the form of user participation that takes place. Given that user influence in design is most important for bespoke systems, this is an issue of great concern.

The organizational setting in which development takes place is an important factor to consider, but is often overlooked (Hornby & Clegg, 1992). Certain practices may be more suitable for some organizations than others. Systems development takes place in a wide variety of contexts, each having different impacts on the conditions for effective user participation (Grønbæk et al., 1993). As such, we need to understand the broader dynamics of participation. There is a need to focus on the 'process' of system development, instead of concentrating solely on the final 'product' to be delivered (Grønbæk et al., 1993). Only by fully understanding the processes involved in development and the problems that need to be overcome can we hope to optimize conditions for the inclusion of human and organizational factors. A case study research approach is useful for this as it can deliver a more holistic and yet detailed understanding of a situation (Clegg et al., in press).

In this paper we describe a case study of a user centred design method in an in-house development situation. The problems for user involvement can be categorized into three interconnecting problem areas, to do with the organizational context, the relationship of the method with other procedures in the organization and the process of the method itself. The key issues underlying the problems are a lack of integrated effort and the incomplete knowledge or experience of those involved and as such, we argue that system development should be seen as knowledge work (Clegg et al., in press). We conclude that these problems might be tackled through organizing development in an integrated development cell; having greater involvement of all parties concerned in the actual design of the development methodology; ensuring thorough piloting and evaluation of it; and managing it with one boundary spanning manager.

2 The Case Study

The case study takes place within a large organization in the UK, operating in a rapidly changing and highly political environment. A computer system was being developed to support the daily administrative activities of several thousand users, nation-wide. This had to incorporate local variations in work practices, as the job in different offices was tailored to the specific needs and requirements of the local area. The new system would replace and extend an old one that already existed in offices.

As a result of dissatisfaction with the current system development approach used in the organization (SSADM), a senior developer within the IT department at head office began to design a more user participative approach. In time help for the approach was recruited from the human factors and network support departments, and approval for its use in this particular development project was eventually gained from more senior managers. This method (which we will call User Involvement Method — UIM) built on some earlier experiments, but essentially was being used for the first time within this organization.

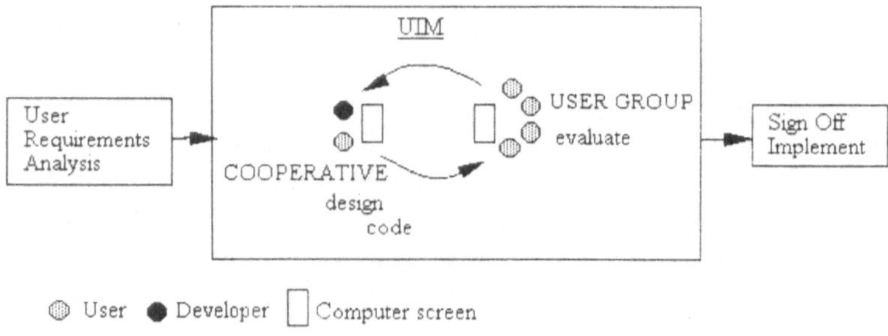

Figure 1: Overview of UIM.

The requirements analysis, had been conducted over the previous two years using SSADM with minimal user involvement. UIM followed on from this, was iterative and focused on design and usability of the system, although many issues of functionality were inevitably addressed. Users were seconded to head office for between one to five weeks and participated in designing prototypes of the new system. There were two main components of the method; a Cooperative and a User Group (see Figure 1). The Cooperative consisted of a user and a developer who jointly designed prototypes. The User Group (UG) was a group of typically 4 to 5 users who evaluated the prototypes designed by the Cooperative.

The process of UIM is described below:

1. The developer and user in the Cooperative were given a section of the user requirements analysis and came to a common understanding about it. They then wrote a detailed task analysis of what sequences of information a user was likely to need to complete this part of their work.

2. This task analysis was then validated with the UG.

3. The Cooperative then designed prototypes of screens and the navigation between them, for this section of the system.

4. The UG validated the screen navigation, mandatory entry fields, cross referenced screens and suggested any changes.

5. The Cooperative made changes to the design of the screens and added database links.

6. The UG evaluated database accesses, did final entry field validations and validated any changes made.

7. The Cooperative made any design changes needed and may have proposed alternative solutions to be discussed with the UG.

8. UGs conducted evaluation using detailed, work based role plays and scenarios that they had designed.

9. Work flowed between the Cooperative and UG in an iterative loop from design, coding to evaluation, several times before sections of the overall system were completed and could be signed off.

The essential aspects of the process were the high degree of interaction and information flow between users and developers and the chance for users to rigorously evaluate the prototypes they helped design. Liaison between the users and developers was managed by a small user support team (two or three people from network services) who dealt with general administration of the method. They were also responsible for recruiting users to work temporarily at head office, introducing users to the new system when they arrived and providing work for them. Although there was a project manager responsible for the development of the software in the IT department, the different parties involved (users, developers, network services, user support and human factors) had different reporting lines and accountabilities, with no formal overseeing manager in charge of UIM itself.

3 Research Methods

The researchers were involved over a period of three months from the end of February to May 1994, ten months into the use of UIM. Our role within the organization was to evaluate the method and make recommendations for improvements. In order to gain a detailed picture of the development situation both past and present, a range of research methods were employed and data were gathered from a range of sources, as described below.

3.1 Semi-structured Interviews

Twelve managers, including some in senior posts, were interviewed to gain a contextual and historical understanding of the development method. Twenty one users from local offices who attended Head Office, during the researchers' involvement, and four out of the nine in-house developers were interviewed about their experiences of UIM. The interviews were audio-recorded and their contents analysed by the three authors for common themes and views.

3.2 Questionnaires

A postal questionnaire was sent to all 87 users who had participated in UIM since its initial use in April 1993. 67 were returned, a response rate of 77%. The questionnaire covered experience and involvement in the method; attitudes and commitment towards UIM; amount of influence they felt they had on the development of the new system, and how the method might be improved. Questionnaires were used so that we could gain information from users who had been involved in UIM in earlier stages. Equivalent questionnaires were distributed to all nine developers involved in this project, for a comparison, and were returned by six of them. Descriptive statistics were conducted on this data using SPSS.

3.3 Video and Observation

Over a three week period towards the end of development (April, 1994), video recordings were conducted of the users working in a UG. This was to gain some understanding of the role of users and their activities whilst evaluating the computer system. In total, 168 hours of video tape were recorded which the authors scrutinized and coded. Preliminary analysis of activities are reported in this paper.

3.4 Tracer Study and Observation

The links between the users and developers in the later stages of development were investigated by conducting a tracer study. This is a method for identifying and describing ongoing organizational processes across time and across different groups. Documentation (evaluation and error reports) from users to developers were tracked, in order to investigate what happened to issues raised by the users. In total, 553 evaluation reports were logged at the organization and viewed by the researchers. In addition, the researchers were able to observe any interactions between users and developers during the study. Selected examples are illustrated in this paper.

4 Findings

The key findings are that historical issues affected the type of participation that took place, such as a cessation of Cooperatives, the introduction of external consultants and a change of deadline. Attitudes towards UIM were positive although there were some criticisms of it from developers. Senior Managers appeared to hold a more cautious view of the new method than the other stakeholders and this lack of support was seen as an impetus for other problems. The changes that needed to be made to the original user specification were highlighted as a problem as well as the problems of selecting users and preparing users and developers for their involvement in UIM. During the later phases of UIM, user activities appeared to be varied, but were not well supported in terms of access to the technical information required. In particular, feedback between users and developers was inefficient during this later phase.

4.1 Historical Overview of UIM

Over its course, UIM, and thus the form of participation changed in nature. The development team started using the new method in April 1993; the system at this stage being designed with character-based screens. In September 1993 the decision was made by senior managers to change to a GUI based system and so some of this previous work had to be restarted. A major change to UIM occurred at the beginning of January 1994, when Cooperatives were disbanded. This was in response to the need to give developers more time to code. User Groups carried on in an evaluative role and were also bringing documentation up to date. Developers and the User Groups were able to have access to each other as and when required, for guidance or help with decisions. Developers tended to prefer this level of interaction with users and felt that the method worked best this way. However, users were much less keen and preferred greater contact with developers.

Around this time, a senior manager became worried that development was taking too long and that the new software was simply replicating old methods of working in local offices. Indeed, developers recognized that the new system was almost becoming a reproduction of the old one, as the old system biased users views of how the new one should operate. As a result the senior manager commissioned some external consultants in January 1994, to develop some additional functionality for the new system. These consultants had conducted a Business Process Re-engineering (BPR) exercise in some local offices the previous Autumn, the results of which had lead to the ideas for the additional functionalities. The consultants said they could deliver these faster than the in-house developers. As such, the outcomes of this BPR exercise were incorporated into development near the end of the process, which potentially limited its scope because the analysis had already been done and much of the system had already been built. In addition, the BPR exercise was only carried out in a few offices in one region, which was also the chosen pilot site for the final system. The consultants used their own system development method for constructing the additional functionalities which involved users from the chosen local offices during the requirements gathering and testing phases only. This method was running in parallel to UIM. However, with the insistence of those working closest to UIM, the users seconded to head office were also able to test these externally developed functionalities. Having external consultants meant that integration of knowledge across the two development groups was more difficult and it also caused bad feelings with those involved in the in-house project.

The consultants promised delivery in May 1994, and so the senior managers brought forward the deadline for piloting the whole system to fit in with this. As such, the original deadline was brought forward by four months. Personal contact between users and developers was reduced further in UIM during this phase as developers were totally engaged in programming and were working a lot of overtime, in order to reach the deadline. Feedback from UGs to developers about the new system was via written communication only and was almost exclusively via the medium of the user support team, who made decisions on how to act upon the feedback. The process became particularly difficult to organize and manage.

4.2 Views of Users, Developers and Managers

The evidence from interview and questionnaire data suggests that overall attitudes to UIM were positive, with 4 of the 6 developers (66%) and 91% of users reporting positive attitudes on the questionnaire. In particular, those managers who were more actively involved with the method (such as the user support team) showed the greatest conviction for its potential benefits and felt strong ownership of it. More senior managers, at a greater distance from the method, held a more cautious view, and felt that the case was as yet unproven. Also, developers who had more investment in the method, in terms of helping in its design or writing the UIM manual felt greater ownership than other developers. Overall ownership was attributed slightly more to the developers than to the users in the questionnaires and interviews.

Developers felt that the good thing about the method was that it enabled them to get answers to business questions, although they were also critical of it. Coordination of work between UGs and Cooperatives was seen as problematic and developers felt they had to spend too much time with users. They felt that there was a lot of repetition of work and confusion about what decisions were being made, and where. Other complaints from developers included the time it took to have a decision ratified by the UG and waiting whilst users argued about what they wanted. However, developers felt that some of the problems were due to the fact that the management needs and resources for involving users, had been under-estimated (i.e. there was a lack of user support). As the organization had almost exclusively used SSADM in the past, there was a lack of knowledge in terms of how best to resource and manage such a high degree of user participation, on such a large project within this environment. This is unsurprising given that they had not attempted user involvement on this scale before.

Selling the method to senior management was one problem highlighted, particularly by managers working most closely with UIM, and was seen as an impetus for other problems that occurred. For instance, it was reported that a lack of senior influence and support in promoting and advertising the new method meant that initially there was a problem of recruiting enough users to participate. There were also delays in getting financial support for the method. Senior managers saw UIM as 'high risk' as it was new and unproven. This may have been partly due to their lack of knowledge about its final outcomes as it was being used for the first time. Although SSADM was seen as problematic by senior managers, it had been organizational policy to use it, and as such was an approved method and considered 'safe'.

One of the outcomes of UIM noted by many managers and developers in the interviews was a virtual re-writing of parts of the original requirements specification. This caused delays because of lengthy change control procedures. Despite this, those with technical training stressed the continuing need for detailed analysis and modelling. However, all parties agreed that an improvement would have been to have greater user participation in the analysis phase, which might have alleviated the need for so many changes.

User influence was reported to be high, particularly when in a Cooperative, i.e. 78% of users felt they had high influence when they were in a Cooperative and 62% felt they had high influence when in a UG. However, one problem noted by members of all parties was selecting representative users. There was a recognized need to involve a variety of users with their different business knowledge from the different regions that the system was to support. This meant a fairly rapid turnover of users was necessary to get the required variation. However, a counter problem highlighted by managers and developers was the long time taken for users to learn and take an active part in development. This highlights a need for more preparation and training. Users often said they were "just getting the hang of things" when they had to leave. IT managers also commented that the developers needed training in communications skills and how to deal with users. Other issues include a lack of feedback and communication during the later stage of development, and delays when users were waiting for work to do.

It must be noted, however, that the above views of the developers and managers in particular, could be more positive towards UIM and more negative towards senior management than they might have otherwise been because the of the involvement of external consultants and the fact that Cooperatives had been disbanded at the time they were interviewed.

4.3 User Activities

From the video recordings and observation, it would appear that the users activities in the UGs, towards the end of development (April, 1994) were varied. They included detecting bugs in the system, checking consistency across screens, designing help screens, entering database materials for trialing, devising work based scenarios and conducting formal evaluation trials with them. These activities may be different to those at earlier stages of UIM, but give an indication of user potential to be involved in diverse activities.

The knowledge they needed to draw upon to complete these activities, not only related to current and future work activities in local offices, but also to what they knew about the rest of the system (such as why different aspects were programmed in), what they knew was technically possible and what was currently happening in the development process. However, the users' knowledge of these more technical aspects was often incomplete and they needed to ask questions about it. This need was not well supported as contact with developers was minimal during this phase. This led to inefficiencies and wasted effort. Another important aspect of the their activity included organizing how their work would be carried out. The method they used in achieving a particular task was at their own discretion which appeared to work effectively. Some users wanted more input into organizing how their work would be carried out within UIM, particularly during periods where there was lack of work, because of system problems or while they were waiting for work to be prepared for them.

4.4 Links between Users and Developers

The tracer study and observation reveal that some feedback from users during the later stages of development (March to May, 1994) was being dealt with by developers (approx. 34%), although quite a large amount had already been filtered out by the user support team as requiring no further action (approx. 28%). Much of this was likely to be due to the development and evaluation cycles being out of synchrony, so that many of the users' reports were already out of date. Users were often evaluating versions of the system that had since been changed. There were also a significant amount of reports outstanding and not resolved (approx. 38%), which had been raised with developers several weeks previously. Lack of direct contact with developers appears to have made the feedback process much less efficient. For instance, screens were being designed without cooperation and immediate feedback from users. This meant that some were sent back to developers due to easily preventable problems such as abbreviations labelling entry fields, that did not make sense to users. Observations of the advantages of direct contact were also made. In one case a developer directly consulted with a user to clarify an error report, so that the fault could be found. This helped to resolve it quickly.

5 Interpretation

In this section we undertake our interpretation of the findings above, by grouping them into problem areas. Firstly it must be recognized that the method represents an enormous amount of effort from various members of the organization through which a great deal of learning has occurred and expertise gained. The resultant system was generally well received by users in the initial pilot sites, more so in the sites that were more involved with the BPR, although there were some bugs that needed to be ironed out. Nevertheless, the process was not without its problems and as such, it seems fruitful to analyse these.

There appear to be three main problem areas arising in the case study which relate to human and organizational issues. These are external factors to do with the organizational context and the relationship with other procedures, as well as those arising within the process of UIM. These and the interconnections between them will be described below.

5.1 The Organizational Context

There was the general difficulty of undertaking any form of large scale development in an organization of this kind, with its massive and widely distributed user population and different, local methods of working. Geographic location is a problem that Grudin (1991) has also noted. Other organizational issues include the fact that there were two different developer groups, which relates to the division of labour problems where opportunities for miscommunication are high (Grudin, 1991); lack of active involvement or support from senior managers; and the organizational policy for SSADM which made it more difficult to introduce the new method.

5.2 Relationship with Other Procedures in the Organization

Here problems include the different nature of the development method used by the consultants; UIM's lack of fit with the SSADM requirements specification; the late incorporation of the BPR outcomes and development of the resultant functionalities. In general, the different procedures here did not integrate well with UIM. As such, this opposes one of the principles of socio technical theory, as the procedures surrounding the method were not congruent to it. This also relates to a point made by Grudin (1991) that managerial preferences for structured design processes work counter to more iterative user involvement.

5.3 Process of UIM

Problems here include the coordination of the method prior to and after the break-down of Cooperatives; optimum contact between users and developers; lack of time to involve users later on; feedback problems and delays in the process. Time and feedback issues are also noted by Grudin (1991). Other problems with the process were a lack of support staff, selection of representative users and the length of their secondments. There were also issues of ownership, knowledge, experience, training and preparation of those involved.

5.4 *Inter-connections*

A key point is that these problems are interconnected, in particular the external organizational factors have an effect on the process of the method. Some examples illustrate this.

For instance, part of the problem of selecting representative users was due to the organizational issue of the size and distribution of the user population and the different local methods of working. This also had implications for the turnover of users seconded to head office, the length of their stay and consequent training and preparation required.

Another organizational issue was the tradition of using SSADM. This can be seen as an impetus for other problems such as the lack of coordination of the components of UIM. Previous exposure and almost exclusive use of SSADM meant that experience and knowledge of how to conduct a process with such a high degree of user participation, in such a project was limited. This in part led to an underestimation of the management needs of the process and resources required. Consequently there was a lack of user support staff which compounded the problems of coordinating the different aspects of UIM. The lack of organizational experience with other methods also meant that UIM was considered 'high risk' which in part led to the lack of support and ownership from senior managers. Indeed, ownership of the method was highest for those most involved in its design or use. Senior management decisions were later made to commission consultants (introducing other procedures to interface with UIM and decreasing its integration) and bring forward the deadline. This in turn led to coordination problems and the lack of time to involve users to the extent they had been.

Nothing can be done about some of the problems within the organization, such as the size and distribution of the user population. However, there are other basic issues that can be acted upon. A common theme and key issue is the lack of integrated effort in the development process. Another key issue is knowledge across all parties involved. These two issues; 'coordinated effort' and 'knowledge', may be seen as critical to the conduct of this method.

6 Conclusions and Implications

In this section we consider the implications of the above view for practice and theory. We argue that system development should be seen as knowledge work and recommend actions that might help to address the problems and the issues of integration and knowledge. Thus, the process should be designed as an integrated development cell, so that all aspects of development from BPR to system testing are undertaken within the same team. There should be greater participation of different parties in the design of the method, particularly senior managers so that they feel more ownership of it, and so that the experience and knowledge held by different parties is included. The process should be managed by one boundary spanning manager, so that all parties are integrated under one person, and so that a senior champion can promote it. In addition, detailed piloting and evaluation of the method is needed to iron out some of the problems. These actions have implications for the concept of user participation.

Our analysis of the case study implies that system development and the development of the process by which this is achieved, should be seen as an attempt at knowledge work (Clegg et al., in press). Coordination and integration of knowledge and expertise is central to the design and operation of such a work system. As can be seen with this case, problems arise when such a work organization is not integrated in a way which constitutes a coordinated effort. From this perspective we recommend four actions that could be taken to overcome some of the problems outlined.

1. *Integrated system development cell.* Firstly, given the problems of integration, the design of the method should follow the notion of a software development cell; a concept borrowed from manufacturing. In this case, the multiple forms of expertise needed for successful development (i.e. analysts, developers, users, human factors experts, BPR specialists) should be incorporated into one development cell. As such, detailed systems analysis, business process re-engineering, design, coding and testing should be undertaken within the same project team. This would conform to the principles of socio-technical systems, in that a highly participative work group should be set up which would help to remove organizational boundaries which impede knowledge sharing and facilitate a more integrated effort. Work should not be contracted out of the cell, but be contracted in, to work within the team, using methods which are congruent with the processes taking place within it.

2. *Greater participation in design of the method.* The new system development method and development cell need to be designed and implemented, and should be done so participatively. With incomplete knowledge held by different parties, there is a greater need for participative decision making or input to how the new method of working could be designed (Vroom & Jago, 1988). Despite the hard work and expertise of the designers of UIM, there was other expertise within the organization which could have contributed. Of particular importance in this case is the input and support from Senior Managers who had the most power and authority to modify or disband the method. Their ideas, such as conducting BPR could have been incorporated from the start. A variety of experts (developers, users, senior managers, human factors, BPR experts etc.) should participate in decisions about various aspects of the method such as how much user support is needed, who to involve and for how long, what training is required, how to involve users in requirements analysis, if and when to involve consultants etc. Greater participation of all those concerned could help to build upon the strengths, positive attitudes and commitment that already exist with those most closely involved in the method and would also help to implement it successfully — e.g. (Ginzberg, 1979).

3. *Having one boundary spanning manager.* The new method needs managing. To facilitate an integrated effort there is a need for one (preferably senior) boundary spanning manager in charge of the development cell, who might be a representative of the user community. This would bring all different parties involved under the same reporting line, instead of having many different ones. Having a senior champion would help with the promotion of UIM throughout

the organization and could also help facilitate the participation of different parties in the design of the method. This relates to Gould & Lewis' (1985) recommendation for integration under one management.

4. *Pilot study and evaluation.* Incomplete knowledge regarding user participation on this scale might be addressed through a more thorough piloting of the method. In this case, although there had been some limited trials, the full process of UIM (with Cooperatives and User Groups) had not been tried out before this development project. A more thorough pilot might help iron out some of the problems and provide greater insight to the management needs, training requirements and outcomes of the method. This would help users, developers and managers with future decision making regarding the process of development. If a pilot had been conducted, it might also have helped to make the case for the method more 'proven' for senior management. The method needs to be developed in an iterative fashion (Gould & Lewis, 1985) with constant review and evaluation of the design of this work system (Cherns, 1987).

The main practical and theoretical message is that we should not just think at the level of user involvement in system design, but look more broadly at organizational involvement in the design of the process itself. This has implications for the concept of 'user participation', as the problem can be reconfigured to that of a knowledge integration and coordination problem, rather than simply a problem of user participation. In addition, the concept of user participation could be expanded to include user input to the design of the process of development. The findings imply that a user's potential should not be underestimated, but should be recognized and supported. As in this case, users' work should be organized to allow them control over the method of performing particular tasks and they should also be provided with all the information they need to do their job, such as technical information.

Consistent with previous work, this study locates the practice of user participation within its organizational context — e.g. (Hornby & Clegg, 1992; Grønbæk et al., 1993) and attempts to apply socio-technical theory to software development — e.g. (Mumford, 1983). Our findings are similar to those found elsewhere, such as Grudin's work in product development organizations, noted earlier. However, there is a need for other detailed case studies to identify problems that exist for different forms of user participation and knowledge integration in different development situations. We also need to investigate the success of those which have tried to overcome their problems. Through a variety of studies we may learn more about the process of active user participation and knowledge integration, and how to improve the conditions for introducing it successfully in different organizational environments.

Acknowledgements

We would like to thank all those in the organization where this study took place who helped with the gathering and interpretation of this data.

References

Browne, D. (1994), *STUDIO: STructured User-interface Design for Interaction Optimisation*, Prentice–Hall.

Cherns, A. B. (1976), "The Principles of Socio-technical Design", *Human Relations* **29**(8), 783–792.

Cherns, A. B. (1987), "The Principles of Socio-technical Design Revisited", *Human Relations* **40**(3), 153–162.

Clegg, C. W., Axtell, C., Damodaran, L., Farbey, B., Hull, R., Lloyd-Jones, R., Nicholls, J., Sell, R., Tomlinson, C., Ainger, A. & Stewart, T. (1996), "The Performance of Information Technology and the Role of Human and Organizational Factors". Report to the Economic and Social Research Council.

Clegg, C. W., Waterson, P. E. & Axtell, C. M. (in press), "Software Development: Knowledge Intensive Work Organisations", *Behaviour & Information Technology*.

Damodaran, L., Ip, K. & Beck, M. (1988), Integrating Human Factors into Structured Design Methodology: A Case Study in the UK Civil Service, *in* H. J. Bullinger (ed.), "Information Technology for Organisational Systems", Elsevier Science, pp.235–241.

Eason, K. (1988), *Information Technology and Organisational Change*, Taylor & Francis.

Ginzberg, M. J. (1979), "A Study of the Implementation Process", *TIMS Studies in the Management Sciences* **13**, 85–102.

Gould, J. D. & Lewis, C. H. (1985), "Designing for Usability — Key Principles and What Designers Think", *Communications of the ACM* **28**(3), 300–311.

Gould, J. D., Boies, S. J. & Lewis, C. H. (1991), "Making Usable, Useful, Productivity-enhancing Computer Applications", *Communications of the ACM* **34**(1), 74–85.

Grønbæk, K., Grudin, J., Bødker, S. & Bannon, L. (1993), Achieving Cooperative System Design: Shifting from a Product to a Process Focus, *in* D. Schuler & A. Namioka (eds.), "Participatory Design: Principles and Practices", Lawrence Erlbaum Associates, pp.79–97.

Grudin, J. (1991), "Systematic Sources of Sub-optimal Interface Design in Large Product Development Organisations", *Human–Computer Interaction* **6**(2), 147–196.

Hackman, J. R., Oldham, G., Jenson, R. & Purdy, K. (1975), "A New Strategy for Job Enrichment", *California Management Review* **17**(4), 57–71.

Hornby, P. & Clegg, C. (1992), "User Participation in Context: A Case Study in a UK Bank", *Behaviour & Information Technology* **11**(5), 293–307.

Kearney, A. T. (1990), *Barriers to the Successful Application of Information Technology*, Department of Trade and Industry.

Mumford, E. (1983), *Designing Human Systems*, Manchester Business School.

Vroom, V. H. & Jago, A. G. (1988), "Managing Participation: A Critical Dimension of Leadership", *Journal of Management Development* **7**(5), 32–42.

Multidisciplinary Modelling for User-Centred System Design: An Air-traffic Control Case Study

Simon Buckingham Shum[1], Ann Blandford[2], David Duke[3], Jason Good[3], Jon May[4], Fabio Paterno'[5] & Richard Young[6]

[1] *Knowledge Media Institute, The Open University, Milton Keynes MK7 6AA, UK.*

Tel: *+44 1908 655723*

Fax: *+44 1908 653169*

EMail: *S.Buckingham.Shum@open.ac.uk*

[2] *School of Computing Science, Middlesex University, London N11 2NQ, UK.*

EMail: *A.Blandford@middlesex.ac.uk*

[3] *Department Computer Science, University of York, York YO1 5DD, UK.*

EMail: {*Duke, Jason*}*@minster.york.ac.uk*

[4] *Department of Psychology, University of Sheffield, Sheffield S10 2TP, UK.*

EMail: *Jon.May@sheffield.ac.uk*

[5] *CNUCE-CNR, Via S.Maria 36, 56126 Pisa, Italy.*

EMail: *F.Paterno@cnuce.cnr.it*

[6] *MRC Applied Psychology Unit, 15 Chaucer Road, Cambridge CB2 2EF, UK.*

EMail: *Richard.Young@mrc-apu.cam.ac.uk*

This paper reports work investigating how user and system modelling techniques can be integrated to support the design of advanced interactive systems, and how such modelling can be effectively communicated to design practitioners in order to evaluate their potential. We describe a large scale modelling exercise concerning a flight sequencing tool for air-traffic controllers. We outline the kinds of system and user analysis possible with the different modelling techniques, and the approach used to integrate and communicate the modelling analyses to the system's designers. We then discuss the value of these techniques against several key criteria. The designers evaluated the modelling positively in many respects, including a commitment to explore further how user modelling can be integrated with their formal methods. We conclude that the scenario of HCI modellers working in collaboration with designers is feasible, and has analytic power.

Keywords: multidisciplinary design, user modelling, formal methods, interaction modelling, air-traffic control.

1 Introduction

1.1 Modelling Techniques for User-centred Design

Over the last six years, the ESPRIT funded AMODEUS Project has been investigating how modelling techniques from software and cognitive engineering can be brought together in the design of advanced interactive systems. We have developed design formalisms for modelling users, systems, their interaction, design rationale, and the multidisciplinary inter-relationships between these formalisms. Summaries and short worked examples of each approach can be found in Buckingham Shum et al. (1994a).

In parallel with developing techniques and exploring ways to integrate them, an explicit concern has been to investigate the obstacles to transferring HCI modelling techniques from research to practice. This strand of the work, conducted by a non-modelling component of the project (i.e. who are not 'stakeholders' in any particular technique), developed a framework which identified a number of key 'gulfs' between HCI modelling research and design practice (Buckingham Shum & Hammond, 1994b), which then motivated specific empirical studies for evaluating the different techniques. These were of two main types: studies *evaluating the usability* of individual techniques, in which different populations of designers were trained to use particular modelling techniques themselves (Blandford et al., 1995a; Buckingham Shum, 1996; Nigay et al., 1995), and modelling exercises in which we provide *HCI 'modelling consultancy'* to external design teams. Two have been reported elsewhere (Bellotti et al., 1995; Buckingham Shum et al., 1994b), and this paper reports a third.

1.2 The Modelling Process

We believe the case study described in this paper to be the largest industrial HCI modelling exercise conducted to date, in terms of the system modelled (a real system with a 100 page formal specification and substantial supporting documentation), the number of modellers (13) and duration of the collaboration with the company (18 months, part time). In this exercise, the modellers were working in a consultancy role, that is, they were doing the modelling and explaining it to the designers. The system in question was an air-traffic control tool called the CERD (Computer Entry & Readout Display), developed by Praxis Systems Ltd. for the UK's Civil Aviation Authority (CAA) as part of its new air-traffic control system.

When collaboration with AMODEUS began the CERD had been delivered to the CAA, and so was no longer a 'live' development project. However, there was a lot of interest by the CERD's designers in the possibility of more rigorously specifying user-relevant properties of systems, and so the CERD represented a safe testbed (from Praxis' point of view). We have reported elsewhere an earlier modelling exercise with a design team developing an audio/video media space in an exploratory research context (Bellotti et al., 1995). This forced us to find ways of deploying and communicating modelling in a domain and culture not normally associated with formal methods. In contrast, Praxis is a company with a strong tradition of using formal methods in large scale system development projects; moreover, whilst it was not surprising that the CERD's chief software engineer was expert in formal methods, so too was the human factors expert, which is much rarer. As such, this offered an ideal design culture in which to trial HCI modelling techniques which:

1. are based on the premise that abstraction and formality have useful roles to play in interactive system design (whether in relation to computational or cognitive information processing); and

2. are more easily grasped by a someone with at least some familiarity with formal mathematical notations.

This modelling exercise was conducted over an 18 month period beginning in January 1994, when the CERD's human factors designer specified a number of issues on which she was interested to receive modelling analyses. In that time, there were two major modelling iterations (Mar–May'94; Jul'94–Feb'95), each ending with a workshop (May'94; Feb'95), at which the modelling was presented and discussed. The CERD's human factors designer attended the first workshop, and was accompanied by the chief software engineer at the second.

In the first round of modelling, the teams worked largely independently and only saw each others' analyses when the compiled modelling report (Buckingham Shum,

1994) was circulated two weeks before the first workshop. This document could be navigated either by type of modelling analysis or by the design issue of interest. The report (which also contains several modelling techniques and analysis of many other design issues not described here) was accompanied by introductory information about each modelling technique.

Following the first workshop, a new technique for integrating user and system modelling was tested, which we called 'collational co-modelling'. The goal of the approach is for modellers together to construct a multidisciplinary understanding of a problem which exceeds the scope or perspective of any one approach. The technique involves an active 'collator' who ensures that relevant approaches contribute to the analysis, tracks emerging themes, and summarizes the contributions (Young et al., 1994). We describe in Section 7 how this was used as a framework within which modellers and designers were able to work together.

The rest of this paper is organized as follows. In Section 2, we introduce the CERD, the system modelled. In Section 3, we describe how the initial formal system modelling analysis (prior to the first workshop) highlighted a potential usability problem ('accidental message deletion'). This raised further issues which were addressable by other modelling techniques, and through a process of co-modelling, three complementary analyses were developed, which we outline in Sections 4–6. Section 7 first clarifies how the collational co-modelling facilitated multidisciplinary analysis, and secondly, describes co-modelling with CERD's designers at the second workshop as an experimental way to communicate the modelling analyses. The designers were asked to provide feedback on the modelling techniques, and in Section 8 we reflect on the issues which arose in our discussions with them on the potential of formal modelling techniques and value of our modelling of the CERD.

2 CERD: An Air-traffic Control Tool

The CERD is the component of an air traffic control station that allows an ATCO (Air Traffic Control Officer) to manipulate the sequence of flights approaching a major airport. The CERD is a touch-sensitive plasma display that presents information to ATCOs as a set of logical screens. Figure 1 shows the structure and content of a CERD screen. The two columns of rectangles are flight records, analogous to the physical flight strips used by ATCOs, providing summary information such as flight number, destination, and calculated time of arrival. The squares are keys for executing various operations (e.g. re-sequencing flights; tidying the display; scrolling left/right). Dashed lines indicate that the key is not currently active.

The user interface for displaying and managing messages was one of the design issues on which the CERD's human factors designer requested modelling analyses. The Message area is at the top of the CERD display. Messages (e.g. notification of a flight diversion) are sent from the central computer and displayed in the single-line message window. The square immediately to the right of the message window displays the number of messages that are pending, including the current one. Messages have three priority levels, and are held in a queue in priority order. If the queue is not empty, the first message is displayed in the message window. It is removed from the queue when the ATCO touches the message area, and the next message, if any,

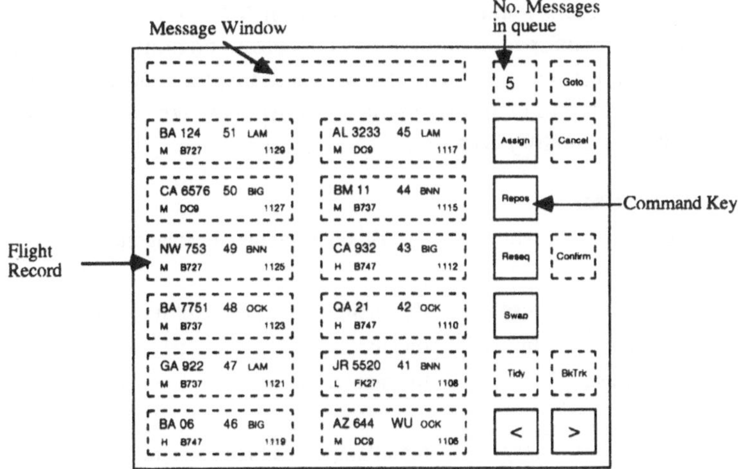

Figure 1: A screen from the CERD.

is displayed. New messages from the central computer are inserted into the queue in priority order, even if this means that the message on display will change without (prior) notice.

As modellers, we were asked by the human factors designer if we thought the messaging interface could be improved, in particular, if more than just the current message should be accessible, and if so, how? This paper describes how analysis of this question led to the detection and analysis of another problem with the way the message interface behaved.

3 York-Interactor Modelling

The York-Interactor Modelling approach (YIM) is a formal specification technique which provides a link between rigorous approaches to software development and user-oriented aspects of interaction. YIM uses the concept of an *Interactor* to organize the formal description of a system into components. In its most general form, an interactor consists of a state and actions that can be perceived and/or invoked by the environment through a number of well-defined interfaces. In practice, it is useful to specialize this view and distinguish one interface, the *presentation*, as that part of the component (state and actions) that can be perceived by a user of the system. Interactors can be used with a range of formalisms, including Z, VDM, and MAL. An introduction to this approach can be found in Duke & Harrison (1995b). A related notion of interactor using the process based LOTOS formalism is described later.

In the CERD analysis (Duke & Harrison, 1995a) the modellers began with the original CERD specification which comprised well documented requirements including a formal model written in VVSL, a modular extension of VDM. This description however was focused on the functional behaviour of CERD, whereas the modellers' interest was in interactive properties of the system. For this reason they re-expressed salient features of the system in Modal-Action Logic, organized around interactors. This specification provided a clear and concise description of the behaviour of the message queue and the message display, and its perceivable and interactive properties. For example, an interactor for message handling was specified as follows (with explanatory comments on the right):

interactor msgs			
	clear:	button	– inherit a button interactor labelled 'clear'
attributes			
	queue:	msg*	– the queue is a sequence of messages
vis	mesg:	[msg]	– one message may be perceivable (optional value)
vis	nr-msgs:	N	– the number of messages is a natural number
actions			
	recv:	msg	– the interactor can receive a message

The above specifies that the 'msgs' interactor inherits a button interactor labelled 'clear' (the inherited button interactor provides simple toggling states of selected/unselected and a 'press' action). The interactor's attributes record the queue of messages, the number of messages, and the displayed message. The latter two are visually-perceivable attributes of the state (indicated by the *vis* attribute). The *recv* action represents a message received by the CERD from the central air-traffic control system.

Key properties of the message system were captured in eight axioms, describing both static relationships (e.g. that the displayed message is the one at the head of the message queue) and dynamic behaviour (e.g. that highest priority messages are moved to the front of the queue, or that pressing the clear button removes the first message in the queue). For example, the axiom below deals with receipt of a new message, 'm'.

$$\text{queue} = x \Rightarrow [\text{recv.m}]\ \text{queue} = (x\ \textit{res}\ \{\ p \mid p > \text{pr(m)}\}) \oplus \langle m \rangle \oplus (x\ \textit{res}\ \{\ p \mid p < \text{pr(m)}\})$$

This specifies that the queue after the receive action consists of, in order:

- The original queue restricted to messages with the same or higher priority than 'm'.
- The new message 'm'.
- Those messages in the original queue with priority lower than 'm'.

3.1 The Accidental Message Deletion Scenario

The process of formally specifying the CERD's state and behaviour prompted the modellers to reason about whether messages could be lost under any circumstances. To answer this they conducted an informal analysis based around scenarios modelled as partially-ordered sets of events. Exploring the scenario in this way suggested that a high priority message could be lost if it was received at 'about' the time that the ATCO was clearing a displayed message. If the ATCO started executing the clear action, they might not notice (or be able to stop) if a new message suddenly appeared on the display. The result of the action would be that the queue remained unchanged, and thus the user might not even notice that a message had been lost. They might attribute the unchanged message line to either a mis-hit of the clear button or a fault in the system.

Clearly such a scenario involved making assumptions about user behaviour and capabilities which are beyond the scope of system modelling. The modelling analyses which follow illustrate how other modelling approaches were able to confirm the above possibility, and shed light on whether the assumptions about users justified concern about accidental message deletion. These modelling analyses are taken from the (more detailed) reports which resulted from the collational co-modelling initiated after the first round of modelling. The details of the co-modelling approach are described in more detail once these other analyses have been outlined.

3.2 LOTOS-Interactor Modelling

The LOTOS-Interactor modelling (LIM) formally specified aspects of both the user and system in terms of internal and external actions, using the LOTOS concurrent notation (International Standards Organisation, 1988) to describe the temporal ordering of actions. The approach focuses on traces of user and system actions, and uses a tool which enables the modeller to formally verify if a specification permits certain traces.

The concept of interactor used in LIM refers to a basic component of a user interface system that can receive input from one side (e.g. the application), and produce output to the other side (e.g. the user). Interactors may have triggers, control events indicating when a result from one side has to be delivered to the other. This concept can be used to reason about system behaviour and its properties at different abstraction levels.

The system specification was modelled by following a method for translating tasks to interactors which has been formally described and applied in another case study (Paterno' & Mezzanotte, 1994) . This resulted in a graphical description of an interactor-based architecture showing inputs and outputs between interactors. Once the interactors had been identified, the LOTOS specification of the corresponding behaviour was obtained by associating each interactor with one LOTOS process, and finally composing the LOTOS expressions in accordance with the graphical description. The final LOTOS specification includes the description of Message handling. The main behaviour of this part is described by the composition of several LOTOS processes, as follows:

```
Behaviour
  (FC[new-msg, change-layout, change-flights-layout]
    |[new-msg] |
    ( ( message-com[new-msg, mod-count, view-msg, ack-msg] (emps,emp,empc)
      |[view-msg, ack-msg]|
        msg-area[view-msg, vis-msg, touch-msg-area, ack-msg]
      )
      |[mod-count]|
      count[mod-count, view-count]|
    )
  )
  ||| GoTo[select-goto-button, high-goto-button, display-referred-flight]
```

Without going into the details of LOTOS or the processes in the above expression, this part specifies that when a new-message (*new-msg* action) is received from the functional core, the system interacts directly with the user with two events, *select-goto-button* and *touch-msg-area* actions.

LIM also models aspects of possible user behaviour as a LOTOS process with internal and external events. *External actions* include the sensation of environmental information (information presented by the system) and the execution of user actions (responses or commands directed towards the system). *Internal actions* include the interpretation of environmental information, and decisions about tasks that need to be performed. These decisions depend upon both the state of the user and their interpretation of the information presented by the system.

For instance, the user, after having realized that a new message has arrived, might wish to select the *goto* button in order to get information on the related flight (shown as *select-actions-to-perform*; (*select-goto-button*)). Alternatively, s/he might touch the area containing the message (*touch-msg-area* action) in order to delete it and to display a new message. A further possibility is to make no response to the system (*do-nothing* action), but add it to other memorized information.

This behaviour could be specified by the following LOTOS expression:

```
process User[...]:noexit:=
read-msg; interpret-msg; decide-task-to-do;
   (select-actions-to-perform;
      (select-goto-button; User[...]
      [] touch-msg-area; User[...])
   [] do-nothing; User[...])
endproc
```

Given a user and a system specification in this form, it is possible to reason about certain properties in order to identify whether some undesired effect can occur. The properties are expressed in Action-based Temporal Logic (ACTL) (DeNicola et al., 1993). ACTL is a branching time temporal logic which means that it can describe alternative future traces of actions. Reasoning about properties of the LOTOS specification was performed by tools for automatic model checking (Paterno' et al., 1994). These tools receive as input the LOTOS specification of the user and the system, and allow the designer to check for different properties expressed in ACTL.

Focusing on the message handling part, the modellers noted that the two entities (the user and the system) only synchronize at particular user interface actions (*select-goto-button* and *touch-msg-area*). However, the action associated with the presentation of a new message (*pres-msg*) does not require synchronization with the user, as the user may fail to attend to that area when the message appears and the system has to evolve its behaviour without having to wait for user synchronization. Thus a different action (*read-msg*) needs to be introduced to explicitly indicate when the user reads the contents of the message area. It is possible to formally check for the possibility that users could accidentally delete the wrong message by verifying the following ACTL property in the LOTOS user and system specifications:

```
E[true{pres-msg} U {true} E[true{true} U {read-msg} E[true{true}
U{pres-msg} E[true{~read-msg} U {touch-msg-area} true]]]]
```

Informally, this means that there is one possible behaviour (*E* operator) where it is possible to have the presentation of a message (*pres-msg*) followed by three sequences:

1. a sequence on which we do not put any constraints (*true*{*true*}), until the user has read the message (*read-msg*);
2. a sequence of transactions on which there are no constraints until a second message has been presented; and
3. a sequence of events on which the only constraint is that the user reads no message (*~read-msg*) and which terminates when the action *touch-msg-area* is performed.

To summarize, the LIM technique gains its power through formal notations supported by automatic checking tools, by allowing designers to formulate precise properties and automatically verify them against the enormous number of interactional traces possible in a complex interactive system. In the CERD example outlined here, we have illustrated the approach's use for analysing the possibility of undesirable interactional sequences between user and system which may have disastrous effects. This represents an interesting pay-off for the intellectual investment which is required to use more formal notations.

4 Interaction Framework Modelling

The *Interaction Framework* (Blandford et al., 1995b) supports an approach to designing and analysing interactive systems which is based on defining properties of interactions in terms which are neutral with respect to the agents involved. These properties are expressed in abstract — sometimes formal — terms. As such, it offers an approach which is not biased by computer system or user concerns, but treats both as equally important. In the design process, we see two roles for interactional requirements: firstly in guiding design ("we want to design an interactive system which has these properties") and secondly in analysing a design ("does the system we have designed satisfy these requirements?").

As described above, the YIM analysis initially identified the possibility of accidental message deletion. However, a similar conclusion can be reached if we start by considering the interaction between the agents involved in this scenario.

When considering the design of the CERD message-viewing interface, the system can be represented as consisting of three agents:

- NAS (the source of messages; we do not consider how NAS gets the information).
- CERD-message-window (receives and displays messages).
- ATCO (reads, responds to and deletes messages).

There are three types of *interactional event*, where an interactional event involves the communication of information between two agents, so (for example) the

Figure 2: Relevant agents in the Interaction Framework modelling of CERD.

CERD displaying a message does not constitute an event until the ATCO reads it. As Figure 2 shows, the event types are:

- Enc: message passes from NAS to CERD.
- Eca: message passes from CERD to ATCO.
- Eac: message passes from ATCO to CERD.

One important interactional requirement is that *for every Enc there is a corresponding Eca* — this is the 'purpose' of the message viewing interface. Then a verification question is: is it possible for this condition to be violated?

1. If the CERD goes down, there will not be any Enc's, but will NAS be aware that messages are not being received by the CERD? This is a question for a system modeller.

2. If the ATCO is not watching the screen, there will not be any Eca's until the ATCO attends to the screen again. What might the consequences be? This is a question for a domain modeller. A user modeller might be required to give an analysis of ways in which to alert the ATCO to the arrival of a new message, but that modeller would need domain information too.

3. If all three agents are available, we consider other circumstances in which there could be an Enc without an Eca.

Let us now focus on a particular violation of the above principle, namely, the accidental deletion of a message from NAS before it has been 'received' by the air-traffic controller via the CERD. As shown in Figure 2, the CERD can receive communications from two other agents. An important consideration is what the consequences of two messages, an Enc and an Eac, reaching the CERD at the same time are. We now consider the detailed design of the message queue. Although the queue actually in use is fairly complex, for simplicity we will assume the following allowable behaviours:

- If message-queue is not empty, then ATCO can read the top of message-queue.
- If message-line is not empty, then ATCO can delete the top message of message-queue.
- If message-line is not empty then NAS can send a message to CERD specifying deletion of any message in message-queue at any time.

- NAS can send a message for CERD to add to the top of message-queue at any time.
- NAS can add a message further down in the message-queue at any time.

In interaction framework terms, events between ATCO and CERD arise in the following circumstances:

- When NAS sends a message that results in CERD displaying a new message at the top of the queue, and ATCO reads that message.
- When ATCO requests deletion of the message at the top of the queue, and CERD deletes that message.
- When ATCO is reading a message and CERD deletes the top message in message-queue in response to a message from NAS, and ATCO reads the next message (if there is one).

As discussed above, we require that ATCO reads any message in message-queue before requesting its deletion, and we observe two occasions when this may be violated:

1. ATCO reads the top message, goes to delete it, but NAS sends a message requesting deletion, which CERD responds to. ATCO instead deletes the next (unread) message.
2. ATCO reads the top message and goes to delete it, but NAS sends a new message for CERD to display at the top. ATCO deletes the new (unread) message and is faced with an apparent repetition of the message he intended to delete.

Interaction Framework cannot predict whether these incidents will actually happen in normal use of the system — we would have to ask system and user modellers for confirmation. Nor can IF predict whether the user would realize that these incidents have occurred, or what timings would cause them — we would again request user modelling advice.

Assuming these problems are real, how can they be averted? An IF approach would be thus:

- Two agents can independently communicate with a third;
- One of those agents can send messages which lead to changes in the state of the third agent without the user being necessarily aware of this;
- The user may form a goal given their understanding of the state but, before carrying out actions towards that goal, the system state may change.
- To avert problems, a 'transitional event' should be introduced. This is an event whose sole purpose is to explicitly draw the attention of one agent to the actions of another where those actions result in an important change in state.

The two problems identified above would now have a transitional event inserted between the actions of the two agents to prevent the user from making an error. They would now look thus:

1. ATCO reads the top message, goes to delete it, but NAS sends a message requesting CERD to delete it. The transitional event is triggered, which the user must participate in before being able to delete the next (unread) message. The user is now aware that the system has deleted the old top message, and so reads the new top message.

2. ATCO reads the top message and goes to delete it, but NAS sends a new message to be added at the top. The transitional event is triggered, which the user must participate in before being able to delete the new (unread) message. Again, the user is aware of the new message and can act appropriately.

The collational co-modelling provided the forum in which the details of implementing the transitional event proposal were discussed by other modellers and the CERD's software engineer. For instance, the modality and timing of such transitional events is dependent on what is technically feasible, and acceptable within the air-traffic control work practices (how often they look at the CERD), and their environment (e.g. no warning sounds except in absolute emergency). We note in passing that ethnographic analyses of air-traffic control would provide the kind of detailed understanding of work practices needed to implement model-based design recommendations.

5 Cognitive Task Analysis

Cognitive Task Analysis (Barnard & May, 1993) is a user modelling approach based on a unified architecture of human cognition called *Interacting Cognitive Subsystems* (ICS). CTA identifies aspects of a design that place heavy demands on the user's cognitive resources such as memory and attention. This information allows the designer to focus upon the features that users will find hardest to learn, and where they are most likely to make errors. The ICS architecture specifies constraints on the way in which different cognitive resources are able to exchange and retrieve information, and the way in which user's models of the task and domain evolve and influence behaviour. Details of the CTA modelling of CERD can be found in May & Barnard (1995).

Once the YIM system modelling analysis of the message queue and display had raised the possibility of accidental message deletion, the CTA user modellers looked for grounds to believe that the ATCOs would act in ways that would cause it to occur. While their techniques did not formally deal with timing issues, the user modellers pointed out that the ballistic nature of motor control meant that actions could not be controlled instantaneously, and that there would be a lag before the formation of an intention to stop an action and its actual halt. If the user's finger was about to touch the display, then even if the user detected a change in the message and attempted to stop their action, the lag might prevent them doing so. Furthermore, there are additional lags between the occurrence of a visual stimulus, the user 'noticing' it, and their forming an intention to stop, all of which would contribute to the likelihood of the problem occurring.

The CTA modellers also considered the likely patterns of action that the ATCO would develop. Since the system orders messages in the queue in terms of type, they pointed out that if the current message is of type 'Data Change' then all of the other messages in the queue are of the same type. From an inspection of the content of these messages, they determined that this type of message predominantly required no action by the user, other than to delete it (the sole exception being certain changes to an aircraft's wake vortex). In these circumstances they argued that the user would develop a pattern of behaviour that would lead them to delete Data Change messages repeatedly, with the action not being under the control of reading (the 'reading' and 'deletion' streams of behaviour would be executed in parallel, rather than in sequence).

One solution to the problem (generated during co-modelling — see below), focused on the lag between the user noticing a display change and their being able to stop a message deletion action, and proposed that all newly presented messages be made unresponsive to touch for a brief period immediately after they appeared. However, the CTA analysis of repetitive deletion as an action stream suggested this might not actually have the desired effect, since the ATCO's action pattern would adapt to take account of the delay. The lack of response to a touch might also cause further problems if there are other lags in the system's feedback of display information, since users may start to 'peck' at buttons until screen changes occur, leading to double-click errors.

6 Collational Co-modelling: Integration and Communication

Collational co-modelling involves:

- direct communication between modellers; and
- iteration of the modelling; together with
- an attempt by a 'collator' to pull together an emerging, multi-disciplinary story.

The iteration requires modellers to re-visit their own analyses in the light of others, and to contribute to other modelling. This process provided us with a way firstly, *to facilitate the integration between different modelling analyses*, and secondly, *to communicate that modelling to the CERD's designers* by involving them in a co-modelling session. These two uses of co-modelling are described in turn.

6.1 Co-modelling to Build a Multidisciplinary Analysis

Once the possibility of accidental message deletion had been raised by the YIM system modellers, co-modelling provided useful process structure for the other modellers to feed in relevant insights to enrich our understanding.

The modelling analyses summarized above resulted from three different kinds of co-modelling: firstly between the modellers by e-mail, who then continued face-to-face, and lastly with the CERD's software engineer face-to-face. Once collated, a co-modelling report highlights the way in which the different models interact to create a richer analysis of a given issue than could be provided by any single model. Below are three extracts (edited for brevity) from the co-modelling report (Young et al., 1994) of the first two sessions. Note how modelling inter-connections which arose during the session are recorded, with references to where the source modelling detail (e.g. [IF: A4] can be found:

S2. The YIM system modelling [YIM: A3] indicates the presence of a potential problem, in so far as it shows that two different agents can update the message display (...) Such a situation suggests the possibility of conflict and timing problems.

S3. An Interaction Framework analysis also spots the problem, from a slightly different perspective [IF: A4]. Looking at the larger picture, IF identifies three relevant agents: NAS (the source of messages), the CERD message system, and the ATCO (...)

S6. Timing constraints from the user modelling can be fed back to the formal system modelling, which can then extend its analysis to reflect questions of timing [YIM: A7]. For example, if UM says that it takes the user 0.5 sec to read a message, then an axiom can be added to the model stating that, following time T, after the user has read the message the time is at least T + 0.5. (...)

The co-modelling then summarizes recommendations for the designers, for instance:

R2. One line of re-design might involve explicit acknowledgement: no message is removed until the user indicates that he has read it [ICS: A16; YIM: A17]. The IF analysis might be helpful in providing some requirements on the way acknowledgement is handled [IF: A4].

Disadvantage: Higher-priority messages will no longer automatically displace lower-priority ones.

This collational co-modelling analysis was extended in the session with the CERD's chief software engineer in several key respects. A specific design solution was proposed which was then pursued in detail, with both modellers and the designer critiquing each others' ideas. On several occasions, the designer rejected modellers' analyses and design solutions as incompatible with air-traffic control practice, or inconsistent with other parts of the CERD's user interface. For example, he was able to advise on the pace of air-traffic control work with CERD (critical for the cognitive modellers), and point out operational system constraints which the system modellers did not know.

6.2 Communicating Modelling to Designers via Co-modelling

In planning the second workshop, the idea arose that collational co-modelling could be naturally extended to include designers (and perhaps also user groups, although this was not feasible in the CERD study). The co-modelling might then be not only enriched by the design team's knowledge of the domain (lacked by the modellers), but co-modelling might serve as a vehicle for communicating the modelling analyses. How successful was this strategy?

Based on the designers' feedback and on analysis of the co-modelling videotapes which we recorded, this first experiment in involving designers in the modelling process leads us to tentative conclusion that co-modelling provides a helpful structure for modeller-designer communication. Firstly, in the meeting, modellers had to explain for the benefit of the designers what they were doing, and clarify the link between their models and their usability analyses. Face-to-face, confusions could be much more quickly resolved than by e-mail or document exchanges. Secondly, the two designers could see first hand how the modellers worked together, using their models to motivate their contributions, and provide answers to each others' questions. They experienced the modelling in a contextualized, dynamic form, in contrast to static modelling documents. The latter contain more detail of the formalism used by the modellers, but our impression (from this and other modelling exercises) is that the degree of understanding which can be reasonably expected of designers on their first encounter with HCI models is often not sufficient for them to benefit from having access to the formalism. Understanding that a formalism and a model underpin what the modellers say is adequate, and thus the most appropriate level to aim for.

7 Assessing the Value of the Modelling

In this final section, we discuss the value of the modelling in three respects, based on our final debriefing discussion with the CERD's designers: the value of the insights we provided; the role of modelling in backing user-centred decision making, and the importance of knowing the scope of each modelling approach in order to maximize the cost/benefit trade-off.

7.1 A Significant Problem was Detected

The accidental message deletion scenario proved to be an issue which CERD's designers had not detected, and which they judged significant enough that they reported the potential occurrence of this problem and the main results of their co-modelling session with us to the CAA team responsible for maintaining the CERD (we are waiting to hear if any design changes are planned as a consequence). Against the criterion of significance, therefore, the content of the modelling was valuable, and its communication to designers was successful, in that they understood the analysis.

7.2 Modelling Adds Technical and Political Weight to Usability Analyses

During discussion about the value of the modelling techniques, the designers said they perceived value both in the specific analyses of the CERD, as well as with regard to HCI modelling techniques more generally. They said the modelling had forced them to consider familiar problems in new ways, and the variety of approaches to tackling them was particularly valuable. In their view, such modelling provided a reasoned basis to support design arguments.

In this respect, the human factors designer noted that the backing behind arguments for user-centred decisions is often perceived to be weaker when competing against other software design criteria, since usability issues can often be difficult to substantiate in formal terms. If a human factors expert can point to a formal modelling analysis to back up her case then it may carry more weight, just as an engineering analysis can appear more persuasive when backed by computational models and equations. So, whilst we would hope that HCI modelling will derive its authority on technical merit, it also assumes rhetorical and hence political power once introduced into design practice.

7.3 Negotiating Modelling's Cost/Benefit Trade-off

In the debriefing discussion, the designers raised the crucial question of whether we are yet in a position to scope the different modelling techniques in order to maximize the cost/benefit trade-off. Praxis is an industry leader in the use of formal methods, and are highly selective in their application of such methods, understanding the strengths and weaknesses of each formalism, and using them only where they expect sufficient payback.

For instance, the human factors designer emphasized the importance of identifying when, where and how HCI modelling techniques should be used:

> "You need to build up that knowledge ... unless people understand what it's going to buy them, it will appear to be very expensive and quite a high risk thing to employ."

This point was elaborated by the chief software engineer:

> "It's very important to do case studies not just to see if we can do it, but what's the cost-benefit ratio? What's really giving the added value?"

Given the industrial experience which these designers have in introducing and deploying formal methods, these issues are surely definitional for HCI modelling's research agenda.

Within the AMODEUS Project, we have been aware of this challenge from the beginning, and have made initial steps towards tackling the cost/benefit trade-off on three fronts:

Software tools to assist in complex modelling: Prototype tools have been developed to assist cognitive and software architecture modelling (May et al., 1993; Nigay & Coutaz, 1992), and automatic verification of formal properties using the LIM approach is now possible (Paterno' et al., 1994), in which the Praxis designers expressed particular interest.

Usability of notations and tools: We have trained practitioners in several of the notations and tools we have developed, and evaluated their use (Blandford et al., 1995a; Buckingham Shum & Hammond, 1994a; Buckingham Shum, 1996; Nigay et al., 1995). These valuations have generated valuable requirements for improving both the approaches, and the way in which they are delivered to designers through training and tools.

Modelling consultancy for design teams: Modelling exercises such as this help us to scope the approaches, and improve our communication of them (what does a given approach seek to do?; what did our modelling of your system conclude?).

This three-pronged attack has generated substantial evidence about modelling techniques which allows us to assess how useful and usable any given technique is. One of the strongest forms of evidence that a technique is approaching maturity is when professional designers continue to show interest after initial exposure to it. Following the CERD modelling exercise, Praxis are committed to further collaboration that will focus on integrating user modelling with their development techniques that already include the use of formal methods.

8 Conclusions

Receptivity to new design techniques is moderated by design culture, where a given culture attracts particular skills and interests, thus fostering particular design practices. The power and influence of design culture on shaping attitudes to proposed new design approaches should not therefore be underestimated. This case study suggests that design organizations already committed to the use of software engineering formal methods are more likely than others to be interested in formal representations of user-relevant aspects of system behaviour, and of user cognition and behaviour. It is also particularly encouraging that the company for whom we provided modelling intend to explore in more depth how to integrate user modelling with their existing formal methods.

The collational co-modelling technique was used with designers for the first time in this case study, and it is too early to draw strong conclusions from these initial sessions. However, both modellers and designers found it a productive way to work together, and it seems to be complementary to written reports as a medium for conveying modelling to designers. Co-modelling supported quick prioritization, clarification and analysis of issues, and provided the designers have confidence in the modellers, can proceed without the designers having to understand fully the theoretical underpinnings of the modelling techniques.

The scenario of usability modellers and designers engaged in multidisciplinary analysis is one conception of user-centred system design in the future. Formal modelling approaches focus on developing useful abstractions and greater precision in the specification and evaluation of interactive systems. In the longer term, these are properties that HCI must acquire if is to develop into a more rigorous, theoretically grounded design discipline. This is not to simplistically proclaim the virtues of abstraction and formality, nor to deny the centrality of intuition and craft skill in both user interface design and the modelling process itself. However, this case study provides evidence that HCI modelling can make valuable contributions to real world system design, and demonstrates one way in which it is feasible and useful for practitioners to work in concert with user and system modellers.

Acknowledgements

We gratefully acknowledge the cooperation of Praxis Systems Ltd. and the UK Civil Aviation Authority in releasing documentation on the CERD system. We are also indebted to Anthony Hall and Sue Appleby at Praxis for the time they gave to this exercise. Only a fraction of the modelling conducted is presented in this paper, and we thank our AMODEUS colleagues whose other contributions have helped to shape our ideas. The AMODEUS-2 Project was funded by the CEC as ESPRIT Basic Research Action 7040.

Note: AMODEUS documents are available at: http://www.mrc-apu.cam.ac.uk/amodeus/

References

Barnard, P. J. & May, J. (1993), Cognitive Modelling for User Requirements, *in* P. F. Byerley & P. J. B. J. May (eds.), "Computers, Communication and Usability: Design Issues, Research and Methods for Integrated Services", Elsevier Science, pp.101–145.

Bellotti, V., Buckingham Shum, S., MacLean, A. & Hammond, N. (1995), Multidisciplinary Modelling in HCI Design ... In Theory and in Practice, *in* I. Katz, R. Mack, L. Marks, M. B. Rosson & J. Nielsen (eds.), "Proceedings of CHI'95: Human Factors in Computing Systems", ACM Press, pp.146–153.

Blandford, A., Buckingham Shum, S. & Young, R. (1995a), User-oriented Design Descriptions for Non-psychologists: Training Software Engineers in the PUM Instruction Language, Working Paper TA/WP44, MRC-APU, Cambridge. AMODEUS-2 Project.

Blandford, A. E., Harrison, M. D. & Barnard, P. J. (1995b), "Using Interaction Framework to Guide the Design of Interactive Systems", *International Journal of Man–Machine Studies* **43**(1), 101–130.

Buckingham Shum, S. (1994), Preliminary Modelling of the CERD Flight Sequencing Tool, Working Paper TA/WP23, University of York. AMODEUS-2 Project.

Buckingham Shum, S. (1996), Analyzing the Usability of a Design Rationale Notation, *in* T. P. Moran & J. M. Carroll (eds.), "Design Rationale: Concepts, Techniques, and Use", Lawrence Erlbaum Associates, pp.185–215.

Buckingham Shum, S. & Hammond, N. (1994a), "Delivering HCI Modelling to Designers: A Framework and Case Study of Cognitive Modelling", *Interacting with Computers* **6**(3), 311–341.

Buckingham Shum, S. & Hammond, N. (1994b), Transferring HCI Modelling and Design Techniques to Practitioners: A Framework and Empirical Work, *in* G. Cockton, S. Draper & G. Wier (eds.), "People and Computers IX (Proceedings of HCI'94)", Cambridge University Press, pp.21–36.

Buckingham Shum, S., Jorgensen, A., Hammond, N. & Aboulafia, A. (1994a), Amodeus HCI Modelling and Design Approaches: Executive Summaries and Worked Examples, Working Paper TA/WP16, University of York. AMODEUS-2 Project.

Buckingham Shum, S., Jorgensen, A., Hammond, N. & Aboulafia, A. (1994b), Communicating and Evaluating HCI Modelling: The ISLE Hypermedia System, Working Paper TA/WP22, University of York. AMODEUS-2 Project.

DeNicola, R., Fantechi, A., Gnesi, S. & Ristori, G. (1993), "An Action Based Framework for Verifying Logical and Behavioural Properties of Concurrent Systems", *Computer Networks and ISDN Systems* **25**(7), 761–778.

Duke, D. J. & Harrison, M. D. (1995a), The Anatomy of the CERD: Human-System Interaction through a Formal Microscope, Working Paper SM/WP55, University of York. AMODEUS-2 Project.

Duke, D. J. & Harrison, M. D. (1995b), Formal System Modelling: Overview and Worked Examples, Working Paper SM/WP44, University of York. AMODEUS-2 Project.

International Standards Organisation (1988), "Information Processing Systems — Open Systems Interconnection: LOTOS — A Formal Description Technique Based on Temporal Ordering of Observational Behaviour". ISO Central Secretariat Report ISO/IS 8807.

May, J. & Barnard, P. J. (1995), A Cognitive Task Analysis of the CERD Exemplar Material, Working Paper UM/WP23, MRC-APU, Cambridge. AMODEUS-2 Project.

May, J., Barnard, P. J. & Blandford, A. (1993), "Using Structural Descriptions of Interfaces to Automate the Modelling of User Cognition", *User Modelling and Adaptive User Interfaces* **3**, 27–64.

Nigay, L. & Coutaz, J. (1992), PAC-Expert: Towards an Automatic Generation of Dialogue Controllers, Deliverable D18, CLIPS-IMAG, Université Joseph Fourier, Grenoble. AMODEUS-1 Project.

Nigay, L., Salber, D., Buckingham Shum, S. & Coutaz, J. (1995), Teaching Trainee and Professional Designers to Use the PAC-Amodeus Software Architecture Modelling Technique, Working Paper TA/WP42, CLIPS-IMAG, Université Joseph Fourier, Grenoble. AMODEUS-2 Project.

Paterno', F. & Mezzanotte, M. (1994), Analysing MATIS by Interactor and ACTL, Working Paper SM/WP36, CNUCE-CNR. AMODEUS-2 Project.

Paterno', F., Leonardi, A. & Pangloi, S. (1994), A Tool-supported Approach to the Refinement of Interactive Systems, *in* F. Paterno' (ed.), "Proceedings of the Eurographics Workshop on Design, Specification and Verification of Interactive Systems", Springer-Verlag, pp.149–160.

Young, R., Blandford, A., Coutaz, J., Duke, D. & May, J. (1994), Collational Co-modelling: An Introduction and an Example from the CERD Interface, Working Paper ID/WP36, MRC-APU, Cambridge. AMODEUS-2 Project.

Costs and Benefits of User Involvement in Design: Practitioners' Views

Stephanie Wilson, Mathilde Bekker, Hilary Johnson & Peter Johnson

Department of Computer Science, Queen Mary and Westfield College, Mile End Road, London E1 4NS, UK.

Tel: *+44 171 975 5231*

EMail: {*steph,tilde,hilaryj,pete*}*@dcs.qmw.ac.uk*

Many design approaches recommend some form of user involvement in the design of interactive systems, although there has been little empirical research directed towards assessing the benefits to be gained, and costs to be incurred, from having users involved during the design process. Moreover, the work that does exist has tended to take a narrow view, considering the gains and losses primarily from an organizational perspective. This paper offers richer definitions of the costs and benefits by which user involvement might be assessed, emphasizing the contrasting views of different 'stakeholders' in the design process. It presents and discusses two empirical studies conducted in the light of these definitions to examine the costs and benefits of user involvement as perceived by design practitioners.

Keywords: user involvement, cost-benefit analysis, user-centred design.

1 Introduction

Throughout the 1980s a central message coming from HCI researchers to computer system designers was to consider system design from the perspective of the user (Norman & Draper, 1986). In this vein, research focused upon developing theories and models of users — e.g. (Barnard, 1987), methods of analysing users' tasks — e.g. (Diaper, 1989; Johnson et al., 1988) and techniques for modelling and analysing user–computer interactions — e.g. (Card et al., 1983; Payne & Green, 1986). These and many other approaches have, by and large, been successful in getting the message across to the software engineering community that user interface design is important and needs to be considered from the users' point of view. A survey of the use of HCI methods in design (Bellotti, 1988) then revealed that while designers recognized the need to consider users in the design of artefacts there was little evidence of any use by designers of the modelling, analysis and evaluation approaches developed by HCI researchers. To address this deficiency, some HCI researchers have put greater efforts into integrating HCI methods with software engineering techniques — e.g. (Lim & Long, 1994). More recent surveys of design practice suggest that designers are beginning to use various analysis and evaluation approaches, perhaps most notably forms of task analysis and methods of usability evaluation, although they still experience problems involving users in the design process (Bekker & Vermeeren, 1993). There are many philosophical, political, methodological and pragmatic issues currently raised around the topic of user and designer involvement in design. The term Participatory Design has emerged — e.g. (CACM, 1993) — as an area of research which considers how users can be 'empowered' in design projects. New methods and techniques are being developed by HCI researchers to enable users to contribute directly to design — e.g. (Schuler & Namioka, 1993; Carroll, 1995).

While many designers are now aware of the need to consider a design from the users' point of view, there may be little direct contact between designers and users, and the extent of access that designers have to users and their work place is often seriously inadequate. One reason for this is that little empirical research has sought to evaluate the benefits to be gained and costs to be incurred from having users involved, or not involved, in design.* Consequently, designers, users and their respective organizations can be reluctant to commit effort to fostering user-designer involvement. In the context of a research project to develop support for user-designer collaboration in HCI design projects, we have begun to investigate the kinds and levels of user involvement that occur in design practice and the mechanisms that might bring about more effective user involvement and user-designer cooperation so as to maximize the usability of the design. This work does not assume that more user involvement in a design project is necessarily better, rather we are investigating the costs and benefits associated with different levels of user involvement in different design situations. Such an analysis can offer insights into the benefits to be gained and costs incurred by increasing the users' contribution to particular design activities and into how design methods may be modified so as to increase the identifiable benefits of user involvement and/or decrease the costs. Further, just as traditional cost-benefit analysis has been used to convince management of the benefits of usability work, our approach to cost-benefit analysis can be used to demonstrate the merits of user involvement to the all various stakeholders — see Grudin (1991) for a discussion on the need to convince stakeholders of the value of user involvement.

Users can be involved in a design project in many ways, ranging from being the actual designers of the system, as is the case in some internal projects, to being the people who are trained on, use and perhaps reject the developed software. We can consider a number of dimensions for user involvement in design, including the

*The term 'design' in this paper covers all the various activities that might occur over the duration of a design project, including modelling, analysis, evaluation, prototyping and implementation activities.

directness, the degree and the design activity. Users may be directly or indirectly involved in a design project, for example, the users may carry out a task analysis of their own work or alternatively a designer or human factors expert may carry out the task analysis. In the former case the user is more directly involved in the analysis than in the latter case. Similarly, users may be included directly in the design team by their actual presence at design meetings, or they may be indirectly involved by receiving written minutes of such meetings. The degree of user involvement distinguishes the number of actual users or surrogate users involved in a project. Surrogate users are people who are not users but who represent the users, for example, marketing staff might be called in to represent users, or union leaders might be called in to represent workers. Finally, the design activities in which users are involved may range from all design activities to one or none.

In the context of our research aims, Section 2 of this paper offers a richer definition of the costs and benefits by which user involvement might be assessed than has been adopted elsewhere. Most notably, our view of costs and benefits goes beyond the purely financial and quantifiable to include other costs and benefits associated with user involvement in design. Further, it takes account of the views of all the stakeholders, not just the organizational view, and it identifies the areas of design where user involvement actually occurs and the stakeholders who are affected by user involvement. A substantial part of the paper is then devoted to reporting the results arising from two on-going empirical studies of design practice (Sections 3, 4 and 5), and to discussing the implications of these results together with some pointers towards future work (Section 6). The results presented here are limited to the costs and benefits experienced by one group of stakeholders, the design practitioners, although the data gathered in the studies includes information about other stakeholders as well. The first study is a cross-sectional survey that identifies the extent of user involvement across different design projects, the types of design activities in which user involvement occurs, and gives some initial indication as to the costs and benefits of user involvement. The second study is a longitudinal study of one design project which provides an in-depth analysis of the designers' perceptions of the nature of user involvement and its associated costs and benefits in that project. In the studies we have sought to identify and characterize the costs and benefits associated with user involvement in design, as experienced by various stakeholders in the context of real world design settings, and as such to provide a timely and novel assessment of the case for user involvement in design.

2 Costs and Benefits

Cost-benefit analysis is a well-established technique whose application to the field of HCI includes the work of Mantei & Teorey (1988), Karat (1990) and Bias & Mayhew (1994). These approaches focus on the costs and benefits of including human factors effort in the design process, often as an argument to convince management of the value and effectiveness of usability work. The analysis methods weigh the financial cost of doing the usability work, arising from factors such as the extra investment of resources (including time and people) required during the design process, against the financial benefits of an improved product, arising from factors such as improved end-user productivity and efficiency or increased sales revenue. There are several distinctions between these approaches and the work reported here, most notably their emphasis on a quantitative, financial assessment and their organizational perspective. Further, for the purposes of our current work, we are interested in the costs and benefits that arise directly as a result of user involvement, or non-involvement, in design, rather the costs and benefits of usability work as a whole. We define costs and benefits as follows:

- A cost is a perceived penalty or disadvantage arising as a result of user involvement in design.
- A benefit is a perceived improvement or advantage arising as a result of user involvement in design.

These definitions raise a number of issues for discussion, each of which is considered in more detail below: who or what experiences the cost or benefit, who perceives the cost or benefit (and the contrasting perceptions of different stakeholders), the design activity with which the cost or benefit is associated and the overall design context in which the observation is made.

A cost or benefit may be experienced by any one or more of a number of possibilities including, but not limited to, the designed product, the design process, and the various stakeholders (users, designers, organizations etc.). The distinctions between these possibilities are not clear cut. For example, if the product 'benefits' from user involvement in some design situation, then any, or all, of the stakeholders might also benefit. Indeed, it would be a strange benefit or improvement to the product if there was no perceivable benefit to any of the possible stakeholders. For example, if the usability of a product is improved then the organization marketing the product may benefit from increased sales, the organization purchasing the product may benefit from increased productivity and the users of the product may benefit from an improvement in their working conditions. Conversely, a stakeholder may benefit from user involvement, without there being any direct benefit to the product — for example, the users may learn more about the work of their colleagues or their organization through their participation in the design process.

The issue is complicated by the fact that what is seen as a benefit by one stakeholder can be seen as a cost by another. For example, an increase in productivity might be perceived as a benefit by the organization which purchases a product but as a cost by the actual users of the product if it leads to redundancies in the workforce. In our assessment of the costs and benefits of user involvement in design, we are not limiting ourselves to an organizational perspective. There are many stakeholders other than the organizations directly involved in the design of a product (e.g. the designers and users), as well as others who are less directly involved (e.g. the future maintainers of a system, post-sales support staff). Hence, the definitions given above emphasize that the costs and benefits considered here are those perceived by the various stakeholders. Every stakeholder has their own goals and prejudices, and it is against these that they perceive the costs and benefits, and judge the trade-offs. The empirical studies presented in Sections 3, 4 and 5 demonstrate how we can investigate the costs and benefits perceived by one of the other groups of stakeholders, the design practitioners.

The costs and benefits of user involvement may be assessed either in terms of the design project as a whole (e.g. increased product development time, improved product usability) or in terms of specific sub-activities within the design process (e.g. increased analysis time, decreased maintenance costs). The latter can be viewed at different levels of granularity, for example, within a single design meeting, or within a design activity such as requirements analysis. Obviously, this is somewhat of an over-simplification, as the successes or failures of any one design activity will have repercussions for those that follow. The empirical studies reported later in this paper examine the costs and benefits both for the overall project and for groups of sub-activities.

Finally, different design projects will have different cost-benefit trade-offs for the stakeholders arising from factors such as different project priorities, different levels of user involvement, or non-involvement, in the various design activities. Hence, the context in which costs or benefits are observed should also be documented. In summary, for our present purposes we describe any perceived cost or benefit of user involvement in design as follows:

- The design context in which the cost or benefit was perceived.
- The person who perceived the cost or benefit and their role.
- To whom or to what the cost or benefit applied, for example:
  - the product (e.g. usability);
  - the stakeholders (e.g. designers, users, organizations, maintainers);
  - the process (e.g. time, cost).
- The design activity for which the cost or benefit was identified.

3 Empirical Studies

Two empirical studies have been conducted to gain a broad overview of the costs and benefits of user involvement experienced in the context of real world design settings. The data from the studies considered here is limited to the costs and benefits perceived by the designers rather than any of the other stakeholders. As mentioned in Section 1, the long-term aim of these studies is to gain insight into the mechanisms that might bring about more effective user-designer collaboration in design. The results will also provide a basis for formulating specific hypotheses to be tested in further empirical studies, for example, whether users find one task modelling notation easier to understand than another. One of the studies reported here aimed to get a broad, though less detailed, view of the costs and benefits of user involvement in a cross-section of design projects, while the other study had a narrower, more detailed, focus on the costs and benefits experienced in just one design project. In both cases, participants were told we were conducting a study of design practice; to avoid introducing bias, our particular interest in user involvement was not mentioned.

3.1 Cross-sectional Study

The cross-sectional study was a survey of design practitioners in Europe and North America, conducted using two complementary approaches: a paper questionnaire was distributed to individuals known to be involved in some aspect of the design of interactive systems, and an interactive, electronic version of the same questionnaire was implemented and made accessible via the World Wide Web. A message requesting responses from design practitioners to the latter was sent to a number of relevant mailing lists and Usenet groups.

The questionnaire was structured into two main sections. The first section asked for general information about the respondents' backgrounds, experience and the organizations for which they worked. It also asked for background information on one design project in which they had been recently engaged (size, people involved, product, customer). The second section of the questionnaire then asked for further details of this design project. Respondents were asked to fill in three tables describing the design process followed on the project, where each table covered a particular category of design activities. The first table asked for details about what were termed 'preparation activities' in design, (for example, defining the problem area, gathering information, task analysis, requirements specification). The second table covered 'design activities' (for example, idea generation, detailed design, prototyping, implementation), while the third covered all 'evaluation activities', irrespective of when they occurred in the design process (for example, reviewing requirements documents, evaluation of prototypes, system testing, usability testing). For each table, respondents were asked to list the design activities in their chosen project that came under this category, the successes and failures of each activity, the people involved in each activity and the benefits and problems associated with the involvement of all of those people.

3.2 Longitudinal Study

The second of the studies was a longitudinal study of one design project. The design project was carried out within a service department of Queen Mary and Westfield College by two externally contracted designers. The initial phase of the project, which formed the basis of the study, was of six weeks duration, and involved the design and prototyping of an office-type application to support the recording and processing of technical queries, a fault log, and an inventory database.

Two members of the research team conducted interviews with each of the two designers individually at ten day intervals, and it is these interviews which form the basis of the analysis reported here. (Other information was also collected during the study which will be used in subsequent analysis: video transcripts of design meetings, interviews with users and copies of all design artefacts used or produced during the course of the project.) A total of 4 interviews, each of 30 to 45 minutes duration, were conducted with each of the two designers. All 8 interviews were recorded on audio tapes which were later transcribed by the same two members of the research team.

In each interview, the designers were asked about what they had been working on during the previous ten days and what they planned to do in the forthcoming ten days. In particular, they were asked about any meetings (with whom, about what), about the problems they had encountered, about the things that had gone well or badly, and what design artefacts had been produced. Additionally, the first interview obtained general information about the designers' backgrounds and their anticipated involvement in the project, while the final interview asked them to summarize their experiences on the project. The designers were not informed of our particular interest in the costs and benefits of user involvement in the design process.

4 The Cross-sectional Study

4.1 Questionnaire Analysis

The survey of design practitioners is ongoing. To date, 10 paper responses and 15 electronic responses have been received and were used in the analysis presented here. Four researchers individually analysed a subset of these completed questionnaires in order to devise a coding scheme for the responses. They agreed upon three categories of costs and benefits that were perceived by respondents to be due to user involvement in the design process: directly stated costs and benefits, indirectly stated costs and benefits and inferred costs and benefits. At this early stage in the research we want to be conservative about the data upon which we base our conclusions, therefore only one of these categories is reported in this paper, directly stated costs and benefits. Directly stated costs and benefits are where the respondents mention that users were involved in an activity and where the perceived costs or benefits were directly identified *by the respondents* as being due to this user involvement. The complete set of questionnaires was then analysed by one researcher in accordance with this coding scheme and the results were then checked by a second researcher.

4.2 Questionnaire Results and Discussion

There was some degree of user involvement in 15 out of the 25 completed questionnaires. As mentioned in Section 3.1, the questionnaire was divided into separate sections for preparation, design and evaluation activities. Out of the 15 questionnaires where user involvement occurred, users were involved in 11 projects in the preparation stage, 6 projects in the design stage and 10 projects in the evaluation stage. A closer look at the results revealed the following findings:

- Users were involved in all 3 activities in 3 projects.
- Users were involved in 2 out of 3 activities in 6 projects: in 1 project users were involved in preparation and design, in 4 projects users were involved in preparation and evaluation and in 1 project users were involved in design and evaluation.
- Users were involved in 1 activity in 6 projects: in 3 projects, users were involved in only preparation activities, in 1 project users were involved in only design activities and in 2 projects users were involved in only evaluation activities.

Table 1 summarizes these figures for user involvement in the 3 activities and shows the numbers of costs and benefits identified for each of the activities. Obviously, there is not a direct relationship between the number of projects where users

Activity	Projects with user involvement	Benefits	Costs
Preparation	11	14	12
Design	6	10	3
Evaluation	10	13	6
Overall	15	3	2

Table 1: Summary of survey results for user involvement.

Activity	Benefits	Costs
Preparation	0	4
Design	0	1
Evaluation	1	1

Table 2: Summary of survey results for non-user involvement.

are involved in an activity and the number of total benefits across projects for that activity. In one project there may have been many costs or benefits associated with user involvement in a particular activity, whereas in another project there might have been very few costs or benefits. The additional 'Overall' category shows that 15 of the 25 projects had some user involvement and documents a small number of costs and benefits which respondents attributed to user involvement in the project as a whole.

Finally, a small proportion of the practitioners who stated that there had been no user involvement perceived this as a cost or benefit for the project (see Table 2). Note here that the costs and benefits are the reverse of those where users are involved. Two practitioners stated that a failure of the project was the lack of user involvement, and a further practitioner said that a failure of their project was that the users' needs were considered too late. The single benefit was concerned with the designer's perception that discussions could be more frank without the user involved.

The questionnaire results show that for this survey of design practice, 15 out of 25 (60%) of the projects described by the practitioners involved users to some degree. This result indicates that for the respondents at least the incidence of user involvement has grown since surveys conducted in the 1980s. As mentioned earlier, the questionnaire was designed to look at design practice in general and any contribution made to the design process by different people rather than targeting user involvement specifically. We believe that the number of respondents filling in the questionnaires who did not experience user involvement on their project demonstrates that the results we achieved are not through practitioners telling us what they thought we might want to hear. However, the sample is relatively small and we are open to the same bias from people who are prepared to fill in questionnaires as any other researcher in any discipline.

4.2.1 Preparation Activities

In the preparation phase, activities such as defining the problem, gathering background information, task analysis, idea generation, requirements definition and analysis all occurred and with a contribution from users. The main contribution of users to these activities was as the providers of information, feedback and discussion, allowing designers to have a better understanding of any relevant information and merging their views with users' views. The users provided information about their tasks, offered suggestions as to future representation of the user interface, enabled a fast generation of ideas and provided likes and dislikes of similar products. The costs were generally due to lack of information on the part of users as to what the designers needed to know and in their heightened expectations of the artefact. For instance, designers say that users are often not able to differentiate information that is important for the designer from unimportant information. Users have problems speaking in general terms, preferring to speak about specific examples. There were also costs when there were different user groups and little consensus across users. Other costs occurred where the lack of information that users possessed about the design process meant that it was hard for them to imagine what the software would be like or to envision design constraints.

4.2.2 Design Activities

In the design phase, a number of activities occurred across the different projects including validation of functional analysis, initial interface design, prototype construction and redesign. The users' contributions generally included activities like identifying interaction issues which had to be addressed by users within the specific application domains, providing ideas and offering a practical view of the design usage. Other user contributions in the design phase were by providing feedback on good and bad points in the design. Therefore the user role here was twofold, providing information to guide design and feedback on initial design ideas. The specific costs related to difficulties the designers experienced in trying to solve problems when there were clearly opposing views, to the users introducing new concepts, and generally to there being too great a volume of feedback. The problem for designers here is that of finding compromizes between different user groups and different stakeholders in the design. In addition the situations seen by some designers as costs might be considered to be the desired consequences of user involvement. For instance, the fact that initial interaction between user and interface meant that the users introduced new concepts could be construed as a benefit of user involvement, it might tighten up the requirements and it has to be expected that requirements will evolve throughout the design. Therefore some of the problems here might relate to mistaken designer expectations of the consequences of user involvement in the activity.

4.2.3 Evaluation Activities

In the evaluation phase, the designers' perceived benefits of user involvement, although there were associated problems, were particularly positive. The benefits highlighted were involvement from users, comments, feedback, suggestions, commitment, criticism, acceptance, improved usability, learning by designers and project leaders, and finally that the feedback was constructive in bringing the user interface closer to tasks for which it was to be used. The costs of user involvement in evaluation seemed to centre on lack of user knowledge about technical limitations of the software, that users had high expectations in terms of how quickly something could be achieved, and that users had too high expectations of user friendliness of the final product and occasionally made ad hoc comments.

4.2.4 Overall

In terms of overall successes or failures within the project, user involvement benefits identified by the respondents were that the users were 'satisfied' and that users accepted, for instance, 'validation of design documents', etc. The costs were that the users were becoming more and more 'exacting', that there were often too many user groups.

5 Longitudinal Study

5.1 Interview Analysis

As mentioned in Section 3.2, a total of 8 interviews were conducted with the designers in the longitudinal case study and used in the analysis to be presented here. One of the interview transcripts was selected for use in initial analysis; four researchers independently analysed this transcript and in subsequent discussions came to agreement as to what should be considered as costs and benefits. Following this, two of the researchers independently coded all eight transcripts in the agreed manner. They then compared and discussed the coding of the eight transcripts until agreement was reached on the costs and benefits identified in the interviews.

All the identified costs and benefits were listed (as quotes from the transcripts) and then grouped according to categories of design activities (overall, preparation, design and evaluation activities). The data was then rationalized to remove multiple references to the same cost or benefit. Finally, each cost or benefit was documented in the manner discussed in Section 2: it was described in terms of the designer (referred to as D1 or D2) who perceived it, to whom and / or to what it applied and the design activity where it was experienced. (Obviously, the design context was the same throughout and was therefore documented separately.)

As in the cross-sectional study, only directly stated costs and benefits were included. Directly stated costs and benefits are where the designers mentioned that users were involved in an activity and they identified some cost or benefit arising directly from this involvement. The designers anticipated certain costs and benefits would arise as a consequence of user involvement in the project, and their comments in the interviews were made in the light of these expectations. In identifying costs and benefits from the interview transcripts, we looked for 'evaluative remarks' which compared the costs and benefits that the designers actually perceived against their expectations. In some cases, the costs and benefits of user involvement were as expected. In other cases, the evaluative remarks indicated that there were either more or less benefits or more or less costs than expected. Finally, we coded remarks where the designers perceived that some unexpected cost or benefit had arisen as a consequence of user involvement in a design activity.

Activity	Benefits	Costs
Preparation	12	6
Design	13	12
Evaluation	7	0
Overall	7	4

Table 3: Summary of results from longitudinal study.

5.2 Longitudinal Study Results and Discussion

In order to position the case study in the context of the design practice survey, it is appropriate to highlight some salient features of the design process.† A cooperative, task-based design approach was followed on the project. The main activities of this approach were: initial discussions and analysis with users and management, analysis and modelling of the users' current tasks (known as task model 1), design and modelling of the users' proposed future tasks (known as task model 2), paper prototyping of an interactive system to support the proposed tasks and software prototyping (implementing the paper prototypes). The design process was cooperative in the sense that it was characterized by a high level of user involvement throughout, with the users actively engaged in the analysis, design and evaluation activities. The stakeholders involved in the project were users, designers, managers and the organization.

Table 3 summarizes the total number of costs and benefits identified in the interview transcripts. The division of the design activities into the same three categories as used in the survey was obtained by asking one of the designers to fill in a copy of the questionnaire, while the 'Overall' category was based on the designers' responses to questions about the design project as a whole. More detailed information about the costs and benefits is presented in Tables 4 to 7. Table 4, lists the costs and benefits identified for the overall process, while Tables 5, 6 and 7 give similar information for the three categories of design activities: preparation activities, design activities and evaluation activities. Each entry in these tables gives a summary of a cost or benefit, shows which of the two designers perceived it (D1 or D2) and indicates to whom or to what the cost or benefit was perceived to apply.

The results show that the designers perceived both costs and benefits arising from user involvement. Rather more costs and benefits were identified for the preparation and design activities than for the evaluation activities. The relatively low figures for evaluation activities may be attributed to the fact that no formal evaluation took place during the phase of the project with which we were involved. Evaluation activities were limited to informal feedback by the users as to the correctness and completeness of the various models used during the design process, most notably, the task models. As for the cross-sectional study, the results are discussed below in terms of the design activities for which the costs and benefits were identified.

† It should be noted that it is not the purpose of this paper to evaluate the design approach; this paper is solely concerned with investigating the consequences of user involvement in the design.

	Summary of perceived cost or benefit	D1	D2	To whom/what
Benefits	The users helped define the scope of the project	×		Design process, scope
	The users contributed design ideas		×	Design process, ideas
	The users provided useful information during the design process		×	Design process, information
	The system, from the department's point of view, was improved by the process		×	Artefact, quality; Organization, work
	The users were happy with the forms that were designed		×	Users, satisfaction
	The users learnt about analysis, task modelling and design	×	×	Users, knowledge
	The users learnt about how the job should be done, and about how each other do the job at present		×	Users, knowledge
Costs	The users had to be educated about design before they could participate in the design activities	×		Designers, time
	The users made unfounded assumptions about the designers' abilities and the effort required to do things	×		Designers, time; Users, expectations
	The designer spent a lot of time chasing the users — sending them email and phoning them	×	×	Designers, time
	The designer put a lot of time and effort into arranging meetings with the users		×	Designers, time

Table 4: Overall design project: Summary of costs and benefits.

5.2.1 Preparation Activities

During the preparation activities (initial analysis and production of task model 1), the users were involved in scoping the project, determining requirements, providing information about their tasks and verifying the information represented in task model 1 (see Table 5). The designers perceived that they benefited during this phase by gathering more information than they had expected from talking to the users, in particular they received unexpected information from some users which other users knew nothing about. They also got early design ideas from the users in return for investing time in explaining the artefacts to the users, organizing and participating in the meetings. The users were active participants in the task modelling and the designers perceived that this caused the modelling process to proceed more rapidly than it would have done had there been less user involvement ("… and the task models were produced very very quickly …"). The designers perceived that the users gained knowledge about the work of their colleagues and the organization ("… a lot of users said independently that the task model was excellent because it showed them for the first time an overview of the department and they were really keen on it"). The users also learnt about analysis and design, and about the notations used, although it cost them time and effort to understand the models and to participate in the meetings. An unexpected benefit was that, based on his experiences during these activities, one of the users was keen to involve some of his colleagues in the design project. The major costs to the designers were the time and effort required to arrange meetings with the users and get them involved in the analysis. Further, the users sometimes misunderstood things about the models, or made incorrect assumptions, which had to be corrected later.

	Summary of perceived cost or benefit	D1	D2	To whom/what
Benefits	One of the users produced additional information that the others knew nothing about during the initial analysis	×		Designers, information
	The users contributed useful information about their work and were actively involved in constructing task model 1	×		Design process, information
	Users contributed design requirements	×		Design process, information
	There was a lot of agreement independently across the different people in the initial analysis	×		TM1, consistency
	The users gained an overview of the department from task model 1 and learnt what was going on for the first time	×		Users, knowledge
	The users were happy because task model 1 showed them how the work of different people fitted together	×		Users, knowledge
	There was more cooperation and involvement from the users than the designer expected	×		Design process, user involvement
	After participating in the production of task model 1, one of the users wanted to invite his colleagues to be involved also	×		Design process, user involvement
	Task model 1 was produced rapidly and went through rapid iterations	×		Design process, time
	The users gained knowledge about each others' work during the initial analysis	×	×	Users, knowledge
	One of the users contributed more useful information than expected during the initial analysis	×	×	Design process, information
	The users contributed design ideas during the interviews		×	Design process, information
Costs	The designers became irritated by their involvement in user disputes	×		Designers, negative feelings
	The designers spent a lot of time arranging meetings and persuading the users to attend during the initial analysis	×	×	Designers, time
	The users misunderstood things about task model 1 which had to be sorted out later on		×	TM1, quality; Design process, time
	The users did not offer their own opinions when constructing task model 1, but agreed with the designers as the analysts		×	TM1, quality
	The users made incorrect assumptions about what task model 1 represented		×	TM 1, quality
	It took time and effort for the users to understand the models		×	Design process, time

Table 5: Preparation activities: Summary of costs and benefits.

5.2.2 *Design Activities*

The users were directly and actively involved in the design activities (production of task model 2 and paper prototyping), where they contributed ideas concerning how their work tasks might be modified, offered design ideas and again verified the information about their work represented in the models (see Table 6). The designers perceived that these activities went well as a result of the direct user involvement and that they rapidly realized a design for the proposed new system which they believed would be easily converted into a software prototype. An unexpectedly high number of costs were mentioned for the design activities. These were largely due to a conflict, arising from old grievances, which took place between rival groups of users

	Summary of perceived cost or benefit	D1	D2	To whom/what
Benefits	Producing task model 2 helped the users to see what others perceived their task to be	×		Users, knowledge
	The users could see an overview of the situation for the first time, what people were doing and what they should be doing	×		Users, knowledge
	The users got together and talked out their differences for the first time	×		Users, conflict resolution
	There was eventually consensus on how the new system should work and what the users future tasks would be	×		TM2, consensus
	The users agreed that task model 2 would be a good new system	×		TM2, consensus
	Very quickly arrived at a model of the proposed new system	×		Design process, time
	Produced a model which the designers hoped could be used as a basis for structuring the software	×		Software prototype, structure
	After the cooperative paper prototyping, the designers had a clear idea of the proposed content of the software prototype	×		Software prototype, information content
	The paper prototyping with one of the users went very well and they sorted out what was going where very rapidly	×		Design process, time
	There was consensus on the paper prototype	×		Paper prototype, consensus
	Users came up with design solutions through discussion of problems during paper prototyping	×	×	Design process, ideas
	The users were happy with the proposed design as a paper prototype		×	Paper prototype, consensus
	The designer perceived the form resulting from the paper prototyping as being completely new and very quick to fill in		×	Paper prototype, quality; Users, time
Costs	Some users wanted to build in functions to check on other users	×		Users, work practice
	One group of users wanted to give another group of users extra work when producing task model 2	×		Users, work practice
	There was a conflict of interest between different user groups concerning who should do what in the new system	×		Users, conflict
	One user felt he was being hassled by the other users and felt unable to make his contribution to task model 2	×		Users, negative feelings
	The designers had to arbitrate and manage conflict between opposing user groups	×		Designers, conflict management
	In one paper prototyping session there was not a lot of cooperation and they didn't produce the intended output	×		Paper prototype, quality
	One of the users was verbose and "went round in circles" in one of the paper prototyping sessions	×		Design process, time
	The designers became irritated with one of the users after his involvement in the paper prototyping sessions	×		Designers, negative feelings
	Users agreed with the designers because they were the analysts, rather than providing their own opinion		×	TM2, quality
	Some of the users did not actually understand task model 2, although they said that they did		×	TM2, quality
	The users made incorrect assumptions about task model 2 and the implementation which required correction later		×	Design process, time
	It took time to convince one of the users to participate in the paper prototyping activity		×	Design process, time

Table 6: Design Activities: Summary of costs and benefits.

	Summary of perceived cost or benefit	D1	D2	To whom/what
Benefits	The users agreed on the fact that task model 2 represented an improved situation	×		TM2, quality
	There was general agreement on the correctness and completeness of task model 1	×	×	TM1, correctness
	The users added things that had been left out and elaborated parts of task model 1	×	×	TM1, correctness
	There was consensus on task model 1		×	TM1, consensus
	The users made comments and corrections to task model 2		×	TM2, correctness
	The users confirmed every field in the paper prototypes		×	Paper prototypes, correctness
	One user suggested changes when evaluating the prototype screens		×	Paper prototypes, quality

Table 7: Evaluation activities: Summary of costs and benefits.

and required additional time and effort to resolve. The conflict concerned how the users' work would be organized under the new system and resulted in disputes during design meetings to the extent that at least one user felt 'hassled' and unable to make any further contribution during a meeting. However, the designers also perceived a benefit in that the users eventually resolved existing differences of opinion about their work ("... for the first time people in the department actually got together and talked out their differences"). As in the preparation activities, a further cost was that users sometimes misunderstood the design models, or made inappropriate assumptions about what they expressed. A final benefit was that the designers perceived that the users again gained knowledge during these activities.

5.2.3 Evaluation Activities

No formal evaluation activities took place during the during the time period covered by the designer interviews, but the users were directly involved in continuous, informal evaluation of the various design artefacts (see Table 7). As the results indicate, all user involvement in this respect was perceived to be beneficial — seven benefits and no costs were identified in the analysis. Notably, user involvement in evaluation was perceived to improve the quality of the design artefacts, by confirming, correcting and elaborating the information.

5.2.4 Overall Activities

Overall, the designers perceived that the design had improved, both in relation to the way the users worked at present and to the design that would have resulted had a different approach, with less user involvement, been adopted. The designers saw this improvement as a benefit to the organization ("I think, for the department, it's more the forms are actually improved through the process, instead of ..."). The designers also saw the fact that old grievances were aired and conflicts were resolved as a benefit to the organization.

The overall perceived benefits to the users were that they gained insights into the workings of their organization, into how others worked and into how others perceived their work. Furthermore, they learned about analysis and design, and were satisfied with the intermediate artefacts and the final design. They did experience costs, because existing conflicts came out in the open and had to be resolved in order to come up with the new design. Some people felt hassled during this process and were worried that they might be given more work or that the new system might be used to check on them. A further cost to the users was that they had to put time and effort into learning and understanding the models used.

The designers perceived that the overall design process went well, apart from how some of the meetings were organized and facilitated. The process had to be adapted in some cases to the users' needs: one user asked for an extra step to be introduced into the approach, and another user suggested changes to the notation so he could understand it better. The artefacts were perceived by one designer to be agreed upon by the users, whereas the other designer wondered whether the users actually understood the models. In later phases of the design process there was evidence to the effect that some things had actually been misunderstood, and that incorrect assumptions had been made, by the users. It then cost time to correct these misapprehensions.

The designers perceived that the overall process was beneficial to themselves: the design process progressed quickly and the artefacts were perceived to be good. The users contributed to the process, offered design ideas and corrected errors in intermediate designs. However, in later phases, the designers sometimes realized that the artefacts were not as good as previously thought, and adjustments had to be made. There were also costs to the designers, most notably in the time and effort devoted to getting the users involved and educating them about the design techniques.

6 Discussion

The cross-sectional study shows the variations in current design practice as to the activities in a design project where users are involved. As might be anticipated, greater incidence of user involvement was found in the preparation and evaluation activities than in the design activities. However, where users were involved in design activities a number of benefits appeared to be the result. The longitudinal study involved rather more user involvement in design activities than is standard in current design practice but likewise indicates various benefits that result. The designers' perceptions of user involvement in evaluation activities were particularly positive in both the studies, suggesting that the value of user evaluation is becoming widely accepted in the HCI community. Overall the designers felt that the quality of both the intermediate artefacts and the final screen designs had benefited from user involvement. No actual usability test has as yet been performed, so it is hard to determine whether there is any truth to their perceptions. Further, the results suggest that the designers perceived that all the stakeholders benefit from user involvement in the design process.

The results indicate that where there is an inclination to involve users and this is looked upon favourably, there are still problems of lack of knowledge and communication between users and designers which result in various costs. These costs have implications for future work on developing techniques that support effective user involvement in design. Many of the costs perceived by the designers arose from misunderstandings or invalid assumptions on the part of the users, their inability to envision future systems or to understand the constraints of technology. Users, in the designers' view, appear unable to grasp the difficulties with which changes can be made and the extra overhead these might involve. Therefore it would seem that to make the most use of user involvement, without costs associated with misunderstanding, it is necessary to educate users to some extent about the designer's task. There is also a need to ensure that intermediate design artefacts and design documents are understood by the users and are expressed in terms that are meaningful in the context of the users' work tasks. This means better communication and representations for communication between users and designers are required, pointing to a need for further research. The results from both studies also indicate that the design process can become a forum for conflict between opposing user groups and that this increases the costs of user involvement to all the stakeholders. The lesson to be learned from this is that design methods which involve users, particularly those that involve groups of users simultaneously, require careful management and facilitation of design meetings so as to prevent situations of open conflict arising. With careful management, the airing of opposing views can be beneficial, highlighting issues that otherwise might not surface until considerably later in the design process, and allowing the participants to negotiate and resolve their differences. This was seen in the longitudinal study, where the designers perceived that the users benefited from talking out their differences for the first time.

The analysis illustrates quite clearly that the trade-offs for each stakeholder differ. For the *designers* it costs time and effort to involve the users, but the quality of the intermediate and final artefacts of the design activities is perceived to be improved. In the case of the *users*, they invest time in the design process (if allowed, able and willing) in return for knowledge about their present work and about design, possibly resolving existing conflicts, and gaining an improved work situation in the future. Whether knowledge about design is actually useful depends on the likelihood of the users being involved in some design project in the future, for example redesigns or new releases. For the *managers*, the trade-off concerns (in this case study) the money invested in the design process vs. the quality of the design, the likelihood of its acceptance by the users and the expectations of more effective work in the future. It is also interesting to contrast the views of the two designers in the longitudinal study. In spite of the fact that these two individuals had similar roles in the design process, there are interesting contrasts in their perceptions. For example, the two designers had different perceptions of how well the users understood the models. They also felt that some approaches that work which well for one user, might not work well for another user.

The analysis of the interviews in the longitudinal study also led to interesting insights into obstacles (factors that prevent the user from making a beneficial contribution to design) and facilitators (factors that enable the users to make a beneficial contribution) of user involvement. A number of such obstacles and facilitators were encountered, although we do not have space to discuss this issue in any depth. The obstacle of having access to users has been discussed extensively by Grudin (1991) and was evident in this study. For example, even though the management agreed in principle to involving users, practical reasons such as the users being busy, unmotivated or on a holiday hindered actual user involvement. Another important obstacle was that the designers did not have sufficient time to involve the users as extensively as intended. Organizing and managing the meetings with the users inefficiently was another factor that hindered effective user involvement. In the cross-sectional survey, the designers reported obstacles arising from management who saw user involvement as an additional, optional activity, and also from marketing staff who thought they knew what users wanted and therefore did not see the necessity to involve the users themselves.

The data gathered in the empirical studies reported here is qualitative in nature. While this was entirely intentional on our part, within behavioural disciplines such as psychology the usefulness of qualitative as opposed to quantitative data has long been debated, see (Morgan, 1996). Although the data highlights important cost-benefit factors beyond the financial and quantifiable, the downside is that it does involve designers introspecting about their own perceptions, and even in some cases undertaking "second order perceptions" of what they feel might be the perceptions of others, e.g. the users. However, these findings will be counter-balanced by further analyses of the longitudinal study in which we intend to identify the costs and benefits perceived by the other stakeholders and to compare these with the designers' perceptions, and also by obtaining objective measures of the usability of the implemented artefact in the context of its use. In addition to the interview data, we have collected design documents and other outputs from the project which will also analysed and compared with the interview data. Finally, we are anxious to collect similar detailed data from further design projects involving different stakeholders to the ones studied here, where there would be different cost-benefit trade-offs for user involvement.

7 Conclusion

The notion of involving users as direct participants in the analysis, development and evaluation of interactive system designs is of growing interest, although the strongest case yet made for such involvement has been in the context of promoting industrial democracy. We are now considering user involvement in more depth to identify how and where such involvement might occur, and the nature of the costs and benefits arising from involving and not involving users in the design process. This paper has offered a view of costs and benefits in line with these concerns, and has reported some initial results concerning the costs and benefits of user involvement in design based on data collected in two of our on-going design studies.

The cross-sectional study identifies the areas of design where users are involved at present and suggests that this occurs more in analysis and evaluation activities, but with some user involvement in prototyping and other design work. The survey further gives us an overview of design practitioners' perceptions of the costs and benefits associated with this involvement. The design interviews from the longitudinal study focused upon the analysis and design activities. These indicated that increased user involvement yielded certain benefits such as rapid production of task models and immediate feedback, but with increased costs such as greater investment of time and the designers becoming embroiled in the users' disputes. The longitudinal study also showed that the trade-offs differ for the different stakeholders.

Clearly these results should not be over-interpreted. The interviews are from only one design project and at present we have only considered the designers' perceptions of the costs and benefits of user involvement. Nonetheless, we believe the results of the studies offer some interesting insights into mechanisms that might bring about more effective user involvement in design. Further, such an analysis offers a rationale to the various stakeholders as to why it benefits themselves, not just their organizations, to involve users in design projects.

Acknowledgements

The authors would like to acknowledge the support of the UK's Engineering and Physical Sciences Research Council for the work reported here (grant GR/K19211, "Supporting Designers and Users in the Creation of Interactive Systems"). We are grateful to the designers who responded to our survey and to the members of the design team who provided us with access during the longitudinal case study.

References

Barnard, P. (1987), Cognitive Resources and Learning of Human Computer Dialogues, *in* J. M. Carroll (ed.), "Interfacing Thought: Cognitive Aspects of Human–Computer Interaction", MIT Press, pp.112–159.

Bekker, M. M. & Vermeeren, A. P. O. S. (1993), Developing User Interface Design Tools: An Analysis of Interface Design Practice, *in* E. J. Lovesey (ed.), "Contemporary Ergonomics: Proceedings of the Ergonomics Society's 1993 Conference", Taylor & Francis, pp.79–84.

Bellotti, V. (1988), Implications of Current Design Practice for the Use of HCI Techniques, *in* D. M. Jones & R. Winder (eds.), "People and Computers IV (Proceedings of HCI'88)", Cambridge University Press, pp.13–34.

Bias, R. G. & Mayhew, D. J. (eds.) (1994), *Cost-Justifying Usability*, Academic Press.

CACM (1993), "Communications of the ACM". Special Issue on Participatory Design, **36**(4).

Card, S. K., Moran, T. P. & Newell, A. (1983), *The Psychology of Human–Computer Interaction*, Lawrence Erlbaum Associates.

Carroll, J. M. (ed.) (1995), *Scenario-Based Design: Envisioning Work and Technology in System Development*, John Wiley & Sons.

Diaper, D. (1989), Task Analysis for Knowledge Description (TAKD), *in* D. Diaper (ed.), "Task Analysis for Human–Computer Interaction", Ellis Horwood, pp.108–159.

Grudin, J. (1991), "Systematic Sources of Sub-optimal Interface Design in Large Product Development Organisations", *Human–Computer Interaction* **6**(2), 147–196.

Johnson, P., Johnson, H., Waddington, R. & Shouls, A. (1988), Task-Related Knowledge Structures: Analysis, Modelling and Application, *in* D. M. Jones & R. Winder (eds.), "People and Computers IV (Proceedings of HCI'88)", Cambridge University Press, pp.35–62.

Karat, C.-M. (1990), Cost-Benefit Analysis of Iterative Usability Testing, *in* D. Diaper, D. Gilmore, G. Cockton & B. Shackel (eds.), "Proceedings of INTERACT'90 — Third IFIP Conference on Human–Computer Interaction", Elsevier Science, pp.351–356.

Lim, K. Y. & Long, J. (1994), *The MUSE Method for Usability Engineering*, Cambridge Series on Human–Computer Interaction, Cambridge University Press.

Mantei, M. M. & Teorey, T. J. (1988), "Cost/Benefit Analysis for Incorporating Human Factors in the Software Lifecycle", *Communications of the ACM* **31**(4), 428–439.

Morgan, M. (1996), "Qualitative Research: A Package Deal", *The Psychologist* **9**(1), 31–32.

Norman, D. A. & Draper, S. W. (eds.) (1986), *User Centered Systems Design: New Perspectives on Human–Computer Interaction*, Lawrence Erlbaum Associates.

Payne, S. & Green, T. (1986), "Task Action Grammars: A Model of the Mental Representation of Task Languages", *Human–Computer Interaction* **2**(2), 93–133.

Schuler, D. & Namioka, A. (eds.) (1993), *Participatory Design: Principles and Practices*, Lawrence Erlbaum Associates.

What You Don't Know Can Hurt You: Privacy in Collaborative Computing

Victoria Bellotti

Apple Computer Inc., 1 Infinite Loop, MS:301–4A, Cupertino, CA 95014, USA.

Tel: *+1 408 974 5206*
Fax: *+1 408 974 0234*
EMail: *bellotti@apple.com*

Privacy is a popular subject in the CSCW literature but has largely been addressed as an issue of security by systems designers. With the growth of networked, multimedia CSCW systems comes an increasing need for better control over how people gain access to one another and to potentially shareable information. This paper poses some challenges for CSCW developers and provides some examples of systems which are beginning to meet such challenges.

Keywords: privacy, access control, collaboration, communication, design.

1 Introduction

A friend at Apple told me a story about how she became a user of 'ShareMon' (Cohen, 1993), a system which gave auditory feedback on your Macintosh, in the form of a knocking-door, opening and closing drawer sounds, creaking noises and a door slamming, to depict activity when someone else remotely logged onto your machine over the network. It also provided auditory feedback or a display to let you know who was logged on. The idea was to provide comprehensible background feedback (awareness) about file-sharing activity over the network. Mac users at Apple and elsewhere routinely set file sharing to support collaboration with named individuals and other users (who log on as guests). My friend told me that, she really liked using ShareMon because she could now see who was using her files and when. However, once she began using ShareMon, she realized that a lot of people (unidentified guests) were going through her directories after hours. She was "absolutely shocked to find out that some people don't have a certain amount of respect". Cohen notes that she was not alone in this reaction and that ShareMon revealed that "all sorts of people were cruising the net looking for stuff" (Cohen, personal communication).

This paper represents an attempt to broaden the debate around the problems of *computer systems design to support privacy*. So far, the majority of the concern about this area has centred around two sets of issues. The first relates to the *security* of communications and computing systems and the second relates to the *legislation* around what is permissible, for whom and when. However, the story above illustrates how privacy can be a serious issue even with legitimate access within secure systems. My aim, therefore, is to introduce a third area of debate on the need for sophisticated and flexible means by which people can control how accessible they are and how much information they want to share with others. Whilst the term 'privacy', in the context of computing, usually gets people very excited about security and legislative issues, there is little debate in the HCI literature on the subject of the user and collaboration related issues of how to manage privacy. Even secure systems which operate within the law do not solve all of the problems raised by these issues. As CSCW technology makes people more accessible to one another and their work more shareable, so new mechanisms are required to enable users to manage personal accessibility to others and to determine what on-line information is shared, with whom and how.

In this paper I will highlight two important distinctions. The first between *information access* and *interpersonal access*, each of which has different implications for what kinds of access control mechanisms are required. The second is between *technical access control* and *social access control*, the former involving technologies which enable, restrict or prevent access and the latter involving the provision of *resources* which make access potentially detectable and thus subject to social governance. Two key resources are *feedback* and *awareness*. Feedback means giving information to system users about how accessible they are and how accessible information is to others. Awareness means providing information about on-line activities which can support social control over access. My aim in this paper is to promote privacy as a design issue for computer supported collaborative work (CSCW) and computer-mediated communication (CMC) systems. I introduce design challenges for information access control and interpersonal access control and provide some examples of systems which are beginning to meet these challenges. Before I make my main points, I want to clear up possible misunderstandings about what privacy might be taken to mean. In the next section, I emphasize the extent of the growing concerns about privacy in the domain of networked and multimedia computing, I provide a flexible definition of privacy for designers to work with and I emphasize that system security does not adequately guarantee privacy, particularly for those who need to have flexible access to one another and to share information widely (as in CSCW and CMC).

2 Privacy Concerns in the Information Age

Current developments in computing and communications technologies are eroding the notion of personal computing as we know it. High bandwidth ATM networks, mobile and location devices (e.g. GPS), wireless and multimedia communications and computing infrastructures also offer new paradigms and platforms for CSCW — e.g. (Want et al., 1992; Weiser, 1991; Gaver et al., 1992; Vetter, 1995; Herring, 1996). Capitalizing on such developments, a variety of researchers have investigated opportunities for supporting interpersonal communication and sharing information on-line — e.g. (Ishii & Kobayashi, 1992; Greenhalgh & Benford, 1995; Minneman et al., 1995). Some of the information which is now available on-line may potentially be of a personal nature. For example, people's locations and movements, what they say, how they behave and what are their areas of professional or non-professional interest are now tractable to computational processing — e.g. (Eldridge et al., 1992; Harper, 1992; Hindus & Schmandt, 1992; Wilcox et al., 1994; Donath, 1995; Zhang et al., 1995; Pentland, 1996). Outside of the research community, many institutions routinely use less up-to-date computing technology to process, match and exploit personal, medical and financial records (Clarke, 1988). Many writers point out the risks associated with the increasing varieties of information which are available and applications which enable access to and utilization of such information — e.g. (Clarke, 1988; Dunlop & Kling, 1991; Reidenberg, 1992; Clement, 1994; Neumann, 1995; Agre & Rotenberg, in press). Some believe that this connectivity and computing power is soon to be, or already being put to use in ways which will pose an unethical threat to people who keep sensitive or personal information on-line (and that is increasingly everyone who uses computers). A great deal of the debate has centred around defining what privacy, the thing we are trying to protect, actually is.

2.1 A Static Norm or an Operational Capability?

Two types of privacy definition are common. I refer to these as *normative* and *operational*. A normative definition involves a notion that there are some aspects of a person's nature and activity which are inherently private and should not be revealed to anyone. (Reiman, 1995) offers such a definition; "privacy is the condition in which others are deprived of access to you", and "For there to be a right to privacy, there must be some valid form that specifies that some personal information about, or experience of, individuals should be kept out of other people's reach. Such norms may be legal." This would presumably mean for designers that, at certain times, people should be accessible to one another and, at others, definitely not. Furthermore, some information should be accessible to others and some should not.

Reiman's definition is not convincing, even from his own arguments. The value of privacy and legislation designed to protect it vary widely both culturally and also legally between countries (Milberg et al., 1995). For example, there has been serious resistance to the idea of carrying and routinely presenting photo ID in the UK based on the view that this an intrusion into people's privacy, whereas France and the USA find this more acceptable. A normative definition of privacy is further problematized because many other personal and contextual factors come into play in deciding if it has been violated. These might include whether two people are related, where something happens (e.g. at home, in the workplace, or in public) and whether someone is aware of what is taking place or mentally competent to give permission. This variability tends to result in lengthy court cases to determine whether a legal violation of privacy has occurred (Privacy Protection Study Commission, 1991), often with plaintiffs being surprised and dismayed to find that there is no legal protection against their complaint (McClurg, 1995). If the law is so complex and unintuitive then it seems that no team of designers, HCI experts and users, or anyone else for that matter, is likely to be able to agree upon who should have access to whom or what and in which circumstances.

A second operational kind of definition of privacy refers to a capability, rather than a set of 'norms'. I refer to this capability as *access control.* For example, (Stone et al., 1983) include in their definition of privacy the "ability of the individual to personally control information about oneself". Similarly, Samarajiva (in press) refers to privacy as "the control of outflow of information that may be of strategic or aesthetic value to the person and control of inflow of information including initiation of contact".* These operational definitions of privacy seem much more practical for CSCW systems designers since they allow for a person's need to make individual, cultural and contextually contingent decisions as to how much information they desire to exchange and when. They also lend themselves readily to the definition of a requirement for the design of access control mechanisms: *Users must be able to know about and control the consequences of their interactions with technology in terms of how visible and accessible they and their information are to others.*

Of course, access control mechanisms can only be trusted if users have guarantees about the security of the system they are using to begin with; i.e. that there is a negligible risk that other users can subvert the system, bypassing control and doing so without being detected.

2.2 *Privacy vs. Security*

Appreciation of the risks of deliberate or even unwitting system subversion in the context of critical and sensitive technological systems has revealed a need for software protection and *system security.* Research in this area is clearly important, since networked computing systems, are vulnerable to unofficial, covert subversion (Mullender, 1989). Consequently, a great deal of design and legislation has been devoted to useful software protection models and standards designed to reduce the risks, such as file protection mechanisms and private- and public-key encryption — e.g. Bowyer (1996) and Denning & Branstad (1996).

Even with secure systems and within the law, however, privacy on-line is commonly invaded, sometimes inadvertently. The ShareMon example with which I began this paper should convince most readers that this is the case. One of the main reasons why this happens is that *people do not generally appreciate what the state of their personal information on-line is with respect to access by others, and thus fail to take steps to control it,* sometimes with serious consequences — e.g. (Forester & Morrison, 1990; Weisband & Reinig, 1995).

*This is based upon Rule (1980) distinction between violations of aesthetic privacy which expose things that victims may feel are inappropriate to reveal to others and violations of strategic privacy which may compromize the victim in the pursuit of his or her interests.

Whilst a lack of *feedback* already causes problems in non-explicitly collaborative computing contexts, it is far more serious for CSCW and CMC. As such systems increasingly support information sharing and communication, it is important for people to understand when they and their information are accessible, when, and to whom. They must also be able to control that access easily and intuitively. Without feedback and appropriate control, even secure systems used by well-meaning work groups will not be trustworthy since it will always be unclear to the individual user who has legitimate access to what (Bellotti & Sellen, 1993).

3 What You Don't Know Can Hurt You

In order to underline the fact that legal and secure systems do not solve the problem of design for privacy, I provide some examples of how common and state-of-the-art CSCW technologies feature inadequate resources for ensuring privacy. In particular, even though many systems are secure, involving only legitimate access and incorporating some access control measures, they still let users down in terms of how privacy is assured:

- *Email: Communication with the wrong person or group.*
  Everyone must be familiar with the reply-to-all problem in email systems, where someone thinks they are replying just to the individual sender but, in fact, they are replying to the entire list of recipients of the message they are replying to. I am probably not the only person who has received email from a friend which was intended to go to someone else and in which, by coincidence, I was the subject matter.

- *Video-Phone: Connecting to the wrong person.*
  Everyone experiences a wrong-number telephone call now and then. This problem can also occur in video mediated communication environments. Fortunately the caller, unlike the email sender, recognizes that the recipient is not whom they expected before they say anything. Email, telephones and videophones share the problem that it is easy to make a mistake in a way which would be unlikely in face-to-face encounters where there are more cues available as to who is being approached or who is likely to receive communicated information.

- *Personal Engagements and Notes: Private information with public access.*
  Many people at Apple use a shared calendar in which public events can be posted under different categories to which others can subscribe. Private notes and events are viewable by the owner only. On one occasion a user 'X' entered an event which was intended to be a private note, but forgot to set the 'private' category and the note was distributed to an entire group using the calendar's default group category. The system's feedback about the public nature of the note X had created was inadequate at the time when it was needed. Even though X saw the note displayed on the calendar later on, the status of the note was not visible. X only discovered that it was being displayed publicly when someone else pointed it out.

- *Dressing and Undressing: Private activity made public.*
Media space[†] users at both Xerox's Palo Alto Research Center (Bly et al., 1993) and Rank Xerox's Cambridge Laboratory (Formerly EuroPARC; (Gaver et al., 1992) have reported various stories in which individuals did not realize or forgot that they were on camera (Dourish et al., in press). There are even examples of people adjusting or removing their clothing in front of the camera (for example, a security guard took off his trousers in front of a camera one evening to sew up a tear). Despite the fact that the people who made these social gaffes knew there was a camera present, they forgot that it was there, or how it worked, or did not appreciate who was connected to it. In one example, a media space veteran 'Y' began changing for sports in front of a camera connected to a colleague's office. Y did so because the colleague had covered their lens as they were also changing for sport. Y had made an erroneous unconscious assumption about reciprocity; "If I can't see you, you can't see me."

- *Misrepresentation: Private activity made public but unintelligible.*
One researcher was 'snapped' in the media space (known as RAVE) at EuroPARC when hugging an unrecognizable person (only visible from the back) by the Portholes system which was used by PARC and EuroPARC to broadcast updated video still images from personal media space nodes to all Portholes users at the two labs. There was considerable speculation as to who the mystery person might be since they strongly resembled someone very well known in Xerox who seemed to be an unlikely candidate for this sort of behaviour.

- *Covertly recording: People recorded while engaged in semi-private behaviour.*
A group of people were exercising within range of a media space camera. One of their colleagues recorded them for amusement. It is likely that many of the people exercising would have been upset if they knew that the recording was made, even though they knew the camera was sending signals continuously to media space nodes around the building.

- *Default recording and processing: Badge applications non-selectively constructing raw data.*
Active badges are wearable devices which can be detected by infra-red sensors hooked up to a computing infrastructure. Badges can direct useful services to their wearers and colleagues (Newman et al., 1991; Harper, 1992; Eldridge et al., 1992; Want et al., 1992). Researchers at EuroPARC wore active badges for a variety of reasons, particularly trying out research applications and to operate a lock which allowed quick entry into the building. A new diary service was offered in which raw data (badge detection events at various sites) was collected and meaningful records of activity were extrapolated (such as X in a meeting with Y in the commons for 30 minutes). One researcher consented to

---

[†] A media space is an AV infrastructure where cameras, monitors, microphones and speakers are set up as special nodes in people's offices enabling them to connect to one another or to cameras in public spaces, or to TV tuners or video players.

try out this service at 3:00pm one afternoon and the next day received a diary which began at 9:00am (6 hours before consent was given). The system was, in fact, extrapolating all badge events, including those of people who had not consented to have service record their movements.

- *Unintentional rejection of access: Failure of newcomers' connections in a media space.*
  The RAVE media space at EuroPARC had an access control setting mechanism for AV connection permissions which were explicitly designed to address users' concerns about privacy (Dourish, 1993). It enabled them to select who could (and could not) make certain kinds of connection to them. While this increased acceptance of the system, it was awkward to manipulate the settings and many users forgot to update their permissions. The result was that when newcomers joined the media space, other people's access settings were such that they would be rejected whenever they tried to connect to them. Some newcomers confronted with this problem assumed that the system was broken and did not mention it to anyone, or when they did, some others also assumed that the system might be at fault.

  This example is different from the others as it shows the other side of the coin of inadequate access control. In this case, legitimate access is unwittingly denied instead of being unwittingly enabled or ongoing. This demonstrates that legitimate access control, whilst often desirable or even essential in CSCW and CMC environments, can be problematic and even obstructive to participation. It must be designed in such a way that people can tell what is really happening when they try to access something or someone. People should also know when they themselves are the target of others' attempts at access. For example, if RAVE users knew that someone was trying to connect to them, but had been rejected, they would probably realize that their access settings needed updating. In fact, information about all current and previous connections to and from one's node is displayed in a window in the RAVE interface, but the information is not easy to see except when one is looking for it.

These examples illustrate a variety of problems with mediated communication and CSCW systems which seem relevant to privacy concerns. Primarily these problems spring from the separation of socially significant activity on-line from actors and separation of information from its owners. When someone does something on-line, they are disembodied (Heath & Luff, 1991; Heath & Luff, 1993) or possibly even dis-associated (Bellotti & Sellen, 1993) from their actions and the results of those actions may not be clearly rendered to the actor or to others. The information the system provides, if any, is diminished or possibly even undetectable.

The result is that people have little way of knowing what the consequences of their actions are in terms of capture and processing by computers and accessibility to others. Sometimes, in media spaces for example, people do not even realize that they are on-line at all! Further, people lack the kind of awareness of the activity of others that is available in physical space, where everyone is embodied and their activity is mostly visible and intelligible.

Thus, on-line collaboration requires that CSCW designers take special measures to design appropriate substitute resources for system users to deal with such issues. ShareMon provides retroactive information about access by others, but with this mechanism, by the time the user finds out about unwanted access it is too late. So, in addition to this, users also require feedback about the current state of affairs in terms of what they are making available to others. ShareMon is a step in the right direction; however, there is far more to be done.

4 Information and Interpersonal Access Control

By now I hope that it is clear that access control, together with appropriate feedback, is important in networked collaborative computing environments. It is needed both to manage one's solitude and to determine what information about oneself and one's work is made available to others. It is not a matter of security (although it demands it), it is a matter of *managing the degree to which secure transactions permit useful access between people and their electronic information.* In computer networks, access tends to be moderated by technical mechanisms which set permissions for users or group members as in the Unix operating system or the Macintosh file sharing mechanism. Such mechanisms are rudimentary compared to those used to manage access in the physical world. This makes them awkward and cumbersome to use and interferes with the sharing and collaboration which is being made possible by high-bandwidth, networked computing and communications technologies.

Much of the concern directed towards protecting people's privacy in distributed and networked computing environments focuses upon access to information (I include raw data, software, personal and impersonal data as classes of information). However, access to individuals themselves also has privacy implications in CSCW and CMC systems. In this section, I outline information access and interpersonal access as two separate issues with somewhat different challenges for technology design. I also provide examples of how recent research in CSCW and CMC has tried to meet some of these design challenges.

4.1 Information Access

Information access implies an action of getting information from somewhere. If the information is from one's own file system, it has few social or privacy implications. However, if it is from some other source it may have anything from limited (as in a shared library) to extreme (as in someone's email folder) social significance. If the action involves obtaining information about a person, this is not interpersonal access unless the individual is dynamically and knowingly involved in giving out that information. Thus, for the purposes of access control, I define a one-way video connection (with no feedback to the site from which video is being sent) as information rather than interpersonal access.

4.1.1 Design Challenges

Different Types of Access to be Controlled: Non-explicitly collaborative systems already support different kinds of information access, typically read and write (and possibly execute as in the Unix operating system) and the owner of the files containing the information can set permissions independently for each file or directory. Designers of flexible CSCW systems, may need to make further distinctions between access such as copy, edit, delete and annotate.

Static Control and Other types of Control: Information access control mechanisms in most existing systems are generally *static*. This means that the controller of the information makes decisions about access permissions at some time independent of the time at which another would-be user attempts access. If people are not given useful feedback about these settings they tend to ignore inappropriate access settings or allow settings to become out-of-date. In this way, static control risks becoming obstructive to collaboration or detrimental to privacy.

Control need not be just a static choice between locking an object or making it freely available. Information controllers may wish to allow access so long as they are notified. Designers might also provide support for negotiated access where an element of dynamism is introduced such that the information controller can receive a request and decide at the time of the request for access (or perhaps at a later time) whether or not to allow it.

Control by Whom: Information access on-line can easily be controlled by people other than its creators. System administrators, for example, may require special access, or take steps to protect other users from unwanted access. First authors in a team of writers collaborating on a paper using a shared editing tool, may wish to exercise editorial control over the rights of other authors to change their own, or each other's text.

Ellis et al. (1991) discuss *system object locking* in groupware for the purpose of concurrency control (to prevent one user's actions in real-time from conflicting with another's). They claim that this kind of default, system locking, is "not only inappropriate for groupware but can actually hinder tightly coupled teamwork". Designers must ensure that control belongs to users and is always flexible enough to support a range of work styles.

Control in Relation to Whom: Information controllers may allow other individuals or software agents different access rights. Further, they may wish to define groups or classes of individuals or agents for which access rights may be collectively set.

Different kinds of Information: Control over access is generally exercised independently in relation to directories and files of information in many operating systems, but it may also be necessary to allow independent control over programs, instructions, arrays, fields, streams of data (e.g. a video signal) and devices (e.g. video cameras). It may also be useful to allow independent access control over different *parts* of an information object.

Identification of users: It is possible to discriminate between information users on the basis of ID (or possibly the IP address of the host machine they use or the router through which they try to obtain access). Whilst interpersonal communications can rely upon the recipient recognizing that the caller is who they claim to be and deciding whether it is appropriate to give out information, in the case of information access, authentication is often necessary to verify the identity of a would-be user.

Feedback: Being able to distinguish between and independently control different kinds of information access to many data sources means that users cannot be expected to remember what their current access control settings are. For example, file-sharing is something which people often forget to set appropriately for the workgroups they collaborate with. As a result, many people (generally unwittingly) make everything public or else they prefer to make most, if not all, of their directories private. Furthermore, it may be the case that, in some settings, another person, or agent, has access control over information one produces. For these reasons, feedback about access control status is extremely important.

Awareness, Accountability and Social Control: This is possibly the most radical challenge to CSCW systems developers. Flexible information access on-line requires that users are not locked out of the things they need access to, which is frequently what results from technical access control mechanisms. Consider a physical world situation in which someone goes through someone else's wallet and their diary; let us assume the owner of the wallet or diary is seriously ill from a drug overdose and some useful information might be found this way to help treat them. It is perfectly acceptable for people to access even very personal information about others, as long as they can give a reasonable account of their behaviour. People are discouraged from illegitimate access when their actions are detectable by others who might censure their behaviour and in this way their behaviour is subject to *social control.*

This, however, will be hard to manage with any degree of confidence unless people, even those one collaborates with, are made *accountable* for their activities on-line in the way that they are in real space. Since people's activity is not inherently visible or intelligible on-line, systems need to be designed to provide *awareness* information about activity of others (Dourish & Bellotti, 1992) which might have implications for privacy. Naturally, awareness information must be carefully designed such that it does not unnecessarily intrude upon the privacy of the individuals whose actions are made visible.

4.1.2 Information Access Control in CSCW

In this section I outline some systems and researchers' recommendations which have begun to meet some of the design challenges for information access control in CSCW systems where information sharing is important, but needs to be regulated to avoid conflicts or privacy problems.

The 'PREP' co-authoring tool (Neuwirth et al., 1990; 1992) offers notified access control to allow co-authors to modify each others' work. PREP also offers users the ability to control access to different parts of a document, which is organized into different types of linked hypertext nodes (called chunks). This means that users might, for example, offer clients access to a proposal document, while withholding access to the budget sections. Shen & Dewan (1992) provide extremely sophisticated access control of shared information for collaborative authoring in their 'Suite' system. Suite defines over 50 different kinds of access over which rights can be varied, such as applying colour, or font changes to content and sharing value changes to content. It also defines inheritance of access rights (for example colour and font access can be inherited from the more general format access). Access rights can also be inherited from classes of users or objects. The definition of different roles for users allows a complex set of access rights to be inferred automatically, however, users are able to fine tune access rights dynamically throughout interaction with the Suite system.

The main problem with Suite is it is unclear how users might deal with the complexity of their access settings. It is also unclear whether this sophistication is justified at the risk of problems giving appropriate feedback and probable user confusion. The authors claim that Suite is an attempt at a simple interface to a complex specification problem but they do not report any user evaluations. It is not clear whether and in what contexts such a sophisticated system might prove worthwhile.

A possible approach to dealing with the complexity of information sharing and access control mechanisms is proposed by Hennessy (1991). She defines the concept of an information domain that reflects existing group structures activities and argues for flexible creation and redefinition of information spaces, roles and corresponding access rights. The idea of a 'project space' as a context for particular shared objects accessible to particular groups of users exploits the natural tendency of people to partition different kinds of work associated with different practices into different spaces. As to how the requisite flexibility that will enable people to create and modify objects, domains and roles should be realized, Hennessy argues, "Whatever mechanism is chosen, it ought to be transparent to the end user".

As mentioned earlier, ShareMon (Cohen, 1993) provides awareness information which can support privacy. Whilst users have no direct feedback about their current information access (file sharing) settings, they get to find out about the consequences of those settings from ShareMon. Other identified users, knowing that their actions are visible to ShareMon users are unlikely to engage in antisocial activity against or invasions of the privacy of those users.

Similarly, Ackerman & Starr (1995) describe a CSCW toolkit, CafeCK, which is capable of generating a range of classes of UI elements called social indicators which display recent or ongoing activity of users (who may not be explicitly working together) in a collaborative system setting. CafeCK presents these social activity indicators as a means of making behaviour more visible. Whilst the aim is not explicitly to moderate access and to control privacy, it is easy to see how such activity indicators could be developed to support social, rather than technical control over information access. An augmented ShareMon or CafeCK might also provide information about unsuccessful attempts at access that could alert people to the need to make something shareable when it is not already.

4.2 Interpersonal Access

I take interpersonal access to mean a social encounter whereby two or more individuals dynamically orient to one another. This need not imply, however, that they engage one another in a focused social exchange. Two people passing in the street, for example, have a weak form of interpersonal access, such that they each make special consideration for the other. This may cause them to allow each other enough space to pass and to avert their gaze. In terms of its implications for privacy, interpersonal access can involve intrusion into someone's solitude, demands on their time and requests for information.

Strongly tied to the notion of interpersonal access is that of *availability*. I use the term availability as a distinct concept from accessibility in the context of CSCW and CMC. It is not the same as accessibility, but is a much more useful term to describe how social engagements are managed. In face-to-face encounters, people are intuitively able to present and recognize signals as to how willing they are to accept a social overture (Goffman, 1963).

4.2.1 Design Challenges

Interpersonal access is implicitly reciprocal by the above definition, involving a mutual orientation of attention between two or more people. Interpersonal access control therefore has some distinct differences in its challenges for designers from those of information access:

Reciprocity: A Defining Characteristic of interpersonal Access: In CMC systems an interpersonal encounter (we'll call this a connection) has to be designed. There is no inherent WISYYSM (When I See [or Hear] You, You See [or Hear] Me) rule built into CMC as there tends to be in the physical world. Whether one designs connections of all kinds to be two-way, or simply provides some proxy feedback about virtual presence when one person connects to another, designers must abide by the rule of reciprocity such that those accessed know that they are accessed (and preferably by whom). If reciprocity is not provided then access is not interpersonal and must be considered to be information access.

Different Types of Access to be Controlled: In the current design of common CMC technologies, such as video-conferencing, there is generally only one kind of access; a two-way connection of indefinite duration.[‡] This limits the potential for interpersonal awareness and communication and particularly for access control. There may be good reasons for designers to provide one-way connections with appropriate feedback to the recipient (such as when one person is using screen space for something else) or low bandwidth exchanges of AV or other information to support mutual awareness (see below).

Availability: People unlike information, require solitude from time to time, they may be more or less prepared for a social encounter and they have an inherent ability to present and interpret social cues as to their current availability. Whilst

[‡] There are alternative kinds of communication system where different kinds of connection are possible. For example, the use of cameras for one-way continuous video surveillance in companies and on private property is becoming extremely common. One-way, indefinite duration, telephone monitoring is used to check quality of service. I do not include these examples here as they do not include a model of legitimate access control.

designers can build features into systems to permit people to reject attempted calls by others, they might also offer a means by which availability can be displayed to others who can then reserve attempts at connections to times when the intended recipient is available.

Note that interpersonal access is inherently subject to social control. Goffman (1963, p.106) speaks of the fact that people's:

> "right to initiate contact is checked by their duty to take [another person's] point of view and initiate contact with him [or her] only under circumstances which he [or she] will easily see as justified."

This is as true for CMC as it is for the physical encounters of which Goffman speaks:

Static and Dynamic Control: People, unlike information, make dynamic decisions about how available they are, whether they wish to exchange information with others and what information they choose to offer. So, for example, the 'ringing' tone of a telephone or video-conferencing call gives the call recipient the opportunity decide on-the-spot if they want a social exchange or to ignore the call if they choose.

Static and dynamic control are each useful for different purposes, but it is interesting to note that dynamic control is not commonly available for information access in existing systems because information owners cannot usually see or respond to others' attempts at access. On the other hand, we are beginning to see communications system features which provide static interpersonal access control in terms of the ways in which some people use answering machine services and also in the development of call screening technologies. People using CSCW and CMC systems who are much more visible to one another may also need static control to be certain of uninterrupted solitude or to engage in private activity at certain times.

Control in Relation to Whom: As with information access, people may allow other individuals different interpersonal access rights. They may also wish to define groups or classes of individuals for which access rights can be set collectively.

Identification: Mechanisms which offer caller ID enable some discriminatory control by connection recipients prior to access. The recipient can decide whether to allow access, based upon their willingness to communicate with certain callers but not others. Unlike on-line information, humans, once they are accessed interpersonally, may recognize a caller or decide that they are legitimate, even if unfamiliar. A connection recipient can decide dynamically and strategically during a connection whether to give out any requested information.

Feedback: The same issues of feedback for information access apply to interpersonal access. People cannot be expected to remember complicated access settings and therefore need feedback about their current status and also about failed attempts at access by others. The RAVE media space example of unintentional rejection in Section 3 illustrates this point.

Mutual Awareness: In the physical world, two people passing in a corridor may, in some circumstances, greet one another and even start a conversation about something of mutual concern. In CMC environments, this kind of serendipitous capability could usefully be supported through the design of appropriate resources. For example, video-conferencing does not currently allow for lightweight, transient connections or general awareness of other people's activity outside of those connections. How then, are remote collaborators to know when others are doing something about which interpersonal communication might be pertinent? For interpersonal communication, designers can provide opportunities for such spontaneous informal encounters but must do so without compromising privacy.

4.2.2 Interpersonal Access Control in CMC

In this section I consider systems and researchers' recommendations which have begun to meet some of the design challenges for wider and more flexible interpersonal access in CMC whilst paying attention to collaborators needs for privacy. The reader should note that all of the systems described here are media spaces where cameras (and perhaps microphones) are on continuously affording a greater range of possible connection services, but demanding more flexible and careful access control than do traditional video-conferencing systems.

The RAVE media space at EuroPARC is an AV infrastructure in which AV nodes in offices are connected to analogue AV switching devices which allow people to make several types of connection from their desktop workstation (Gaver et al., 1992). Interpersonal connections include a glance — a short one-way, video only connection; a vphone — an open ended, two-way AV connection; and an office-share — a long term, two-way, AV connection. There is also a background connection which is available to public areas with a camera in them.[§]

Unwanted access in this system is controlled by mechanisms far more sophisticated than those available for a standard video-conferencing system. As mentioned in Section 3, to preserve a sense of privacy and trust in RAVE, if users do not specify otherwise, the system defaults to a rejection of any kind of incoming connection from any other user but fails to provide sufficient feedback about this behaviour.

At their personal nodes in their offices users can exercise the same kind of dynamic control for a vphone connection as one can with a video-conferencing call, but with the added advantage of seeing the name (not just the number) of who is calling. Furthermore, they can exercise independent static access control over each connection in terms of who they will allow to make it. Audio cues can also be requested to warn of impending glance connections (a non-speech signal, either a knocking or opening door sound) and who is making them (a speech signal saying the name of the caller). In this way control over glance connections (which is more like information access if the recipient does not get to see or hear the caller) is also socially manageable since people are identifiable to the recipient and thus accountable for making them. In this way those making connections are deterred from making a nuisance of themselves unless they can give a good account of their behaviour.

[§]This provides one-way video access, but there is no reciprocal video signal being sent to the public space to show who is looking which makes this video information access rather than interpersonal access.

The office share connection has no acceptance protocol like that of the vphone, nor does it have any alerting audio cues associated with it like the glance connection. The reason for this is that office shares are a service offered for long term arrangements made between the participants. Permissions for these are rarely granted and once given, the connections can last for days, weeks or even years (Dourish et al., in press).

The display of availability as an alternative to technical interpersonal access control mechanisms in CMC systems is illustrated by the Portholes system (Dourish & Bly, 1992) where low resolution frame-grabbed video images of media space users are taken from their office cameras and updated every few minutes in a window on screen. Users of Portholes are able to tell if other users are on the phone, in a discussion with someone, or working alone and can make informed judgements about how available they are for communication.

The CAVECAT media space (Mantei et al., 1991) models availability in the form of four different levels, depicted by four selectable door states (open, ajar, closed and locked). Once selected these are displayed above each media space users' name in a window which is the interface to this media space. Here every user's current availability is displayed and the user can select AV connections to any one of them by clicking on either a glance or connect button positioned beneath each user's door. However, in this case availability is confounded with accessibility since selecting a door state determines which connection buttons are displayed to others. When the user selects an open door both glance and connect buttons are displayed beneath their door icon. When they select an ajar door, only connect is displayed and so on.

Notice that in this system, the static control mechanism offered is easier to use in a dynamic fashion than RAVE's mechanism. CAVECAT users can quickly make themselves very accessible, or completely inaccessible, just by clicking one button. On the other hand, only RAVE users are able to choose who in particular they want to have connect to them.

Tang et al. (1994) describe Montage, a media space with no static access control. Nor is there an explicit acceptance protocol for dynamic acceptance or rejection of calls like RAVE's vphone. Instead they base access control around a model of informal access to offices along a corridor. When a user connects to another user, they select a glance connection and then a name from a menu. A two-way video-only connection is established with a small video window on each person's screen. After this, the connection lasts for about 8 seconds before fading away. At any time during the connection either party can press an audio button to begin two-way audio and establish a connection of indefinite duration. Either party can also select a visit button that enlarges the video windows through which they view each other.

Privacy and access control in this system are afforded by having video connections fade in gradually allowing recipients to compose themselves and by making the initial connection period into an explicit phase wherein the caller gauges the availability of the other as one might by popping one's head around an office door. If the recipient seems to be unavailable, the caller discreetly fades away.

Smith & Hudson (1995) describe the use of specially processed speech signals as an indication of ongoing activity in a media space whilst distorting the voices so that what is being said is unintelligible. This technique allows collaborators in a media space to gain some mutual awareness of the ongoing conversations amongst other users which they might not wish to interrupt or might like to request to join in, whilst preserving the privacy of the conversants.

In a similar vein to Hennessy (1991) in Section 4.1.2, Clement & Wagner (1995) highlight the necessity for designers to consider how collaborators often need or wish to maintain separation from each other in the course of their work. In reference to both information access and interpersonal access, they assert, "there should be technical facilities for allowing participants to erect, shift, blur, harden, dissolve and strengthen the boundaries to communication spaces". Like other researchers, they emphasize the need for flexibility of access control in CMC and CSCW systems. Clement & Wagner also make it clear that systems which disrupt existing boundaries, by making people and their work more accessible to one another and by permitting new boundaries to be constructed, often need to be evaluated in practice over time before their ultimate success can be determined. This was certainly true of RAVE (Bellotti & Dourish, in press).

5 Some Concluding Remarks

In this paper I have defined a number of challenges for CSCW designers to ensure that privacy is not invaded when users have increased access to one another and share more information. I have also provided some examples of how recent CSCW and CMC systems designers have begun to meet some of these challenges. I wish to conclude by making some final points which I believe designers of CSCW technology should bear in mind.

Firstly, I believe that, in the domain of design for privacy and access control there is a great deal to learn from the physical world in which we interact with others. Sociologists such as Goffman and Giddens have much to say that is worth attending to in the design of systems which are intended to support social interaction and collaboration — e.g. (Goffman, 1963; Giddens, 1990). The notion of social control, in particular, draws upon lessons learned from sensitivity to the ways in which people intuitively interact with one another in face-to-face settings. Furthermore, studies of interactions and behaviour in physical and computer-mediated settings, such as those reported by Clement & Wagner (1995), are necessary before and after the installation of potentially intrusive technology into work or other contexts. Indeed, it may be that the very manner in which new technology is implemented can affect how people feel about their privacy — e.g. (Dourish, 1993).

Secondly, I want to emphasize my earlier distinction between normative and operational definitions of privacy. A normative definition of privacy presupposes, incorrectly as it turns out, that some kinds of information and some aspects of behaviour are inherently private or not to be shared. Designers who build rigidity into systems, for example, by enforcing roles for collaborators (Sandhu et al., 1996) or by having fixed private or public spaces (even if these are based upon observations), may well be creating obstacles to collaboration which may only emerge over time as people come to trust their system or to try to adapt it to new uses. Uses of innovative CSCW and CMC systems tend to evolve over time — e.g. (Bellotti &

Dourish, in press). Therefore designers should provide, not fixed roles or private and public spaces, but *the capability for users to define such things at will.*

Thirdly, the notion of social control as an alternative to technical control is one which may raise some concerns about risks of exposure of sensitive information, perhaps through unintentional access. For example, we are probably all familiar with the immense feeling of embarrassment that occurs when someone, perhaps a friend and perhaps not, reveals some excruciating intimate detail about us which we would rather were kept a secret. Social control is inherently risky and it is thus a question of making a trade-off between the risks involved and the potential obstacles imposed if we resort to technical control and locking mechanisms. Naturally there will be some cases where only technical control will do (for example, if one wants to protect very personal email), but technical control should not be the preferred default mechanism in collaborative environments amongst trusted colleagues.

Finally, I hope that my arguments have succeeded in broadening readers' views about design to support privacy which has, so far, largely been restricted to technical aspects of system security and legal aspects of what is permissible. Privacy is a key design consideration and measures taken to deal with it appropriately can also improve the flexibility with which people achieve wider communication, mutual awareness and closer collaboration in CSCW systems.

Acknowledgements

I would like to thank the following people for their support in the preparation of this paper: Phil Agre, Paul Dourish, Bill Gaver, Lorin Hawley, Scott Minneman, Yvonne Rogers, Heiko Sacher, Rohan Samarajiva, Bill Walker and last, but not least, Blake Ward.

References

Ackerman, M. & Starr, B. (1995), Social Activity Indicators: Interface Components for CSCW Systems, *in* G. Robinson (ed.), "Proceedings of the ACM Symposium on User Interface Software and Technology, UIST'95", ACM Press, pp.159–168.

Agre, P. & Rotenberg, M. (eds.) (in press), *Technology and Privacy: The New Landscape*, MIT Press.

Bellotti, V. & Dourish, P. (in press), Rant and RAVE: Experimental and Experiential Accounts of a Media Space, *in* K. Finn, A. Sellen & S. Wilbur (eds.), "Video-mediated Communication", Lawrence Erlbaum Associates.

Bellotti, V. & Sellen, A. (1993), Design for Privacy in Ubiquitous Computing Environments, *in* G. de Michelis, C. Simone & K. Schmidt (eds.), "Proceedings of ECSCW'93, the 3rd European Conference on Computer-Supported Cooperative Work", Kluwer (Academic Press), pp.77–92.

Bly, S., Harrison, S. & Irwin, S. (1993), "Media Spaces: Bringing People Together in a Video, Audio and Computing Environment", *Communications of the ACM* **36**(1), 28–47.

Bowyer, K. (1996), *Ethics and Computing: Living Responsibly in a Computerized World*, IEEE Computer Society Press.

Clarke, R. (1988), "Information Technology and Dataveillance", *Communications of the ACM* **31**(5), 498–512.

Clement, A. (1994), "Considering Privacy in the Development of Multi-Media Communications", *Computer Supported Cooperative Work* **2**(1/2), 67–88.

Clement, A. & Wagner, I. (1995), Fragmented Exchange: Disarticulation and the Need for Regionalized Communication Spaces, *in* H. Marmolin, Y. Sundblad & K. Schmidt (eds.), "Proceedings of ECSCW'95, the 4th European Conference on Computer-Supported Cooperative Work", Kluwer (Academic Press), pp.33–49.

Cohen, J. (1993), 'Kirk Here:' Using Genre Sounds to Monitor Background Activity, *in* S. Ashlund, K. Mullet, A. Henderson, E. Hollnagel & T. White (eds.), "Proceedings of INTERCHI'93", ACM Press, pp.63–64.

Denning, D. & Branstad, D. (1996), "A Taxonomy for Key Escrow Encryption Systems", *Communications of the ACM* **39**(3), 34–40.

Donath, J. (1995), Visual Who: Animating the Affinities and Activities of an Electronic Community, *in* "Proceedings of Multimedia'95", ACM Press, pp.99–107.

Dourish, P. (1993), Culture and Control in a Media Space, *in* G. de Michelis, C. Simone & K. Schmidt (eds.), "Proceedings of ECSCW'93, the 3rd European Conference on Computer-Supported Cooperative Work", Kluwer (Academic Press), pp.125–137.

Dourish, P. & Bellotti, V. (1992), Awareness and Coordination in Shared Workspaces, *in* J. Turner & R. Kraut (eds.), "Proceedings of CSCW'92: Conference on Computer Supported Cooperative Work", ACM Press, pp.107–114.

Dourish, P. & Bly, S. (1992), Portholes: Supporting Awareness in Distributed Work Groups, *in* P. Bauersfeld, J. Bennett & G. Lynch (eds.), "Proceedings of CHI'92: Human Factors in Computing Systems", ACM Press, pp.541–547.

Dourish, P., Adler, A., Bellotti, V. & Henderson, A. (in press), "Your Place or Mine? Learning from Long-term Use of Video Communication", *Computer Supported Cooperative Work*.

Dunlop, C. & Kling, R. (eds.) (1991), *Computerization and Controversy: Value Conflicts and Social Choices*, Academic Press.

Eldridge, M., Lamming, M. & Flynn, M. (1992), Does a Video Diary Help Recall?, *in* A. Monk, D. Diaper & M. Harrison (eds.), "People and Computers VII (Proceedings of HCI'92)", Cambridge University Press, pp.257–269.

Ellis, S., Gibbs, S. & Rein, G. (1991), "Groupware: Some Issues and Experiences", *Communications of the ACM* **34**(1), 39–58.

Forester, T. & Morrison, P. (1990), *Computer Ethics*, MIT Press.

Gaver, W., Moran, T., MacLean, A., Lövstrand, L., Dourish, P., Carter, K. & Buxton, W. (1992), Realizing a Video Environment: EuroPARC's RAVE System, *in* P. Bauersfeld, J. Bennett & G. Lynch (eds.), "Proceedings of CHI'92: Human Factors in Computing Systems", ACM Press, pp.27–35.

Giddens, A. (1990), *The Consequences of Modernity*, Stanford University Press.

Goffman, E. (1963), *Behaviour in Public Places*, Free Press.

Greenhalgh, C. & Benford, S. (1995), Virtual Reality Tele-conferencing: Implementation and Experience, *in* H. Marmolin, Y. Sundblad & K. Schmidt (eds.), "Proceedings of ECSCW'95, the 4th European Conference on Computer-Supported Cooperative Work", Kluwer (Academic Press), pp.165–180.

Harper, R. (1992), Looking at Ourselves: An Examination of the Social Organization of Two Research Laboratories, *in* J. Turner & R. Kraut (eds.), "Proceedings of CSCW'92: Conference on Computer Supported Cooperative Work", ACM Press, pp.330–337.

Heath, C. & Luff, P. (1991), Disembodied Conduct: Communication through Video in a Multi-Media Office Environment, *in* S. P. Robertson, G. M. Olson & J. S. Olson (eds.), "Proceedings of CHI'91: Human Factors in Computing Systems (Reaching through Technology)", ACM Press, pp.99–103.

Heath, C. & Luff, P. (1993), Disembodied Conduct: Interactional Asymmetries in Video-mediated Communication, *in* G. Button (ed.), "Technology in Working Order", Routledge, pp.35–54.

Hennessy, P. (1991), Information Domains in CSCW, *in* J. Bowers & S. Benford (eds.), "Studies in Computer Supported Cooperative Work", Elsevier Science, pp.299–311.

Herring, T. (1996), "The Global Positioning System", *Scientific American* **274**(2), 44–50.

Hindus, D. & Schmandt, C. (1992), Ubiquitous Audio: Capturing Spontaneous Collaboration, *in* J. Turner & R. Kraut (eds.), "Proceedings of CSCW'92: Conference on Computer Supported Cooperative Work", ACM Press, pp.210–217.

Ishii, H. & Kobayashi, M. (1992), ClearBoard: A Seamless Medium for Shared Drawing and Conversation With Eye Contact, *in* P. Bauersfeld, J. Bennett & G. Lynch (eds.), "Proceedings of CHI'92: Human Factors in Computing Systems", ACM Press, pp.525–532.

Mantei, M., Becker, R., Sellen, A., Buxton, W., Milligan, T. & Wellman, B. (1991), Experiences in the Use of a Media Space, *in* S. P. Robertson, G. M. Olson & J. S. Olson (eds.), "Proceedings of CHI'91: Human Factors in Computing Systems (Reaching through Technology)", ACM Press, pp.203–208.

McClurg, A. (1995), "Bringing Privacy Law Out of the Closet: A Tort Theory of Liability for Intrusions in Public Places", *North Carolina Law Review* **73**(3), 989–1088.

Milberg, S., Burke, S., Smith, H. & Kallman, E. (1995), "Values, Personal Information, Privacy and Regulatory Approaches", *Communications of the ACM* **38**(12), 65–74.

Minneman, S., Harrison, S., Jansson, W., Kurtenbach, G., Moran, T., Smith, I. & van Melle, W. (1995), A Confederation of Tools for Capturing and Accessing Collaborative Activity, *in* "Proceedings of Multimedia'95", ACM Press, pp.523–534.

Mullender, S. (1989), Protection, *in* S. Mullender (ed.), "Distributed Systems", ACM Press, pp.117–132.

Neumann, P. (1995), *Computer Related Risks*, Addison–Wesley.

Neuwirth, C., Chandok, R., Kaufer, D., Erion, P., Morris, J. & Miller, D. (1992), Flexible Diff-ing in a Collaborative Writing System, *in* J. Turner & R. Kraut (eds.), "Proceedings of CSCW'92: Conference on Computer Supported Cooperative Work", ACM Press, pp.147–154.

Neuwirth, C., Kaufer, D., Chandhok, R. & Morris, J. (1990), Issues in the Design of Computer Support for Co-authoring and Commenting, *in* D. G. Tatar (ed.), "Proceedings of CSCW'90: Conference on Computer Supported Cooperative Work", ACM Press, pp.183–196.

Newman, W., Eldridge, M. & Lamming, M. (1991), PEPYS: Generating Autobiographies by Automatic Tracking, *in* M. Robinson, L. Bannon & K. Schmidt (eds.), "Proceedings of ECSCW'91, the 2nd European Conference on Computer-Supported Cooperative Work", Kluwer (Academic Press), pp.75–188.

Pentland, A. (1996), "Smart Rooms", *Scientific American* **274**(4), 68–76.

Privacy Protection Study Commission (1991), Excerpts from Personal Privacy in an Information Society, *in* Dunlop & Kling (1991), pp.453–468.

Reidenberg, J. (1992), "Privacy in the Information Economy: A Fortress or Frontier for Individual Rights?", *Federal Communications Law Journal* **44**(2), 195–243.

Reiman, J. (1995), "Driving to the Panopticon: A Philosophical Exploration of the Risks to Privacy Posed by the Highway Technology of the Future", *Santa Clara Computer and High Technology Law Journal* **11**(1), 27–44.

Rule, J. (1980), *The Politics of Privacy: Planning for Data Systems as Powerful Technologies*, Elsevier Science.

Samarajiva, R. (in press), Interactivity as Though Privacy Mattered, *in* Agre & Rotenberg (in press).

Sandhu, S., Coyne, E., Feinstein, H. & Youman, C. (1996), "Role-based Access Control Models", *IEEE Computer* **29**(2), 38–47.

Shen, H. & Dewan, P. (1992), Access Control for Collaborative Environments, *in* J. Turner & R. Kraut (eds.), "Proceedings of CSCW'92: Conference on Computer Supported Cooperative Work", ACM Press, pp.51–58.

Smith, I. & Hudson, S. (1995), Low Disturbance Audio for Awareness and Privacy in Media Space Applications, *in* "Proceedings of Multimedia'95", ACM Press, pp.91–97.

Stone, E., Gardner, D., Gueutal, H. & McClure, S. (1983), "A Field Experiment Comparing Information-Privacy Values, Beliefs and Attitudes Across Several Types of Organizations", *Journal of Applied Psychology* **68**(3), 459–468.

Tang, J., Isaacs, E. & Rua, M. (1994), Supporting Distributed Groups With a Montage of Lightweight Interactions, *in* R. Furuta & C. Neuwirth (eds.), "Proceedings of CSCW'94: Conference on Computer Supported Cooperative Work", ACM Press, pp.13–34.

Vetter, R. (1995), "ATM Concepts, Architectures and Protocols", *Communications of the ACM* **38**(2), 30–38.

Want, R., Hopper, A., Falcao, V. & Gibbons, J. (1992), "The Active Badge Location System", *ACM Transactions on Office Information Systems* **10**(1), 91–102.

Weisband, S. & Reinig, B. (1995), "Managing User Perceptions of Email Privacy", *Communications of the ACM* **38**(12), 40–47.

Weiser, M. (1991), "The Computer for the 21st Century", *Scientific American* **265**(3), 94–104.

Wilcox, L., Kimber, D. & Chen, F. (1994), Audio Indexing using Speaker Identification in Automatic Systems for the Identification and Inspection of Humans, *in* "Proceedings of the International Society for Optical Engineering SPIE 2277", IEEE, pp.149–157.

Zhang, H., Low, C., Smoliar, S. & Wu, J. (1995), Video Parsing, Retrieval and Browsing: An Integrated and Content-based Solution, *in* "Proceedings of Multimedia'95", ACM Press, pp.15–24.

Computer-Supported Cooperative Work

Behavioural Patterns of Collaborative Writing with Hypertext — A State Transition Approach

Chaomei Chen

Department of Computer Studies, Glasgow Caledonian University, Glasgow G4 0BA, UK.

Tel: *+44 141 331 3288*
Fax: *+44 141 331 3277*
EMail: *C.Chen@gcal.ac.uk*

This study investigates behavioural patterns of collaborative writing with a hypertext system by using a state-transition approach. State-transition models are empirically developed for capturing the dynamic nature of collaborative writing. Users were frequently engaged in tasks such as exploration, organization, and editing, whereas the use of collaborative support functions was transient in nature. The study shows that state-transition analysis is an important approach to task analysis, requirements engineering, and human-computer interaction studies. This study has produced some valuable experiences and lessons for researchers and practitioners in collaborative writing.

Keywords: collaborative writing, user models, Markov analysis, task analysis, hypertext.

1 Introduction

Collaborative writing presents a significant challenge to the design and use of information technologies that support group work (Kraut et al., 1992). Collaborative writing involves a wide range of tasks and activities. The nature of collaborative writing with computer systems is yet to be fully understood (Sharples et al., 1993). It is important for designers and users to understand the process of computer supported collaborative writing and how the organization of the work is affected.

Sequential data analytic techniques have been used to build descriptive and predictive models in task analysis and protocol analysis (Cooke et al., in press). These models represent the flow of interactive events between users and computer systems. These models provide valuable means of software engineers to identify weaknesses in systems design, to suggest design alternatives, and to allow a variety of comparisons across different groups of users and even different systems.

Task analysis of using hypertext-based systems has been recognized as one of the most important challenging issues in HCI and CSCW (Nielsen, 1989; Chen & Rada, 1996). With a suitably grain-sized state space, state-transition modelling approach used in this study can be a useful tool of building a task taxonomy.

In many collaborative writing systems, knowledge is represented and organized in a shared, hypertext-based workspace. The shared workspace serves as an essential medium of sense making and mutual understanding among co-authors (Chen & Rada, 1995; Whittaker et al., 1993). Co-authors may communicate with each other through the shared workspace as well as communicate directly (Miles et al., 1993).

In this study, we investigate behavioural patterns of a group of users working with a such shared workspace for collaborative writing. We expect that these patterns can lead us to a clearer understanding of collaborative writing. In particular, do experienced users have different patterns from inexperienced users? How do they differ? Are these behavioural patterns affected by the organization of knowledge in such workspaces? The work is significant in that it addresses methodological issues of research in collaborative writing as well as issues concerning the design of a collaborative writing system. The work adapts state-transition analytic techniques to the area of collaborative writing and the work itself may provide useful experience for researchers in CSCW and highlight important aspects to be further studied in the future.

1.1 Collaborative Writing

Computer support for collaborative writing is in its formative stage of design and evaluation. Irish & Trigg (1989) identified three levels of interaction among co-authors with a hypertext system as procedural, annotational, and substantive. Kraut et al. (1992) characterized the dynamics of collaborative writing in terms of tool-selecting behaviour as co-authors respond to a changing situation.

Writing Environment (WE) is a hypertext-based system for writing technical and scientific documents (Smith et al., 1987). The system was based on a cognitive theory of writing, which conceptualizes writing as a sequence of cognitive modes engaged by a writer (Smith et al., 1993). A writer may engage in a mode of exploring ideas, organizing concepts, drafting, or revising drafts. The strategy of the writer is reflected by the sequence of modes that the writer uses. The WE system provides four system modes to support six cognitive modes. For example, exploratory thinking is supported in a *network* mode of the system and organizational thinking is supported in a tree mode. SEPIA is another example of hypertext-based co-authoring system which is based on a cognitive model of writing (Haake & Wilson, 1992). However, little has been available in the literature regarding the experiences of its users or empirical studies with the system.

Neuwirth et al. (1990) suggested that merely providing users with a shared hypermedia may not be adequate for users to organize their collaborative writing.

Neuwirth et al. (1994) defined several parameters of interaction for document reviewing. They noted that collaborative technologies increasingly relax the boundaries of who, where, when, and what information will flow across a shared workspace. They emphasized the role of a flexible environment in which these parameters of interaction can be observed and configured. They are building descriptive models based on these parameters to represent some aspects of the flow of collaborative writing and to experiment with different approaches in different writing groups.

Olson et al. (1993) compared groups of designers using *ShrEdit*, a shared editor, with groups who worked with conventional whiteboard, paper, and pencil. Their study suggested that a shared workspace may help the convergence of collaboration in a small group. Olson et al. (1994) characterized the sequential structure of interactive behaviours through statistical and grammatical techniques.

1.2 The MUCH System

The MUCH system supports collaborative authoring of scientific papers, allows knowledge sharing and reuse, and streamlines electronic publishing. A series of versions of the MUCH system have been implemented on Hewlett Packard UNIX graphical workstations. The latest one was developed with Andrew Development Toolkit (ATK). The most significant difference between the latest version of the MUCH system and previous versions is that the Andrew version supports a What-You-See-Is-What-You-Get (WYSIWYG) multimedia editor. Chen et al. (1994) developed a model of collaborative writing with the MUCH system. Readers are referred to else where for detailed account of the MUCH system (Zheng & Rada, 1994).

The user interface of the MUCH system consists of an outline window and a node content window. The Outline Window displays an outline of the hypertext, which is generated by the traversal algorithm. The Display Window shows the content of the focal node selected from within the Outline Window. The MUCH system provides a set of functions through its user interface for various tasks, such as manipulating the underlying semantic-network and editing the contents of nodes. These functions form a framework for users to interact with the collaborative hypertext. Some basic functions of the MUCH are as follows:

- *Unfold*: To expand the existing hierarchical view from a node entry in one-step forward breadth-first traversal. All the nodes associated with the focal node are added to the view.
- *Read*: To load and display the content of a node which has an entry in the existing hierarchical view.
- *Lock*: To lock the content of the focal node for editing, but concurrent users still can read the content with Read function.
- *Info*: To display evolutionary information regarding the currently visited node.
- *Update*: To save changes since the last Update or since the latest Lock a nd to release the updated content to the update manager in the server, which will subsequently update the screens of all the concurrent users who are on the same node.

The selection credit of a node is to reflect the degree of interests shown to the node. Previous experiences with student users show that they had attempted to make the heading of a node distinguished in the hierarchical view in order to attract more visitors to their nodes and achieve a high score of the selection credit.

2 Dynamic User Modelling

Exploratory sequential data analysis (ESDA) is a rapid advancing collection of observational methods in human-computer interaction (Sanderson & Fisher, 1994). These methods include task analysis, protocol analysis, process tracing, and interaction analysis.

2.1 Sequential Data Analysis

Sequential data of user behaviour can be automatically captured as users interact with a computer system. Previous studies in interactive information systems have used this type of data substantially (Qiu, 1993; Marchionini, 1989; Chapman, 1981; Penniman, 1975). Using this type of data allows researchers investigate a dynamic process non-obtrusively.

Siochi & Hix (1991) used an empirical technique to search for recurring patterns for heuristic evaluation of user interfaces and suggested that the technique is useful in uncovering design problems with various interfaces. If one were guided by theory, by analysis of an interface design, or by prior statistical analysis, one could extend the technique to study patterns from complicated situations.

Smith et al. (1993) used automated protocol analysis in their study to analyse the strategies of professional writers using the *WE* system. Writers' behaviour was automatically captured in time-stamped logs. These logs were analysed with a cognitive grammar. Interactive behaviours were mapped into various classes of cognitive activities of writers.

Markov chain models have been used to study behavioural patterns with information retrieval, on-line database search, and other activities with an interactive system. Qiu (1993) found that interactive behaviours of users with static hypertext can be adequately described by a second-order Markov chain. Empirical evidence and experienced writers suggest that collaborative writing may consist of substructures as planning, drafting, and revising. More detailed understanding is needed.

2.2 State Transitions and Markov Models

Table 1 shows a sequence of interactive events, in a simplified format, recorded by a built-in program in the MUCH system. The time series data corresponds to a segment of a 2-hour session of a user with a particular authoring space. The user was editing the draft of a co-authored book.

The sequence of 22 events was observed over a 10-minute interval. In general, a much longer time series can be expected. We use this sequence to illustrate the procedure of data collection and encoding. Five types of events appeared in this short session: (A) Unfold, (B) Reading, (C) Lock, (D) Update, and (E) Quit. The session can be coded as the follows:

AAABCDBCDBCDBCDBCDBCDE

Time	Event	Target Node of the Transaction
14:39:30	Unfold	Courseware Development Coordination and Reuse
14:39:32	Unfold	University Examples
14:39:36	Unfold	MIT's Athena Project
14:40:23	Read	University Examples
14:40:39	Lock	University Examples
14:41:33	Update	University Examples
14:41:43	Read	MIT's Athena Project
14:42:06	Lock	MIT's Athena Project
14:42:37	Update	MIT's Athena Project
14:42:41	Read	TUDOR
14:42:58	Lock	TUDOR
14:43:27	Update	TUDOR
14:43:33	Read	Physical Geography Tutor
14:43:49	Lock	Physical Geography Tutor
14:44:52	Update	Physical Geography Tutor
14:44:59	Read	Purdue's Escape
14:45:11	Lock	Purdue's Escape
14:45:37	Update	Purdue's Escape
14:45:49	Read	Organizational Issues
14:46:40	Lock	Organizational Issues
14:47:43	Update	Organizational Issues
14:49:09	Quit	Organizational Issues

Table 1: A sequence of user actions from a short session with the MUCH system.

There are 3 As, 6 Bs, 6 Cs, 6 Ds and 1 E in the sequence.

A transition matrix represents state transition probabilities from column states to row states. Each element in this matrix represents how many times a state of A, B, C, D, or E at time t was followed immediately by one of these 5 types of states at time $t + 1$. A 5×5 matrix of transition frequencies is normalized by dividing each of its row frequencies by the respective row sum. This yields a matrix P. The element (i, j) in the matrix P is the probability of being in the state j at time $t + 1$ given that the process is in the state i at time t. The elements of P are called sequential, transitional, or conditional probabilities.

The transition probability matrices are estimated from the observed counts of each event recorded by computer logs. The ultimate transition probabilities are the mean of corresponding transition probabilities of all the individual users.

3 Method

Dynamic user models in this study are built on Markov chain models of sequential data recorded in the logs. Markov chain models are represented by log-linear models. These log-linear models are subsequently analysed.

3.1 Tasks and Data Collection

A sequence of behavioural events of a user is a list of observed interactions between the user and the interface. This sequence is called an activity list in the field of Task Analysis in HCI (Diaper & Addison, 1991). Task sequencing can be highly contingent in interactive work. Interactive events of users in sessions with the MUCH system were logged over 7 active workspaces for three months. Users were involved in drafting and editing several co-authored manuscripts as research papers and textbooks. The MUCH system was used as a workstation-based word processor as well as a network organizer. Writing tasks, for instance, were divided into smaller tasks, such as writing and organizing a number of hypertext nodes. Collaboration was based on the shared workspace among co-authors.

The occurrence of each event was recorded with the following information: the name of the responding function in the MUCH system, the time of the occurrence, and the heading of the current node. Each workspace was identified at the beginning of a session.

The sample contains more than 20,000 transactions for each database. Researchers in the MUCH group and a class of graduate students at the University of Liverpool were included. Users were divided into two groups according to the total number of transactions of each user during the period of observation. The total number of transactions of an active, or regular user of the MUCH system ranges from 1,500 to 9,000. For an infrequent, or occasional user, the figure is less than 1,000.

The percentage breakdowns of user behaviour are listed in Table 2. The most frequently occurred transactions are Unfold, Reading, Local, Fold, and Update. The occurrences of these actions are at least 10 times more than the rest of actions.

The consent of individual users was obtained for analysing the data. Users were notified at the beginning of each session that a recording was in operation. A total of 24 interactive functions of the MUCH system were combined into a state space of six states — constructing, browsing, reading, awareness, writing, and printing. The categorization was based on the function model of the MUCH system and a preliminary analysis of the most predominant tasks observed. Finally, the analysis includes a four-state state space to reveal the overall patterns of interaction.

3.2 Analysis and Modelling

Statistical Package for the Social Sciences (SPSS) is used for the analysis. Markov models were specified in terms of hierarchical log-linear models. Log-linear models are used to compute expected counts according to the structure characterized by the model. A detailed description of using log-linear models in Markov analysis can be found in Bishop et al. (1975).

Previous studies mainly focused on information retrieval tasks in a static information space — there are few changes in the organization of information. In contrast, this study involves tasks such as content writing and structure authoring, as well as navigating and searching. Collaborative writing processes are expected to be dynamic and have complexity at least to the same extent as an interactive search process. In addition, this research classifies the state space and maps individual states to the modality of collaboration.

Transaction	Occurrences	Percentage
Total	12089	100.0
Unfold	4383	36.3
Read	3136	25.9
Lock	1301	10.8
Fold	1210	10.0
Update	1188	9.8
Delete	184	1.5
Quit	174	1.4
Modify	150	1.2
Info	90	.7
Rename	84	.7
Save	66	.5
CreateNote	63	.5
Send	20	.2
Refresh	15	.1
word	8	.1
Preview	4	.0
Print	4	.0
users	3	.0
Check	2	.0
MakeOutline	2	.0
author	1	.0
browser	1	.0

Table 2: Interactions with the Groupware & Hypertext authoring space. Entries in the lower sub-table are not included in further analyses.

By taking into account existing findings on behavioural patterns with interactive systems, the analysis in this study hypothesizes that the sequential structure of user behaviour with a collaborative authoring hypertext, such as with the MUCH system, is essentially a second-order Markov chain.

Markov models of the third- or lower order are examined to determine the appropriate order of the Markov chains. Three major hypotheses were as follows:

- *Hypothesis 1*: The sequential structure of interactive behaviours of users working with the MUCH system can be adequately represented by a second-order Markov chain.
- *Hypothesis 2*: Regular users and occasional users have significantly different strategies in interacting with the MUCH system. The differences should be noticeable between corresponding one-step transition probability matrices.
- *Hypothesis 3*: The organization of the shared knowledge in the hypertext is a significant factor for regular users on their behavioural patterns.

This study examines first-order Markov chain models to reveal the significance of sequential characteristics of user behaviours as the patterns in first-order chains are preserved in higher-order chains (Penniman, 1975; Qiu, 1993).

3.3 *Aggregated State Space*

The MUCH system supports more than 20 types of events through its user interface. Some of them have occurred frequently, while some have only occasionally occurred. One technique used in Markov chain analysis and log-linear models is to lump closely related states into a new, summarizing state such that the original state space can be replaced with a smaller state space without losing much information — e.g. (Qiu, 1993; Olson et al., 1994). As a result, there will be fewer sampling zeros in the new transition matrix. Log-linear models based on the aggregated state variables are expected to have a better goodness-of-fit statistics.

Each aggregated state variable consists of individual transaction events which characterize particular modalities of collaborative writing. Inter-modality transitions are described by corresponding state transitions in the new state space. Primitive states are aggregated according to their goals, relationships defined in the function model of the MUCH system, and their state transition probabilities. For instance, two frequently co-existing events may be combined as a new, more abstract state. A four-state space at the highest level is generated as follows:

- Local Content: composing tasks.
- Global Structure: organizing tasks.
- Global View: browsing tasks.
- Awareness: group awareness tasks.

On the other hand, discussions of one-step transitions are included whenever appropriate in the study so as to provide the reader with sufficient details and interpretations with intuitive appealing.

4 Results

Log-linear tests showed that an interactive process with the MUCH system is a second-order Markov chain. The process can be adequately modelled by a second-order Markov chain (Pearson's $\chi^2 = 660.86$, df = 780, p = 0.9992), but not by first-order Markov chains ($\chi^2 = 6523$, df = 102, $p < .0001$). The tests were based on transactions from both regular and occasional users, i.e. experienced and inexperienced users.

4.1 *Patterns in One-step Transitions*

A full-scale transition probability matrix for the *Groupware & Hypermedia* authoring space is given in Table 3. The transition matrix indicates two types of interactive events between users and the system. The central Type I interactions include Unfold (UNF), Read (RED), Lock (LOK), Fold (FLD) and Update (UPD). All the events in this group communicate each other. The auxiliary Type II interactions are transient in that

	UNF 19	RED 14	LOK 9	FLD 6	UPD 20	DEL 5	MD 10	INF 8	REN 16	SAV 17	SND 18	FRS 15	QIT 13
19	**.686**	**.164**	**.012**	**.120**	**.006**	.003	.001	.001	.000	.000	.000	.001	.004
14	**.088**	**.458**	**.283**	**.041**	**.005**	.035	.034	.015	.017	.013	.002	.001	.009
9	**.030**	**.056**	**.215**	**.012**	**.666**	.000	.000	.005	.030	.010	.001	.000	.011
6	**.465**	**.140**	**.005**	**.362**	**.005**	.002	.002	.000	.001	.002	.000	.004	.012
20	**.061**	**.541**	**.056**	**.078**	**.218**	.001	.003	.003	.001	.003	.002	.000	.026
5	.628	.022	.000	.005	.000	**.339**	.005	.000	.000	.000	.000	.000	.000
10	.773	.002	.000	.007	.000	.000	**.200**	.000	.000	.000	.000	.000	.000
8	.101	.326	.056	.067	.067	.000	.000	**.315**	.011	.000	.000	.000	.056
16	.759	.000	.060	.012	.000	.000	.000	.000	**.133**	.000	.000	.000	.036
17	.108	.262	.046	.031	.000	.000	.000	.000	.000	**.231**	.000	.000	.323
18	.006	.404	.000	.000	.006	.000	.058	.000	.000	.000	**.520**	.000	.006
15	.286	.239	.000	.000	.000	.000	.000	.000	.000	.000	.000	**.475**	.000
13	.000	.000	.000	.000	.000	.000	.000	.000	.000	.000	.000	.000	**1.00**

Table 3: The transition probability matrix of the first order 13-state Markov chain.

users usually do not move within in the group in an adjacent step. Instead, the process is likely to return to Type I behaviours. This pattern is shown in the table — in the upper left sub-matrix all the transition probabilities are positive, but in the lower right sub-matrix the non-reflexive transition probabilities are essentially zero.

Persistent events suggest that the MUCH system has been essentially used for hypertext reading and writing tasks. Task events for constructing the structure of the hypertext information space or for communicating among co-authors are categorized as transient events because:

1. cross-state transition probabilities are essentially zero; and
2. inner-group transition probabilities are positive (i.e. from a transient state to a persistent and vice versa).

Patterns of interactive behaviours with the Groupware & Hypermedia authoring space suggested that users either persistently worked in one of the four modes with the MUCH system, or they moved from social, contextual modes to independent working modes.

The *Class* authoring space was used by graduate students enrolled in an MSc in Information Systems in 1994. The state transition probabilities were based on 8,386 valid direct manipulation events. Users were slightly more likely to work within the node content window than to the overview window in this workspace (.50 to .46). The probability of a persistent action on the focal node is .631, while a persistent action in the overview is .613.

The transition matrix shows that awareness seeking tends to lead the process into actions on the local node:

$$Prob(LocalContent \mid Awareness) = .468$$

whereas changing the organizational structure of the workspace is likely to be followed by an action on the overview:

Prob(GlobalView | GlobalStructure) = .813

The matrix shows that the transitions are not symmetry between independent work modes (I:LC and GV) and loosely coupled modes (J:AW and GS) (i.e. $P_{IJ} < P_{JI}$), suggesting that there is a strong tendency of the process returning to the independent working mode.

Comparing with the matrix for the *Class* database, users of *Groupware & Hypermedia* are 4 times more likely to be constructing or modifying the structure of the database organization than seeking contextual awareness (odd ratio = 4.). In contrast, users of *Class* are 5.5 times more likely to seek contextual awareness than to work on the organization of the database.

In summary, users are predominantly engaged in transactions which are particularly related to the content of a chosen hypertext node (P = .520). To a less extent, users are engaged in transactions which manipulate an overview to the organization of hypertext databases, and provide entry points to the databases (P = .437). Users are much less likely to move into states such as seeking contextual awareness or constructing the databases (P = .020 and P = .018, respectively).

If the state LC and GV characterize an independent mode of working, and AW and GS characterize a loosely-coupled mode, users of the MUCH system are 25 times more likely to be engaged in the independent mode than in a loosely-coupled mode (odd ratio = 25.18). The interactive process moves from one mode to another in an unbalanced way — the process has a strong tendency to return to the independent mode once it enters into a loosely-coupled mode. Therefore, in general, users tend to use the databases in the MUCH for exploring and organizing ideas for writing, but not use these databases as much as a space for discussion and coordination.

4.2 *Effects of Users' Experiences*

A log-linear model was used to compare the second-order Markov chains between the two groups of users with the *Groupware & Hypermedia* authoring space. The level of users' experience has significant effects on the transition patterns they use. The second-order Markov chains for active users and inactive users are significantly different (Pearson's $\chi^2 = 2298.35$, df = 28, $p < .001$). Differences of behavioural patterns between active users and inactive users were also found with the *Management* workspace ($\chi^2 = 66552.86$, df = 22, $p < .001$). Markov chains of regular and occasional users are significantly different across seven hypertext databases (Pearson's $\chi^2 = 5880.91$, df = 180, $p < .001$). Differences between the two groups were specified by corresponding λ parameters in log-linear models.

Figure 1 shows how the behavioural patterns differ between experienced and inexperienced users with the Management database. The global view played a central part in the behavioural patterns of experienced users, labelled as experts in the figure, in contrast to its role for novices. The global view absorbs users' actions from other categories of interactive behaviours. In addition, experienced users appeared to be more stable as they worked in a particular category. Inexperienced users were less likely to remain in a state longer than experienced users.

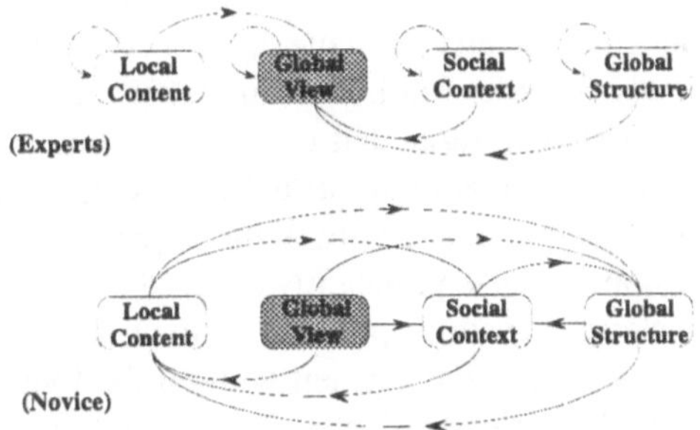

Figure 1: The behavioural patterns of users with the management database.

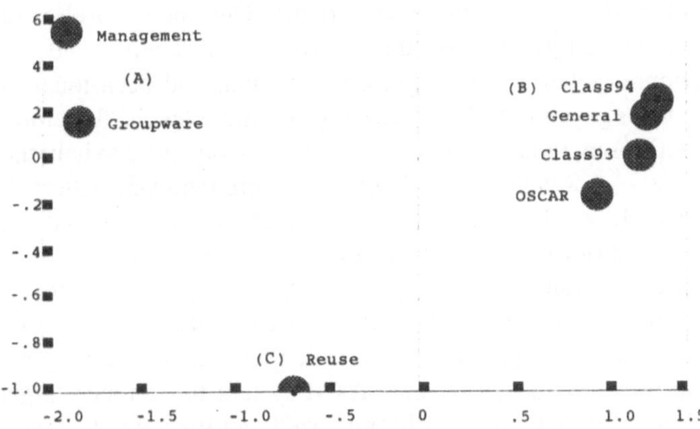

Figure 2: Classification of hypertext databases according to the similarity of corresponding Markov chains. (Stress=0.0386, RSQ=0.9950).

4.3 *Classification of Behavioural Patterns*

The organization of an authoring space significantly affects the way that it is used. The influence was compared between the processes from two workspaces (Pearson's $\chi^2 = 19052.12, df = 1296, p < 0.001$). Databases were grouped into three clusters by the similarity of associated processes (see Figure 2). Second-order transitions were aggregated in each cluster to characterize user behaviour which corresponds to the three clusters of workspaces. Cluster A includes the Management and Groupware databases; Cluster B includes the General database, a database for a joint project, and databases for students in classes; and Cluster C contains the software reuse database. Log-linear models specified significant differences in patterns of user behaviour associated with these clusters.

5 Discussion

Studies in hypertext information retrieval have shown that the use of a static hypertext can be modelled as a second-order Markov chain. This study shows that the use of a dynamic hypertext can also be modelled by a second-order Markov chain. This finding provides important information for us to have a clearer understanding of collaborative writing and its complexity in terms of the sequential structure. In our study, regular users and occasional users significantly differed in their behavioural patterns and corresponding one-step transition probability matrices revealed how they are different. Regular users were more persistent with all the four states. In particular, regular users are more likely to use Global Views continuously than occasional users. Therefore, regular users tend to access wider areas in the shared workspace. Previous empirical studies in laboratory settings have found that experienced users of hypertext systems tend to use browsing strategies more than inexperienced or novice users (Carmel et al., 1992). Experienced users tend to explore wider areas in a hypertext network, whereas inexperienced users tend to use backtrack to minimize the effects of getting off the main search paths. Our behavioural models therefore provide important information on the environmental requirements. For instance, these behavioural patterns may suggest that regular and occasional users because they tend to be engaged in tasks at different cognitive levels; therefore, they would demonstrate different requirements of tools in the workspace to help them.

Browsing ⟶ Reading ⟶ Writing is a predominant pattern in our study. Qiu (1993) has shown that in her read-only hypertext system a predominant pattern for information retrieval tasks has the structure of Querying ⟶ DisplayTitle ⟶ DisplayArticle. Browsing ⟶ Browsing ⟶ Browsing accounts for 17.68% of the second-order transitions, but merely 2.13% in Qiu's study. These differences may depend on whether the hypertext is used for collaborative authoring or information retrieval purposes. For instance, the MUCH system has a much larger number of nodes and links and they are loosely organized and they are changing. Browsing, therefore, affords an appropriate, heuristic strategy to approaching the evolving information space.

These comparisons can inform designers the potential weaknesses and alternatives for improvement. For instance, using browsing excessively in the MUCH system indicates the need of more efficient and more acceptable searching and locating mechanisms. In fact, the MUCH system provided a filtered view of the shared hypertext and users can alter the configuration to meet particular needs. However, users have hardly used the feature mainly because they found that a filtered view tends to undermine the sense of context in the hypertext.

6 Conclusion

The results of the study have some practical implications for collaborative writing research and related areas. This study reveals that how to choose the unit of analysis, i.e. the grain-size of states, is a fundamental issue that has to be systematically addressed in the future. One lesson we learned from the study is that the grain-size of the state space essentially depends on the goal of a particular study, researchers' existing knowledge of the particular domain, and theories and empirical findings on which researchers can build their new framework. A fine-grained state space may preserve more detailed information, whereas a coarse-grained state space may be suitable for obtaining a clear overview, which is particularly important at formative stages of systems design and evaluation.

The study also shows that state-transition models can be a useful tool for researchers to formulate specific hypotheses regarding a particular behavioural pattern or a relationship between a behavioural pattern and some outcome measures. Such experience should be useful for researchers and practitioners to understand the nature of collaborative writing and to inform designers to produce more appropriate tools.

To understand collaborative writing, one needs to take into account both social and technological aspects of the dynamics. Naturally, some aspects of collaborative writing cannot be adequately captured by quantitative approaches. They may be more suitable for qualitative approaches. For instance, how is the mutual understanding changed among individuals interacting with a shared workspace throughout collaborative writing? How do they organize and coordinate their work? What does the interrelationship between an organization and computing technologies evolve? Markov chain models constructed in this research are suitable for capturing and examining the dynamics of collaborative writing to the extent as users interact with collaborative hypertext and use the MUCH system as a tool.

The method used in our study can be extended to deal with situations where a large number of users are involved via a shared workspace. Further work is needed to incorporate additional aspects of collaborative writing into the descriptive-predictive models, including synchronous communication, the use of multimedia, dynamically matching the allocations of roles and tasks.

Acknowledgement

The author would like to thank the members of the MUCH group at the University of Liverpool for their collaboration and Dr Liwen Qiu at the University of Western Ontario for her valuable advice on Markov analysis.

References

Bishop, Y. M., Fienberg, S. E. & Holland, P. W. (1975), *Discrete Multivariate Analysis: Theory and Practice*, MIT Press.

Carmel, E., Crawford, S. & Chen, H. (1992), "Browsing in Hypertext: A Cognitive Study", *IEEE Transactions in Systems, Man and Cybernetics* **22**(5), 865–884.

Chapman, J. (1981), "A State Transition Analysis of Online Information Seeking Behavior", *Journal of the American Society for Information Science* pp.325–333. September.

Chen, C. & Rada, R. (1995), Understanding Collaborative Authoring in Shared Workspaces, *in* K. Nordby, P. H. Helmersen, D. J. Gilmore & S. A. Arnessen (eds.), "Human–Computer Interaction — INTERACT'95: Proceedings of the Fifth IFIP Conference on Human–Computer Interaction", Chapman & Hall, pp.277–282.

Chen, C. & Rada, R. (1996), "Interacting with Hypertext: A Meta-analysis of Experimental Studies", *Human–Computer Interaction* **11**(2), 125–156.

Chen, C., Rada, R. & Zeb, A. (1994), "An Extended Fisheye View Browser for Collaborative Writing", *International Journal of Human–Computer Studies* **40**(5), 859–878.

Cooke, N. J., Neville, K. J. & Rowe, A. L. (in press), "Procedural Network Representations of Sequential Data", *Human–Computer Interaction.*

Diaper, D. & Addison, M. (1991), User Modelling: The Task Oriented Modelling (TOM) Approach to the Designer's Model, *in* D. Diaper & N. Hammond (eds.), "People and Computers VI: Usability Now! (Proceedings of HCI'91)", Cambridge University Press, pp.387–402.

Haake, J. & Wilson, B. (1992), Supporting Collaborative Writing of Hyperdocuments in SEPIA, *in* D. Lucarella, J. Nariard & M. Nariard (eds.), "Proceedings of Hypertext'92", ACM Press, pp.138–146.

Irish, P. & Trigg, R. (1989), "Supporting Collaboration in Hypermedia: Issues and Experiences", *Journal of the American Society for Information Science* **40**(3), 192–199.

Kraut, R., Galegher, J., Fish, R. & Chalfonte, B. (1992), "Task Requirements and Media Choice in Collaborative Writing", *Human–Computer Interaction* **7**(4), 375–407.

Marchionini, G. (1989), "Information-Seeking Strategies of Novices Using a Full-Text Electronic Encyclopedia", *Journal of the American Society for Information Science* **40**(1), 54–66.

Miles, V. C., McCarthy, J. C., Dix, A. J., Harrison, M. D. & Monk, A. F. (1993), Reviewing Designs for a Synchronous–Asynchronous Group Editing Environment, *in* M. Sharples (ed.), "Computer Supported Collaborative Writing", Springer-Verlag, pp.137–160.

Neuwirth, C., Kaufer, D., Chandhok, R. & Morris, J. (1990), Issues in the Design of Computer Support for Co-authoring and Commenting, *in* D. G. Tatar (ed.), "Proceedings of CSCW'90: Conference on Computer Supported Cooperative Work", ACM Press, pp.183–196.

Neuwirth, C., Kaufer, D., Chandhok, R. & Morris, J. (1994), Computer Support for Distributed Collaborative Writing: Defining Parameters of Interaction, *in* R. Furuta & C. Neuwirth (eds.), "Proceedings of CSCW'94: Conference on Computer Supported Cooperative Work", ACM Press, pp.145–153.

Nielsen, J. (1989), The Matters that Really Matter for Hypertext Usability, *in* "Proceedings of Hypertext'89", ACM Press, pp.239–248.

Olson, G. M., Herbsleb, J. D. & Rueter, H. H. (1994), "Characterizing the Sequential Structure of Interactive Behaviors through Statistical and Grammatical Techniques", *Human–Computer Interaction* **9**(3/4), 427–472.

Olson, J., Card, S., Landauer, T. & Olson, G. (1993), "Computer-supported Co-operative Work: Research Issues for the 90s", *Behaviour & Information Technology* **12**(2), 115–129.

Penniman, W. (1975), A Stochastic Process Analysis of Online User Behavior, *in* "Information Revolution: Proceedings of the 38th American Society for Information Science Annual Meeting", ASIS, pp.147–148.

Qiu, L. (1993), "Markov Models of Search Patterns in a Hypertext Information Retrieval System", *Journal of the American Society for Information Science* **44**(7), 413–427.

Sanderson, P. M. & Fisher, C. (1994), "Exploratory Sequential Data Analysis: Foundations", *Human–Computer Interaction* **9**, 251–317.

Sharples, M., Goodlet, J., Beck, E., Wood, C., Easterbrook, S. & Polwman, L. (1993), Research Issues in the Study of Computer Supported Collaborative Writing, *in* M. Sharples (ed.), "Computer Supported Collaborative Writing", Springer-Verlag, pp.9–28.

Siochi, A. C. & Hix, D. (1991), A Study of Computer Supported User Interface Evaluation using Maximal Repeating Pattern Analysis, *in* S. P. Robertson, G. M. Olson & J. S. Olson (eds.), "Proceedings of CHI'91: Human Factors in Computing Systems (Reaching through Technology)", ACM Press, pp.301–305.

Smith, J. B., Smith, D. K. & Kupstas, E. (1993), "Automated Protocol Analysis", *Human–Computer Interaction* **8**(2), 101–145.

Smith, J. B., Weiss, S. F. & Ferguson, G. J. (1987), A Hypertext Writing Environment and its Cognitive Basis, *in* "Proceedings of Hypertext'87", ACM Press, pp.195–214.

Whittaker, S., Geelhoed, E. & Robinson, E. (1993), "Shared Workspaces: How do they Work and When are they Useful?", *International Journal of Man–Machine Studies* **39**(5), 813–842.

Zheng, M. & Rada, R. (1994), "MUCH Electronic Publishing Environment: Principles and Practices", *Journal of the American Society for Information Science* **45**(5), 300–309.

Workspace Awareness in Real-Time Distributed Groupware: Framework, Widgets, and Evaluation

Carl Gutwin, Saul Greenberg & Mark Roseman

Department of Computer Science, University of Calgary, 2500 University Dr NW, Calgary, Alberta T2N 1N4, Canada.

Tel: *+1 403 220 6015*

Fax: *+1 403 284 4707*

EMail: *{gutwin,saul,roseman}@cpsc.ucalgary.ca*

URL: *http://www.cpsc.ucalgary.ca/projects/grouplab/*

The rich person-to-person interaction afforded by shared physical workspaces allows people to maintain up-to-the minute knowledge about others' interaction with the task environment. This knowledge is *workspace awareness*, part of the glue that allows groups to collaborate effectively. In real-time groupware systems that provide a shared virtual space for collaboration, the possibilities for interaction are impoverished when compared with their physical counterparts. In this paper, we present the concept of workspace awareness as one key to supporting the richness evident in face-to-face interaction. We construct a conceptual framework that describes the elements and mechanisms of workspace awareness, and apply the framework to the design of widgets that help people maintain awareness in real-time distributed groupware. Our evaluation of these widgets has shown that several designs improve the usability of groupware applications.

Keywords: workspace awareness, real-time groupware, shared workspaces, widgets, CSCW.

1 Introduction

Recent work has shown how a shared physical workspace (such as a chalkboard, a control panel, or a tabletop) and the artifacts in that space act as stage and props for rich person-to-person interaction (Brinck & Gomez, 1992; Segal, 1994; Tang, 1991; Tatar et al., 1991). Information available in and through the physical workspace allows people to maintain an awareness of others' locations, activities, and intentions relative to the task and to the space — awareness that enables them to work together more effectively. We call this workspace awareness: the collection of up-to-the minute knowledge a person holds about the state of another's interaction with the workspace (Gutwin et al., 1995; Gutwin & Greenberg, 1996). As will be shown, workspace awareness helps people move between individual and shared activities, provides a context in which to interpret other's utterances, allows anticipation of others' actions, and reduces the effort needed to coordinate tasks and resources.

Recently, real-time distributed groupware has been developed to emulate aspects of physical workspaces — e.g. (Baecker, 1993; Greenberg et al., 1995). Its goal is to let people who are in different places work together at the same time in a shared *virtual* workspace. However, interactions in groupware workspaces are impoverished when compared with their physical counterparts, partly because support for maintenance of workspace awareness is not yet a design priority for groupware designers.

In our work building real time groupware, we want to support the rich interaction that is possible in a traditional shared workspace. Consequently, we are looking closely at the concept of workspace awareness, with the goal of supporting its maintenance through special groupware widgets. We believe that if such widgets can help people maintain their workspace awareness, the system can better support the subtle, fluid, and facile interaction that is evident in face-to-face collaboration.

The purpose of this paper, therefore, is to present and apply the concept of workspace awareness. We begin by presenting scenarios from an observational study we carried out, in order to explain what workspace awareness is and how it works in face-to-face situations. Next, we set out the problems of supporting workspace awareness in groupware, and then describe previous work on awareness in CSCW. The paper then outlines a conceptual framework of workspace awareness, specifying the elements that comprise it and the mechanisms used to maintain it in face to face settings. We apply the framework to the design of a variety of widgets that we have constructed in GroupKit, a groupware toolkit (Roseman & Greenberg, 1996). The widgets serve both to illustrate the possibilities of computer support for workspace awareness, as well as the difficulty in designing adequate replacements for our natural awareness mechanisms. Finally, we report on initial results from usability evaluations of four widgets.

2 Workspace Awareness

This section looks at what workspace awareness is and how it works in actual face-to-face situations, and then considers the problems of supporting awareness in groupware.

2.1 Episodes from a Study of Group Interaction

To help us understand workspace awareness, we observed pairs of people working together over a physical workspace. Each pair was assigned the task of composing a two-page layout of a newspaper using materials we provided — paper articles, pictures, and headlines. The episodes that follow are a composite of those that we saw in our observational studies. Each episode shows how people contribute to or benefit from awareness of one another in the workspace:

- *Mixed-focus collaboration.* Linda and Mark start the task together, with both attending to the same part of the workspace. As they talk, they decide that Linda will work on page one and Mark on page two, and they determine roughly which objects will go on each page. They then shift their focus of attention to their individual pages, and start laying out the material. As work progresses, their focus shifts back and forth between individual and shared activity, and between different parts of the layout.

- *Lightweight information gathering.* Mark's attention is briefly drawn from his own work by Linda moving objects back and forth in her area. With a quick glance, he notices that she is working on article one, that she has moved from the top left part of the page to the top right, and that she appears to be having trouble getting two columns of the story to fit into the available space.

- *Integration of information with previous knowledge.* Linda notices Mark move over to work on the headlines at the top of page 1. Recalling the instructions that the editor had given them earlier, she says, "Let's not forget to leave space for that picture that they want in there."

- *Anticipation of another's actions.* Mark watches Linda position her first article down the length of the page, and thinks that this may be the way she plans to position all of her articles, so he speaks up: "Um, I think we should decide on sort of a consistent layout for the two pages together because I'm doing things in the top half and the bottom half, and it looks like you're going all the way down the page."

- *Using awareness of activity.* Linda knows that Mark is working on article two, so when she finds a column from that story hiding under the desk, she hands it to him, saying, "I think this is one of yours."

- *Interpreting references.* Mark and Linda are busy with their own tasks when Mark says, "Do you think that this should go down here?" Linda glances over to see what he is pointing at and then says: "It'd look OK, but I'm not sure it'll fit." Later, Mark hears the sound of paper being cut with scissors, and without looking up, says, "Can I have those when you're done?"

These episodes are ordinary and commonplace, and none of them on their own has any great effect. However, they are made possible by workspace awareness, and though small, will be joined by many other moments of opportune collaboration. Taken together, these actions allow a group to be significantly more effective than an individual. Workspace awareness lowers the overhead of working together, creates new opportunities for collaboration, and provides people with a larger context for their actions (Dourish & Bellotti, 1992).

As the above scenario shows, workspace awareness can be seen both as a product and a process. The product is the state of understanding about another person's interaction with the workspace, that allows people to interpret events, anticipate needs, and interact appropriately. The process is the continuous cycle of extracting information from the environment, integrating this information with existing knowledge, and using that knowledge to direct further perception. The maintenance of workspace awareness involves several human cognitive processing skills including pre-attentive processing, attention allocation, perception, working memory management, comprehension, and projection (Endsley, 1995). These skills are the basis for higher-level mechanisms such as gaze awareness (Ishii & Kobayashi, 1992), gestural communication (Tang, 1991), and deictic reference (Tatar et al., 1991).

While the process and product of workspace awareness in a face-to-face situation seem trivial, things become far less clear when trying to support workspace awareness in a real-time groupware system.

2.2 Workspace Awareness Problems in Groupware

When shared activity moves from a face-to-face setting to distributed groupware, many things change that impair people's abilities to maintain workspace awareness:

- The perceivable environment shrinks drastically. Where people could see all of a fairly large physical workspace, they now have only a tiny viewport through the computer screen.

- Some means of communication are weakened: our hands' capabilities for expression are only poorly approximated with a mouse cursor (Hayne et al., 1993), and speech loses much of its audio quality and directional component over typical voice links.

- Common ways of interacting with computer applications, such as through menus or function keys, hide actions that are visible in a physical workspace.

- Computer systems cannot handle many of the ingrained perceptual and physical abilities that we use to maintain workspace awareness in a face-to-face setting, and must replace them with means of perceiving the environment that are comparatively slow and clumsy.

- Groupware approaches that allow participants to control their own views of the virtual workspace (Stefik et al., 1987) can further obscure people's locations and activities.

- Video techniques that bring people's hands and bodies into the virtual workspace are limited by scalability and resolution problems (e.g. most cannot handle more than two people) (Ishii & Kobayashi, 1992).

Within this strange new situation, the groupware designer must try and recreate the conditions and cues that allow people to keep up a sense of workspace awareness. Unfortunately, many of the things that supported workspace awareness in face-to-face situations disappear in the transition to a groupware setting. For example, in the page-layout example discussed above, people made use of peripheral vision, rapid glances, three-dimensional sound, and the ability to see the entire workspace, none of which would be available in a groupware system. Whereas face-to-face interaction has inherent mechanisms and affordances for maintaining workspace awareness, the groupware designer is faced with a blank slate — any support for building or maintaining workspace awareness must be explicitly determined and built into the groupware system.

It is not immediately obvious what information people need to maintain workspace awareness, or how that information should be presented within a groupware system. We have been forced to look more closely at these issues, and the next sections present the work that we have done in bringing together knowledge about workspace awareness that can be used in designing groupware widgets. The product of our investigations is a conceptual framework of workspace awareness that is detailed below. First, however, we step back for a moment to show the context that this framework fits into. The following paragraphs describe awareness in group work more generally and how various kinds of awareness have been looked at in CSCW research.

3 Related Work on Awareness

People are aware of many different things when they work in groups, some of which relate to the group, and some to the task or situation more generally.

For example, people maintain awareness of an association of people, their reasons for being together and their shared knowledge, which we call *organizational awareness*. Organizational memory is one way of tracking organizational awareness — e.g. (Conklin & Begeman, 1988). Another example is *task awareness*, which involves understanding the purpose of a task, the specific goals and requirements of the group in pursuing the task, and how the task on hand fits into a larger plan. Project management software is one type of system that supports task awareness. *Situation awareness* is another area that has been extensively discussed in the human factors community — e.g. (Adams et al., 1995; Endsley, 1995), and refers to the state of knowledge that an individual requires to operate or maintain a complex and dynamic system (such as an aircraft or a nuclear generating station).

Within CSCW, researchers have proposed four types of awareness that apply more specifically to groups working face to face, and these are shown in Figure 1. We use a Venn diagram to indicate that these different kinds of awareness overlap, inform one another, and interact during group work.

Informal awareness of a work community is the general sense of who's around and what they are up to — the kinds of things that people know when they work together in the same office. Informal awareness is the glue that facilitates casual interaction. CSCW researchers have attempted to provide this sense of social presence to distributed groups through the use of media spaces — e.g. (Baecker, 1993). Media

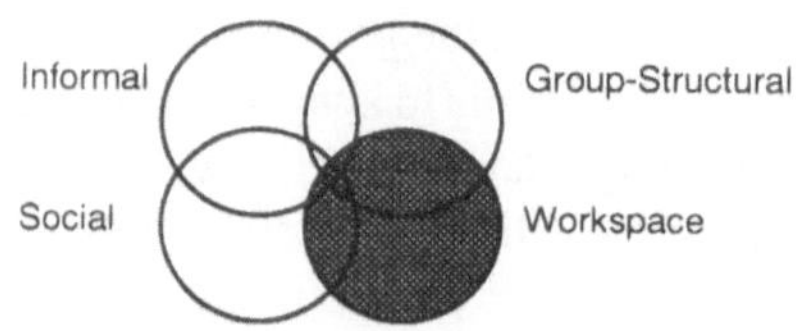

Figure 1: Types of awareness in group work.

spaces use long-term links that show continuous video or snapshots of offices and common areas at a remote site.

Social awareness is the information that a person maintains about others in a social or conversational context: things like whether another person is paying attention, their emotional state, or their level of interest. Social awareness is maintained through conversational cues such as back-channel feedback, and through non-verbal cues like eye contact, facial expression, and body language. The maintenance of social awareness in distributed groups has been explored in CSCW through desktop video-conferencing — e.g. (Borning & Travers, 1991), video tunnels (Buxton, 1993), or the mixing of video and computational workspaces to allow eye contact within a work-surface (Ishii & Kobayashi, 1992).

Group-structural awareness involves knowledge about such things as people's roles and responsibilities, their positions on an issue, their status, and group processes. CSCW research has looked at support for meeting rooms — e.g. (Valacich et al., 1991), group decision-making — e.g. (Kraemer & Pinsonneault, 1990), representation of arguments and positions — e.g. (Conklin & Begeman, 1988), floor control — e.g. (Greenberg, 1990), and explicit roles — e.g. (Leland et al., 1988).

This brings us to workspace awareness, different from the other forms in Figure 1 because of the integral part played in the collaboration by the workspace. When interaction happens in a workspace, maintaining knowledge about others' interaction with the space and its artifacts becomes highly relevant. Workspace awareness has also been recognized in CSCW research (although under different names), and our work builds directly on these efforts — e.g. (Baecker et al., 1993; Beaudouin-Lafon & Karsenty, 1992; Dourish & Bly, 1992; Dourish & Bellotti, 1992).

4 A Framework of Workspace Awareness

We have built a conceptual framework of workspace awareness that structures thinking about groupware interface support. We believe the framework necessary because groupware designers face two operational problems:

1. They must know what awareness information a groupware system should capture about another's interaction with the workspace.

2. They must consider how this information should be presented to other participants.

Element	Relevant Questions
Identity	Who is participating in the activity?
Location	Where are they?
Activity Level	Are they active in the workspace?
	How fast are they working?
Actions	What are they doing?
	What are their current activities and tasks?
Intentions	What are they going to do?
	Where are they going to be?
Changes	What changes are they making?
	Where are changes being made?
Objects	What objects are they using?
Extents	What can they see?
Abilities	What can they do?
Sphere of Influence	Where can they have effects?
Expectations	What do they need me to do next?

Table 1: Elements of workspace awareness.

The framework presents a set of basic ideas that are critical for the design of awareness support, and that allow techniques for widget designs to be identified, described, and compared. The following sections detail the parts of the framework: first, the elements that make up people's workspace awareness, and second, the mechanisms that they use to gather awareness information.

4.1 Elements of Workspace Awareness

The first part of the conceptual framework is a list of elements that people may keep track of when they work with others in a shared space (see Table 1). Workspace awareness in a particular situation is made up of some combination of these elements (although we do not claim to have covered all the elements used in all situations).

The elements are for the most part common sense things that can be seen in many kinds of workspace collaboration, and can be related to questions that people ask themselves during group work (column 2). Awareness of identity is simply knowing who you are working with, and often, the answer to "who is participating?" is obvious based on seeing and hearing others in the room. The other questions in the table show that several of the elements can be put into two rough groups — one that relates to what is happening and one that relates to where it is happening. Elements that deal with 'what' involve the amount of activity, the nature and content of actions, the changes that are made to artifacts, people's capabilities for action, and their expectations for action from each other. Those dealing with 'where' involve where in the workspace people are focusing, the extents of what they can see, where they are making changes, the particular objects that are being used, and the extended area within which they can indirectly cause changes to the workspace (through connections and constraints between artifacts).

These elements provide a basic vocabulary for thinking about awareness requirements and groupware support. Designers can use the framework to analyse existing face-to-face situations. For example, the group page-layout activity described earlier required that people stayed aware of where on the page others were working and of large movements of artifacts, but not of small changes to the placement of the columns. In addition to considering which elements are more or less important in a particular situation, there are several further ways that a designer can assess how elements are used. For example:

- Several elements relate to the past as well as the present. For example, awareness of past activities or past location is useful in many situations, especially when someone needs to bring themselves up to date on what has been going on in an area of the workspace.
- Awareness elements can constrain one another. For example, knowing where someone is working can limit what they can be doing.
- Some elements can be further specified in terms of the granularity at which the information is useful. For example, in a task that does not involve much close interaction, participants may only maintain a general idea of where others are working.
- Awareness information will vary in character depending on the situation. For example, location information can be relative to a participant, absolute in terms of the workspace, or determined by the semantic structure of the artifacts (such as section numbers in an outline).

Several CSCW projects have implemented various support for elements of workspace awareness, although often in an application-specific, limited, or ad-hoc manner. Research has considered elements such as view location — e.g. (Baecker et al., 1993; Beaudouin-Lafon & Karsenty, 1992), fine-grained location — e.g. (Tang, 1991; Hayne et al., 1993), content of activity — e.g. (Beaudouin-Lafon & Karsenty, 1992; Dourish & Bellotti, 1992; Stefik et al., 1987), presence — e.g. (Ellis et al., 1991; Sohlenkamp & Chwelos, 1994), changes — e.g. (Ellis et al., 1991; Sohlenkamp & Chwelos, 1994; Stefik et al., 1987), and activity level — e.g. (Ackerman & Starr, 1995).

4.2 Workspace Awareness Mechanisms

After considering elements of workspace awareness, the next part of the framework looks at how people obtain the information that updates their state of knowledge. Determining precise mechanisms in face-to-face situations is difficult, however, since they can be subtle, hard to observe (sound cues, for example), or buried within several layers of inference. Instead, we present a general set of information-gathering mechanisms that have been discussed in previous literature, and discuss how they are used for maintenance of workspace awareness:

- *Direct communication.* People explicitly communicate information about their interaction with the workspace; this communication is primarily verbal, although gestures (Tang, 1991) and deictic references (Tatar et al., 1991) are also common.

- *Indirect productions.* People commonly communicate through actions, expressions, or speech that is not explicitly directed at the other members of the group, but that is intentionally public (Dourish & Bellotti, 1992; Heath & Luff, 1991).

- *Consequential communication.* Watching or listening to others as they work provides people with a great deal of information about their interaction with the workspace (Segal, 1994).

- *Feedthrough.* Information can also be gathered by observing the effects of someone's actions on the artifacts in the workspace (Dix et al., 1993).

- *Environmental feedback.* People also perceive higher-level feedthrough from the indirect effects of another's actions in the larger workspace. For example, in a control room situation, seeing some measured value decrease can provide evidence that another member of the team has initiated a particular procedure.

Groupware designers must consider how information about various elements is transmitted and gathered, and must allow people to continue using natural mechanisms like those listed above, or others specific to particular domains and situations. With knowledge of these mechanisms, and of how they are used to maintain different elements of awareness, a designer can begin to create techniques and widgets that provide people with appropriate information about others in a virtual workspace.

By setting out elements and mechanisms of workspace awareness, the conceptual framework provides a vocabulary and a starting point for thinking about and designing groupware support. The following section describes several widgets that were designed using the framework, and outlines the results of a usability study carried out to evaluate their effect on a groupware application.

5 Workspace Awareness Widgets

We have used the conceptual framework above in the design of many groupware widgets that help people maintain workspace awareness (Gutwin et al., 1995; Gutwin et al., 1996). We have initially concentrated on awareness of identity, location, and actions, three elements that are particularly relevant to relaxed-WYSIWIS ('what you see is what I see') groupware (Stefik et al., 1987). In these systems, people can change the location or representation of their view onto the workspace to suit the needs of their immediate task. Relaxed-WYSIWIS view sharing is more natural and more flexible, but because people may not see the same thing, they can lose track of who else is in the workspace, where they are, and what they are doing.

The following paragraphs focus on four inventions that illustrate a range of approaches to helping people keep track of others in a relaxed-WYSIWIS workspace: radar views, multiple-WYSIWIS views, workspace teleportals, and the WYSIWID ('what you see is what I do') display.

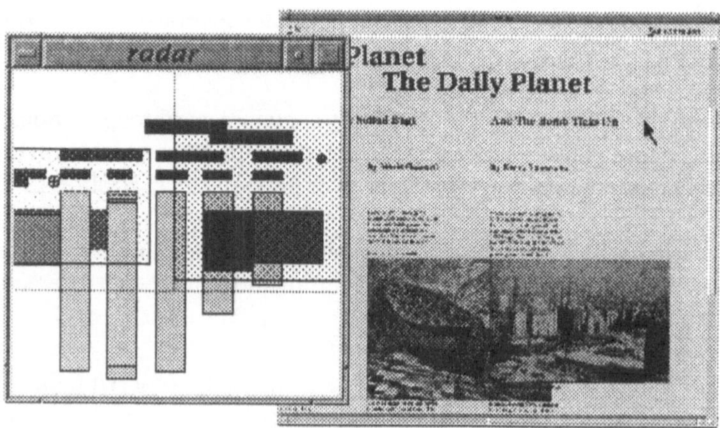

Figure 2: Radar view of a newspaper layout editor, with view outlines (dotted rectangles) and telepointers (crossed circles). The main view is shown reduced in size at right.

5.1 Radar Views

Radar views are a class of widgets based on miniature overviews of an entire workspace. These miniatures have been seen in video games and some groupware systems — e.g. (Baecker et al., 1993). Our basic radar view (see Figure 1) adds information about other people's interaction with the workspace to this miniature. Since the overview provides a spatial representation of the workspace, location information is a natural addition. The radar display shows the extent of what each person can see by marking view outlines (inspired by SASSE's text overview (Baecker et al., 1993)) and also shows finer-grained location by including miniature telepointers that represent each person's mouse cursor (Hayne et al., 1993). These additions support awareness of another person's general and specific location in the workspace.

The radar view also supports awareness of activity. The radar shows all movement of and changes to artifacts in the workspace, which provides information about others' actions with feedthrough. Adding telepointers to the display adds a second source of information about what people are doing and where they are working. Telepointers in the radar also allow for gestural communication and deictic references even when people's main views are different. In addition to these techniques, it is easy for groupware designers to provide task-specific feedback about types of activity, such as selection of objects or use of different tools.

The basic radar view conveys identity by showing each participant's view outline and telepointer in a unique colour. One problem with this approach is that it can be difficult to sort out which view rectangle belongs to whom. To simplify interpretation, we have constructed a 'portrait radar' that attaches names or pictures to the view rectangles, allowing more natural identification (see Figure 2). The portraits sit behind the artifacts in the display, so this portrait radar is most useful in sparse

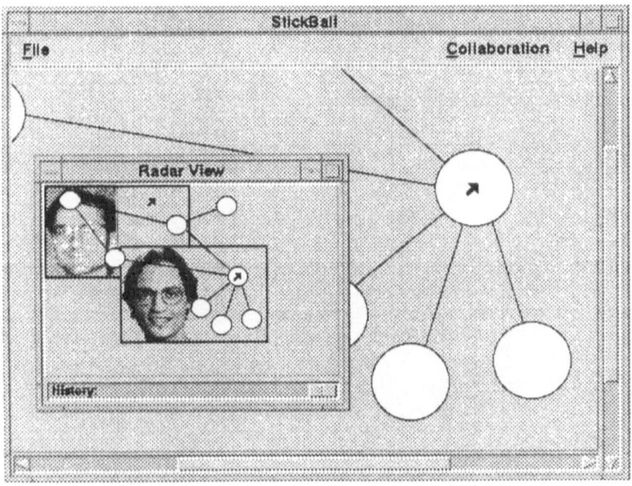

Figure 3: Portrait radar on a graph editor. The radar window is inset over the main view.

workspaces or where artifacts are transparent. In future, we may replace these static pictures with live video images.

5.2 *Multiple-WYSIWIS Views*

Radar views provide only a low resolution representation of others' views, especially if the workspace is large. If more detail about the artifacts in each participant's view is required, our multiple-WYSIWIS widget can be used, which shows a scaled-down duplicate of each person's view of the workspace (see Figure 4). All of the other person's actions in the workspace, including cursor movement and manipulation of artifacts, are visible within the display. This widget provides some of the benefits of the WYSIWIS approach by once again giving the group a common (though composite) view of the workspace, but still allows people individual control of their main views.

5.3 *The 'What You See Is What I Do' Widget*

In some cases, people need to see detail about another's actions at full size. Since limits on screen space usually preclude a full-size duplicate of another person's view, we have designed a 'what you see is what I do' (WYSIWID) widget that provides full-size details, but shows only a limited part of the other person's view (Figure 5).

The widget shows only the immediate context around another person's cursor, since most actions in graphical applications will involve the mouse. As a person moves their cursor on a remote machine, the background of the widget pans to keep the display centred around the pointer.

5.4 *Workspace Teleportals*

Finally, in some situations people wish to see another person's entire view in full size. We have created graphical and textual workspaces where pressing a mouse button temporarily 'teleports' the user to another person's location, returning to their

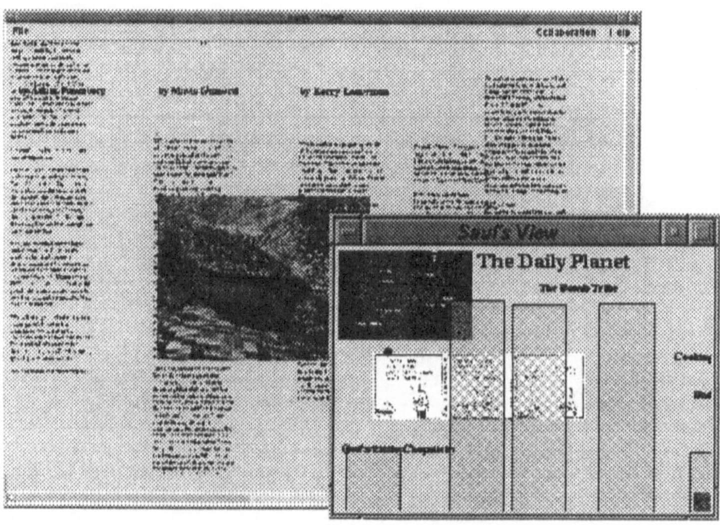

Figure 4: Multiple-WYSIWIS view. The main view at left shows the local user's view of the workspace; the inset window shows a remote participant's view.

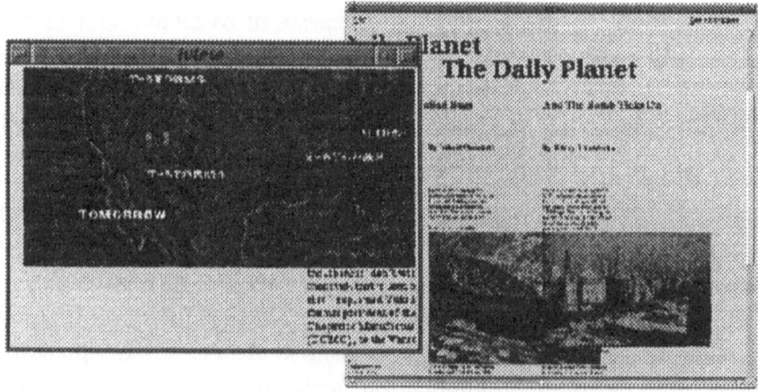

Figure 5: The 'what you see is what I do' widget. The inset window at left shows a full-scale but limited area around a remote user's cursor; the local user's main view, reduced in size, is shown at right.

Widget	Awareness of identity (who is in the workspace)	Awareness of location (of view, extents, focus, and changes)	Awareness of actions (objects used, changes made, activity level)
Radar view and Portrait radar	participants indicated by unique colour (or by picture)	view extents shown with outlines superimposed on miniature of workspace telepointers show fine-grained location	movement and changes in miniature view (at low resolution) telepointers show activity and allow gesturing (at low resolution)
Multiple-WYSIWIS view	each scaled-down view identified by participant's name	view location must be determined from knowledge of workspace view extents represented by size of scaled view telepointers show fine location	movement and changes shown in each scaled-down view (moderate resolution) telepointers show activity and allow gesturing (moderate resolution)
WYSIWID display	widget shows remote participant's name	view location must be determined from knowledge of workspace view extent not shown full size shows precise location of remote cursor	all actions shown in full detail
Workspace teleportal	window title shows the name of participant who is being 'visited'	view location must be determined from knowledge of workspace view extents not shown main-view telepointers show precise location	actions shown in full detail, but are only visible after teleporting telepointers show activity and allow gesturing

Table 2: Summary of workspace awareness support provided by the widgets.

original view when the button is released. This technique allows people to 'glance' at another's work area without much effort. This device is difficult to show in a figure, but works by rapidly scrolling to the remote participant's location when the mouse button is pressed, and then scrolling back again when upon release.

5.5 Summary

As a summary, Table 2 compares the widgets in terms of the three workspace awareness elements mentioned above (identity, location, and activity). Since the widgets support other elements as well, these are listed parenthetically within the main categories. The table summarizes the techniques used in the widgets to help people maintain awareness in relaxed-WYSIWIS groupware systems.

One key difference between the widgets is that they show a gradual transition from favouring global context to favouring local detail. Although they all support

Group	System 1	System 2
1	Basic	Radar
2	Radar	Basic
3	Mini	WYSIWID
4	Scrollbar	Basic
5	Radar	Mini
6	Mini	Scrollbar
7	Radar	Radar + WYSIWID
8	Radar	Basic

Widget	# Pairs
Basic	4
Scrollbar	2
WYSIWID	2
Miniature	3
Radar	6

Table 3: System configurations and total pairs for each widget.

awareness of identity, location, and activity, the tradeoffs in their design imply that they will be useful to different degrees in particular groupware applications. We have tested how well three of these widgets, the radar view, the workspace teleportal, and the WYSIWID display, worked in one groupware system. The next section briefly outlines the initial results of a usability study carried out to evaluate these widgets.

6 Usability Evaluation

We conducted a study of a shared workspace system that incorporated various awareness widgets, in order to evaluate how well our designs supported the maintenance of workspace awareness. We were particularly interested in knowing whether information in the widgets was easy to interpret, whether they distracted users from their tasks, and whether users thought that the displays were worth the screen space that they used.

We constructed a relaxed-WYSIWIS groupware editor for manipulating the layout of a two-page newspaper page, similar in spirit to the setup of the face-to-face situation described earlier. About one third of the total workspace could be seen at a time on a 19-inch computer monitor. The system provided simultaneous access to the shared workspace for multiple participants, and allowed users to move pictures, headlines, and columns of text. Eight pairs of undergraduate and graduate computer science students participated as subjects. Each pair completed two layout tasks, each limited to fifteen minutes and each using a different system configuration. In different conditions, as shown in Table 3, the layout editor provided either a basic shared workspace, including telepointers and the workspace teleportals, or the basic workspace augmented with one of several awareness widgets:

- A multi-user scrollbar, which shows each person's view location as a coloured bar beside the regular horizontal and vertical scrollbars of the workspace.
- A workspace miniature, which is similar to the radar view but shows only the workspace objects, not the participants' view rectangles or telepointers.
- A radar view, as shown in Figure 2.
- A WYSIWID view, as shown in Figure 5.

The multiple-WYSIWIS and portrait radar views were not used, as they will be part of a later evaluation. Data collected in the study included experimenter observation, videotape of the sessions, questionnaires filled out by the subjects after each task, and records from an interview conducted at the end of the session.

In general, all pairs completed their tasks and produced reasonable layouts. We observed a variety of working styles, ranging from 'divide and conquer' to tightly coupled collaboration. Regardless of the style, there was evidence that the pairs maintained an awareness of each other's use of the workspace, and acted on that information to collaborate with their partner and complete their task. We observed that subjects did make use of the various awareness widgets, and they reported that several of the widgets provided useful awareness information. In particular, most subjects greatly favoured the conditions that included the two widgets that were based on a miniature of the workspace.

Subjects made considerable use of the radar view, the miniature, and the teleportal. Subjects liked these displays, and found them to be useful for maintaining awareness of their partner. The radar view was distracting to only one of the eight people who used it, and it was universally considered easy to interpret, possibly because its overview mimics the workspace. All of the subjects who used the radar view reported that it was well worth the screen space it used, both because it kept them up to date on their partner, and because it also provided information that was useful to them as they carried out their individual tasks. The teleportal used no screen space at all, and while this is of course economical and non-distracting, it provides no visual affordance to novice users that teleportation is possible. Several subjects reported that they would have used the teleportal more often, but that they forgot that it was there.

Subjects were less enthusiastic about the WYSIWID display, complaining that it was difficult to determine what was going on within it. The problem may have arisen from the somewhat jumpy animation that the display exhibited; however, there were other problems with the fit between the WYSIWID and the layout task that may have reduced its usefulness. The task did not demand that participants make precise actions, or that they monitor the small details of what others did, and so the full-size but limited-context view was likely too focused for the requirements of the task.

Subjects also found the multi-user scrollbar to be less useful than the other widgets. Two factors in this display may have led to problems: first, it shows location on an abstract scale that does not allow a simple determination of actual workspace location or of what others can see; and second, the widget provided location information in two dimensions (horizontal and vertical) that forced users to mentally integrate the information in order to determine someone's actual location.

Overall, the displays that provided a bigger picture (especially the radar view) were found to be more appropriate, even though they contained less detail. When compared with the plain shared workspace condition, subjects always preferred having the extra awareness information, and often seemed to engage in more interaction about the task (this observation is currently being explored further). The radar view was successful in enriching the kinds of interaction that happened in the shared workspace, and one subject went so far as to remark "it was just like working over a big table."

7 Conclusions and Future Work

In this paper, we have presented the concept of workspace awareness as a critical design concern for real-time groupware, and have constructed a conceptual framework that gives designers a starting point for building awareness support into groupware. We also showed several awareness widgets that we have built using the framework, and discussed how they affected the usability of a realistic shared-workspace groupware system. Our evaluation reinforces our beliefs that workspace awareness is a significant part of collaboration, and that workspace awareness can be supported through groupware widgets. This research presents several avenues for further work, including:

- Expanding and validating the framework through additional studies of face-to-face groups.
- Building additional awareness widgets for other elements and mechanisms, such as a fish-eye view that smoothly integrates radar and detail views (Greenberg et al., 1996b).
- Further evaluating the widgets, both in terms of the framework and in usability studies of realistic applications.
- Investigating other issues of applying the framework to groupware, such as the possibilities of going beyond existing face-to-face mechanisms for maintaining awareness.

Although the widgets make clear advances in supporting particular awareness elements and mechanisms, much work needs to be done before groupware workspaces approach the richness and simplicity of face-to-face interaction.

Acknowledgements

We are grateful to the Natural Sciences and Engineering Research Council of Canada and to Intel Corporation for financial assistance.

References

Ackerman, M. & Starr, B. (1995), Social Activity Indicators: Interface Components for CSCW Systems, *in* G. Robinson (ed.), "Proceedings of the ACM Symposium on User Interface Software and Technology, UIST'95", ACM Press, pp.159–168.

Adams, M., Tenney, Y. & Pew, R. (1995), "Situation Awareness and the Cognitive Management of Complex Systems", *Human Factors* **37**(1), 185–104.

Baecker, R. (ed.) (1993), *Readings in Groupware and Computer-supported Cooperative Work*, Morgan-Kaufmann.

Baecker, R., Nastos, D., Posner, I. & Mawby, K. (1993), The User-centred Iterative Design of Collaborative Writing Software, *in* S. Ashlund, K. Mullet, A. Henderson, E. Hollnagel & T. White (eds.), "Proceedings of INTERCHI'93", ACM Press, pp.399–405.

Beaudouin-Lafon, M. & Karsenty, A. (1992), Transparency and Awareness in a Real-time Groupware System, *in* M. Green (ed.), "Proceedings of the ACM Symposium on User Interface Software and Technology, UIST'92", ACM Press, pp.171–180.

Borning, A. & Travers, M. (1991), Two Approaches to Casual Interaction over Computer and Video Networks, *in* S. P. Robertson, G. M. Olson & J. S. Olson (eds.), "Proceedings of CHI'91: Human Factors in Computing Systems (Reaching through Technology)", ACM Press, pp.13–19.

Brinck, T. & Gomez, L. (1992), A Collaborative Medium for the Support of Conversational Props, *in* J. Turner & R. Kraut (eds.), "Proceedings of CSCW'92: Conference on Computer Supported Cooperative Work", ACM Press, pp.171–178.

Buxton, W. (1993), Telepresence: Integrating Shared Task and Person Spaces, *in* Baecker (1993), pp.846–852.

Conklin, E. J. & Begeman, M. (1988), gIBIS: A Hypertext Tool for Exploratory Policy Discussion, *in* D. G. Tatar (ed.), "Proceedings of CSCW'88: Conference on Computer Supported Cooperative Work", ACM Press, pp.140–152.

Dix, A., Finlay, J., Abowd, G. & Beale, R. (1993), *Human–Computer Interaction*, Prentice–Hall International.

Dourish, P. & Bellotti, V. (1992), Awareness and Coordination in Shared Workspaces, *in* J. Turner & R. Kraut (eds.), "Proceedings of CSCW'92: Conference on Computer Supported Cooperative Work", ACM Press, pp.107–114.

Dourish, P. & Bly, S. (1992), Portholes: Supporting Awareness in Distributed Work Groups, *in* P. Bauersfeld, J. Bennett & G. Lynch (eds.), "Proceedings of CHI'92: Human Factors in Computing Systems", ACM Press, pp.541–547.

Ellis, S., Gibbs, S. & Rein, G. (1991), "Groupware: Some Issues and Experiences", *Communications of the ACM* **34**(1), 39–58.

Endsley, M. (1995), "Toward a Theory of Situation Awareness in Dynamic Systems", *Human Factors* **37**(1), 32–64.

Greenberg, S. (1990), Sharing Views and Interactions within Single-user Applications, *in* F. H. Lochovski & R. B. Allen (eds.), "Proceedings of the Conference on Office Information Systems", ACM Press, pp.227–237.

Greenberg, S., Gutwin, C. & Cockburn, A. (1996), Awareness through Fisheye Views in Relaxed WYSIWIS Groupware, *in* R. Bartles (ed.), "Proceedings of Graphics Interface'96", Canadian Information Processing Society, pp.28–38.

Greenberg, S., Hayne, S. & Rada, R. (1995), *Groupware for Real-Time Drawing: A Designer's Guide*, McGraw-Hill.

Gutwin, C. & Greenberg, S. (1996), Workspace Awareness for Groupware, *in* M. Tauber (ed.), "Companion Proceedings of CHI'96: Human Factors in Computing Systems (CHI'96 Conference Companion)", ACM Press, pp.208–209.

Gutwin, C., Greenberg, S. & Roseman, M. (1996), Workspace Awareness Support with Radar Views, *in* M. Tauber (ed.), "Companion Proceedings of CHI'96: Human Factors in Computing Systems (CHI'96 Conference Companion)", ACM Press, pp.210–211.

Gutwin, C., Stark, G. & Greenberg, S. (1995), Supporting Workspace Awareness in Educational Groupware, *in* J. L. Schnase & E. L. Cunnius (eds.), "Proceedings of Computer Supported Collaborative Learning '95", Lawrence Erlbaum Associates, pp.147–156.

Hayne, S., Pendergast, M. & Greenberg, S. (1993), "Implementing Gesturing with Cursors in Group Support Systems", *Journal of Management Information Systems* **10**(3), 43–61.

Heath, C. & Luff, P. (1991), Collaborative Activity and Technological Design: Task Coordination in London Underground Control Rooms, *in* M. Robinson, L. Bannon & K. Schmidt (eds.), "Proceedings of ECSCW'91, the 2nd European Conference on Computer-Supported Cooperative Work", Kluwer (Academic Press), pp.65–80.

Ishii, H. & Kobayashi, M. (1992), ClearBoard: A Seamless Medium for Shared Drawing and Conversation With Eye Contact, *in* P. Bauersfeld, J. Bennett & G. Lynch (eds.), "Proceedings of CHI'92: Human Factors in Computing Systems", ACM Press, pp.525–532.

Kraemer, K. & Pinsonneault, A. (1990), Technology and Groups: Assessments of the Empirical Research, *in* J. Galegher, R. Kraut & C. Egido (eds.), "Intellectual Teamwork: Social Foundations of Cooperative Work", Lawrence Erlbaum Associates, pp.373–404.

Leland, M., Fish, R. & Kraut, R. (1988), Collaborative Document Production using Quilt, *in* D. G. Tatar (ed.), "Proceedings of CSCW'88: Conference on Computer Supported Cooperative Work", ACM Press, pp.206–215.

Roseman, M. & Greenberg, S. (1996), "Building Real-time Groupware with GroupKit, A Groupware Toolkit", *ACM Transactions on Computer–Human Interaction* **3**(1), 66–106.

Segal, L. (1994), Actions Speak Louder than Words: How Pilots Use Non-verbal Information for Crew Communications, *in* B. Adelson, S. Dumais & J. Olson (eds.), "Proceedings of CHI'94: Human Factors in Computing Systems", ACM Press, pp.21–25.

Sohlenkamp, M. & Chwelos, G. (1994), Integrating Communication, Cooperation, and Awareness: The DIVA Virtual Office Environment, *in* R. Furuta & C. Neuwirth (eds.), "Proceedings of CSCW'94: Conference on Computer Supported Cooperative Work", ACM Press, pp.331–343.

Stefik, M., Bobrow, D., Foster, G., Lanning, S. & Tatar, D. (1987), "WYSIWIS Revised: Early Experiences with Multiuser Interfaces", *ACM Transactions on Office Information Systems* **5**(2), 147–167.

Tang, J. (1991), "Findings from Observational Studies of Collaborative Work", *International Journal of Man–Machine Studies* **34**(2), 143–160.

Tatar, D., Foster, G. & Bobrow, D. (1991), "Design for Conversation: Lessons from Cognoter", *International Journal of Man–Machine Studies* **34**(2), 185–210.

Valacich, J., Dennis, A. & Nunamaker, Jr., J. (1991), "Electronic Meeting Support: The GroupSystems Concept", *International Journal of Man–Machine Studies* **34**(2), 262–282.

Using Distortion-Oriented Displays to Support Workspace Awareness

Saul Greenberg[†]**, Carl Gutwin**[†] **& Andy Cockburn**[‡]

[†] *Department of Computer Science, University of Calgary, 2500 University Dr NW, Calgary, Alberta T2N 1N4, Canada.*

Tel: *+1 403 220 6087*

Fax: *+1 403 284 4707*

EMail: {*saul,gutwin*}*@cpsc.ucalgary.ca*

[‡] *Department of Computer Science, University of Canterbury, Christchurch, New Zealand.*

Tel: *+64 3 364 2774*

EMail: *andy@cosc.canterbury.ac.nz*

Desktop conferencing systems are now moving away from strict view-sharing and towards relaxed 'what you see is what I see' (relaxed-WYSIWIS) interfaces, where distributed participants in a real time session can view different parts of a shared visual workspace. As with strict view-sharing, people using relaxed-WYSIWIS require a sense of *workspace awareness* — the up-to-the-minute knowledge about another person's interactions with the shared workspace. The problem is deciding how to provide a user with an appropriate level of awareness of what other participants are doing when they are working in different areas of the workspace. In this paper, we propose distortion-oriented displays as a novel way of providing this awareness. These displays, which employ magnification lenses and fisheye view techniques, show global context and local detail within a single window, providing both peripheral and detailed awareness of other participants' actions. Three prototypes are presented as examples of groupware *distortion-oriented displays*: the *fisheye text viewer*, the *offset lens*, and the *head-up lens*.

Keywords: awareness, magnifying lenses, fisheye views, distortion-oriented displays, desktop conferencing, groupware.

1 Introduction

Real-time distributed groupware allows people who are geographically separate to work together at the same time through computers. These systems provide a shared virtual workspace where conference participants can see and manipulate work artifacts. The shared workspace typically contains groupware tools such as a shared sketchpad or drawing system — e.g. (Greenberg et al., 1992), multi-user text editors — e.g. (Baecker et al., 1994), idea organizers — e.g. (Tatar et al., 1991) or multi-user games. In addition to the workspace, a groupware system is likely to incorporate facilities for communication over audio and video links.

Unfortunately, groupware workspaces cannot yet match the diversity and richness of interaction that their physical counterparts afford. In particular, virtual workspaces make it more difficult to maintain a sense of awareness about who else is in the workspace, where they are operating, and what they are doing. In a physical workspace, people use peripheral vision, auditory cues, and quick glances to keep track of what goes on around them. In a groupware system, the visual field is greatly reduced, and many of our normal mechanisms for gathering information (such as glancing) are ineffective since the required information may be absent from the display.

In addition, the way that a groupware system supports view sharing can further impair people's abilities to stay aware. Recent groupware systems have relaxed the strict 'what you see is what I see' (WYSIWIS) model where all participants see exactly the same view of the workspace at all times (Stefik et al., 1987). The relaxations give people control over their own view of the workspace, and thus allow them to work in a more natural style, shifting their focus back and forth between individual and group work. Relaxed-WYSIWIS, however, can contribute to a loss of awareness since, when views differ, people can lose track of where others are and what they are doing in the workspace. One technique to support awareness in relaxed-WYSIWIS provides users with two separate windows: a normal-sized view of one's own working area; and a 'radar' overview that shows a miniature of the entire workspace, typically overlaid with boxes that represent each participant's viewport — e.g. (Smith et al., 1989; Baecker et al., 1994). While these work well in some tasks (Gutwin et al., 1996; in this volume), the separate windows introduce a physical seam between local and global contexts that a user may find difficult to integrate, and the radar miniature may not have enough resolution to show the necessary details of another's' activity.

In this paper, we propose *distortion-oriented* displays as a mechanism for presenting awareness information. These displays show both global context and local detail within a single window. They work by scaling most or all of a workspace to fit within a window, and then distorting (or magnifying) a region to show its detail. When applied to groupware, the distortion-oriented display provides both peripheral and detailed awareness of other participants by showing their position and actions in the global context, and by distorting the area around their work to see the details of the interaction.

In the following subsection we briefly review the workspace awareness requirements that groupware systems should satisfy.

Workspace Awareness

When people work together, they maintain an awareness of others that helps them coordinate activity and find opportunities to collaborate — e.g. (Dourish & Bellotti, 1992). This awareness, which we call *group awareness* (Gutwin et al., 1995; Gutwin & Greenberg, 1996), is part of the "glue" that allows groups to be more effective than individuals. Group awareness is made up of several kinds of knowledge about what is happening in one's collaborative environment, as summarized below.

Informal awareness of a work community is basic knowledge of who is around in general (but perhaps out of sight), who is physically in a room with you, and where people are located relative to you. *Group-structural awareness* involves knowledge about such things as people's roles and responsibilities, their positions on an issue, their status, and group processes. *Social awareness* is the information that a person maintains about others in a social or conversational context: things like whether another person is paying attention, their emotional state, or their level of interest. The fourth kind of group awareness is *workspace awareness*, which involves knowledge about how the others in the group interact with the shared workspace. In a face-to-face interaction, the shared workspace is often the tabletop and whiteboard, where people bring artifacts such as documents to the table, pass them to each other, point and gesture around them, use tools to modify them, and make notes on white-boards.

We define workspace awareness more precisely as the up-to-the minute knowledge a person requires about another group member's interaction with a shared workspace if they are to collaborate effectively. While it is less easy to define exactly what knowledge people require, the first column in Table 1 in Section 4.2 summarizes a few of the more essential elements comprising awareness, phrased as questions (the framework is reviewed in (Gutwin et al., in this volume) and more fully in Gutwin et al. (1995)). These awareness factors include information on the following important items: the *identity* of those in the workspace, their *location*, their *activity*, and the immediacy of *changes* with which others' activities are communicated. The elements in this table provide heuristic guidelines for the development of the awareness prototypes, as described in Section 3.

The following section presents a brief background on distortion-oriented displays. Section 3 then introduces three prototypes that demonstrate the application of distortion-oriented views in groupware: the *fisheye text viewer*, the *offset lens*, and the *head-up lens*: a video is also available that illustrates their dynamics (Greenberg et al., 1996a). The paper closes by discussing both the strengths and weaknesses of using distortion-oriented displays to support group awareness

2 Distortion-oriented Displays

A central concern in information visualization is how a system can present both global structure (that provides overview and context) and local detail (that reveals information in the user's area of interest). Distortion-oriented displays allow visualization that merges the global view of the information and the local detail of interest to the user. These displays can be categorized into two approaches: magnifying lenses, and fisheye views. Each are briefly discussed below.

2.1 *Magnification Lenses*

When a paper document contains details too small for people to read, they can use a magnifying lens to enlarge a portion of it. Similarly, a magnifying lens metaphor can be applied to computer displays. At its simplest, consider a large workspace that is scaled to fit within a single window. This provides the viewer with a sense of the global context but poor detail. When the viewer points to an area of interest on the display, a separate "lens" window containing a magnified view of that area appears on top of the original one.

Computer-based magnifying lenses surpass their physical metaphors. Stone et al. (1994) introduce the Magic Lens: a movable filter that affects the appearance of objects viewed through it, in ways that go far beyond simple magnification. Aside from scaling, they have applied the Magic Lens to show a variety of information: different renderings of pictures; state information of objects that is normally hidden; additional structures such as grids; selective detail of a view; and so on. They also show how a lens can be turned into a *click-through tool*, which modifies a user's input over the transformed region being viewed. A taxonomy of such see-through tools is given by Bier et al. (1994).

2.2 *Fisheye Views*

Fisheye views are computer visualization techniques that provide both local detail and global context in a single display (this concept was originally coined a *bifocal display* by Spence & Apperley (1982). Unlike magnification lens techniques, where entities are either magnified or not, fisheye views display the global context and local detail on a continuous 'surface'. The user chooses a point of focus where they wish to see local detail: this area is visually emphasized, and the remainder of the data is made less visually important.

Fisheye views have been used to visualize data in many domains. Furnas (1986) created systems for viewing and filtering structured program code, biological taxonomies, and calendars. Egan et al. (1989) used a type of fisheye view in Superbook, a text-based electronic book, to provide the now familiar notion of an expandable table of contents. Sarkar & Brown (1992) implemented graphical fisheye views for networks of nodes such as cities on a map.

Although fisheye techniques are normally used to emphasize a single focus point, multiple focus points can also be supported. Sarkar et al. (1993) built displays based on the metaphor of a rubber sheet, where several different focal points could be 'pushed forward' for emphasis. In addition, this system gave the user direct control over the amount of screen space used for objects in the areas of interest. Schaffer et al. (1996) also provided for multiple focal points in hierarchically-clustered networks.

3 Applying Distortion-oriented Views to Group Awareness

In this paper, we suggest that distortion-oriented views can also be applied to groupware as well as conventional information visualization. We contend that distortion-oriented views are well-suited to groupware because of their ability to provide awareness of others' actions in the workspace within a single window. To achieve this awareness, the positions and coarse actions of all participants are displayed within the global context, while the magnified areas present the local details of each participant's particular interaction.

To illustrate how this can be done, we present three prototypes: the *fisheye text viewer*, the *offset lens*, and the *head-up lens*. This section describes the awareness features provided by the prototypes. The limitations of these systems, and our plans for further work, are discussed in Section 4.

3.1 Fisheye Text Viewer

The fisheye text viewer (Greenberg et al., 1996b) supports awareness by assigning one focal point to each participant, and by giving each person the ability to tailor the magnification function of any of the focal points. It reveals the location of others within its workspace, and illustrates how details of other people's activity can be presented via multiple focal points. To demonstrate the fisheye text viewer, we first present how it works as a single-user system, and then how it works as a multi-user system.

3.1.1 Single-user Fisheye

The viewer uses a fisheye lens to present a text document, as illustrated in Figure 1a (left side). Most of the document is shown at a very small font, which gives the person a sense of the document's global structure. The user views local detail by selecting a focal point within the document, either by clicking the mouse on a line of text or by moving the scrollbar. If the scrollbar is used, the effect is that of sliding an optical lens up and down over the document. In Figure 1a, the user has selected line 157 as the focal point, and this line is shown in a large font. The surrounding 20 lines gradually decrease in size until the default background size is reached.

Users can tailor the shape and the magnification of their fisheye lens with the control panel shown on the right side of Figure 1a. First, they can adjust the font size of the background (global) text or have it removed entirely. Second, users can change the shape of the lens that magnifies text around their focal point, using a custom-built lens control. The black area of the control represents a cross-section of the lens; users increase the magnification function by moving any of the curve's points rightwards, or leftwards to decrease it. The curve is constrained to be always convex and symmetrical. As the lens is manipulated, the magnification function is immediately applied to the document.

3.1.2 Groupware Fisheye

The fisheye text viewer is also a groupware system that lets several people view the same document. Each person's view is relaxed-WYSIWIS, allowing each individual to set their own focal point on the document.

Workspace awareness is supported by representing each participant's focus in the document. Referring to the awareness factors in the first column of Table 1, identity and location information are presented by marking others' focal points with their chosen colour. In addition, the text around other participants' focal points is also magnified. Thus, activity awareness is provided through each user's view of the other participants' focal points. Figure 1b illustrates this: there are three focal points

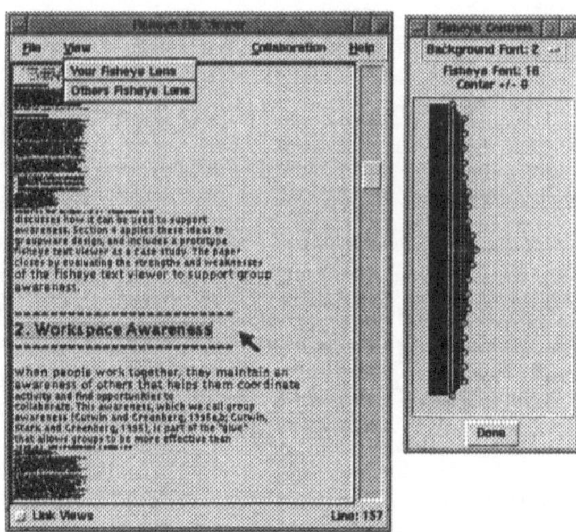

a) The single user version of the Fisheye Text Viewer.

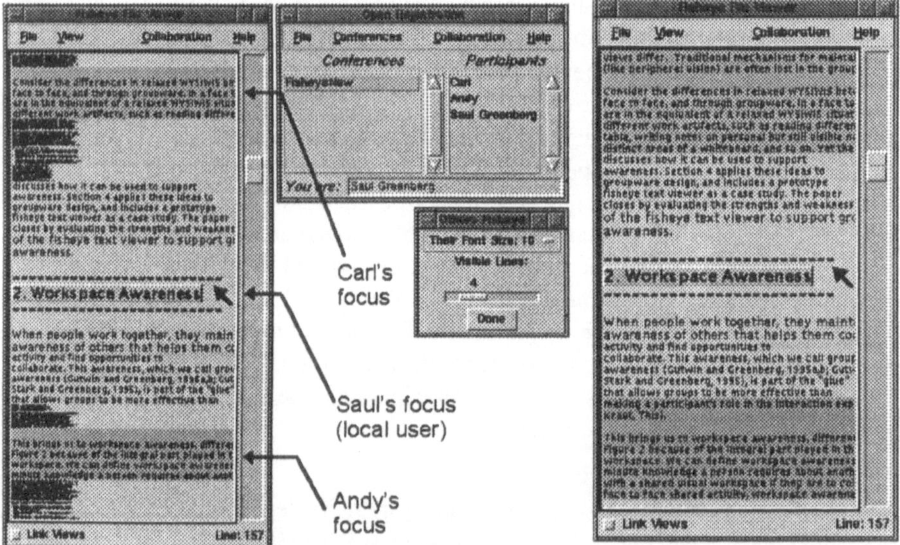

b) Groupware fisheye with multiple focal points and global context. c) Removing global context.

Figure 1: The groupware fisheye text viewer.

with corresponding magnified regions, the centre region belonging to the user and the surrounding two representing the other participants. Their locations in the global context and the detail of their work are clearly, and immediately, visible to the other participants.

A user can also change the magnification function applied to their view of other people's focal points — albeit in a simpler fashion — via the control panel on the middle right of Figure 1b. Moving the slider adjusts the range of the magnified region (here, to four lines), and a menu allows the font size of that region to be set (here set to 10 point font).

These fisheye controls allow users to flexibly allocate screen space for their own work or for the display of awareness information, as their tasks require:

- If only location information is required, a user can turn off the magnification of other participants' focus points. Their location will still be indicated through colour, but no detail will be shown. No extra screen space is used.
- When finer-grained awareness is desired, both location and detail can be progressively controlled by increasing the magnification around the other participant's focus, as well as the extent of the region being magnified.
- When people are working far apart in the document, a 'split window' effect can bring them closer together. This is achieved by making the global view invisible, thus displaying only the regions surrounding each focal point. For example, Figure 1c shows a split window effect using the same focal points and document seen in Figure 1b.
- For tightly-coupled collaboration, people can align their views to something closer to a strict WYSIWIS situation in two ways. First, moving their own focal point onto another person's focal point is appropriate for quick and spontaneous interaction. Second, people can link their views by clicking a check button on the viewer (Figure 1b & c, bottom left). This option lets all participants share a common focal point; if any user changes the focus, it will be changed on all other displays as well. View linking supports longer and more tightly coupled collaborations.

The fisheye text viewer has also been modified to cluster location information based on the document's semantic structure. For example, a code-viewing application places remote focal points on the name of the subroutine where that person is working, instead of showing the actual (and perhaps less meaningful) line of code.

3.2 *The Offset Lens*

The Offset Lens is a magnification-oriented system that allows participants to view and concurrently edit a shared graphical workspace. Figure 2 shows the Offset Lens in use. Nodes in the graph represent arbitrary 'grains' of information — for instance, pages in a hypertext document, a concept map, or independent design decisions and their associated rationale. The workspace is scaled so that the entire graph fits the window, and thus contains the entire 'global context'. In this section, the offset lens is first explained as a single-user system, and then as a groupware system.

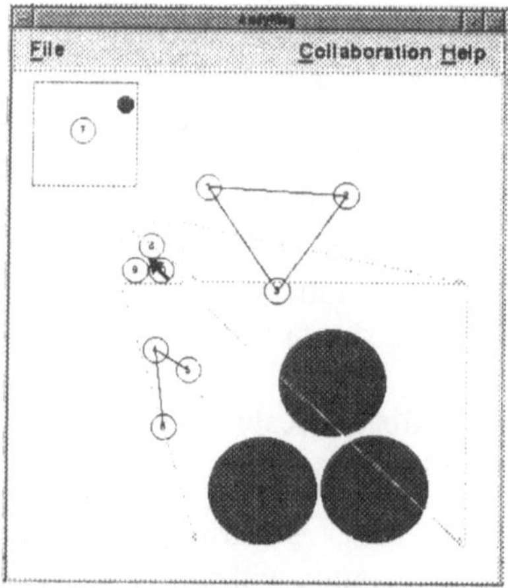

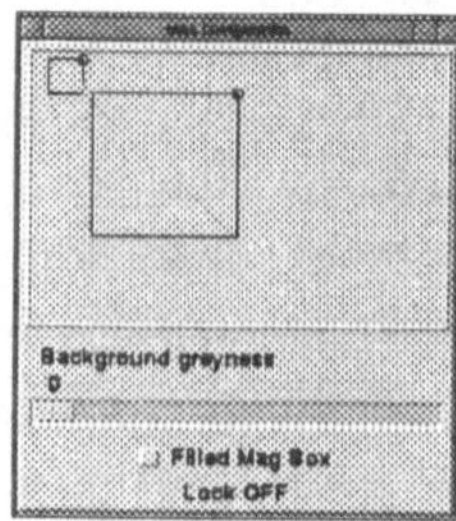

Figure 2: The Offset Lens, showing the magnification and offset controls on the right.

3.2.1 Single-user Offset Lens

The global context is directly editable, and the user can add new nodes and edges (lines) to it by clicking or dragging with the mouse. The user also has a magnification lens layered over a sub-area of the workspace, shown in Figure 2 as the bordered projected area on the bottom right. This lens shows the 'local detail' (the magnified nodes and lines around a person's cursor): the lens' position on the display follows the cursor as one moves around the global context, and the contents of the local detail continually update to show the new sub-area beneath the lens. As a single user system, it is similar in spirit to Ware & Lewis' (1995) DragMag image magnifier (the original Offset Lens, created before we saw the DragMag, was changed to include some of DragMag's single user features).

Like the global context, the local detail region is editable. Editing the local detail requires the user to lock the magnification lens' position onto the current focus (by clicking with the right-hand mouse button). Subsequent editing actions, identical to those at the global-level, take effect at the current magnification level. The cursor location and editing actions are immediately reflected, to all users, in the global context. The user can therefore see the consequences of edits in both the local detail and global contexts.

The user can alter several of the lens properties through the control panel (Figure 2, right window): the size of the lens; the position of the lens relative to the focal point; and its transparency:

1. The balance between global view and local detail is adjusted by directly setting the size of the magnifying lens. While the magnification factor remains constant, the area magnified by the lens (and thus the size of the lens) can be enlarged or made smaller.

2. A true magnifying lens, positioned over an unmagnified region, occludes some of the unmagnified nodes beneath the lens. This tends to hide the connections between thc local detail and global context. To mitigate this problem, the system allows a user to offset the magnified image away from the focus by dragging the magnifier to a new position (Figure 2, right window). When the offset is zero, the magnified image is placed on top of the focus. Adjusting the amount of offset moves the lens from the focal point, eventually allowing simultaneous views of the area of interest in both global and local contexts.

3. The global context and local detail are drawn as two elements that can compete for attention, and a user may want to adjust their visibility to suit the task on hand. The Offset Lens allows this adjustment in two ways. First, the magnifying lens can be set to transparent or opaque, set by selecting the 'Filled Mag Box'. For instance, the task of browsing the work surface is easier if one can see through the magnifying lens, while focusing on local detail is easier if the lens is opaque. Second, the visibility of the global context can be controlled by having it drawn at different grey levels. By adjusting a slider, the greyness moves from black to white and the global context becomes less visible and the local detail stands out further.

3.2.2 Groupware Offset Lens

The groupware Offset Lens uses relaxed WYSIWIS. All users see the same representation of the global context, including immediate updates following editing actions. However, each user's local detail (the images within their magnifying lenses) is not shared, allowing participants to focus on whatever part of the workspace they wish to view. Telepointers are also supported for gesturing and location awareness.

Referring to the awareness factors in Table 1, location awareness is provided by revealing to the other participants the position of each user's magnification lens on the global context. The identity of each user is determined by uniquely colouring their lens (another user is shown by the rectangle in Figure 2, top left). Activity and temporal awareness are provided by the immediate updates of editing actions on the global context. Additional location and activity awareness is available when a user is editing within their local detail (rather than in the global context). This information is communicated by small telepointers on the global context which provide an indication that the user is focused on a specific region and intends to carry out editing actions.

Through this combination of awareness mechanisms, each user can monitor the global context and stay aware of their colleagues' presence, their region of activity, where they are currently pointing to, and what actions they are doing. By not showing everyone's magnified views, a person's display is left uncluttered. Of course, people can align their magnified views when sharing of detailed information is required.

3.3 Head-up Lens

The Offset Lens takes the local and global views of a workspace, and merges them into a single display that shows both views at the same time. The Head-Up lens, which is a graph editor, takes this one step further, by layering and resizing both the

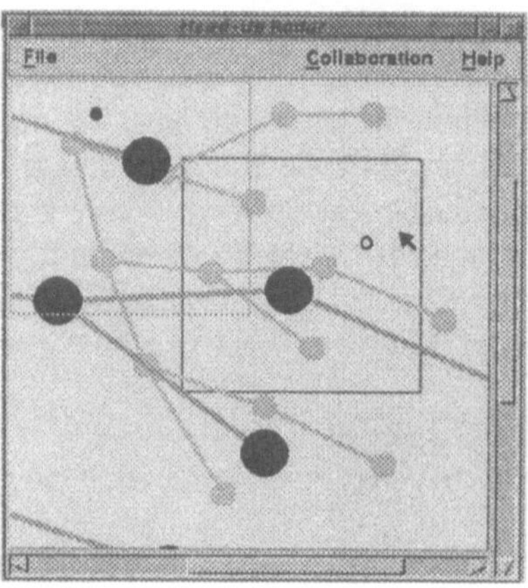

Figure 3: The Head-Up Lens.

views to fit the window exactly. It is a "transparent layered user interface", as defined by Harrison et al. (1995).

3.3.1 *Single-user Head-up Lens*

As with most head-up displays, our lens provides a two-level view of the workspace. It is illustrated by the graphical editor in Figure 3. Like the Offset Lens, the global context shows the entire workspace, scaled to fit the size of the window exactly. The foreground shows the local detail which is a viewport onto a sub-area of the background global context. The location of the user's viewport onto the global workspace is controlled through scrollbars and other conventional interface mechanisms. The two primary differences between the Head-Up Lens and the Offset Lens are that, first, the Head-Up interface is simpler because there is no need to raise or position the lens, and second, the user is unable to edit the global context directly in the Head-Up system.

3.3.2 *Groupware Head-up Lens*

As with the Offset Lens, uniquely coloured rectangles on the global context show the view extents of the local and remote participants, providing location and identify awareness. For example, the foreground viewport in Figure 3 is reflected by the middle-right rectangle in the background. When someone moves their foreground view, their rectangle slides around the background, showing where they are currently located. In addition, miniature telepointers in the background (drawn as small circles) give some indication of what object others are focusing on, proving activity awareness. The telepointers on the global context in both the Offset and Head-Up Lens systems also allow limited gestural communication even when participants do not share the same local view. To reduce the amount that activities on the global context intrude on a person's attention on the local-detail objects, the background is "ghosted out" in light grey.

4 Discussion and Further Work

The previous section described the interfaces and features of three prototypes for providing workspace awareness in groupware. The current implementations are intended to be point systems indicating what is possible and emphasizing the technical feasibility of group-awareness in distortion-oriented displays. In this section we identify the limitations of the prototypes, focusing on inadequacies in their interfaces and on mismatches between the awareness facilities they provide and those identified as desirable in Section 2. This discussion serves as a specification of our further work as we iterate from point-systems to evaluable working prototypes.

4.1 Assessing the User Interfaces

Although it is premature to run formal usability studies on the prototypes, the design team has experimented with each system. Our aim in assessing the interfaces is to remove the large grain usability flaws to ensure that subsequent usability analysis identifies problems with the support for workspace awareness rather than symptoms of lower-level interface errors.

Of the three prototypes, the fisheye-text viewer has the most polished interface. Users had few problems in changing their focal points and tailoring the focal properties of the lenses. The primary limitation of the fisheye prototype is functional, in that its editing facilities are rudimentary.

The most fundamental problem of the Offset and Head-Up Lens systems is that users are required to mentally integrate the magnified and unmagnified planes of work. The fisheye viewer does not suffer this problem so severely because the magnified regions appear on a continuous plane. Finding effective ways to balance people's need to both focus and divide their attention on transparent layered interfaces is a research issue in its own right, as now being explored by Harrison et al. (1995).

More generally, the interface to the Offset Lens is complex when compared to the two other systems. This is primarily due to the large number of user customizable features, but in addition, special interface measures are required to let a user edit both the global and local regions. The user has to select a mode which locks the lens onto the display, and directs user input to the local-detail region. Unfortunately, the locked lens makes it difficult to interact with objects that lie just outside the magnified area. This problem is partially resolved by the small telepointer which shows the user's area of action on the global context. An alternative (unimplemented) solution to the locking problem is based on Bier et al.' (1994) two-handed input techniques — one hand is used to move the lens over the display, while the other hand controls the mouse cursor and the interaction to the area either inside or outside the lens.

The interface to the Head-Up Lens is simpler, but more constrained, than that of the Offset Lens. The locking problems are resolved because editing is only possible on the local detail layer. This limitation would be straightforward to remove by adding a toggle that flips global and local layers, and by redirecting the input to the global level. This modification would, however, come at the cost of additional interface complexity. Other powerful, but complex, controls in the Offset Lens are not available in the Head-Up Lens. These include controls for the lens' size, magnification function, and the degree of shading used to obscure the global-context.

Despite its interface simplicity, the Head-Up Lens suffers problems similar to the Offset Lens, as well as a few others. Of particular note is the problem that changes in the global context, caused by the actions of others', can interfere and annoy a person concentrating on their local detail.

Some of the potential problems described above are repairable, others are ingrained in the fundamental approach of the particular distortion-oriented technique. The ultimate viability of the systems, and the degree to which these *potential* problems affect users, has yet to be determined through user testing

4.2 Assessing the Workspace Awareness

Generally, the systems satisfy the criteria for location and activity awareness (where and what) more successfully than the criteria for identity and temporal awareness. In assessing the user interfaces of the prototypes, issues of awareness have already been raised: for instance, the fact that others' actions can impinge on a user's local detail in the Head-Up Display. There are many other trade-offs and problems in the awareness mechanisms supported by the three prototypes, as summarized in Table 1. Each of the forms of awareness is briefly discussed below.

4.2.1 *Identity Awareness*

All the systems use colour coding as the main method of identifying participants. Each user, therefore, has a cognitive burden of mapping from colours to individuals. In our experience, this is not a problem as the small size of the group and the natural verbal and gestural deixis between participants strongly reinforce the colouring identification scheme. However, mapping could be difficult if the group is large or meets infrequently, or if speech channels are not immediately available. Another problem in the use of colouring occurs when overlapping colours obscure each other. This problem affects the fisheye text viewer most seriously, as large blocks of text may be coloured: in the two lens systems, only the bounding boxes of the lens regions are coloured. A partial solution to this problem would be to allow mouse actions within a region to pop up the names of those currently working in the area.

4.2.2 *Location Awareness*

Extensive use of telepointers and moving viewports provide rich information on the region of participants' activity in each of the systems. Because all participants' locations are embedded in the global view, it is easy for a user to situate exactly where others are working.

Awareness affords opportunities for tightly-coupled interaction, and as a consequence the ability to couple locations (and therefore views) would be useful. Currently, only the fisheye text viewer provides an explicit facility for tightly coupled views of the workspace. Thus, in the Offset and Head-Up Lens systems, users who wish to work directly on the same section of the workspace must make the necessary view adjustments independently to ensure that their focal regions are similar. Future versions of the Offset and Head-Up Lens systems will provide a view linking option, similar to that in the fisheye text viewer.

<table>
<tr><th>Awareness Element</th><th>Fisheye Text</th><th>Offset Lens</th><th>Head-Up Lens</th></tr>
<tr><td rowspan="2">Identity
Who is participating?</td><td rowspan="2">✔ Visible as coloured region and as enlarged font
✘ One coloured region may overlap another
✘ Area may be out of view</td><td colspan="2">✔ Coloured viewport and cursors of others visible in global context
✘ May be occluded by magnified objects</td></tr>
<tr><td>✔ Lens may be offset to see what is below it</td><td>✘ Foreground image must be scrolled to a clear area to make the occluded background visible</td></tr>
<tr><td>Location
Where are they working?
What can they see?
What are they pointing at?
Where can they have effects?</td><td>✔ Focal point shown as coloured lines within global context
✔ Area around the focal point enlarged
✔ Focal point can act as cursor
✘ Enlarged area does not represent actual viewport size</td><td colspan="2">✔ All viewport shown within global context as coloured boxes
✔ Small cursors shown in global view
✘ Images within viewport may be too small to determine what a person can see</td></tr>
<tr><td>Activity
What are they doing?
What are their intentions?
What changes are they making?</td><td>✔ Area around the focal point enlarged, with details clearly visible
✘ Text cursor not shown
✘ Area may be scrolled out of view</td><td colspan="2">✔ Changes made in detailed view immediately visible in global view
✔ Fine-grained movement of small cursors in global view indicates intent
✘ Global view may not have enough detail to make changes and cursor movement comprehensible</td></tr>
<tr><td>Temporal immediacy
When have changes been made?</td><td colspan="3">✔ Changes are shown as they are made
✘ No ability to replay past events
✘ Can miss changes in the global view when attending the local view</td></tr>
</table>

Table 1: Assessing the prototypes with respect to awareness criteria.

4.2.3 Activity Awareness

By implementing multiple focal points, the fisheye text viewer is able to show details of what is happening in each person's focus. In addition, the text viewer's tailorable lenses allow users to make their own decisions about allocating screen space, letting them trade awareness information for screen space and greater individual focus when their tasks require it. However, the region of other participants' activity may be scrolled out of view if the document is large. In contrast, in the Offset and Head-Up Lens systems, the scrolling problem does not occur because the global context reveals the entire workspace at all times. The lens systems are, however, susceptible to another problem — in a very large workspace, the global context may lack the detail to provide useful activity awareness.

The counter-side to activity awareness is clutter. When focusing on the details of their personal work, users are likely to want a dedicated view that masks background activity. The tailorable lens in the fisheye text viewer allows the user to suppress information about the activity of others, and the Offset Lens allows the user to mask out the global context. The Head-Up Lens, as currently implemented, makes no user configurable allowance for the suppression of activity information, but this could be easily repaired at the cost of additional interface complexity.

4.2.4 Temporal Awareness

Although all show updates as soon as they are made, none of them support awareness over a period of time. If a user leaves the session for a period, or misses a sequence of updates because the region was obscured or scrolled out of view, there is no support for finding out what has changed, for replaying the sequence of actions, or for finding out who did what.

4.3 Summary

Assessing the prototypes' support with respect to the awareness criteria is useful in helping us identify potential problems prior to end-user evaluation. What is clear is that the distortion-oriented techniques do, at least in theory, support many awareness needs. Of course, there is no guarantee that users can use this information in practice. The benefits and problems that emerge in actual use are yet to be determined in usability studies.

5 Conclusions

In this paper, we have identified the lack of workspace awareness as a major limitation in current relaxed WYSIWIS groupware. The critical factors in workspace awareness were discussed, and distortion-oriented visualization techniques were proposed as a technology for satisfying many awareness requirements. Distortion-oriented techniques are promising because they allow awareness information to be integrated within large information spaces, while minimizing the demands on screen real-estate.

The three prototype groupware applications described in the paper demonstrate novel ways that distortion-oriented displays can provide people with a sense of group awareness. The capabilities of these systems were assessed with respect to the workspace awareness criteria. While much work remains to be done, we believe that the awareness facilities demonstrated by these systems will ultimately improve the usability of real-time distributed groupware.

These distortion-oriented awareness tools are all derived from single-user equivalents. We believe that these techniques will be *at least* as useful as their single-user counterparts, for the groupware extensions make no constraints on single-user use. We also believe that leveraging these techniques to support group work will make them even more beneficial.

Availability

GroupKit (Roseman & Greenberg, 1996), the toolkit used to implement the awareness prototypes, is available via anonymous ftp. The actual systems described in this paper are either included in the release, or available from the authors.

site:	ftp.cpsc.ucalgary.ca
directory:	pub/projects/grouplab/software
http:	http://www.cpsc.ucalgary.ca/projects/grouplab/home.html
mailing list:	groupkit-users@cpsc.ucalgary.ca

Acknowledgements

This research is (gratefully) supported in part by Intel Corporation, and the National Engineering and Research Council of Canada. Neville Churcher and Mark Roseman contributed in one way or another to this work.

References

Baecker, R., Glass, G., Mitchell, A. & Posner, I. (1994), SASSE: The Collaborative Editor, *in* B. Adelson, S. Dumais & J. Olson (eds.), "Proceedings of CHI'94: Human Factors in Computing Systems", ACM Press, pp.459–460.

Bier, E. A., Stone, M. C., Fishkin, K., Buxton, W. & Baudel, T. (1994), A Taxonomy of See-through Tools, *in* B. Adelson, S. Dumais & J. Olson (eds.), "Proceedings of CHI'94: Human Factors in Computing Systems", ACM Press, pp.358–364.

Dourish, P. & Bellotti, V. (1992), Awareness and Coordination in Shared Workspaces, *in* J. Turner & R. Kraut (eds.), "Proceedings of CSCW'92: Conference on Computer Supported Cooperative Work", ACM Press, pp.107–114.

Egan, D. E., Remde, J. R., Landauer, T. K., Lochbaum, C. C. & Gomez, L. M. (1989), Behavioral Evaluation and Analysis of a Hypertext Browser, *in* K. Bice & C. H. Lewis (eds.), "Proceedings of CHI'89: Human Factors in Computing Systems", ACM Press, pp.205–210.

Furnas, G. (1986), Generalized Fisheye Views, *in* M. Mantei & P. Orbeton (eds.), "Proceedings of CHI'86: Human Factors in Computing Systems", ACM Press, pp.16–23.

Greenberg, S., Gutwin, C. & Cockburn, A. (1996a), Applying Distortion-oriented Displays to Groupware, Videotape available from the authors.

Greenberg, S., Gutwin, C. & Cockburn, A. (1996b), Awareness through Fisheye Views in Relaxed WYSIWIS Groupware, *in* R. Bartles (ed.), "Proceedings of Graphics Interface'96", Canadian Information Processing Society, pp.28–38.

Greenberg, S., Roseman, M., Webster, D. & Bohnet, R. (1992), "Human and Technical Factors of Distributed Group Drawing Tools", *Interacting with Computers* **4**(1), 364–392.

Gutwin, C. & Greenberg, S. (1996), Workspace Awareness for Groupware, *in* M. Tauber (ed.), "Companion Proceedings of CHI'96: Human Factors in Computing Systems (CHI'96 Conference Companion)", ACM Press, pp.208–209.

Gutwin, C., Greenberg, S. & Roseman, M. (1996), Workspace Awareness Support with Radar Views, *in* M. Tauber (ed.), "Companion Proceedings of CHI'96: Human Factors in Computing Systems (CHI'96 Conference Companion)", ACM Press, pp.210–211.

Gutwin, C., Stark, G. & Greenberg, S. (1995), Supporting Workspace Awareness in Educational Groupware, *in* J. L. Schnase & E. L. Cunnius (eds.), "Proceedings of Computer Supported Collaborative Learning '95", Lawrence Erlbaum Associates, pp.147–156.

Harrison, B., Ishii, H., Vicente, K. & Buxton, W. (1995), Transparent Layered User Interfaces: An Evaluation of a Display Design to Enhance Focused and Divided Attention, *in* I. Katz, R. Mack, L. Marks, M. B. Rosson & J. Nielsen (eds.), "Proceedings of CHI'95: Human Factors in Computing Systems", ACM Press, pp.317–324.

Roseman, M. & Greenberg, S. (1996), "Building Real-time Groupware with GroupKit, A Groupware Toolkit", *ACM Transactions on Computer–Human Interaction* **3**(1), 66–106.

Sarkar, M. & Brown, M. H. (1992), Graphical Fisheye Views of Graphs, *in* P. Bauersfeld, J. Bennett & G. Lynch (eds.), "Proceedings of CHI'92: Human Factors in Computing Systems", ACM Press, pp.83–91.

Sarkar, M., Snibbe, S. S., Tversky, O. J. & Reiss, S. P. (1993), Stretching the Rubber Sheet: A Metophor for Visualizing Large Layouts on Small Screens, *in* "Proceedings of the ACM Symposium on User Interface Software and Technology, UIST'93", ACM Press, pp.81–91.

Schaffer, D., Zuo, Z., Greenberg, S., Bartram, L., Dill, J., Dubs, S. & Roseman, M. (1996), "Navigating Hierarchically Clustered Networks through Fisheye and Full-zoom Methods", *ACM Transactions on Computer–Human Interaction* **3**(2), ?–?

Smith, R. B., O'Shea, T., O'Malley, C., Scanlon, E. & Taylor, J. (1989), Preliminary Experiences with a Distributed, Multi-Media, Problem Environment, *in* J. Bowers & S. Benford (eds.), "Proceedings of ECSCW'89, the 1st European Conference on Computer-Supported Cooperative Work", Computer Sciences House, pp.19–34.

Spence, R. & Apperley, M. D. (1982), "Data-Base Navigation: An Office Environment for the Professional", *Behaviour & Information Technology* **1**(1), 43–54.

Stefik, M., Bobrow, D., Foster, G., Lanning, S. & Tatar, D. (1987), "WYSIWIS Revised: Early Experiences with Multiuser Interfaces", *ACM Transactions on Office Information Systems* **5**(2), 147–167.

Stone, M. C., Fishkin, K. & Bier, E. A. (1994), The Movable Filter as a User Interface Tool, *in* B. Adelson, S. Dumais & J. Olson (eds.), "Proceedings of CHI'94: Human Factors in Computing Systems", ACM Press, pp.306–312.

Tatar, D., Foster, G. & Bobrow, D. (1991), "Design for Conversation: Lessons from Cognoter", *International Journal of Man–Machine Studies* **34**(2), 185–210.

Ware, C. & Lewis, M. (1995), The DragMag Image Magnifier, Videotape at the CHI'95 Video Program, ACM SIGCHI.

Working by Walking Around — Requirements of Flexible Interaction Management in Video-supported Collaborative Work

Steinar Kristoffersen & Tom Rodden

Cooperative Systems Engineering Group, Computing Department, Lancaster University, Lancaster LA1 4YR, UK.

Tel: *+44 1524 65201*

Fax: *+44 1524 593608*

EMail: {*steinar,tam*}*@comp.lancs.ac.uk*

This paper considers the effects of video-based communication systems on individual, local mobility in the everyday, practical 'space' of work. The notion of video as a vehicle that transcends physical space in an unproblematic fashion is carefully considered. Previous academic research has emphasized how video can extend and enhance the working environment. We found, doing a focused ethnography in the Customer Service Centre of a large high street bank, that video, in a trade-off between 'real' and 'virtual' mobility, restricted the use of personal, workaday, physical space. Issues thus raised for the design of video-based communication systems are: physical mobility in workaday space during interactive sessions; modal and temporal switching between and within different media; articulating and supporting collaborative work with private activities; and, accommodating alternating tasks.

Keywords: video, communication, multimedia, space, mobility, CSCW.

1 Introduction

This paper is concerned with how people in the workplace manage their social and professional interaction *with* and *within* a personal, physical as well as logical, working environment. Work is articulated and accomplished *in* and *by* this space. The notion of an enhanced or extended 'space' mediated by video is critically examined in this perspective, and some implications for design are drawn.

The relatively recent development of commercial multimedia products has allowed systems that have previously existed only in the domain of research laboratories to move into the workplace. Introduction, adoption and use have not been unproblematic, however. This paper is based on an ethnographic study in a major, high street, UK bank. The bank is in the process of introducing a 'Video Link' to facilitate communication between specialists in a Customer Service Centre, and the customers and clerks in the branches. The Customer Service Centre came into existence as part of an ongoing centralization effort in the bank, responding to the perceived globalization and competitiveness of the industry. Managerial opinion at the bank suggested that, in most of its business domains, it was facing harder competition; from specialized or low-cost, 'telemarket'-based businesses, increased globalization; through the European Economic Agreement, and a more mobile, less loyal customer base; probably linked to uncertainties in the employment market.

The bank wishes to reduce the back-log of customer queries by reducing paperwork and putting the customer, in the branch, 'directly' in contact with the specialists. Video is perceived as a suitable, technical solution. The bank is interested in exploring video as a medium for more efficient selling and administration, compared to the telephone- or document-driven work of today, as well as a symbol of the advanced, service-oriented organization that "puts the customer first". The introduction of the Video Link has, however, been problematic, for many reasons (Hughes et al., 1995). The problem that we wish to address in this paper is the ways in which video-based communication systems potentially reduce the degrees of freedom, logically and physically, for the users in the Customer Service Centre. Moreover, a design framework is suggested to address the problem in future implementations of video conference systems for these, and similar settings. It is not, in this paper, our concern that the Video Link is potentially obtrusive, or has few mechanisms to ensure privacy. Our concern is the ways in which video potentially interferes with the natural, workaday use of the personal, physical space for people whose work is unpredictably dynamic and mobile.

Early work with video defined the 'media space' as an electronic setting in which groups of people could work together, even when they were geographically or temporally dispersed (Stults, 1988). A similar research effort was undertaken by Bellcore, focusing on the 'virtual hallways' of media space. Key concepts are social browsing, proximity and unplanned interaction (Root, 1988; Fish et al., 1993). For many researchers in the field, this has become the equivalent of supporting the ability to meet informally, claiming that this is a critical aspect of productive group work (Fish et al., 1990; 1992). Some of these assumptions have little relevance in the bank (Kristoffersen & Rodden, 1995).

The research philosophy adopted for the empirical work in the Bank, was broadly that of ethnomethodologically informed ethnography. The aim of ethnography is to describe what happens in a selected setting, from (or as close to as possible) the participants own perspective (Hammersley & Atkinson, 1993). The distinguishing characteristic of this approach is the researcher's involvement in the organization; describing the circumstances, practices, conversations and activities that comprise the 'real world' character of everyday work settings. The purpose of such investigations is to provide a rich understanding of what takes place in the workplace during an ordinary working day. Ethnography relies on the participation of the researcher in the daily life of the organization, either covertly or overtly, collecting through observation, listening, and questions any data that might add to the understanding of the research question. The 'naturalistic' approach suggests that the object of our study should be the phenomenon of interest in its 'natural' state, i.e. not an experiment designed to control and isolate variables. Based on a single setting, ethnography does not yield results that are easily generalizable. Having said that, ethnography can produce findings that are 'typical' and relevant for practical purposes (Hammersley, 1992). Our claim is that, as a paper-based open plan office with an intermediate, but critical level of computerization, the bank's service centres are typical for many medium-to-large corporations.

This migration of video-based communication technology from the research labs to the complex world of work offers the opportunity for a general reflection on the core conceptual underpinning of many of these systems. However, given the recent introduction of the Video Link in our example, we are not yet in a position to carry out longitudinal studies. Furthermore, in several situations into which the bank has deployed the Video Link, the use frequencies have been low. There is little evidence that the usage has 'stabilized', or even that the new medium will be adopted at all. Given our commitment to study the use of video in realistic settings, redesigning the 'experiment' is not an option, neither is assigning to 'samples' artificial tasks for which they are allocated the Video Link tool. Rather, the fact that the Video Link is not used much becomes, in the methodological framework we employ, simply more data, adding to our understanding of the phenomena that we study.

2 Working Mobility in the Bank

2.1 The Customer Service Centre

The organizational unit reported on in this section is the Regular Payments Unit (RPU), part of the recently established Customer Service Centre in the bank. Approximately 20 people work in the unit, including the manager and supervisors. The following section is an account of how work is performed *without reference to the Video Link*, most of the time relying on written documents and telephones for communication. We offer the account because we believe that it provides important pointers to problems pertaining to video-based communication system in use at this workplace. Although designated 'specialists', some are 'job sharing' or 'part-timers', and their experience and commitment vary (some have been with the bank 'always', others are looking for 'a way out'.) The specialists' title is Senior Machinist Officer (SMO), a reminder of the previous division of labour in which they were responsible for operating the 'back office' business machines. While most staff have previous banking experience, young people without the 'back office' background of the SMOs are currently being brought in. The RPU are responsible for setting up and cancelling standing orders and direct debits, as well as dealing with any ensuing queries and complaints. Traditionally, the customers would approach their local branch about problems, queries, or complaints pertaining to their accounts. Since the SMOs no longer work in the branches, the customers' queries are recorded on dedicated forms (Query Forms) by the clerks, alongside with the information necessary for the SMO to resolve the query. Increasingly, the customer will approach the Customer Service Centre directly using a 'free-phone' service offered, in which Telephone Liaison Officers (TLOs) record the queries. In the long run, the bank aims to replace parts of an expensive branch network with 'home banking'. This approach has not proven unproblematic, however, since clerks and TLOs are recruited not for their specialist knowledge, but rather for their ability to sell the bank's products. The managers suspect that the consequence has been that too many, and badly formulated moreover, queries have been forwarded to the SMOs. When information essential to successful resolution of a query is found to be lacking, the account holder has to be addressed again with further risk of alienation and lost custom. The Video Link is therefore also introduced to alleviate the problematic asides of the new organization of work, reducing the number of errors and time needed for completion, as well as the amount of paperwork.

The specialists are allocated a set of queries every morning, albeit that their 'routine' work setting up, checking and cancelling contracts, is considered more important. But not always; some customers and some queries are 'urgents'. Local knowledge aids the supervisors and SMOs in recognizing important customers, suspicious wordings and amounts that require immediate action. The 'ideal' day will start by completing the necessary, everyday routine, followed by query handling. Most of the time SMOs respond to demands from supervisors, managers, peers, clerks, and customers, making the best out of the time and resources available. Much work is event-driven, either in the form of customers phoning through on the external lines, or as interruptions from colleagues. Often queries cannot be completed in one push, simply because other people are involved. Customers, business managers, and other clients are sometimes unavailable, lack the essential information, or occasionally simply don't know the answer to a query. The expected average for query handling is 10 minutes per query, or 4 in an hour. Our impression, however, is that, at best, this is an optimistic estimate. The specialists maintain a log for all their work, in which information needed to process each query is entered as well. Generally, little autonomy is awarded the specialists, and they are supposed to consult the manager or other supervisors in exceptional cases.

The one-page Query Forms have fields defined for the essential information, but are completed in a close to 'free-form' manner, the back-side being used as well when there is too little space, or the categories and tick-boxes do not fit the cases. The QFs can either be filled in by the TLO or by the branch staff.

The physical layout of the office is important, in particular the distance between specialists and manager/supervisors, the manual archives, and the single VDT terminal connecting this unit to the centralized transaction register. The manager/supervisors often need to sanction decisions made by the specialists. The archives are consulted frequently because all correspondence and documentation are kept there, either sorted chronologically, or by customer name. The VDT terminal can be queried, asynchronously (or rather, synchronously, but very slowly — it takes many minutes before a result is produced), for individual transactions yielding reference numbers, account number, amounts, etc. This essential information is often missing from the Query Forms.

In this environment, people are continuously moving around, discussing cases with each other, particularly and obviously if the cases relate to special experience or competencies. The ability of this dedicated space to allow workers to interleave tasks, to stop and start as new information comes to hand from a variety of sources; to monitor the work of others, to consult colleagues and intervene when necessary; is central to the practical accomplishment of work in the Service Centre. During one working day, I observed a SMO work with the 4 queries that she was assigned. One clearly visible, and important element in terms of the 'orderliness' of the work, is the way that cases are interleaved, worked in parallel, suspended, and part-initiated by all parties involved in the 'collaborative' effort; managers, specialists, branch clerks and customers.

The following list shows the actual sequence, or ordering, of one day's query handling, as seen from the perspective of one of the specialists:

1. The P. Brothers — Use the VDT.
2. Amend a SO.
3. Dr & Mrs S.
4. Call from branch manager — 'Verbal query'.
5. The P. Brothers — Talk to colleague.
6. The big telephone bill.
7. The Zoo.
8. Vodac.
9. Dr S. is on the phone.
10. The Zoo is on the phone.
11. Approached by colleague about overdraft in branch.
12. The big telephone bill.
13. Routine transactions.
14. Vodac.

To illustrate the use and 'affordances' of space let us briefly consider two of the cases observed (The P. Brothers and Dr & Mrs S.) during the study. 'Interaction management' details are included, but each case is discussed on its own for ease of reading. Bear in mind that this is not an attempt to exhaustively summarize the field studies, the descriptions are offered as illustrations of how work is performed in the CSC.

In the first example, the accountant for a company, the P. Brothers Ltd. had phoned in a query about two items on a statement on behalf of 'the brothers':

1. *The TLO had taken the query, and filled in the Query Form. The core of the matter was that the company did not acknowledge two debits on their account statement, and they "suspected fraud!" The amounts and the dates were correctly entered on the form (according to the specialist this was exceptional in itself), but it had no reference numbers.*

Resolving the case of the P. Brothers Ltd. involved qualified guessing based on experience, the perusal of the paper record, and searching in the VDT connected system. The paper records were extracted from the manual archived approximately 15 yards away from her desk. The specialist had to leave her desk also to use the 'old-fashioned' transaction register to retrieve the reference number, using the date as input for the VDT query.

2. *Cheryl 'suspended' this case by walking over to the VDT to enter a query to the micro film system about the transactions that the P. Brothers were suspicious about. She needed more detailed information, and the transaction was too old to be found in the transaction register system. While waiting for the VDT to respond, she started working on the next case, leaving only a note on the VDT keyboard, with the reference number for this VDT query, saying that she had a 'job' running on the machine.*

The purpose was to gather all essential information about the 'suspicious' transaction. The specialist returned to her desk whilst waiting for the VDT to display the results.

3. *Sometime later, whilst simultaneously engaged in other work, and after collecting the output from the P. Brothers Ltd. query; the specialist asked a colleague (located at the desk behind her), whose speciality was fraud rather than standing orders, about credit and debit cards and the use by shops of the rented card transaction register machines. At this point the specialist thought she had recognized the reference numbers as a format generated by exactly such transactions.*

The colleague's desk was the next immediately behind her own, so all she had to do was turn around and ask.

4. *She contacted the debit card help line, using the telephone, with a number given to her by her colleague, where they told her that, "yes, she was right", the code on the account statement was for a service charge on two card transaction register machines used for the processing of Access and VISA transactions.*

In the next instance, customers Dr & Mrs S., had queried two similar debits that appeared on their account, suspecting that a debit to the ABC Building Society had been drawn twice.

1. *The TLO had written on the query form that the customers had not made any amendments to their standing orders lately. (From experience such changes often produce errors.) However, this proved to be untrue, as the specialist discovered by retrieving the file from the archive, since a note requiring their standing order to the building society to be amended was in their file.*

Again, the SMO left her desk to get documentation from the archives.

2. *The specialist checked the list of standing orders on their accounts, in the database accessible from her personal workstation, and found three entries registered on the ABC Building Society. One of them had been changed recently. She suggested that a mistake had been made, that perhaps someone had amended the wrong standing order, thereby bringing a standing order for £12.75 up to £226.57, because she had found a printout of an old standing order in the file, with a reference number matching the new one. The one that should have been amended (if the working hypothesis so far was correct) was still active, drawing a monthly £223.23 from the account.*

Because of the bank's concern with maintaining good customer relations, the most important thing in cases as this is to refund the customer, after which the specialist called the building society, and explained about the overpayment.

3. *She filled in two forms, one to debit the 'suspense account', the other to credit the customer's account. She called the building society, and explained about the over-paying. However, while talking to the person in the building society, she began to look increasingly puzzled, later appearing quite irritated saying that she "didn't think the person there was very bright".*

After finishing this conversation she told me she suspected something was very wrong here, because the person in the Building Society said the customer only had two payments to them, one for the mortgage, the other one an endowment insurance. If this was the case it should have been only two, not three sets of contracts. She wondered if one of the contracts, a Direct Debit, had once been a Standing Order that hadn't been cancelled when the new contract was set up. However, if this was the case, why hadn't the customer noticed? A new working hypothesis is thus introduced.

4. *In this situation, the specialist was using the Query Form all the time, she scribbled down a prioritized 'to do' list on it and ticked them off as she completed each item. She talked loudly to herself, (or perhaps to me?) "Take it easy, it's important to get this right, and avoid starting a new complaint, ...". She repeated to herself that "yes, the customer was now refunded, and so she would have to write a letter to the building society to reclaim the overpaid money". To do this she brought up a template for this type of request on the screen, unfortunately the template addressed the letter to the customer and so she changed the addressee, and wrote the letter, practically from scratch. She arranged for the letter to be printed and then went into the SO entry system to amend the contract details.*

However, working with the query had revealed that something else was wrong here, and it wasn't obvious what it was. The SMO couldn't from the manual file find out what the two other contracts were for, and whether or not one really should have replaced the other. So which contract should really be amended? The only solution would be to call the customers at the number they had left on the Query Form.

5. *The specialist finally managed to get hold of the doctor on the telephone, and he told her that the £36 DD was for Endowment insurance, but that he didn't know what the £12.75 SO had once been. She called the building society again to confront them, the person on the other end doing most of the talking, and then she said "Dr S. lied to me, this item is in fact not an Endowment insurance."*

These fieldwork excerpts illustrate in a direct and tangible manner the need for individual mobility and flexibility in the 'real' space of the Service Centre. Members of the centre make use of the affordances of the space in a real and direct way throughout their query handling activities. The physical freedom allows them to manage and interleave the tasks constituting their work to allow the highly contingent nature of queries to be handled in a flexible and direct manner. The space and layout of the Service Centre are central to the practical accomplishment of the work at hand. Until recently customers who accessed the Service Centre on the telephone were unaware of the nature of the space in the Service Centre.

Clearly video can be intrusive in the respect that it opens up the SMOs workplace to the customer, but that is not the main concern of this paper. The point we make is that the specialist relies on locally and globally dispersed resources (e.g. the VDT, the archives, fax-machines, telephones, etc.), people (colleagues for advice, managers for sanctioning, branch clerks hosting the customer, etc.), and organizations (external service providers, clients, branches, building societies, etc.), that because of the specialists' new role as *producers of synchronous*, tightly coupled video presentations would have to be accessed differently. Current video-based communication systems do not offer support for this type of flexible, unpredictable, dynamic, distributed, and situated management of interaction. Our findings are aligned with the claim by Heath et al. (1995, p.84) that:

> "In particular, the principle concern in media space research with supporting (mediated) face-to-face communication, has inadvertently undermined its ability to reliably support collaborative work"

Indeed, with more relevance for the Video Link than for media space research in our opinion.

2.2 The Video Link — Training

The Video Link is introduced into a workplace characterized by the need for flexible interaction management and unpredictable individual mobility in 'real space', as excerpts from the fieldwork clearly demonstrate. The bank presumes that the SMO is able to initiate, resolve, and conclude the query in 'real-time', thereby not only increasing customer satisfaction, but also reducing the administrative overhead. Eventually, efficient new routines for query handling may evolve. However, during an ethnography of training sessions for SMOs that eventually would be allocated to the Video Link 'team', we found indications that rather than augment the space of members of the Service Centre, video can constrain the individual mobility and flexible management of the personal space in work-settings.

The example of use presented below was gathered from an early training session. The bank's research department employed external consultants to do a series of training sessions for the sites where video was introduced. In this session the bank's research department in London had provided a list of 'simple', example, queries for the specialist's attention and assumed the role of the customer in the branch on the Video Link. Excerpts from the fieldwork data illustrate and clarify both the nature and scope of the problem.

The example case reported here is concerned with the 'winding up', or deleting, the account of a deceased person. Here the 'customer', is the (pretence) spouse of the deceased, and he is in the branch to transfer the money to his own account. Before the call was invoked the specialists briefly discussed how to handle this case, because neither of them were 'expert enough'.

Strict legal compliance has to be observed in cases like this. Partly due to the increased specialization in the centre, only two people are authorized to deal with them.

1. *The practical problem that the specialist now faces is that the branch, as part of a marketing effort as much as an attempt at shifting the responsibility, have already told the customer that they would let them talk to an expert. The branches don't generally have the expertise themselves to detect which cases most specialists can handle directly.*

2. *Furthermore, the 'customer' has also waited for 2–5 minutes for the call to be set up.*

The obvious action to take in a 'telephone supported' space, would be to put the customer on hold, and then walk off to find the expert. If the expert could deal with the case immediately, then the call could simply be transferred. If the experts were both busy, the specialist would take the customer's number, and promise that the right people would call him back. This would be a relatively light-weight operation, and of little inconvenience to the customer. This is no longer the case as the customer has waited to become introduced to the link, and has effectively been promised instantaneous access to an expert, i.e. immediate *positive* action.

Clearly, video, as part of an organizational re-orientation, has put the customer, as well as the specialist and the branch clerk, in a new situation inasmuch as the expectations of instantaneous responses and lasting, tightly coupled interaction are much higher.

3. *The trainer suggested that they could get hold of the "circumstances person" and get them to contact the branches straight away. The problem for the specialist is that she has to do this in a way that doesn't take away her image as an expert.*

The problem, therefore, for the SMO (and the centre) is that any such apparently 'evasive action' would quickly attenuate the customer's confidence in the competencies they advertize. These aspects obviously trouble the specialists during this training session. One of them 'drops out' of the frame without noticing (and neither do her colleague and the trainer).

4. *The specialist is very nervous, but she manages to concentrate on looking straight into the camera. She leans forward a lot. She seems very insecure from how she talks, when she tells the customer about how "the senior expert will contact her later today", the pitch of her voice rises as if it was a question.*

Both SMOs both look increasingly uncomfortable and insecure in the 'designed-to-be-simple' cases, with the quality of promises and advice rapidly declining as they become 'stuck' in front of the camera. The focus on the 'customer', and the consciousness of knowing that the customer is looking at them seems to make the telephone residing on the desk 10 inches from them an 'invisible' option for local, point-to-point communication, which is what they would normally do in similar situations.

In summary, the specialists involved became increasingly uncomfortable and insecure during the 'designed-to-be-simple' cases, with the quality of promises and advice rapidly declining as they became 'stuck' in front of the camera. In our interpretation, the main problem experienced by the users was that the resources of the ordinary, workaday space; e.g. colleagues to ask for advice, managers to decide on exceptional cases (which they almost all turned out to be, after all), and documentation from the archives, were no longer available to them because they were 'on the air'. The focus on the customer, and knowing that the customer had been offered the added value of 'facing' them, made the telephone sitting on the desk only 10 inches from them an 'invisible' option for local, point-to-point communication, which is what they would normally use in similar situations.

2.3 The Video Link — Real Use

In a 'real' use situation, with an actual customer, a similar situation occurred, confirming our suspicion that the work ordinarily carried out by bona fide competent specialists, require a more elaborate and flexible interaction management than the Video Link and current division of labour of which it is part, can offer today:

1. *At 12, the specialist gets a live call on the link.*

2. *The specialist receives info before call about "items on statement", account number, customer's name Mrs Middlemiss, ("that's going to be a bit of a mouthful").*

3. *The specialist invokes the accounts and transactions registration system, and checks the account before starting the Video Link session.*

   (i) *"Sound and picture OK?"*

   (ii) *"My name is J, ..."*

4. *Recounts the problem.*

5. *Customer with baby on her lap.*

6. *"I have your details right here, so I'll just take a look at it and see what I got".*

7. *Checking both customer accounts.*

8. *Quite long concentrated silences in which the specialist is hammering away on the keyboard.*

9. *She explains to the customer how the Bank is organized; CSC, each operator serving three branches, keyed on transaction with wrong sort-code, "downstairs-upstairs" (The entries are keyed downstairs).*

   (i) *Got customer's number.*

   (ii) *Got convenient contact time.*

   (iii) *Same account number in a different branch (West Kirby), customer is in Wallasey.*

   (iv) *The specialist is aware of the "no eye contact" problem, she told me she thought the customer had been weary of the technology.*

The crucial parts of this excerpt are when the specialist 'defines' the problem based on the available information. She determined that the case could not be solved by herself. She explained to the customer what went wrong (that one of the processing staff forgot to key in the branch's sort code to override the terminal's default, with the result that all her transactions were registered on the wrong sort-code). Then, she made an appointment (getting the telephone number and a convenient time) to contact the customer again once she had resolved the query. It is also relevant to the constraints and possibilities within our design space of future applications, that the 'problem' is anchored in two different branches. Potentially, the need to contact and interact with a geographically dispersed, even wider group could arise, during the interview with the customer.

3 Design Implications

For most people, the ability to move around freely and flexibly in their local environment is not a privilege, but rather a necessity. However, using the Video Link, this mobility could become restricted. Our work suggests that designers should critically revisit their models of video-supported communication. Below, we discuss four issues that designers of video-based communication systems should take into consideration.

The first issue; *physical mobility* implicates at least two design considerations:

1. What is the 'scope' of the cameras that are being used for a 'presentation', and how can the user influence it during a session.

2. In the case of recording from an open office; who 'owns' the (public) devices? Who determines what is captured and where it is broadcast? This issue bears resemblance to the 'floor-control' mechanism of computer conference applications.

The 'floor' and 'scope' needs to be signalled to potential 'extras' that might inadvertently become part of the presentation. Compared to the 'control' design issue in (Bellotti & Sellen, 1993), the public nature of the open office increases complexity and the need for in-session negotiation of resources.

The second issue brought to attention is the need for *modal and temporal switching*. One possible requirement (e.g. in a situation where a customer is interviewed and an 'exceptional' issue arises demanding the instantaneous, but brief attention of a manager) is for the Video Link to allow a second connection to be set up without dismounting the current. Most applications today do not allow a new participant to be added to the 'conference' that is running. It is possible, using the IP multicast addressing scheme, but unfortunately with loss of privacy (IP multicast is broadcast, and 'everyone' can listen to the network traffic). Current video-communication systems usually take the physical address and port number to transmit to as start-up parameters, offering either unicast (i.e. UNIX sockets) or multicast communication. Additional conference processes can generally not be invoked because the first instance running (successfully) has made the physical devices unavailable on the hardware library level (i.e. the device is 'locked').

The third design concern; *allowing collaborative work to be articulated by private activities*, is clearly demonstrated in the note-taking and planning activities performed by the SMOs. Not all work we do is cooperative, and even during cooperative sessions we sometimes wish to do work that is unrelated to the other participants, or for some other reason is temporarily private. Due to the customer-oriented work of the specialists, this requirement will be 'hard' to satisfy; after all video is 'sold' as a vehicle for direct access and more 'tightly coupled' interaction than can be offered by the telephone. In some situations it could be appropriate to share documents in preparation between the centre and the branches. This proposal was, however, rejected by the bank's research department in collaboration with user representatives, simply because "they were sold at the other end as experts" and didn't feel comfortable about sharing *mistakes* with customers, in that context.

The fourth design issue is *persistence*, e.g. representing the interview as an entity that could be stored in permanent memory, containing the necessary information to resume. Typically, this requirement could address the need to work on several cases simultaneously, as we saw the SMOs do in the centre. Instead of starting from scratch, the contact information, related electronic documents, the quality specification, etc., could be 'contained' in the connection, making it possible to re-enter the 'conference' where it was suspended, instead of *restarting* it.

4 Conclusion

The problem addressed in this paper is that video communication imposes limitations in the individual, physical space, with reduced degrees of freedom and inflexible interaction management. The limited ability to manage interaction *in the personal, physical space* across video connections is particularly problematic for the adoption of video technologies within real world work settings. We believe that the existing models of so-called 'media spaces' are insufficient. Without the ability to manage the interaction, users of video based communication systems are left with fewer resources to 'get the job done', in situations where the demands of the job involve talking to colleagues, getting 'OKs' from managers, searching and retrieving manual documents from shared archives, filing in forms and mailing letters. Albeit based on one focused ethnography, the aspects outlined above are characteristic of most office work. Multiple cameras (e.g. *'bird's view'*), cannot unproblematically alleviate the situation due to problems of privacy and intrusiveness. With video, the remote customer potentially 'reaches into' the physical space without a presence of her own, causing significant disturbances to the work taking place (Heath & Luff, 1991). Mutual referencing and the transfer of local context between sites are made harder as well, upon introducing several cameras for each site ("establishing and sustaining a mutually compatible frame of reference can prove deeply problematic" (Bellotti & Sellen, 1993)).

The centrally switched model of video based systems, ISDN-based, analogue or digital on local area networks, are problematic inasmuch as connections can either be *created*, knowing in advance the physical address of information provider and information consumers alike, or *destroyed*, freeing the devices and controlling software for new connections. This creates awkward interaction management, not only because taking down and putting up connections is time consuming, but, mainly, because movement in the office space is hard to predict.

We suggest a design framework that could be used to draw attention to important issues in the design of video-based communication systems. Our preliminary set of requirements for such systems includes the ability to explicitly manage and transfer video connections between machines, for instance when moving from the personal workstation to archives or common office equipment like faxes or dedicated terminals. A 'floor control' and 'scope report' mechanism could make the control & feedback framework suggested by Bellotti & Sellen (1993) more cogent for open offices and public spaces. The participants should be able to perform 'add', 'delete', and 'modify' on an existing connection without breaking and re-initializing it, simply because these moments are swiftly dealt with in interpersonal communication, but still, we think, important enough to warrant support. When discussing privately the ongoing case, or to accommodate interruptions, it should be possible to 'hold' and 'resume' a connection. Interesting aspects of *presence* in media space arise, and will be pursued in future research. Integration with the telephone will become important in the customer oriented work performed in the bank, since at present, most external agents don't have a compatible video kit. In an 'extended office space', privacy concerns will have to be addressed throughout and thoroughly. In the case described in this paper, such matters are complex not only because of the customer-oriented matter of their work, but because the privacy of an individual office is the privilege of very few.

Introduction of video-based communication has, in this particular, but, we believe, typical, open office environment not been entirely successful. More research, design, development and experimental use are required to produce useful systems. The eventual success and utility of video in such settings depend, at least, on a richer set of mechanisms to manage the interaction in video 'space'.

5 Further Work

Work is ongoing to implement the requirements that we outlined above. In the first 'demonstration', current common approaches to video 'conferencing'; UNIX unicast on sockets and IP multicast, will be pushed to their limits in prototypes informed by the field studies. From these assessments of the technology, new requirements of multimedia and network technology will, alongside with a new set of models of their design, implementation and use, most likely, surface.

Acknowledgements

Financial support for this work was provided by the Research Council of Norway as part of project 100268/410, and Norsk Regnesentral, from which the author is currently on leave. The Committee of Vice Chancellors and Principals is gratefully acknowledged for the ORS Award 1995/1996. Thanks are due to the specialists in the CSC and their managers for patiently and openly allowing us to learn about their work, as well as the Video Link project leader and our contacts in the Bank's research department. I would also like to thank my colleagues at Lancaster for useful comments. Particular thanks are due to Mark Rouncefield for his support during the fieldwork.

References

Bellotti, V. & Sellen, A. (1993), Design for Privacy in Ubiquitous Computing Environments, *in* G. de Michelis, C. Simone & K. Schmidt (eds.), "Proceedings of ECSCW'93, the 3rd European Conference on Computer-Supported Cooperative Work", Kluwer (Academic Press), pp.77–92.

Fish, R., Kraut, R., Root, R. & Rice, R. (1993), "Video as a Technology for Informal Communication", *Communications of the ACM* **36**(1), 48–61.

Fish, R. S., Kraut, R. E. & Chalfonte, B. L. (1990), The VideoWindow system in Informal Communications, *in* D. G. Tatar (ed.), "Proceedings of CSCW'90: Conference on Computer Supported Cooperative Work", ACM Press, pp.1–11.

Fish, R. S., Kraut, R. E., Root, R. W. & Rice, R. E. (1992), Evaluating Video as a Technology for Informal Communication, *in* P. Bauersfeld, J. Bennett & G. Lynch (eds.), "Proceedings of CHI'92: Human Factors in Computing Systems", ACM Press, pp.37–48.

Hammersley, M. (1992), *What's Wrong With Ethnography?*, Routledge.

Hammersley, M. & Atkinson, P. (1993), *Ethnography: Principles in Practice*, Routledge.

Heath, C. & Luff, P. (1991), Disembodied Conduct: Communication through Video in a Multi-Media Office Environment, *in* S. P. Robertson, G. M. Olson & J. S. Olson (eds.), "Proceedings of CHI'91: Human Factors in Computing Systems (Reaching through Technology)", ACM Press, pp.99–103.

Heath, C., Luff, P. & Sellen, A. (1995), Reconsidering the Virtual Workplace: Flexible Support for Collaborative Activity, *in* H. Marmolin, Y. Sundblad & K. Schmidt (eds.), "Proceedings of ECSCW'95, the 4th European Conference on Computer-Supported Cooperative Work", Kluwer (Academic Press), pp.83–99.

Hughes, J., Kristoffersen, S., O'Brien, J. & Rouncefield, M. (1995), The Organisational Politics of Meetings and their Technology — Two Case Studies of Video Supported Communication, *in* "Proceedings of the First IFIP WG8.6 Working Conference". Leangkollen, Oslo, Norway, 14th–17th October.

Kristoffersen, S. & Rodden, T. (1995), Multimedia Support of Collaboration in a Teleservice Team, *in* H. Marmolin, Y. Sundblad & K. Schmidt (eds.), "Proceedings of ECSCW'95, the 4th European Conference on Computer-Supported Cooperative Work", Kluwer (Academic Press), pp.293–308.

Root, R. W. (1988), Design of a Multi-Media Vehicle for Social Browsing, *in* D. G. Tatar (ed.), "Proceedings of CSCW'88: Conference on Computer Supported Cooperative Work", ACM Press, pp.25–38.

Stults, R. (1988), Experimental Uses of Video to Support Design Activities, Technical Report SSL-89-19, Xerox PARC.

Multimedia

Matching Media to Goals: An Approach Based on Expressiveness

David Williams, Iain Duncumb & James L Alty

Department of Computer Studies, Loughborough University, Loughborough, Leicestershire LE11 3TU, UK.

Tel: *+44 1509 222681*
Fax: *+44 1509 211586*
EMail: *{D.M.L.Williams,I.P.Duncumb,J.L.Alty}@lboro.ac.uk*

This paper addresses the problem of output media selection in the design of human-computer interfaces. Particular emphasis is placed on the effect that the chosen medium has on the nature and effectiveness of the interactions that can take place. A novel approach is suggested in an attempt to gain an insight into why particular media allow certain goals to be achieved more effectively. This approach borrows ideas from linguistics and logic, and views media as formal representational systems. Out of this approach is developed the notion of expressiveness; the amount of abstraction a representation system affords a referent domain. The approach suggests that it is the congruence between the representation required by the goal and the expressiveness afforded by the media that largely determines the effectiveness of the interface. To give an example of this approach, three VCR user interfaces are discussed in terms of expressiveness.

Keywords: multimedia, user-centred design, expressiveness, goal decomposition, VCR programming.

1 The Media Selection Problem

It is a truism that any interaction between a computer and a human relies on the mediation of the machine's internal state and means of suggesting its use to the user. This begs the question; "how do we represent this internal state to the user?". Multimedia technologies, such as digital audio and video, bit-mapped graphics and high speed animation, have greatly increased the number of output options available. This expansion of the interface design-space makes poor medium choices more likely.

To attempt to remedy this situation, research in a variety of fields from social science to computer science has attempted to identify the important indices of this choice. Whilst all approaches are not computer-based, in every case the goal of effective communication is paramount. Work concerned with goal and task descriptions for interactive and didactic systems (Casner, 1991; Maybury, 1993; Remus, 1984; Andre & Rist, 1993; Alty et al., 1992), data descriptions (Roth & Mathis, 1990; Mackinlay, 1986; Arens & Hovy, 1993), automatic presentation design (Casner, 1991; Arens et al., 1988; Mackinlay, 1986), perceptual characteristics of users (Casner, 1991; Buttiegeig, 1989), characteristics of media (Bertin, 1983; Tufte, 1983; Alty & Rijkaert, 1994; Hunt, 1989; Lohse et al., 1990), hardware constraints (Alty & Rijkaert, 1994), terminology (Frolich, 1992; Arens & Hovy, 1993; Nigay & Coutaz, 1992), demonstrates the multi-disciplinary nature of multimedia research, each group having its own motivations and goals. One result of such multi-disciplinary approaches is a divergence in the definition of terms, such as medium, modality and channel, which are often used interchangeably depending on the focus of study. This lack of a unified terminology makes it necessary to define such terms at the beginning of any discussion. The following definitions will therefore be used throughout this paper:

Medium: Representational system or language with its own distinct syntax, semantics and pragmatics.

Multimedia: Communicating using a number of different media simultaneously.

A further factor is identified by the artificial intelligence community by Levesque (1988, p.357), who suggests that:

> "Problem solving is all about choosing the right representation of the problem."

This reminds us that HCI is essentially design for the support of problem solving at the interface. With this view, media are only deemed useful if they aid in the solution of some goal in some mediated domain. The media provide a view of the task world that can vary greatly according to the type of media used. This seriously affects the viewer's exploration strategy and eventual solution to the presented problem.

2 Media Seen as Representation Systems

Since media vary in their physical manifestation and interpretation, addressing the media selection process requires a fundamental discussion of media as representation systems. By taking this mechanistic approach, the reasons for media choice in particular problem scenarios can be grounded in what differentiates between media.

Palmer (1978) provides a starting point:

- Structure of the represented domain.
- Structure of the representing domain.

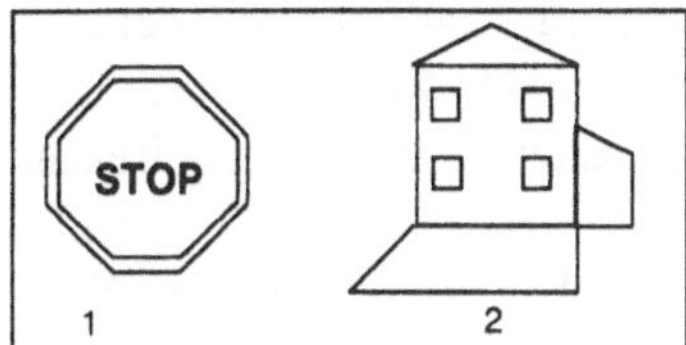

Figure 1: Pictogram(1) and multi-dimensional icon(2) representations.

- Aspects (entities) of the represented domain.
- Aspects (tokens) of the representing domain.
- Correspondences or mappings between the represented and representing domains.
- Key terminology that allows mappings to be understood.

Palmer suggests that this description is applicable to any representational system. However, the description is only sufficient if one is considering systems where tokens encode entirely by virtue of their form through perceivable variations in dimensions, e.g. size, shape, colour. Since a dimension can have only one perceived value at a time, Bertin (1983) describes these tokens as *monosemic*; a collection of dimensions denotes one and only one domain referent (this does not apply if tokens have temporal variations in form, i.e. animation, in which case further information can be conveyed by the speed and type of temporal transformations). *Monosemic* describes a range of instances from one-dimensional icons (Figure 1(1)), to multidimensional icons (Figure 1(2)). The strength of these representation systems is that once the corpus of dimensional mappings and/or referents is learnt, the system can be accurately interpreted (e.g. {Number of windows} = {Number of bedrooms}, etc.). However, Arens & Hovy (1993) identify restrictions on these properties. They suggest the number of encoding dimensions of monosemic systems is severely limited, since they are restricted by their perceptual nature; only so many dimensions can be used as encoders without confusion and with a limited resolution.

Alternatives to monosemic representation systems are *polysemic* systems (e.g. linguistic systems). These representations encode information in a different way that is not constrained by their physical form. Consequently they can have a paucity of perceptual encoding dimensions. Such systems are limited to sequences of concatenated *marks*, either strung together in one-dimensional space for written language, or in time for spoken language (*mark* applies to the perceivable constituents of the language that make up the tokens or words of a linguistic system. These in turn carry meaning). Linguistic systems rely on complex abstract systems to dictate valid structure and meaning. A representation instance is not the result of *n-ary* relational mappings to the domain (e.g. {size, shape} = {value, type}). It is defined by a complex transformational grammar and a many-faceted semantic system. There may also be proclivities of usage defined by pragmatics.

Thus to interpret these systems correctly requires an understanding of:

- The conceptual meaning of tokens as defined by lexical semantics, i.e. a dictionary.
- The domain meaning of tokens as defined by the represented domain.
- Which token sequences make sense.
- The domain meaning of acceptable token sequences as defined by structural semantics.
- The effect of domain context on meaning (Barwise & Perry, 1983).

As a result of this highly complex knowledge-base, such systems are able to be polysemic and therefore, in certain circumstances, ambiguous. They can use more than one token sequence to refer to the same domain entity or event.

However, Goodman (1968) points out that such ambiguity can be avoided in linguistic systems. Such representational systems are called notations to distinguish them from their polysemic, linguistic counterparts. Goodman argues that this distinction must be made because the lexicon of this type of representation system is not ambiguous; a given referring token has one, and only one, referent in the represented world. Examples of such systems are computer languages, where declarations refer to one variable and one variable only. However, such systems still retain the abstract syntax and semantics defined above.

In summary, we have made an important distinction between monosemic and polysemic systems. Monosemic systems make their n-ary interpretation rules *visible*. In doing so they become tied to their physicality and are restricted in what they can represent. On the other hand, polysemic systems are not bound by physical constraints but suffer from a need for their users to learn complex underlying interpretation rules. Of course, there is a continuum of representation systems between the two. Between the extremes are linguistic systems where the abstract syntax is made simpler (e.g. computer languages), or where token systems are extended by keys and terminologies allowing representation beyond form, e.g. geographical maps, conceptual graphs (Sowa, 1979).

3 Media Supporting the Solution of Tasks

If we are to practise user-centred interface design (Norman & Draper, 1986), then our approach should focus on supporting the goal(s) which users must achieve during their interaction with the computer (Card et al., 1983, pp.192–228). This approach will involve an analysis of the component tasks and sub-tasks that define the information required to support user interaction and define system feedback.

There are many ways in which the interface designer can support users in achieving their goals. Weir (1991) describes three possibilities with particular reference to domestic systems:

- One-shot command approaches.
- Intelligent control approaches.
- Intelligent dialogue approaches.

As Woods (1991) points out, the representations chosen to convey the system's state to the user, determine the type and sequence of tasks and actions that are required to satisfy goals. For any goal we must identify how it can best be achieved within the above constraints. Implicitly this is asking for the interface representations to provide a user-system dialogue that makes the goal reachable. We suggest that the key is the ability of the representation system to convey the maximum amount of relevant domain information in the most economical way.

An Example: Euler's Circles

Work by Stenning et al. (1994; Stenning, 1994; Stenning & Oberlander, 1995), indicates that it is the monosemic/polysemic distinction that dictates how representation systems can support problem solving. It is suggested that although an abstract medium has an unlimited ability to represent a domain, understanding can be problematic because the encoding mechanisms are hidden.

As an application of this theory, Stenning examines an abstractive graphical representation that has been proven to aid problem solving more than a polysemic linguistic representation system (Grossen & Carnine, 1990). The chosen system is Euler's Circles (Euler, 1772), which was designed to support syllogistic reasoning (the part of logic which deals with relationships between sets, e.g. if all A are B and some B are C, what are consistent relationships between A and C?). The difficulty of syllogisms lies in the need for the problem solver to consider variations of initial premises (*all A are B* implies variations A and B, ¬A and B, ¬A and ¬B). This is followed by studying the resulting combinations of *premise* pairs (for more detail see Stenning & Oberlander (1995)). This is an example of how a prohibitively large state-space, which a problem solver must explore, places intolerable burdens on short-term memory.

Stenning argues that the success of Euler's Circles is firstly due to its use of what at first sight would appear to be a monosemic system, i.e. {point, circle} = {member, set}. However, only those diagrams that represent *maximal* models of the premises (i.e. a single diagram capturing all types consistent with the premise) are considered. Secondly, on top of this isomorphic representation system an additional 'x' symbol is added to denote *minimal* types (directly defined by the premise rather than consistent with it). This allows a simple graphical algorithm for cancelling or leaving these marks when premise pairs are combined (for more detail see Stenning (1994)). The graphical algorithm reduces the solution to a one-pass process; the representation has trivialised the solution of what was a complex goal by using the Euler Circle representation system. In the context of our discussion this work brings out two important and related points.

Firstly, the abstraction made possible by the minimal region 'x' marking on the *maximal* models, extends the monosemic system into an abstractive, polysemic system. This can now convey a number of domain states in a single representation system instance, and allow the processing of these states when premises are combined. As a result of this, the syllogistic reasoning goals are made humanly tractable. Secondly, due to this abstraction, the task required to identify valid solutions becomes a trivial topological and sub-region marking task. The beauty of Euler's systems is that the encoding mechanism of the Euler's Circles makes this possible. It is a clear example of the representation making the task trivial by reducing the number of domain states that must be individually represented.

What Stenning identifies is the abstractive ability of a medium. This allows one instance of the representation system to encode more than one *state-of-affairs* in the domain. An abstractive system is therefore much more economical in its conveyance of information. This ability is particularly useful when the number of states within the domain state-space to be visited for a solution is large. The previously mentioned syllogisms form a large state space and many other domains have this property. More tangible examples are provided by Moray (1986) and Sanderson & Verhage (1989), who focus on the control of large process-control systems, e.g. chemical and power generation plants. They point out how the vastness of the problem solving state space is dealt with by operators, who learn to mentally abstract over these state spaces, allowing them adequately to control the system.

Further advantages of abstraction over several domain states are identified by Grossen & Carnine (1990). They found that graphical aids for problem solving elevated the success of novice students to the level of experts, who had used a linguistic representation. Experts used heuristics to allow them to consider possible problem states. The novices were given the same advantage by the graphical-aid because it abstracted over the domain, compacting multiple states into single representation instances.

4 Expressiveness as a Measure of Media Abstraction

We have shown abstraction to be essential in the support of problem solving in complex domains and can now define the notion of expressiveness. This notion is intended to quantify the maximum amount of goal-oriented domain information that a given representation system can convey to the user.

Other work has touched on this idea. Mackinlay (1986) has suggested expressiveness as a measure of the match between primitive isomorphic representation systems, such as bar-charts and scatter plots, and simple statistical tasks defined over a discrete numerical domain. The representation systems considered by Mackinlay do not abstract over the domain and so can be seen as having low expressiveness. They are monosemic systems; one state of the domain is encoded by one instance of the representation system. The work of Schubert (1976) provided a formalized view of representational expressiveness by using monadic predicate calculus. The expressiveness of a medium, in this case semantic networks (Brachman, 1979; Woods, 1975), was gauged by what aspects of the predicate logic could be captured.

Low Expressiveness

MARS (Minimal Abstraction Representation System) e.g. graph, table
"can only express one model of the domain"

|

LARS (Limited Abstraction Representation System) e.g. Euler's Circles
"can express several models, but not in an arbitrary dissection of the state space"

|

UARS (Unlimited Abstraction Representation System) e.g. natural language
"can express arbitrary positions of the state space"

High Expressiveness

Figure 2: Classification of representational systems.

Both of these approaches treat representation systems independently of the domain they convey and the tasks they support. Stenning argues that this is meaningless since it is the domain that determines how the representation system must be interpreted. Mackinlay's work offers a caveat to this, since it considers media that are already defined at their most primitive level. This allows his argument to move from the syntactic implications of their pre-defined form (e.g. located marks on axes) to the semantic repercussions of this syntax. This is in contrast to Stenning's work, which moves in the opposite direction defining first how the representation should be interpreted, as determined by the domain that defines the syntax (i.e. its semantic interpretation).

The two approaches are at odds due to their motivations. Stenning's starting point is to reveal why certain representation systems work best in certain situations. Mackinlay is more pragmatic in his approach as he attempts to match systems to data by virtue of their form, rather than some abstract concept of computational tractability advocated by Stenning (1994). Both authors have highlighted two important approaches to representation selection:

- Representation systems that are accepted as primitive, can be defined in terms of what they are able to represent independent of the task, e.g. a numerical axis.

- For complex domains, one should start with a domain description. Goals should then be considered in terms of what tasks will most easily provide the solution, and the representation should be chosen which affords this solution.

In summary, we define expressiveness as the number of goal-relevant states of the represented domain that a representation system can capture. It is a result of the constraints at all levels, which are part of a representation description.

Stenning & Oberlander (1995) classify different representational systems along a continuum, as shown in Figure 2. The terms MARS, LARS and UARS are labels given to areas of the continuum.

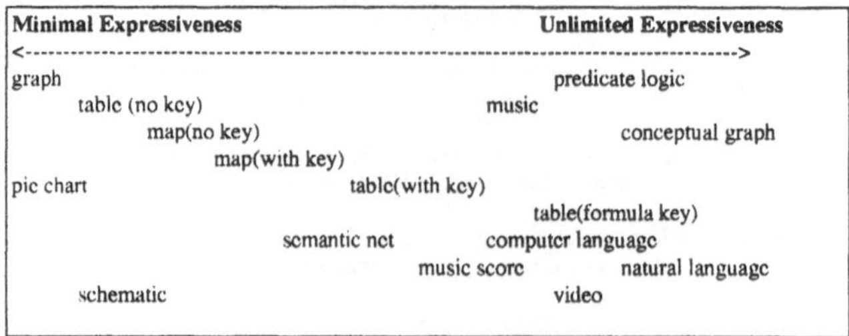

Figure 3: Tentative expressiveness continuum.

4.1 Ranges of Expressiveness

Since Figure 2 describes a continuum, it is interesting to consider finer expressiveness distinctions between representation systems. For example, although graphs and tables can both be regarded as minimally expressive (i.e. they can only represent one domain state per representation instance), there is a subtle difference. The ordinal nature of the graph axes enforces an ordering restriction on domain data that is not required in the tabular representation.

Further distinctions are shown in Figure 3, which shows how additions to representation systems can increase or decrease their expressiveness, e.g. adding key terminology to table cells as in spreadsheet applications. This is an important characteristic when one is attempting to choose suitably expressive media for domain and goal descriptions, e.g. ordering table rows and columns allows trends between object dimensions to be easily seen.

5 Expressiveness and Goal Accomplishment

At the outset of this paper, we suggested that the key to good user interface design was choosing an interface representation that would allow the user's goals to be satisfied. We can now discuss this in terms of fixed or modifiable representations that have a certain expressiveness. In our brief look at Euler's circles, we saw how choices in the representation transformed the goal accomplishment from a memory-intensive solution to a topological *one-pass* graphical algorithm. The key is that this was a result of the expressiveness of the medium (circle representation system) *matching* the abstraction required by the reasoning goal. The syllogisms required some abstraction over domain states (syllogism variations) and the representation system provided this abstraction.

We must now show the utility of this method in a more tangible domain. This will allow us to demonstrate the utility of the expressiveness approach and provide indications of where to develop our thinking.

6 Applying our Approach to Video Cassette Recorder Programming

The VCR is often cited as an example of poor user-interface design (Norman, 1988), and a number of subsequent studies have proposed improvements to the interface. Thimbleby (1991) identified four categories of problems associated with VCRs and concluded that if designers followed guidelines addressing these, VCRs could be made much more usable. Similar conclusions were reached by Hoffberg (1991). Plaisant & Shneiderman (1992) treated VCR programming as an instance of a class of home scheduling problems and developed a standardized interface employing direct manipulation.

The convergence of the TV and Personal Computer technologies offers new media for addressing the VCR usage problem. VCR programming is therefore an interesting domain for testing our ideas on expressiveness and effectiveness. Three different types of programming interface are considered.

6.1 Two Conventional VCR Programming Interfaces

An Akai VCR (model VS-G64EK-N) is analysed as an example of a conventional interface, providing on-screen entry of programme details. The TV screen is used to show the schedule, with the user inputting the start/stop times and TV channel of the programme to be recorded. Cursor control keys on the remote hand-set are used to navigate.

The same VCR also provides programming via VideoPlus numbers. These numbers are input into the hand-set, where they are converted to times, dates and TV channel prior to transmission to the VCR unit.

6.2 Prototype Drag and Drop Programming System

Figure 4 shows the main screen of a proposed drag and drop interface. The programme *Chandler Co.* has been selected for recording and is being dragged across the screen.

Four columns of TV channels are shown against a clock time scale and a separate column, initially empty, displays those programmes selected for recording. Buttons positioned above and below the clock time scale, are used to scroll the display to show earlier or later programmes. Programmes are selected for recording by clicking and dragging into the record column, and further programmes selected are arranged by the system in chronological order. Recording is cancelled by dragging the programme out of the record column and dropping anywhere else on the screen.

6.3 Results of a User Evaluation

Duncumb (1995) prototyped the drag and drop interface using Visual C++ on a PC and carried out usability comparisons with the conventional systems. In summary, the results suggested that the new interface was quicker to use, provided better quality output and was favoured by users. It was interesting that although the conventional time/date entry system required more key presses compared to VideoPlus, users preferred the former because meaningful information was being manipulated.

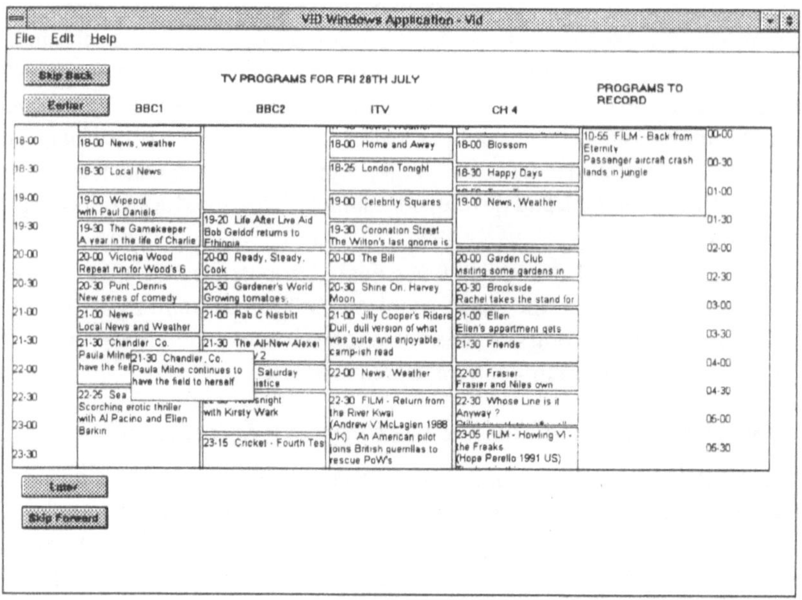

Figure 4: The main screen of the drag and drop interface.

7 Analysis of the VCR Interfaces in Terms of Expressiveness

Any allocation of media in the interface requires the description of the target domain and the tasks. However, in the chosen example media have already been suggested. Therefore we restrict our discussion to noting the differences in the way the interfaces support the programming task as opposed to the ideal task solution. All descriptions are grounded in terms of the expressiveness approach, which accesses semantic and syntactic characteristics of the chosen representation systems.

7.1 Video Programming Domain Description

The TV programming domain can be seen as a database that holds programme instances. They are frames of the following form:

Programme:

Title: *name (1–max_name_length)*
Start Time: *time (24 hour)*
End Time: *time (24 hour)*
Date: *date (dd/mm/yy)*

Channel: *channel (1–4)*
Description: *text (1–max_length)*

We assume primitive *name, hour, minute, date, channel* and *text* types. The domain holds many programmes, related by time and channel. As well as this object description, some global semantic criteria must be obeyed:

- Program scheduling is usually continuous i.e. there is a programme on at all times on all channels.
- No two programmes can share the same time-slot on the same channel.
- Programmes appear contiguously in time.

7.2 Conventional On-screen System

Once the desired programme has been found from an external source (e.g. TV schedule), its details must be entered by the following procedure, which uses a representation based on a slot filling process for start-time, end-time, channel and day. The slots can be filled in any order. When the slots have been filled the entire programme can be viewed and corrected if necessary. The system also allows a number of programme memories to be viewed in a table. The table is stepped through and a chosen programme can be shown in detail. The number of steps required to enter programme details corresponds to approximately 18 key presses.

At first glance this seems like a text-based, tabular, MARS representation as it can only represent one entity of the domain at a time, i.e. a programme or set of programmes. However, because the semantic information required is limited to times and channels, it represents *any* programme that has these criteria. Thus it allows some abstraction over the domain, effectively creating a LARS. Unfortunately, users do not need this additional expressiveness since they are interested in specific programme titles at specific times. Users are forced to undertake programming with a semantically weak set of programme criteria, which does not contain the unique programme name. What is required is a representation that can convey the key criteria that uniquely identify a programme, effectively having minimal expressiveness.

7.3 VideoPlus System

Once the desired programme has been found from an external source, its details must be entered by the following procedure. A code number is entered which carries the programme details in a coded impenetrable form. Time, channel, and day slots are filled automatically from this coded number and the entire programme can be viewed and corrected if necessary. The system also allows a number of programme memories to be viewed in table format. The table is stepped through and a chosen programme can be shown in detail.

The system attempts to improve usability by cutting down the number of control actions required to enter programme details. The code numbers are interpreted as instances of a MARS uniquely mapping to domain entities, but the mapping is unknown to the user and so the code carries no overt semantic information. Once the code is entered, the programme details appear as a LARS programme record, as with the conventional on-screen system. Like highly expressive systems, the code has meaning beyond its form, relying on a hidden algorithm to encode its meaning. However, it still remains a LARS because it carries time-slots rather than unique programme names. It is the lack of interpretation knowledge for the code representation system that causes problems for users. They have no idea of the mapping between the representation system and domain and so the code carries semantic information only for the machine.

7.4 Drag and Drop System

A Personal Computer is used to show programmes in the same format as a TV schedule. This can be scrolled through to find earlier and later programmes. The tape is represented by an area to the right of the programme details. To record a programme the user selects it with a mouse and drags and drops it into the tape area.

The drag and drop system uses a MARS that is semantically restricted by denoting *all* programme details to remove any ambiguity, and mirroring the temporal and channel ordering of domain information. This semantic restriction causes a reflexive syntax that represents programmes as discrete objects. The chosen form is textual information in boxes whose position defines start-time, end-time and channel number against horizontal and vertical positional axes. This allows users to select and move objects that have meaning directly relevant to the programming domain, i.e. objects representing unique programmes. In this way, no abstraction is needed so it is best that none is given.

7.5 General Discussion

The first two systems fail because they do not represent the information at a level congruent with the task. What a user requires is a representation that exactly mirrors the domain, specifically the temporal and channel ordering of programmes. This is achieved in the drag and drop system by using a minimally expressive representation.

A corollary of presenting *all* of the domain information on screen in the drag and drop system is that the direct-manipulation interaction paradigm is made possible. The semantic objects, which the user deals with in the domain space, are all available in a graphical form for manipulation. The programming task is now transformed to a search, select, drag and drop, and the deletion task to a drag and drop.

In summary, the third system shows that a user can best achieve a goal by perceiving a view of the domain which provides enough abstraction, i.e. is expressive enough for the goal. If this is not the case then errors will be made, as the experimental results suggested. Furthermore, by providing the correct level of expressiveness the interface reduces the goal solution to a search, drag and drop, which is all that the programming task requires. The right choice of representation allows the task solution to be as simple as possible, which is the objective that the interface designer should strive for.

8 Conclusions and Further Work

This paper has addressed the need for user-interfaces to support the goals of the user within the context of the interaction. In the user- interface, the representation chosen to convey goal-orientated information may contain many different representation systems (multimedia), but can be generalized in terms of its expressiveness. Expressiveness is defined as the amount of abstraction of a domain a given representation system can convey. This property is a result of the semantic and syntactic description of the representation system, which dictates how it is interpreted by a user.

We have discussed the trade-off between the ease of use of a representation system and its level of expressiveness. We argue that there is utility in the definition of the expressiveness that a problem domain requires in its representation to make tasks tractable. This description can then be matched to media (representation systems). Although simple, the VCR example demonstrated this by the quality of the match identified in the drag and drop system that determined how well the system supported the user's goal. We suggest that it was the correct choice of media that allowed this.

Further work is continuing (Williams, 1996), which will develop the expressiveness approach in two directions. Firstly, the approach will be applied to more complex goals within a large state-space. By examining the use of many different media in problem solving, the expressiveness criterion can be investigated for different media-goal complexity matches (or mismatches). Secondly, the effect of expressiveness on the mental models formed of domains is being investigated. It is hoped this will provide an insight into the effect that different media have on internalization of domain information and how this relates to the expressiveness of the chosen representation.

Acknowledgement

The first author is funded by the EPSRC.

References

Alty, J. L. & Rijkaert, M. (1994), "Process Operators Multimedia Intelligent Support Environment". Final Report, ESPRIT Project 239.

Alty, J. L., Bergen, M., Craufurd, P. & Dolphin, C. (1992), Can Multimedia Interfaces Become a Benefit rather than a Feature, *in* C. Hurnung (ed.), "Proceedings of 2nd EuroGraphics Workshop on Multimedia", Eurographics Press, pp.27–50.

Andre, E. & Rist, T. (1993), The Design of Illustrated Documents as a Planning Task, *in* Maybury (1993), pp.94–116.

Arens, Y. & Hovy, E. (1993), On the Knowledge Underlying Multimedia Presentations, *in* Maybury (1993), pp.280–306.

Arens, Y., Miller, L., Shapiro, S. C. & Sondheimer, N. (1988), Automatic Construction of User Interface Displays, Internal Report IS-51, University of Southern California Information Science Institute.

Barwise, J. & Perry, J. (1983), *Situations and Attitudes*, MIT Press.

Bertin, J. (1983), *Graphics and Graphic Information Processing*, Walter de Gruyter.

Brachman, R. J. (1979), On the Epistemological Status of Semantic Networks, *in* N. Findler (ed.), "Associative Networks: Representation and Use of Knowledge by Computers", Academic Press, pp.3–50.

Buttiegeig, M. A. (1989), Emergent Features in Visual Display Design for Two Types of Failure Detection Tasks, PhD thesis, EPRL, University of Illinois.

Card, S. K., Moran, T. P. & Newell, A. (1983), *The Psychology of Human–Computer Interaction*, Lawrence Erlbaum Associates.

Casner, S. M. (1991), "A Task Analytic Approach to the Automated Design of Graphic Presentations", *ACM Transactions on Graphics* **10**(2), 111–151.

Duncumb, I. (1995), User Evaluation of a Novel Concept for Programming the Timer on a Video Cassette Recorder, Master's thesis, Loughborough University of Technology, UK.

Euler, L. (1772), *Letters to a German Princess: Vol 2 On Various Subjects of Physics and Philosophy*, Birkhauser.

Frolich, D. (1992), The Design Space of Interfaces, *in* L. Kjelldahl (ed.), "Proceedings of 2nd EuroGraphics Workshop", Springer-Verlag, pp.53–69.

Goodman, R. (1968), *The Languages of Art*, Bobbs-Merrill.

Grossen, G. & Carnine, D. (1990), "Diagramming a Logic Strategy: Effects on Difficult Problem Types and Transfer", *Learning Disability Quarterly* **13**, 168–182.

Hoffberg, L. (1991), Designing User-interface Guidelines for Time-shift Programming on a Video Cassette Recorder (VCR), *in* "Proceedings of the Human Factors Society 35th Annual Meeting", Human Factors Society, pp.501–504.

Hunt, M. J. (1989), Speech is More than Just an Audible Version of Text, *in* M. M. Taylor, F. N. Neel & D. G. Bouwhuis (eds.), "The Structure of Multimodal Dialogue", Elsevier Science, pp.287–299.

Levesque, H. J. (1988), "Logic and the Complexity of Reasoning", *Journal of Philosophical Logic* **17**, 355–389.

Lohse, J., Rueter, H., Biolsi, K. & Walker, N. (1990), Classifying Visual Knowledge Representations: A Foundation for Visualisation Research, *in* A. Kaufman (ed.), "Proceedings of Visualisation'90", IEEE Publications, pp.131–138.

Mackinlay, J. (1986), "Automating the Design of Graphical Presentations of Relational Information", *ACM Transactions on Graphics* **5**(2), 110–141.

Maybury, M. T. (ed.) (1993), *Intelligent Multimedia Interface Design*, MIT Press.

Moray, N. (1986), "Acquisition of Process Control Skills", *IEEE Transactions in Systems, Man and Cybernetics* **16**(4), 497–504.

Nigay, L. & Coutaz, J. (1992), A Design Space For Multimodal Systems: Concurrent Processing and Data Fusion, *in* P. Bauersfeld, J. Bennett & G. Lynch (eds.), "Proceedings of CHI'92: Human Factors in Computing Systems", ACM Press, pp.172–178.

Norman, D. A. (1988), *The Psychology of Everyday Things*, Basic Books.

Norman, D. A. & Draper, S. W. (eds.) (1986), *User Centered Systems Design: New Perspectives on Human–Computer Interaction*, Lawrence Erlbaum Associates.

Palmer, S. E. (1978), Fundamental Aspects of Cognitive Representations, *in* E. Rosch & B. B. Lloyd (eds.), "Cognition and Categorisation", Lawrence Erlbaum Associates, pp.259–303.

Plaisant, C. & Shneiderman, B. (1992), "Scheduling Home Control Devices: Design Issues and Usability Evaluation of Four Touchscreen Interfaces", *International Journal of Man–Machine Studies* **36**(3), 375–393.

Remus, W. (1984), "An Empirical Investigation of the Impact of Graphical and Tabular Data Presentations on Decision Making", *Management Science* **30**(5), 533–542.

Roth, S. F. & Mathis, J. (1990), Data Characterisation for Intelligent Graphics Representation, *in* J. C. Chew & J. Whiteside (eds.), "Proceedings of CHI'90: Human Factors in Computing Systems", ACM Press, pp.193–200.

Sanderson, P. M. & Verhage, A. G. (1989), "State Space and Verbal Protocols for Studying the Human Operator in Process Control", *Ergonomics* **32**(11), 1343–1372.

Schubert, L. (1976), "Extending the Expressive Power of Semantic Networks", *Artificial Intelligence* **7**(2), 163–198.

Sowa, J. F. (1979), Semantics of Conceptual Graphs, *in* R. Brachman (ed.), "Proceedings of 17th Meeting of Computational Linguistics", IEEE Publications, pp.39–44.

Stenning, K. (1994), Logic as a Foundation for a Cognitive Theory of Modality Assignment, Internal Report HCRC/RP-51, University of Edinburgh Cognitive Science Unit.

Stenning, K. & Oberlander, J. (1995), "A Cognitive Theory of Graphical and Linguistic Reasoning: Logic and Implementation", *Cognitive Science* **19**(1), 97–140.

Stenning, K., Inder, I. R. & Neilson, I. (1994), Applying Semantic Concepts to Analysing Media and Modalities, Internal Report HCRC/RP-61, University of Edinburgh Cognitive Science Unit.

Thimbleby, H. (1991), "Can Anyone Work the Video?", *New Scientist* **129**(1757), 48–51.

Tufte, E. R. (1983), *The Visual Display of Quantitative Information*, Graphics Press.

Weir, G. (1991), Interacting with Complex Devices, *in* J. L. Alty & R. Coombs (eds.), "HCI for Complex Tasks", Harcourt Brace Javanovich, pp.1–21.

Williams, D. M. L. (1996), Multimedia, Mental Models and Complex Tasks, *in* "CHI'96 Companion", ACM Press, p.65. Paper presented at CHI'96 Doctoral Consortium.

Woods, D. D. (1991), The Cognitive Engineering of Problem Representations, *in* J. L. Alty & R. Coombs (eds.), "HCI for Complex Tasks", Harcourt Brace Javanovich, pp.169–188.

Woods, W. A. (1975), What's in a Link? Foundations for Semantic Networks, *in* D. G. Bobrow & A. M. Collins (eds.), "Representation and Understanding", Academic Press.

DAVID: A Multimedia Tool for Accident Investigation

Mauro Pedrali[†] **& Remi Bastide**[‡]

[†] *ARAMIIHS — CNRS, 31 rue des cosmonautes — ZI du Palays, F-31077 Toulouse Cedex, France.*

Tel: *+33 61 39 68 14*
Fax: *+33 62 24 77 80*
EMail: *pedrali@soleil.matra-espace.fr*

[‡] *LIS — Université Toulouse 1, Place Anatole France, F-31042 Toulouse Cedex, France.*

Tel: *+33 61 63 35 88*
Fax: *+33 61 63 37 98*
EMail: *bastide@cix.cict.fr*

Investigations on several real life accidents have revealed the increasing causal role played by humans, and the importance of the context of human actions. Accident analyses should therefore concentrate not only on system failures but also on what we call human factors investigations. We propose an approach based on a method for retrospective analysis of accidents. The aim is the identification of erroneous actions and their related causes. A prototype software-tool implementing the method is to be integrated with an existing video editor and a database in a multimedia environment.

Keywords: accident investigation, root cause analysis, errors taxonomy, video analysis.

1 Introduction

Accidents' investigations of the last decade have revealed the increasing role played by humans both at the very beginning and during the accident. Investigators noticed this aspect especially in occasion of accidents having putted population into risk (Three Mile Island, Bhopal, Zeebrugge, Strasbourg).

Among the main difficulties encountered in accident investigations are the complexity of human actions, their great flexibility with respect to system performances, and their connections with the social context and the environment. The context of sub-optimal human performance can be better understood by thorough, competent investigation of these factors (Harle, 1994), that are commonly known as Human Factors.

Accident investigations ought to refer to a combination of different approaches: not only analysis of system failures, but also human factor analyses supported by state-of-the-art tools. We propose a support system based on three main components, namely:

- A method for retrospective analyses of accidents.
- A software tool implementing the method.
- A multimedia environment incorporating the tool.

The method (Pedrali & Cojazzi, 1994) allows the detection of the operator's erroneous behaviours that contributed to the accident, and the identification of possible triggering causes. The method has already been applied to two aeronautical accidents: One involving an A320, near Strasbourg in January 1992; and the other involving a DC9-30, approaching Zurich airport in November 1990 (Pedrali et al., 1995).

The software tool implements the method, and permits indexation and analysis of video sequences concerning erroneous behaviours. The multimedia environment combines the resources of a video editing desktop with a database, in order to organize the selected video sequences and to store them together with the analysis results.

The objective of our research is to support accident investigations with a multimedia tool. This tool helps in investigating not only why an accident occurred, but also in explaining how the different factors noted during the analysis could lead to the accident.

We will provide a brief summary of the accident investigation domain, a description of the method, and finally an explanation of the multimedia environment and of the tool.

2 Accident Investigation: Aims and Resources

The main purpose of investigations is to prevent other accidents from occurring; there is no higher outstanding issue in accident investigation than *prevention*. Nevertheless, effective accident prevention measures require more than identifying *Who* did *What*, *When* and *Why* (the *4Ws*). What is needed is a better understanding of the context in which operators encounter accident-conducive circumstances, as well as a valid method of analysis to detect those factors — system and/or human related — which played a role in the accident.

Different approaches have been used. In the aeronautical domain for example, the conceptual model SHEL (Software, Hardware, Environment, Liveware) facilitates the data collection task, by focusing on operators and on their relations with the other components of the traditional human–machine–environment system (Edwards, 1972; Hawkins, 1984; 1987). Root Cause Analysis (RCA) methods retrospectively study accidents having involved human actions, with the specific goal of investigating the causes of erroneous actions (Leplat & Rasmussen, 1987). Another approach consists of seeing accidents as caused by triggering events coupled with weaknesses existing at the organizational level (maintenance failures, personnel selection, management deficiencies), respectively called unsafe acts and latent failures (Reason, 1990). While unsafe acts set off the accident latent failures prepare the conditions; therefore, investigation efforts should concentrate on investigating both the latent weaknesses in the system and the triggering events.

However, this may be not enough; the method that we propose goes further. Not only the 4Ws ought to be discovered, but investigators should also understand *How* these 4Ws are involved in the operator's process of cognition, that eventually gives rise to what we commonly call 'human error'.

3 The RCA Method

The Root Cause Analysis (RCA) method is subdivided in two parts, namely: Erroneous Action Identification (EAI); and Causal Analysis (CA). In the first part (EAI), the investigator makes a chronological reconstruction of the accident/incident and detects the erroneous actions performed by the operator(s) involved in the accident/incident. These actions are the manifestations of erroneous behaviours, i.e. the final result of an erroneous cognitive process, whose triggering causes will be investigated in the second part of the method (CA).

The reason for this subdivision is methodological: incorrect actions in context need firstly to be singled out before looking for their causes. The EAI is not only preparatory to the CA, but it is also the main reference when performing the CA.

3.1 Erroneous Action Identification (EAI)

This part of the method is devoted to the identification of those actions that *deviated* from the expected evolution of the events. They can be seen as symptoms of a general mis-functioning of human–machine and/or human–environment interaction. These actions are not necessarily erroneous: they may not be erroneous deviations from a prescribed procedure; the analyst determines it throughout the following phases: Data Collection, Event Time Line and Deviation Detection.

3.1.1 Data Collection

The analyst gathers all the material concerning the evolution of the accident in this phase. It is important to collect information regarding not only the actions the operator(s) have accomplished, but also all the data available on the instrumentation, such as signals, cues and so on. Sources of data can be audio/video recordings, incident forms, elicitation of operators and experts.

1	2	3	4	5
Time	Available information or stimulus	Event signalled	Knowledge and/or belief state component	Intention

6	7	8	9	10
Expectation	Decision/Action	Source for Decision/Action	Immediate feedback	Comments

Table 1: The Event Time Line table (Pew et al., 1981).

3.1.2 Event Time Line

The analyst structures the data collected in the previous phase in a working table, which will detail a time-oriented representation of the accident/incident and will help him/her to detect the erroneous actions. Not only must the analyst consider overt actions that were taken but also the intentions, the expectations of the operators and what they believed about the states of the system, at selected times. This concept was originally proposed by Pew et al. (1981) and it can be suitably employed in any accident analysis.

Table 1 shows the Event Time Line table; the description of the column categories that we provide is taken, with minor changes, from the work of Pew.

Time (Column 1). It refers to the occurrence of the various signals/alarms or actions taken; it represents the elapsed time since the first significant event (at time zero).

Available information (Column 2). Identification of caution/warning panels, status sensor and, where known, their location on the various control panels and workstation. They represent both stimuli to the actions identified on the right columns (i.e. Event signalled, Knowledge and/or belief state component) and information that could have produced these stimuli.

Event signalled (Column 3). Description of system events that are signalled by the occurrences of alarms and states identified in the left column (Available information).

Knowledge and/or belief state component (Column 4). Context related information where decisions/actions were taken/performed by operators. The information briefly characterizes both the operators' system knowledge whose actions were based upon, and the operators' beliefs concerning the scenario they were faced with.

Intention (Column 5). Characterizations of the overall operators' strategy or intention with respect to the system/scenario that produced the overt decision/action (Column 7).

Expectation (Column 6). Expected outcomes of particular decision/action.

Decision/Action (Column 7). Descriptions of the specific action, given the previous columns' contents.

Sources for Decision/Action (Column 8). Elements of training, passed experience that could have contributed to the decision/action taken/performed.

Immediate feedback (Column 9). Information providing the most immediate contribution of decision/action taken/performed.

Comments (Column 10). Analyst's observation concerning the validity of the operators' knowledge and/or belief states and the correctness of intentions, expectations, actions and decisions.

3.1.3 Deviation Detection

> "From the point of view of accident analysis, of highly proceduralized human–machine systems, it can be reasonably said that each deviation from the procedures, written or even tacit ones, is a potential error." (Cojazzi & Pinola, 1994)

At this stage, actions performed by operators that deviated from the prescribed procedure should be detected. Since a procedure may not always be very detailed — not being conceived as a step by step description of tasks and goals — deviations are often difficult to detect. Besides, operators' decisions may sometimes demand a trade-off between two or more parallel procedures or even, in certain cases, the procedure does not exist and they have to invent a new one.

The sequence of actions reconstructed by the Event Time Line is compared with the procedure. From the comparison, deviations are subdivided into *justifiable* actions, and *unjustifiable* actions. The distinction is necessary because actions that are not usually envisaged are often unavoidable owing to particular circumstances. This is the case for example in exceptional weather conditions or, more often, in the case of inadequate functioning or failure of an instrument. However, only the deviations that cannot be 'justified' are the *erroneous actions*, in terms of error manifestations.

3.2 Causal Analysis (CA)

In the second part of the method, the analyst investigates causes of human erroneous actions using a taxonomy of human errors to be described below. These causes may be either the result of latent failures or simply related to momentary conditions (triggering events).

The taxonomy was originally proposed by Hollnagel & Cacciabue (1991) and it is described here with reference to an updated version.

Human action analysis needs to be based on a classification or taxonomy of human errors, on a method of analysis, and on a model or paradigm of human behaviour (Cacciabue et al., 1993). While the use of a classification scheme is necessary to put event descriptions in a common form, the method is important to

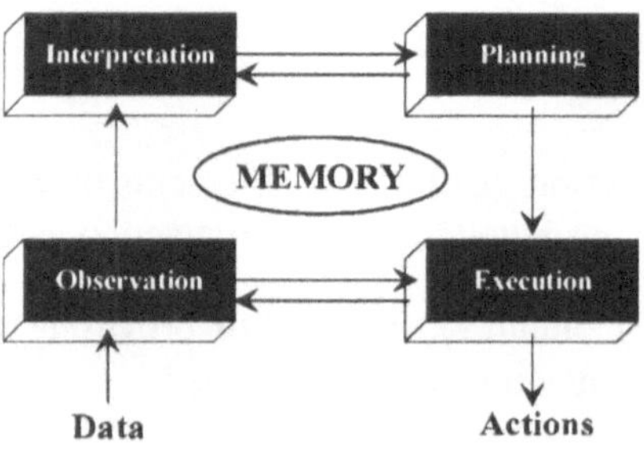

Figure 1: The SMoC (Hollnagel & Cacciabue, 1991).

ensure that the classification is used in a uniform way; the model provides a basis for the classification.

The employed taxonomy is coupled with a model of cognition, and it clearly distinguishes between effects and causes of erroneous behaviours.

3.2.1 *The Cognitive Model*

The reference cognitive model is the SMoC (Simple Model of Cognition). Four cognitive functions outline the process of cognition (Observation, Interpretation, Planning and Execution) and are connected with each other as schematically represented in Figure 1.

The two fundamental features of the SMoC are:

1. the distinction between what can be observed and what can be inferred; and
2. the cyclical nature of human cognition (Hollnagel & Cacciabue, 1991).

What can be observed is related to the phases of Execution and Observation, such as the execution of a particular action, or the perception of a signal. What can only be inferred is related to the phases of Planning and Interpretation. Indeed, we can deduce how operators have interpreted a signal or a system state only by observing their behaviour.

The cyclical nature means, for instance, that an action can be preceded by a choice (in the planning phase), or by the interpretation of an observed sign, which could be the consequence of a previous action.

3.2.2 *The Taxonomy*

The taxonomy of human errors is the 'core' of the root cause analysis method. It consists of four tables in relation with the four cognitive functions of the SMoC. Each table contains a set of pre-defined errors categories, typical of a particular function (Execution, Planning, Interpretation and Observation).

The taxonomy is used to investigate triggering causes of erroneous actions. The analysis is performed by starting from the *manifestation* of erroneous actions, which

General Effect (GE)	Specific Effect (SE)	Internal Cause (IC)	External Cause (EC)
Phenotypes	Phenotypes	PRCs (Link Functions) to PLN GE	SRCs

Table 2: The Execution (EXE) table.

is called *Phenotype* (Hollnagel, 1991), and by following back the process of cognition that ended up with the execution of these actions.

Causes are subdivided in 'System-related Causes' (SRC), or external causes, and 'Person-related Causes' (PRC) or internal causes. PRCs and SRCs are the categories contained in the taxonomy tables.

SRCs refer to conditions that are external to the operator and that can be ascertained in an objective sense, (e.g. inadequate procedures, equipment failures, management problems). PRCs refer to internal conditions that cannot be directly observed and that are typical of cognitive processes (e.g. memory failure, distraction). SRCs may trigger or modify a PRC; however, they are not necessarily involving in an erroneous behaviour (PRCs can be the only causes).

3.2.3 The Method

The method ensures the uniform use of the taxonomy. In the beginning, the analyst classifies the erroneous action according to one of the phenotypes contained in the General Effect or Specific Effect column of the Execution table (this will depend on the amount of information available on the erroneous action). Causes of this erroneous action can be Person-related and/or System-related, as shown in Table 2.

At each stage of the taxonomy, an effect can be triggered by different causes. These causes are searched by following a well-defined set of rules which apply to all the four tables:

1. effect classification — General or Specific; and
2. causes identification.

Thus, the analyst explores four possible paths, shown in Figure 2, but none of them excludes the others; they are:

1. Effect → Person-related cause (General Function) → System-related cause.
2. Effect → Person-related cause (General Function).
3. Effect → System-related cause.
4. Effect → Person-related cause (Link Function).

In the first case, the effect is triggered by a PRC that was set off by a SRC. In the second and in the third case, the effect is only triggered respectively by a PRC and a SRC. While in the first three cases the analyst detects causes within a specific table, in

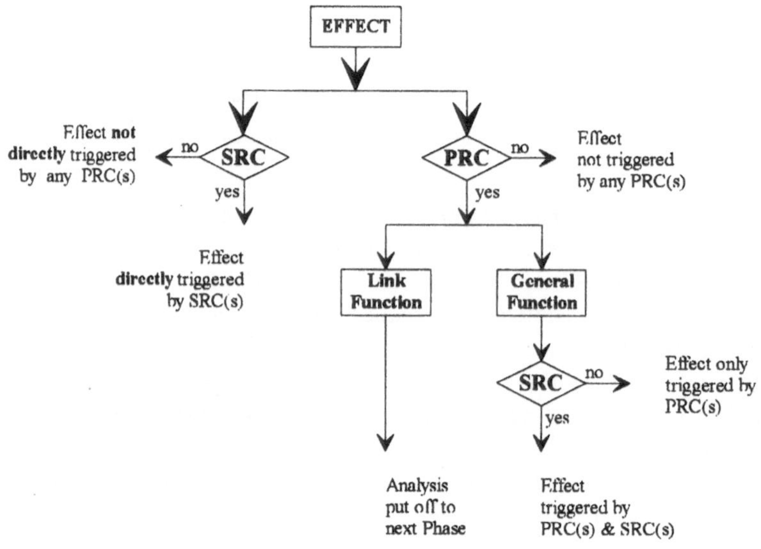

Figure 2: Taxonomy application.

<table>
<tr><th>General Effect (GE)</th><th>Specific Effect (SE)</th><th>Internal Cause (IC)</th><th>External Cause (EC)</th></tr>
<tr><td rowspan="2">PRCs (Link Functions) from EXE IC</td><td rowspan="2">Specific Functions</td><td>PRCs (Link Functions) to INT GE</td><td rowspan="2">SRCs</td></tr>
<tr><td>PRCs (General Functions)</td></tr>
</table>

Table 3: The Planning (PLN) table.

the fourth one the analysis is put off to another table. PRCs — Link Functions connect two tables: what is a 'cause' in one phase is an 'effect' in the other.

In the Execution table, if a PRC (Link-Function) is chosen, the analysis is postponed to the Planning table, and it continues from the General Effect column. In the corresponding Specific Effect cell, there are the effects typical of the Planning (Specific Functions) whose causes can be Person-related (General and/or Link Function) and/or System-related (Table 3).

The analyst performs the analysis throughout the tables following the same rules, until all the root causes of the phenotype are found. The results obtained from the phenotype analysis are a reconstruction of the incorrect process of cognition in terms of PRCs and SRCs connections. The Interpretation (INT) and Observation (OBS) tables are structured according to other templates.

General Effect (GE)	Specific Effect (SE)	Internal Cause (IC)	External Cause (EC)
PRCs (Link Functions) from PLN IC	Specific Functions	PRCs (Link Functions) to OBS GE	SRCs
		PRCs (General Functions)	

Table 4: The Interpretation (INT) table.

General Effect (GE)	Specific Effect (SE)	Internal Cause (IC)	External Cause (EC)
PRCs (Link Functions) from INT IC	Specific Functions	PRCs (General Functions)	SRCs

Table 5: The Observation (OBS) table.

An example will clarify further on the use of the taxonomy, and will show how the different tables are exploited when investigating erroneous actions causes.

3.3 Example

The example is taken from the applications of the method made to two aeronautical accidents (Pedrali et al., 1995). In this case, the aim was not to give another interpretation of facts. Instead, the interest was to understand how the different factors noticed by the official commissions of inquiry could play a role in the pilots' cognitive processes. These processes led the pilots to deviate from the prescribed procedures and to ignore those signs and signals that could have induce them to recover from errors.

3.3.1 The Strasbourg Accident

The accident involved an Airbus A320, flying from Lyon-Satolas to Strasbourg-Entzheim, on 20th January 1992. Approaching the Strasbourg area, the crew was informed by the automatic terminal information service on the runway in use. However, while the captain decided an indirect approach, the air traffic control (ATC) expected a direct one. When they realized their conflict of expectations, it was too late for the ATC to clear an indirect approach immediately. Eventually, the crew accepted radar vectoring (for a direct approach), but because this was not precise, the captain (the pilot flying) failed to properly intercept the final approach axis. Therefore the descent was not begun at the nominal point at which it is supposed to. At that time, the rate of descent increased to about 3300 ft/m instead of the normal 800 ft/m, but the crew appeared not to be aware of this. The cockpit activity focused on the approach axis and on the aircraft configuration until the impact (Paries, 1994).

3.3.2 Error Analysis

The commission of inquiry concluded that, besides the abnormal rate of descent, considered as the pivot event of the accident, there were a number of inappropriate actions the pilots made. We focused on one of them to give an idea of how error

General Effect (GE)	Specific Effect (SE)	Internal Cause (IC)	External Cause (EC)
Omission (The announcements corresponding to an important altitude vs. distance check are not performed)		**No choice made** (⇒ **GE-PLAN**)	

Table 6: Execution Phase (EXE).

General Effect (GE)	Specific Effect (SE)	Internal Cause (IC)	External Cause (EC)
No choice made	**Decision paralysis** (Pilots' attention is devoted to the alignment with the centreline)	**Incorrect recognition of state** (⇒ **GE-INT**) ***Time compression*** ***Work-overload***	***Procedures*** *(Owing to the lack of a level, three main tasks are to be executed in a short period of time)*

Table 7: Planning Phase (PLN).

General Effect (GE)	Specific Effect (SE)	Internal Cause (IC)	External Cause (EC)
Incorrect recognition of state (The pilots did not realize about the abnormal rate of descent)	**Unfamiliar situation** (This kind of approach is not commonly performed)	**Failure to notice signal/alarm** (⇒ **GE-OBS**) ***Lack of training*** *(The pilots are not at ease with the VOR/DME approach)*	

Table 8: Interpretation Phase (INT).

General Effect (GE)	Specific Effect (SE)	Internal Cause (IC)	External Cause (EC)
Failure to notice signal/alarm The pilots did not remark the excessive values on the instrumentation: Altimeter Flight Director, vs. Indicator, Pitch Altitude Indicator)		***Lack of training***	***Interface*** *(The power of alert of the instrumentation is very poor)*

Table 9: Observation Phase (OBS).

causes were found. We consider the omission of an important altitude vs. distance check that was not performed; Tables 6, 7, 8 and 9 show the reconstruction of the process of cognition that led to this phenotype.

This error was classified as an *Omission* (Phenotype) whose cause was the PRC *No choice made* (Link Function).

At the Planning phase this category is more specifically classified as a *Decision paralysis* (Specific Function) — at that time the crew attention was completely devoted to the interception of the centreline. The decision paralysis was caused by:

1. The PRCs *Time compression* and *Work overload* (General Functions) triggered by the SRC *Procedures* — three main tasks had to be executed in a short period time.

2. The PRC *Incorrect recognition of state* (Link Function).

At the Interpretation phase, the "incorrect recognition of state" can be seen as an Unfamiliar situation (Specific Function) — this kind of approach (VOR/DME) is not commonly performed. The *unfamiliar situation* was probably caused by:

1. The PRC *Lack of training* (General Function) — the pilots were not at ease with the VOR/DME procedure.

2. The PRC *Failure to notice signal* (Link Function).

At the Observation phase, the "failure to notice signal" refers to the fact that the pilots did not notice the excessive value on the instrumentation. This was caused by the PRC *Lack of training* (General Function) probably triggered by the SRC *Interface* — the power of alert of the involved interface is poor.

The process of cognition can be more clearly represented as a flow-chart diagram. Figure 3 shows the four phases and the connections between the different causes; arrows' orientation indicates the direction of the analysis (from the phenotype up to the causes).

4 DAVID

A software tool called DAVID (Dynamic Analysis of VIDeo) implements the root cause analysis method. The purpose is to support accident investigation with a work station, permitting retrospective analyses of videos about accidents involving the human activity in complex systems (e.g. cockpits, nuclear power stations and air traffic control rooms). However, we envisage its use in the training domain as well. Operator activities are very often recorded during a simulator session (e.g. pilot training), DAVID can be thus exploited by trainers during debriefing sessions. This will help them identify and understand trainees' problems arising during critical phases of the simulation.

The principle of DAVID is the following: starting from a set of video recordings concerning operator activity, the analyst selects all the video sequences related to incorrect behaviours and arranges them for Erroneous Action Identification (EAI). The data contained in the sequences are organized and the information the analyst has

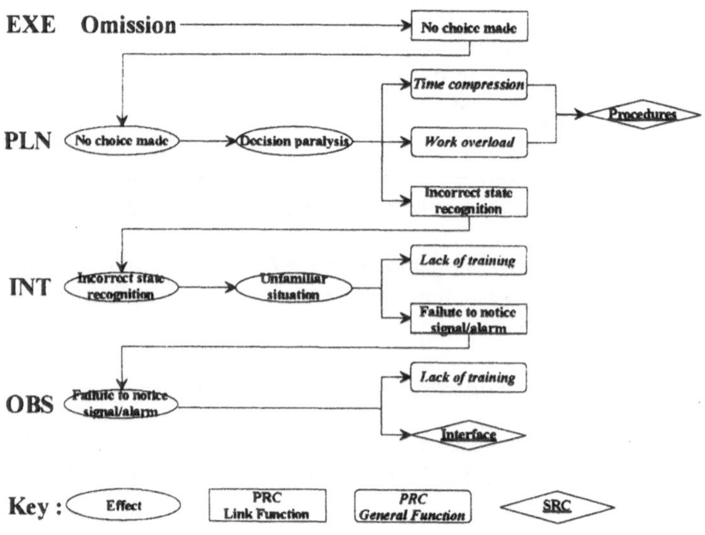

Figure 3: Flow chart.

inferred is exploited in Causal Analysis (CA). DAVID is therefore composed of two parts supporting the two phases of the method; however, we cannot go further into its description without introducing the multimedia environment that incorporates it.

5 DAVID and the Multimedia Environment

The multimedia environment is based on a set of *Editors*, *Analysers* and a *Database*. Editors are tools allowing the selection of video sequences and the organization of data contained therein. The analyst treats the information inferred from these data by an Analyser in order to obtain analytical results.

Since each Editor and each Analyser implement specific methods for human activity studies (co-operation between agents, communication, etc.) they are strictly related to each other. The analyst organizes data for a specific Analyser, but this does not prevent the analysis of the same set of video sequences from different points of view, i.e. by different Editors/Analysers. The selected sequences, the information inferred from data as well as the results of analyses are stored in the database, at three different levels, respectively called level-0, level-1 and level-2. Figure 4 shows the architecture of the environment.

5.1 *Video Analysis — The Editor's Role*

Video analysis is carried out as follows. The analyst begins by examining a set of video tapes; this task is accomplished by means of an Editor. Useful information is very often spread out all over the recording, and this does not facilitate its collection

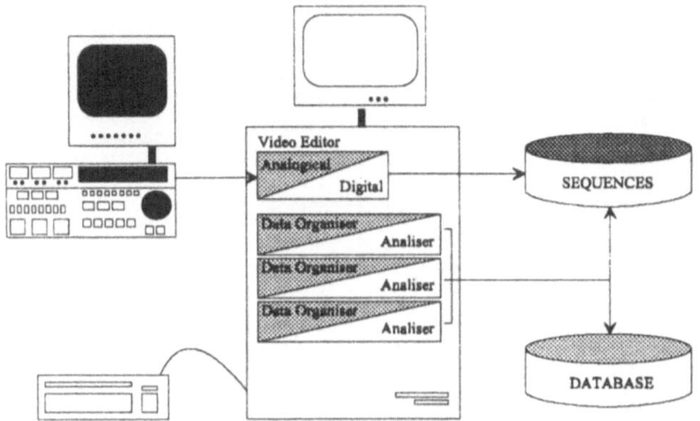

Figure 4: Architecture of the environment.

and its organization. This is the reason why Editors are composed of two sub-Editors, respectively called *Video Editor* and *Data Organizer*. While the Video Editor is basically used for sequence selection, the Data Organizer helps in the data organization. Actually, since the selection is always carried out by the same mechanism, the Video Editor is unique and common to the other Data Organizers that do characterize a specific Editor.

The Video Editor is the Video Machine — Digital Player/Recorder that has been developed by FAST Electronic GmbH. It is a desktop both for *linear* and for *non linear* video editing, but in our case, it is exploited essentially for non linear editing: source material (video cassette) is firstly digitized on a hard disk providing an immediate access to precise instants of the recording. After having selected a number of sequences, the analyst builds scenarios for video analysis through a set of video editing operations (e.g. digital effect, titles and graphics implementation, time-code-oriented editing, audio mixing, etc.).

The Data Organizer helps the analyst in the correlation of data scenarios. The main purpose is the deduction of as much information as possible on the human activity that has been recorded and that will be analysed further on by means of an Analyser.

Since the root cause analysis method was conceived from the onset as a self standing one, its implementation within the environment demanded some modifications. The role of the three phases in the EAI has therefore changed in order to be combined with the Video Editor.

5.1.1 Video Editor's Role in DAVID

The analyst selects a number of sequences relevant to the root cause analysis. These sequences concern critical actions — with regard to the foreseen procedures — that have been performed by the operators. The analyst extracts a number of 'clips'

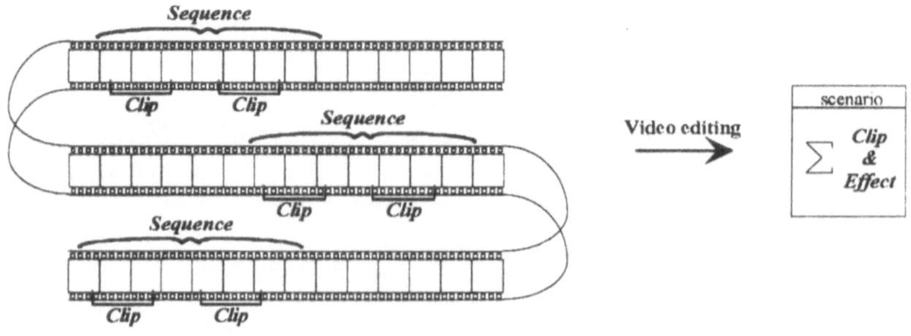

Figure 5: Process of video editing.

(pieces of recording) within these sequences, each one identifying the beginning and the end of a particular action. Scenarios are then built by composing the desired clips and by adding special effects (picture in the picture, text, sound commentaries, etc.) as shown schematically in Figure 5.

5.1.2 Data Organizer's Role in DAVID

The Data Organizer implements the three phases of Erroneous Action Identification (Data Collection, Event Time Line and Action Detection) in order to prepare the information for the Causal Analysis. However, the introduction of the Video Editor necessitated some changes. The Data Collection phase can be already considered as accomplished to some extent after the digitization on the hard disk. Nevertheless, despite the fact that we can retrieve a lot of data from a video, we must remember that some types of data concerning the accident are inaccessible from a video recording. This is the case for flight parameters (speed, attitude, altitude, engines, etc.) recorded by the Digital Flight Data Recorder that is installed on board an aircraft. These data also need to be taken into account to have a complete idea of the accident dynamics.

As regards the Event Time Line phase, it is basically based on Table 1; however the main goal now is the grouping and the correlation of all data pertinent to a specific scenario. Since we now have the video of the accident, we will not use the Event Time Line to reconstruct what happened.

The Deviation Detection phase is carried out as foreseen, i.e. the analyser still compares procedures and scenarios. If a video concerning the procedure is available, the comparison is directly done by the Video Editor. In this case, the analyst puts the two videos side by side (the scenario and the procedure) so that deviations can be more easily detected. They are then classified as justifiable or as unjustifiable.

DAVID data organizer consists of table similar to the Event Time Line that is filled by the investigator when examining the scenario. Since Erroneous Action Identification is not only preparatory to Causal Analysis but will support it too, the Data Organizer interface is conceived so that it can be called from the Causal Analysis interface to provide information for the analysis of the erroneous action.

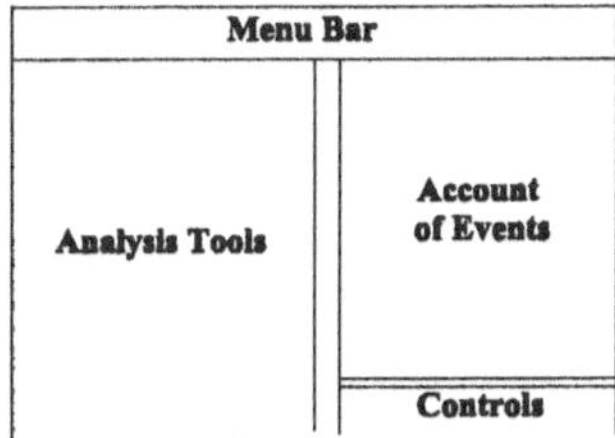

Figure 6: Analyser interface (overall view).

5.2 Video Analysis — The Analyser's Role

The investigator will have a number of scenarios, each one concerning one or more erroneous actions. These actions are procedures deviations that have been classified 'unjustified' and therefore incorrect or erroneous.

We made a few changes to implement the Causal Analysis in DAVID; two steps are still foreseen, namely: classification of the erroneous actions according to the given phenotypes list, and investigation of the triggering causes along the four phases of the cognitive model. As we stated, the analysis purpose is not only investigating the causes of an erroneous action, but also the reconstruction of the process of cognition that led to it.

The main component of the Causal Analysis is the taxonomy, whose structure has basically remained the same, i.e. four tables (for each phase of the cognitive model) subdivided in four columns (General and Specific Effect, Internal and External Causes). However, we tried to simplify their representation in the interface and therefore its use. The analyst is guided through the different tables, by showing him only one column at a time. Figure 6 provides an overall view of the interface.

While the left side is devoted to the analysis, the right one provides a chronological representation of the erroneous cognitive process related to its phenotype. On top, a menu bar displays the interface functions, some of which are directly accessible from the control box in the left side corner.

5.2.1 How to Use

In the following, we will expose how the interface is used to analyse errors. References are made to the example reported in paragraph 4.3.2.

At the beginning of the analysis, the analyst enters a brief description of the selected erroneous behaviour, which appears above "ACCOUNT OF EVENTS"; in this case, the action is described as "*An important altitude vs. distance check is not reported*".

After that, the selected action is classified according to a set of pre-defined phenotypes displayed in a list below "PHENOTYPES". The phenotypes are the General/Specific Effects belonging to the taxonomy table related to the Execution phase, which is recalled on the interface by "PHASE: EXECUTION (EXE)".

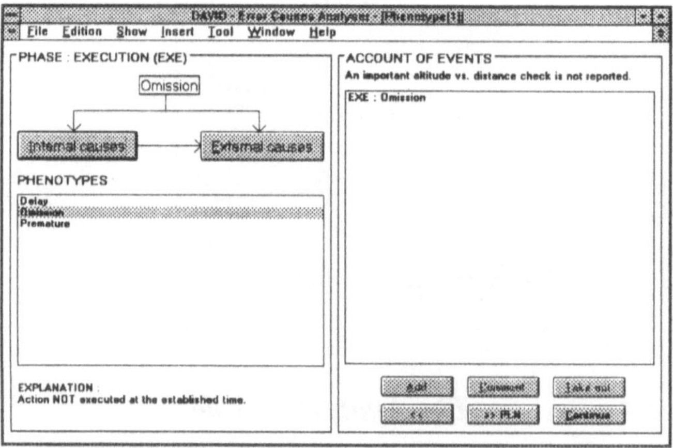

Figure 7: Selection of a phenotype.

Since in the example the error was classified as an omission, the phenotype '*Omission*' is chosen in the "PHENOTYPES" list and it is added (button 'Add') in the "ACCOUNT OF EVENTS" list. When an effect is selected, its name appears in a label over the 'Internal/External Causes' buttons, as shown in Figure 7.

By clicking on the 'External Causes' or 'Internal Causes' button, the corresponding list of internal causes (Person-related cause) or external causes (System-related cause) related to the selected effect appears below; in the example "INTERNAL CAUSES (EXE)" appears.

We remind that the possible cause/effect connections are those foreseen by the rules exposed in paragraph 3.2.3:

1. Effect → Internal cause → External cause.
2. Effect → Internal cause.
3. Effect → External cause.
4. Effect → Internal cause/Link Function (followed by: → PLN, → INT, → OBS).

The selection of a category is supported by an explanation appearing when the analyst clicks on the left side list. During the analysis, it is possible to associate to each element displayed in the "ACCOUNT OF EVENTS" list a commentary as well as the related piece (video) of scenario, as shown in Figure 8.

In the control box, three buttons provides the following interaction within the "ACCOUNT OF EVENTS" list: adding a category (button 'Add'); taking a selected category out (button 'Take out'); adding a commentary ('Comment').

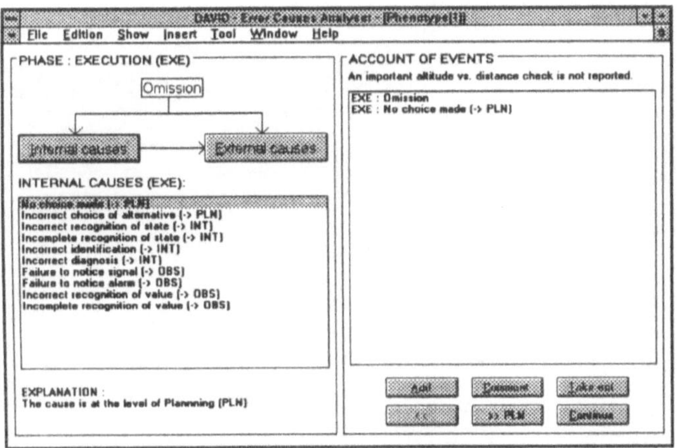

Figure 8: Selection of Internal Causes (link function).

Three others allows to navigate throughout the four taxonomy tables. Since a scenario can contain two or more erroneous action, different phenotypes can be analysed at the same time.

5.3 *Video Analysis — The Database's Role*

The database is structured according to a relational data model, which stores the taxonomy elements (Phenotypes, Person-related causes and System-related causes); the information inferred from the different Data Organizers (DO); and the results obtained from the Analysers. The database has been developed using Microsoft Access.

The database is structured on three levels (0, 1 and 2) corresponding to the three steps of the video analysis, i.e. selection, editing and analysis of sequences. The results obtained from of each step are stored separately. Recall that every Editor is composed of a common Video Editor and of a particular Data Organizer which is specific to each Analyser.

The elementary component of DAVID is the scenario, the final result of a video editing (done by the Video Editor) that is stored at level 0 of the database. Actually, what is stored at this level is not the scenario itself but its 'address'. An address identifies the beginning and the end of a scenario that can be placed either on the hard disk or on a tape.

In the analysis of an accident, the analyst decomposes it in different scenarios that are compared with the corresponding procedures in order to detect the deviations. The Data Organizer supporting the Erroneous Action Identification permits this, and the information inferred are stored at level 1 and they are exploited by the Analyser.

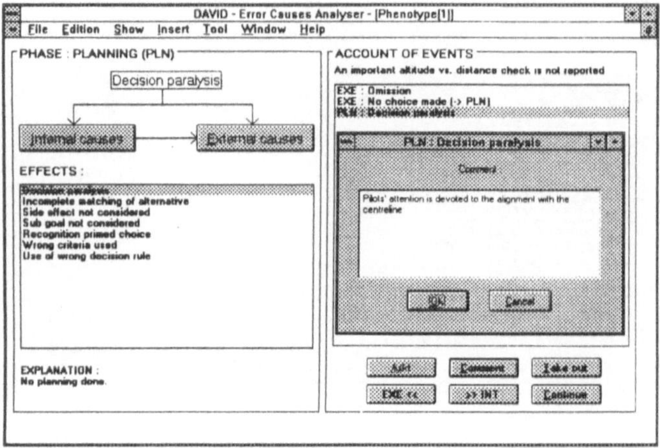

Figure 9: Selection of an effect.

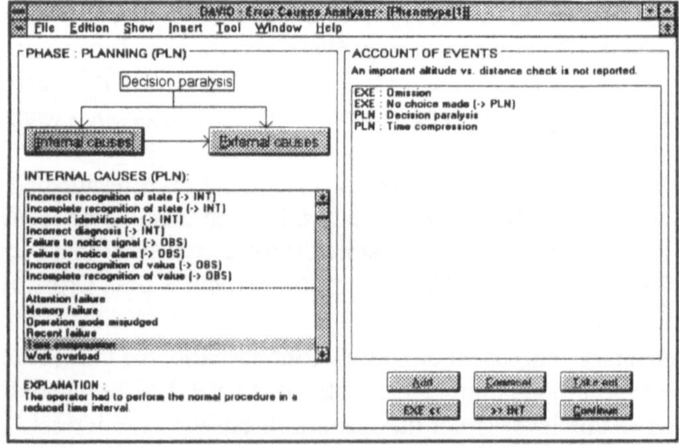

Figure 10: Selection of an Internal Cause.

Eventually, by mean of the Analyser supporting the Causal Analysis the causes of erroneous actions are investigated. The analyst is able to reconstruct the operator's process of cognition that led to an erroneous action through a cause/effect connection. Results obtained from the analysis are stored at level 2 of the database.

5.3.1 Storing and Retrieval

We have introduced the concept of 'layer' in the storing and retrieval of the information. The layers are implemented in terms of relational views. The multimedia environment is planned to incorporate several Editors and Analysers that are supposed to be used on the same set of sequences, but whose final results (in terms of data organization and analysis) are assumed to be stored separately. This will permit a general user of the multimedia environment to analyse the same situation by methods implemented into different tools.

The storage at different levels provides a better data organization both in terms of their origins (from a specific Editor and/or Analyser) and in terms of their 'richness'. The idea of gradual enriching of information (from level 0 to level 1 and 2) is usefully exploited at the retrieval phase. Indeed, supposing that investigators have to find information concerning a phenotype, they can be interested in watching all the scenarios related to this phenotype. In this case, the database will retrieve the addresses corresponding to these scenarios (level 0).

If the investigator desires to go deeper in the request, wishing to know about the procedure deviation involved, the database will find the answer at level 1.

If the request is more specific, what kind of external and/or internal causes, the answer is found deeper at level 2.

6 Conclusion and Future Works

We have presented a tool, named DAVID, aimed at supporting the error analysis task for accident/incident investigations. A multimedia environment incorporates this tool, together with a video editor system and a database. The tool implements a root cause analysis method that is principally based on a taxonomy of human erroneous actions.

We believe that our tool may substantially improve the task of error analysis, as it allows not only for the detection of erroneous action causes, but also for a dynamic reconstruction of the process that led to these errors. Moreover, the integration of the method within a multimedia environment enriches the error investigation process, enabling the analyst to better exploit the enormous amount of data typical of real life accident investigations.

The environment is generic enough to encompass other types of human factor analysis which exploit multimedia data, such as verbal protocols or co-operative work analyses.

At the technical level, we are working on enhancing the integration of the commercial video editing environment we use with the rest of our platform, in order to provide a seamless integrated interface that can reduce the requirements for training for error analysts.

References

Cacciabue, P. C., Pedrali, M. & Hollnagel, E. (1993), Taxonomy and Models for Human Factors Analysis of Interactive Systems: An Application to Flight Safety, *in* "Human Factors Digest No.9: Proceedings of the 2nd ICAO Flight Safety and Human Factors Symposium", number 243-AN/146 *in* "ICAO Circular", International Civil Aviation Organization, pp.270–279.

Cojazzi, G. & Pinola, L. (1994), Root Cause Analysis Methodologies: Trends and Needs, *in* "Proceedings of PSAM II".

Edwards, E. (1972), Man and Machine: Systems for Safety, *in* "Proceedings of British Airline Pilots Association Technical Symposium", British Airline Pilots Association.

Harle, P. G. (1994), Investigation of Human Factors: The Link to Accident Prevention, *in* N. Johnston, N. McDonald & R. Fuller (eds.), "Aviation Psychology in Practice", Avebury Technical, pp.127–148.

Hawkins, F. H. (1984), Human Factors in Education in European Air Transport Operations, *in* M. Nijhohff (ed.), "Breakdown in Human Adaptation to Stress: Towards a Multidisciplinary Approach", Vol. 1, Commission of the European Communities.

Hawkins, F. H. (1987), *Human Factors in Flight*, Gower Technical Press.

Hollnagel, E. (1991), The Phenotype of Erroneous Actions: Implications for HCI Design, *in* G. R. S. Weir & J. L. Alty (eds.), "Human Computer Interaction and the Complex Systems", Academic Press, pp.73–121.

Hollnagel, E. & Cacciabue, P. C. (1991), Cognitive Modelling in System Simulation, *in* "Proceedings of the 3rd European Conference on Cognitive Science Approaches to Process Control", University of Wales, pp.1–29.

Leplat, J. & Rasmussen, J. (1987), Analysis of Human Errors in Industrial Incidents and Accidents for Improvement of Work Safety, *in* J. Rasmussen, K. Duncan & J. Leplat (eds.), "New Technology and Human Error", John Wiley & Sons.

Paries, J. (1994), Ætiology of an Accident: A Case Study of the Human Factors Aspects of the Mont Sainte-Odile Crash, *in* "Proceedings of the ICAO Regional Seminar on Human Factors and Flight Safety", International Civil Aviation Organization.

Pedrali, M. & Cojazzi, G. (1994), A Methodological Framework for Root Cause Analysis of Human Errors, *in* N. Johnston, N. McDonald & R. Fuller (eds.), "Human Factors in Aviation Operations: Proceedings of the 21st Conference of the European Association for Aviation Psychology (EAAP)", Vol. 3, Avebury Aviation, pp.143–148.

Pedrali, M., Cojazzi, G. & Cacciabue, P. C. (1995), A Methodology for Retrospective Analyses of Accidents Involving Human Factors, *in* R. S. Jensen & L. A. Rakovan (eds.), "Proceedings of the 8th International Symposium on Aviation Psychology", Vol. 2, Ohio State University, pp.1278–1283.

Pew, R. W., Miller, P. C. & Feeher, C. E. (1981), Evaluation of Proposed Control Room Improvements through Analysis of Critical Operators Decision, Technical Report NP 1982,891, EPRI.

Reason, J. (1990), *Human Error*, Cambridge University Press.

A Web StoryBase

Mary Beth Rosson, John M Carroll & David Messner

Department of Computer Science, Virginia Polytechnic Institute and State University, Blacksburg, VA 24061 0106, USA.

Tel: *+1 540 231 6470*

EMail: *rosson@vt.edu,carroll@cs.vt.edu,dmessner@vt.edu*

We describe the Web StoryBase, a system using HTML forms technology to collect and share stories and story annotations from users of the World Wide Web. We analyse usage data collected over a period of 26 weeks, from the perspective of how the system was advertised, contributed to, and browsed. We also discuss several themes extracted from the reported Web experiences: usability, learnability, diversity, communication, just-in-time information, capture and fun.

Keywords: Internet, networks, World Wide Web, HTML forms, stories, user experience.

1 Introduction

The World Wide Web (WWW) is emerging as a highly diverse and dynamic information system with the potential for great impact on our lives. In fact, this impact is occurring so rapidly that HCI researchers have had little time to understand and facilitate the process, despite our evident interest (e.g. the NII panel from CHI'95). A few studies have begun to appear, for example, chronicling a specific user's experience (Britton & Reyes, 1994), the design of a particular Web interface (Nielsen & Sano, 1994), and the demographics of the Web user population (Pitkow & Recker, 1994). However, we still know remarkably little about how people are using and reacting to this information resource.

The StoryBase project began with an opportunity: the emergence of HTML forms technology transformed the Web from a strictly browsing environment to a potentially interactive one. We conceived of a system that would at once allow us to

Private Webs
keywords: networks, usefulness
author: Austin Hicklin
email: hicklin@webstation.com
date: Mon Aug 07 07:54 1995
annotations: 1 **last:** Mon Aug 21 12:24 1995

Figure 1: A typical story index listing. The user reads the story by following the title link (underlined); email can be initiated through the email address link.

experiment with a collaborative Web application, and to gather specific information about the experiences users are having with the Web. Our project extends Flanagan's 'critical incidents' method (Flanagan, 1954); we attempted to gather and present users' stories of personally significant Web usage episodes. Thus our initial hope was to provide a rich, qualitative 'snapshot' of why and how people are using the Web, while that use is emerging and evolving.

We first describe the StoryBase system. We then discuss the usage of this system from a variety of perspectives: the usage activity itself, characteristics of the stories that were submitted and annotated, and themes we discovered in the story content.

2 The StoryBase

The Web StoryBase is an interactive repository of stories that relate users' experiences with the World Wide Web (http://hci.ise.vt.edu/storybase/story/). The home page (like all pages in the system) is generated by a Perl CGI script: it contains a welcome and orienting paragraph, along with an index of submitted stories. This index lists the stories in chronological order of submission date. Each entry contains a story's title, date of submission, the number and most recent date of annotations, and keywords (see Figure 1). Entries contain optional fields for a story's author and email address. Selecting a story title causes that story to be displayed, followed by its annotations (also in chronological order).

Contributors follow a 'Compose' link from the main page to submit a story; from individual story pages they use an 'add an annotation' link to submit annotations. Submission is supported by a forms-based dialog, in which the story title, content (which can of course include embedded HTML tags), keywords, and optional identifying information are obtained. Contributors are also asked to indicate whether or not they wish their submissions to be public.

The StoryBase was designed with several high-level goals in mind. We wanted the application to be inviting: we needed to be able to catch the attention of casual Web surfers, enough to stop and browse and perhaps contribute a story or annotation. Thus we made an effort to develop an attractive welcome page with a few evocative images for browsing and composing stories. However, we also attempted to not overwhelm or distract users with complex and flashy graphics; our intention was to highlight the story material, not the user interface used to present it.

From our own experiences using the Web, we expected that people would browse or submit material only if these tasks were very easy — as easy as moving on to another Web adventure. Thus we streamlined the browsing task by providing considerable summary information in the story index (see Figure 1). For example, author and annotation data as well as story title can be used in selecting stories to browse. Although the process for submitting stories or annotations is constrained by HTML forms technology (users must submit filled-out forms prior to receiving feedback), we provided tips for less experienced users (e.g. a suggestion to cut and paste text from their own text editor), as well as an offer to submit stories received through standard email.

To make the story submission process more rewarding, the system supports the personalization of contributions. For example, although we seeded the StoryBase with a small set of descriptive keywords, a story author may add terms that better describe his or her experience. Authors are also encouraged to include HTML tags in their stories, which allows them to provide pointers to Web resources of interest to them. If a contributor submits an email address, we automatically convert this into a 'Send-to' tag, which in appropriate Web browsers can be used to send an email reply.

If a contributor provides email contact information, we send a 'thank you note' acknowledging the contribution to the StoryBase; we send this not only as an expression of thanks, but also as a reminder and additional advertisement for the system. If a story is annotated, we again use email to notify the story author, hoping to facilitate direct collaboration among users if appropriate.

Although we have no yardstick against which to measure the overall 'success' of the StoryBase, we have informal evidence that it has been well received. A number of visitors to the site have sent email complimenting us on the idea and its implementation, for example:

> "Well, I've just spent most of a day surfing around to different annotation sites, and I came back here. Your software is by far the nicest, friendliest and cleanest I've seen."

Several users have requested bits of the underlying technology so as to emulate it in other applications; in fact, one user made a contribution simply to audition it for his own needs:

> "Mac, schmac, windows schmindows, it all works out in the end. Just wanted to see how this annotation setup works. Very impressive. I plan to steal this idea!"

We ourselves have adapted it to another application, the OOPSLA'95 Virtual PhD Forum (http://hci.ise.vt.edu/phd/VirtualForum), as well as using it as a source of ideas for a more elaborate network-based sharing system, the BEV HistoryBase (Carroll et al., 1995).

In March 1995, after 3 months of beta-testing within our local networks, we advertised StoryBase on the Yahoo and NCSA *What's New* pages, two heavily used 'launching pads' for Web exploration. As further evidence of its positive reception, it was subsequently picked up by several 'hotspot' services, most notably Delphi

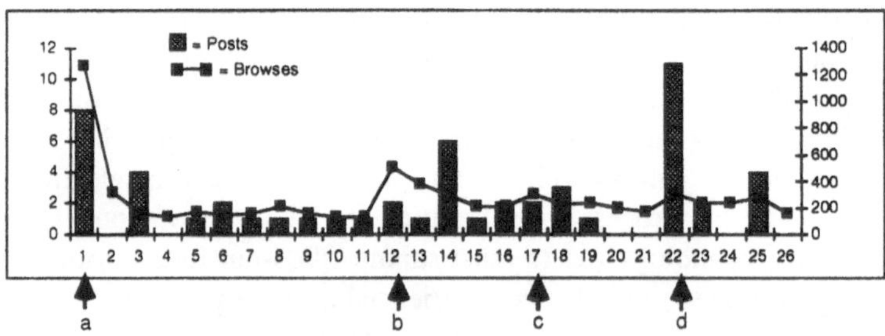

Figure 2: Browses and posts for the 26 weeks from 3/6/95 to 9/1/95. The arrows indicate points at which we 'advertised' the StoryBase in various ways: a) on Yahoo and NCSA Mosaic What's New; b) on announcements.chi; c) on comp.infosystems.www.announce; d) via direct email to 47 'interested' colleagues.

Innovative Web Sites, the Collaboration sites of the World Wide Web Consortium, and GEnie Hotspots.

3 Browsers and Contributors

When we conceived of the story-sharing project, we had two concerns: first that we would be flooded with contributions from Web users all over the world; and second, that no one would come. Over a period of 26 weeks that we gathered weekly measures of system activity, 6863 pages were browsed, and 55 posts were made — an average of 261.8 browses and 2.1 posts per week and a browse-to-post ratio of about 125:1. Given the novelty of this type of application, we have no way of assessing what 'normal' activity is: people came, but we were not overwhelmed.

Our initial experience with StoryBase involved local users, largely students in the Computer Science Department at Virginia Tech. During the first 3 months of operation (Dec 1994 through Feb 1995), we received 14 posts consisting of 5 stories and 9 annotations. These numbers convinced us that the contributions were likely to accrue slowly, so we decided to open the site for public use, and in parallel to investigate informally the effects of several types of 'advertisement'.

The browse and post data summarized in Figure 2 depict usage data for the 26 weeks from 6 March through 1 September. As one would expect, there is a general tendency for the levels of browsing and posting to be related ($r = 0.47$). However, the pattern of browsing and posting activity does seem to be influenced by the type of advertising that we did.

Week 1 coincided with the appearance of the StoryBase site on the NCSA Mosaic *What's New* listing (it had appeared the week before on the Yahoo listing used by Netscape). Although we do not have data for the weeks prior to these ads, the drop-off in subsequent weeks suggests that they had a pronounced effect on StoryBase use. We do not know how the number of browses during our first week of data collection (1270) compares to the activity a site can expect when first listed. For example, these lists are alphabetized, and we made an effort to place ourselves near the top by naming our site 'An Authorable StoryBase'; this may have increased attention to our offering. Despite the large number of accesses, however, only 8 posts were made during that week (a ratio of approximately 160:1).

A similar but less dramatic effect was observed for the invitation sent in Week 12 to announcements.chi (a listserv that reaches about 800 users): a local peak of 500 browses was observed, but only 2 posts were made (although it is possible that at least some of the posts in the following two weeks were a delayed reaction to this solicitation, see Figure 2). This ratio (250:1) is not unlike that observed in the first week, with many users seemingly curious about the system, but not interested or experienced enough to make a contribution.

In contrast to the first two solicitations, the Week 17 post to the comp.infosystems.www.announce newsgroup seemed to have very little effect on usage activity: the number of browses (298) for that week was modestly greater than that of the preceding week (209), but posting seemed relatively unaffected. It may be that as Web hotspot and searching services increase their coverage and sophistication, this more traditional announcement mechanism is becoming less important; it is also likely that the high traffic on this site reduces attention paid to any one posting.

In Week 22, the first author sent out direct email solicitations to 47 individuals known to be interested and involved in Web activities. These messages were 'form letters' but began with a personalized salutation. As the figure shows, this technique had a major impact on the number of postings: the 294 browses and 11 posts yields a ratio of approximately 27:1, almost an order of magnitude greater than that observed in week 12.

This dramatic increase in submissions seems likely to be due to the individualized nature of the solicitation. The 47 persons contacted in this fashion are active members of the CHI community and most had probably received the general invitation sent out over announcements.chi. But the person-to-person invitation elicited participation where the general notice had not. As one contributor put it in a follow-up email message:

> "Okay ... that was fun. I think your 'personal note' strategy is helpful; I have to admit that I knew about your StoryBase before but had never taken the time to put up a story."

4 The Stories

We received 31 story submissions over the 38 week period from Dec 9 through Sep 1. Four of these were omitted from the StoryBase, three because their content had nothing to do with Web experiences, and one because it consisted merely of a list of links to the submitter's own Web pages. Of the 27 remaining stories, 22 related a specific Web experience while 5 reported a more general Web reaction or perspective.

We carried out several qualitative analyses of the stories to better understand their content and their impact on the evolving StoryBase. At a high level, we categorized the basic content of the stories to begin to articulate the kinds of experiences users felt were worth sharing with others. We also looked at the use of author-selected keywords as descriptors of the content. Because a large portion of activity involved annotations, we spent some time trying to understand what kinds of stories were

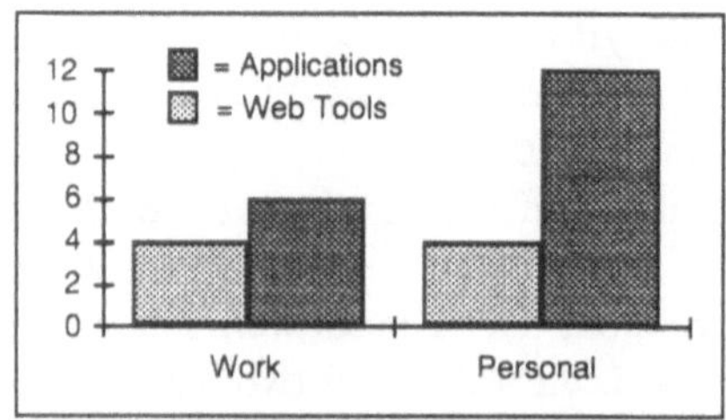

Figure 3: Stories broken down by the context and content of the experience reported.

most likely to evoke comments from other users. Finally, we examined story and annotation content in more detail to extract users' views on the ways in which the Web is contributing to their lives and how it should evolve.

4.1 Story Categories

We first searched for general characteristics that seemed to reflect distinctions among stories. One such distinction was in the *context* of the story — the author's work vs. his or her personal life; a second was in the *content* — a focus on Web tools vs. the application of these tools. Examples of Web-tool stories include a description of hotlist problems and of delays during link navigation; examples of application stories include using the Web to find a publisher and retrieving travel information for a family vacation. Figure 3 summarizes the breakdown of stories into these general categories.* While the number of stories is still too small to warrant strong inferences concerning these general categories, it is interesting that a high number of stories (62%) describe a Web experience from the author's personal life. If this is a genuine trend, it may be indicative of the extent to which the Web has permeated individuals' lives, or perhaps their surprise at the extent to which it has. It may also reflect an implicit assessment of what characterizes a good story to share: self-disclosure is a powerful technique for evoking response from others (Archer, 1980).

Another general characteristic we considered was the *tone* of the story, either positive or negative (our orienting paragraphs encouraged stories of both types). Of the 27 stories, we judged 16 (59%) to be generally positive in tone, 11 negative. Again, our small numbers qualify this observation, but at the least it suggests that users are as willing to recount good things about this new technology domain as to complain about it. Of more interest was our observation that *none* of the stories focusing on Web tools were positive. This may reflect a general tendency of users to reflect on the tools they are using only when the tools become 'present-to-hand' through 'breakdowns' (Heidegger, 1962). The inverse of this — that only 2 of the Web applications stories had a negative tone to them — may reflect the current euphoria users seem to be feeling with respect to Web resources.

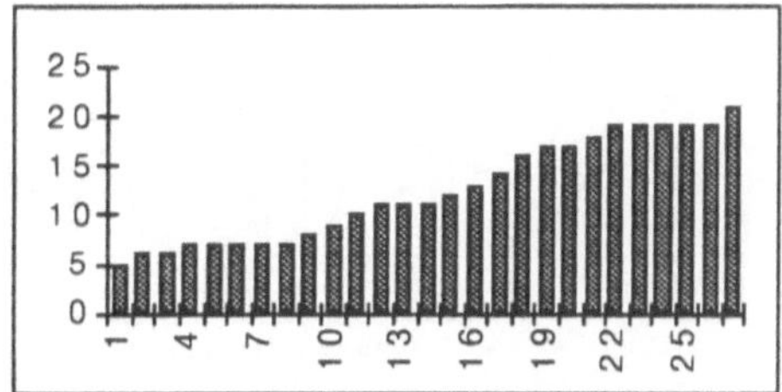

Figure 4: Expansion of keyword set across stories. Terms in order of addition are: immensity, frustration, happiness, anger, amazement, confusion, sound, dudgeon, usability, network, fool, dupe, futures, contacts, behaviour change, description, usefulness, surfing, hotspots, awesome, and dream come true.

4.2 Keyword Distribution

Another view of the submitted stories is through the terms authors used to describe their contributions. The choice of one or more keywords was optional, but only 2 authors elected not to so-describe their submission. The addition of new keywords was also optional, and 13 of the 27 story authors elected to do this, with most adding just one new term. We 'seeded' the keyword set with 5 generic terms: immensity, frustration, happiness, anger, and amazement. Authors contributed an additional 16 terms for a total of 21 over the 27 stories (Figure 4).

On average, authors selected 2.3 terms; the mode was 2 and the maximum was 11. As one would expect, there was a tendency for authors to select more keywords as the set available increased: during the submission of the first 14 stories, the keyword set increased to 11, with an average of 1.5 selected for each story; during the remaining 13 stories, the keyword set grew to 21, and an average of 3 terms were selected.

An informal examination of the keywords (see caption in Figure 4) suggests that they are weighted more toward positive aspects of stories; only 6 of the 21 (frustration, anger, confusion, dudgeon, fool, dupe) have a negative tone, with three of these coming from our original set, and one of them (anger) never used at all. This may simply reflect the slightly higher number of stories with a positive tone, or it may reflect a desire of authors to be more specific in categorizing their positive experiences.

Of interest to the future of the StoryBase is the extent to which keywords can be used as retrieval or story organization cues. Our welcome page explains that as the number of stories increases, we expect to offer alternate views. One such view could be based on keywords; we plan to use keywords both to organize stories by content and to contract the size of the top-level listing (which is now at the grain of individual stories). Our examination of keyword use suggests several considerations for this plan.

*One story did not fit into this 2x2 categorization; it was an allegorical tale emphasizing at once the attractiveness but also immensity of Web navigation, entitled "The Silk Road".

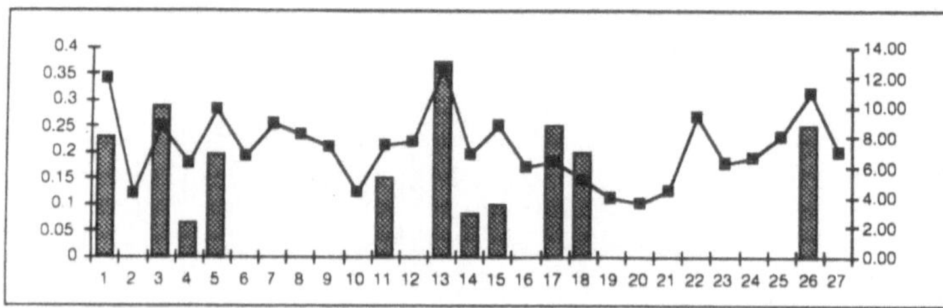

Figure 5: Weekly browse and annotation rates for the 27 stories. The measures have been normalized by the number of weeks the story had been a part of the StoryBase at the time of data collection; for example story 1 had been in the system for 38 weeks, story 14 for 20 weeks, and story 27 for 1 week.

We ended up with almost as many keywords as stories, causing us to wonder about the scalability of this particular feature. It may be that the addition of new terms will taper off, as the list gets longer and more difficult to scan; unfortunately, at that point we may not serve authors' desire to be specific in describing their stories. Indeed, our initial inclination would be to change the dialog so that users simply enter keywords in a free-form fashion without worrying about whether they correspond to terms already in the system. It will be interesting to track the expansion and possible asymptotic character of the set over a longer period.

The relatively large set of keywords also leads us to doubt the usefulness of the full term set in grouping the stories: offering users 21 categories within which to access the 27 entries would indeed provide a content-oriented browsing structure, but would do little to reduce the size of the highest-level listing. Clearly we will need to be more selective in the keywords used for this grouping purpose.

As a first pass at such a selective process, we examined the relative 'coverage' of individual keywords. We found that the smallest set of keywords covering all 27 stories included eight terms: amazement, happiness, frustration, immensity, network, fool, behaviour change, and hotspots. Given this set, 11 stories would appear under more than one category. In contrast to the full set of 21 terms, this group of eight seems likely to produce a noticeable filtering effect for users. Again, it is too soon to know how useful these terms will be as the set of stories grow, but we plan to automate and evaluate such a selection of 'high filter value' terms. We are also considering more complex schemes that would introduce sub-categories as a function of overlap in term use.

4.3 To Annotate or Not

The capability for annotating submitted stories is an important feature of our design: submission of a story for sharing is an indirect act of collaboration, but annotation of a specific individual's story is a more direct collaborative act. Indeed, we attempted to reinforce this implicit collaborative relation by notifying authors of annotations to their stories. Thus another 'view' of our results is the characterization of stories that did or did not receive annotations.

Stories with High Annotation Rate			No Annotations but High Browse Rate	
Title	Post Rate	Browse Rate	Title	Browse Rate
BoneHeads on the Web (13)	0.37	12.59	Yahoo! The Hotspot is a Cool Monastery (22)	9.33
Shouldn't have Bought a Mac (1)	0.23	11.87	Oh My Faux Pas (7)	8.90
Hot List Haemorrhage (5)	0.20	9.84	How I discovered free tech support (8)	8.12
URLs in USA Today! (3)	0.29	8.79	One out of three beats two out of three (25)	8.00

Table 1: Titles and Individual Activity Measures for Eight Stories (numbers refer to story submission order, see Figure 4).

A summary of activity specific to stories appears in Figure 5. All stories were browsed to some extent; the weekly browse rates ranged from 3.6 to 12.6. However, not all of the stories were annotated: the weekly annotation rate for the 11 stories receiving comments ranged from 0.06 to 0.37, but 16 stories had no posts.

So what does attract browsing and annotation activity? For the case of browsing, our best guess is that it is the title. This makes intuitive sense: the title is probably the most salient feature displayed in the story index (although as a story is annotated, the mere presence of annotations might be enough to invite browsing).

As Figure 5 suggests, stories that are browsed more often tend also to be annotated more often ($r = 0.61$): perhaps the 'interestingness' of the title attracts browsing, and once browsed, a story is more likely to be annotated. However, as the figure also suggests, this is not all that is going on. The browse-annotate relationship breaks down at times (e.g. look at story 22 in Figure 4), suggesting that factors other than title interestingness are contributing to annotation behaviour.

To provide some insight into possible other factors, we have displayed in Table 1 the titles and usage data for eight stories. On the left are the stories with the highest overall annotation rate; not surprisingly, they also have high browse rates. On the right are four stories that had relatively high weekly browse rates but no annotations.

One factor apparent in the table is controversiality — one would naturally expect stories with controversial content to evoke more dialog. Thus, the titles of the first two stories on the left in Table 1 suggest controversy, while none of those on the right do so. However, one story attempted to provoke controversy ("The Web is Dead: Long Live the Web"), including an explicit request for opinions, but has received no responses thus far. Further, only a few of the stories raised controversial topics, so we expect that other factors must also be in operation — cf. Shirky (1995), that newsgroup users tend to respond when they disagree.

Posting a controversial theme can be seen as an implicit request for discussion. Other stories seem to be making similar implicit requests: for example, several of the stories receiving annotations included some reflective introductory remarks before launching into the narrative, perhaps serving to set a discussion 'agenda'. The hot list story raised a specific problem, and evoked a number of solution-responses.

We also speculate that stories pitched at a 'medium' level of abstraction may be more successful in evoking responses from others. So, for example, though the "Web is Dead" story explicitly requested opinions, its topic was rather abstract and

Theme	Story content suggesting theme
Usability	absence of common style; hot lists; navigation; response time
Learnability	poor documentation; how to get new users hooked
Capture	being drawn into an overly long or complex investigation
Diversity	movies, airplanes, travel, etc. — wide range of material on the Web
Communication	increased contact with friends; hopeful outreach, future trends
Just-in-Time Info	project information; literature reference; travel planning; product support
Fun	hobby information; practical joke

Table 2: Summary of themes extracted from story and annotation content.

philosophical. In contrast, the highly-annotated stories concerning URLs and hot lists are concrete topics to which many users can relate.

At the other extreme, many non-annotated stories reported very specific personal experiences (e.g. a friend's pointer to a picture of a favourite airplane). These stories are interesting to read (and in the case of the Yahoo! story in Table 2, may provide useful Web pointers), but they may be too context-specific to evoke a reaction or sharing of similar experiences (although note that the literature on self-disclosure, would predict otherwise; (Archer, 1980)).

5 Tools, Applications and Practices

We had two main research interests when we initiated the StoryBase project, one to study the design and use of forms-based collaborative authoring, and another to extract Web experiences from users that might have implications for the future use and evolution of Web-based tools, applications and practices. To pursue the second of these goals, we have analysed the content of submitted stories and annotations for frequent or interesting patterns or themes (see Table 2).

5.1 Usability

We were surprised at the relatively small number of usability concerns expressed in the stories. Our starting assumption was that problems using Web tools would be a major source of contributions; our focused solicitations to members of the CHI community heightened this expectation, and we were curious to what extent concerns evident in personal stories would map to those identified by more systematic usability investigations — e.g. (Britton & Reyes, 1994). However, only five stories raised usability concerns, and two of these were 'seed' stories we contributed to get the system going!

Two stories commented on the failure of many Web authors to follow basic 'style' guidelines. This is not a surprising situation, given the rapid growth in Web-empowered contributors combined with the almost total absence of monitoring or control. Style guides are becoming available, e.g.:

http://info.med.yale.edu/caim/StyleManual_Top.html

but as one story relates, a common way to get started is to copy and modify a colleague's page. This copy/edit strategy has been observed in other 'programming' situations (Rosson & Carroll, 1991; in press), and while it can provide a fast track to productivity, one would expect that the quirks of a convenient example might persist in the learners' own authoring efforts.

Another usability concern covered problems with the hot list feature (which adds sites to a menu for convenient navigation; in Netscape Navigator this is called a 'bookmark'). Problems with hot list creation and management have been noted before (e.g. the list quickly gets long and is difficult to scan; there are no organizing mechanisms; (Britton & Reyes, 1994)). Of interest in our study is that this story was one of the more extensively annotated ones, with several of the responses suggesting useful approaches to hot list problems (e.g. a technique for combining a Mosaic hot list and a set of Netscape bookmarks). In this sense, the story and its annotations reflect a sort of communal problem-solving; the exchange of expertise might also be viewed as an ad hoc "Answer Garden" (Ackerman, 1994), emphasizing the communicative functions of the StoryBase.

A third concern revolved around the difficulties in (re)finding information of interest, especially when it is similar or partially overlapping with other resources. The rapid evolution of powerful search tools — see for example:

http://www.opentext.com:8080/omw-comp.html

may address these problems, although perhaps at the cost of learning effective use of query procedures.

A final issue raised was the unpredictable and often long delays in navigating links, especially to more remote sites. That story came from a user working with Mosaic; the now very popular Netscape Navigator addresses this issue to some extent, providing considerably more feedback about the progress of link navigation, as well as providing a more robust cancellation feature.

5.2 Learnability

Several stories dealt with the general issue of learning or teaching others about the Web. Two stories discussed problems learning enough about HTML to be able to create their own pages, and commented that there was little available in terms of literature that could help in this. To a great extent, this can be attributed to the speed with which HTML authoring has become available to the general public, as compared to the time it takes for quality books to be written and published. Ironically, most of the helpful information is available *on the Web*, making the initial introductory experience a sort of Catch-22. Also of interest are the 'support group' annotations that appeared in response to these stories — again in contrast to Shirky's (1995) observation that users tend to contribute to newsgroups only when they disagree.

Another learnability theme was the question of how to get friends and colleagues 'hooked'. The suggestion was to select an area of intense interest that you know is well-represented on the Web, and to use exploration of that material as a first introduction.

5.3 *Capture*

Several stories described what might best be characterized as Web capture or entrapment: a user, who may or may not be an experienced Web user, is drawn into the Web on a search for something, and ends up spending an excessive time pursuing links. One user described a successful one-week search for information that was available right down the hall. Another described a student who unwittingly 'expanded' an assignment to include a document *plus all of its links*.

5.4 *Diversity*

A very common theme across stories was the incredible diversity of information that is now commonplace on the Web. Examples include stories describing URLs for entertainment, a restaurant, a monastery, a (hardcopy) publisher inviting work, airplanes for sale, and state tourism information. One of the most annotated stories was the tale of seeing a URL in USA today; other users were eager to share similar experiences. Given the current explosion of Web services, it is not surprising to find this as perhaps the most frequent reaction across users.

5.5 *Communication*

Another feature of many stories was the extent to which the Web supports communication, and especially contact among friends (Rheingold, 1993; Shirky, 1995). One story involved serendipitous discovery of long-lost friends, suggestive of a new 'Small World' mechanism. Another told how the Web was used to publish hopeful notes from Sarajevo: hopeful in the sense that the authors had no way of knowing whether the intended recipients would see the messages, but were eager to try anything, even the rather exotic and long-shot method of Web publishing, to communicate with loved ones.

5.6 *Just-in-time Information*

The diverse and dynamic nature of the Web, combined with now much-improved search tools and organized collections, makes the Web a wonderful resource *at the time* a question or need arises. Several stories recounted such situations — for example, finding just the right reference for a paper while under deadline pressure, obtaining travel information as you are ready to begin your vacation, looking up needed project information in a new job.

5.7 *Fun*

Finally, a few of the stories simply reflected the enjoyment users are finding in their interactions with this new and growing information resource. The airplanes example concerned a friend's pointer to something he knew the author had been dreaming about. Another story and its annotations related how a 'fakemail' mechanism was used to pull a practical joke on a friend.

6 Summary and Conclusions

We have described a variety of StoryBase analyses — user interaction rates, the general tone of submitted material, annotation behaviour, and some of the Web experience themes apparent in the stories. We will close by emphasizing a few key points and discussing our plans for future work.

First, we have provided an early picture of the relative frequency of browsing vs. contributing to Web pages: in our data the overall proportion was approximately 125:1. This general lopsidedness is consistent with the reports of others studying network communities (Rheingold, 1993). However, we were also able to demonstrate that by interjecting a personal communication, we could produce a major adjustment in this ratio.

Second, users clearly were ready and willing to use our system for communication, rather than simply information provision. Many stories described personal experiences of users involving friends and family. Users often responded to questions or problems with bits of their own expertise or supportive comments. Nonetheless, highly personal stories often did not attract annotations. This observation is of special interest in light of the well-known effects of self-disclosure on communicative response in dyads or small groups (Archer, 1980). It may be that the asynchronous nature of the StoryBase communication process, combined with users' physical remoteness, defuses the impact of self-disclosure.

Finally, there was a relatively small number of stories containing usability 'critiques'. We did collect 2–3 such stories (not counting our own), and the usability issues did tend to evoke discussion from readers who had their own views or fixes for the problems. But for the most part, stories described efforts to use the Web to accomplish something, whether it be work or fun, and many authors attempted to convey their excitement and amazement at how useful they were finding the Web to be in their lives. It may be that at this early stage of Web technology evolution, users tend to overlook many of the glitches they experience while exploring the constantly expanding boundaries of what is possible.

In future work, we plan to investigate alternative access structures for the stories, perhaps based on the keyword analyses described earlier. We also expect to contrast the experiences revealed through this casual and open-ended forum with those obtained through more traditional user observations. Recently we have discovered another 'story' project, a collection under development by Farnet (http://www.farnet.org/). That project uses email and gopher technology, rather than forms and HTML, and its goals appear to be directed specifically at 'success' stories; nonetheless, it will be interesting to compare the two collections.

Finally, we are interested in the role that the StoryBase might play as a collaborative history system. Elsewhere (Carroll et al., 1995) we are exploring the contributions of a shared database of community reflections and plans on the development and maintenance of community bonds. In a sense, the StoryBase can be seen as a concrete step toward creation of such a shared archive for the very large community of World Wide Web users.

References

Ackerman, M. (1994), Augmenting the Organizational Memory: A Field Study of Answer Garden, *in* R. Furuta & C. Neuwirth (eds.), "Proceedings of CSCW'94: Conference on Computer Supported Cooperative Work", ACM Press, pp.243–253.

Archer, J. L. (1980), Self-disclosure, *in* D. M. Wegner & R. Vallacher (eds.), "The Self in Social Psychology", Oxford University Press, pp.183–204.

Britton, D. R. & Reyes, A. A. (1994), Discovering Usability Improvements for Mosaic: Application of the Contextual Inquiry Technique with an Expert User, *in* "Electronic Proceedings of the 2nd World Wide Web Conference: Mosaic and the Web". http://www.ncsa.uiuc.edu/SDG/IT94/Proceedings/HCI/britton/britton_reyes.html.

Carroll, J. M., Rosson, M. B., Cohill, A. C. & Schorger, J. (1995), Building a History of the Blacksburg Electronic Village, *in* G. Olson & S. Schuon (eds.), "Proceedings of Designing Interactive Systems Conference: DIS'95", ACM Press, pp.1–5.

Flanagan, J. C. (1954), "The Critical Incident Technique", *Psychological Bulletin* **51**, 28–35.

Heidegger, M. (1962), *Being and Time*, Harper and Row.

Nielsen, J. & Sano, D. (1994), SunWeb: User Interface Design for Sun Microsystem's Internal Web, *in* "Electronic Proceedings of the 2nd World Wide Web Conference: Mosaic and the Web". http://www.ncsa.uiuc.edu/SDG/IT94/Proceedings/HCI/nielsen/sunweb.html.

Pitkow, J. E. & Recker, M. (1994), Results from the First World Wide Web Survey, *in* "Electronic Proceedings of the 2nd World Wide Web Conference: Mosaic and the Web". http://www1.cern.ch/PapersWWW94/pitkow-survey.ps.

Rheingold, H. (1993), *The Virtual Community: Homesteading on the Electronic Frontier*, Addison–Wesley.

Rosson, M. B. & Carroll, J. M. (1991), Active Programming Strategies for Reuse, *in* O. M. Nierstrasz (ed.), "ECOOP'93 — Object-Oriented Programming", Vol. 707 of *Lecture Notes in Computer Science*, Springer-Verlag, pp.4–20.

Rosson, M. B. & Carroll, J. M. (in press), "The Reuse of Uses in Smalltalk Programming", *ACM Transactions on Computer–Human Interaction.*

Shirky, C. (1995), *Voices from the Net*, Ziff-Davis Press.

Session Length and Subjective Satisfaction in Information Kiosk Research

Jorma Sajaniemi & Ismo Tossavainen

Department of Computer Science, University of Joensuu, PO Box 111, FIN-80101 Joensuu, Finland.

Tel: *+358 73 1513101*

Fax: *+358 73 1513290*

EMail: *saja@cs.joensuu.fi*

Information kiosks introduce a possibility to test usability of computer based services with a large number and a wide variety of users. In this paper, we are interested in evaluating user's subjective satisfaction, hopefully using automatic log analysis techniques. Based on usability data collected in an information kiosk study conducted in a housing fair, we show that subjective satisfaction cannot be predicted based on session lengths. However, subjective satisfaction can be combined with session length to find user groups having important qualitative differences that can be exploited in usability analysis.

Keywords: usability research, usability analysis, usability kiosk, subjective satisfaction, methodology.

1 Introduction

The new digital media is emerging in homes, libraries, shopping centres and other places where ordinary people live their daily lives and spend their free time. New technology makes computer based multimedia and telematic services available to people of all ages having vastly different training, experience, and personal characteristics and capabilities, particularly in the area of computer use. In a couple of decades the computer literacy will be much better than today but there will always be people who face the computer for the first time in an environment with no one around to assist them. Moreover, today and during the next 5–10 years, the success of mass production multimedia and telematic services will depend on people who are novices in the computer area. The crucial point for the producers and distributors of multimedia and telematic services will be the number of people that will start using and consuming these services.

Usability research has so far been conducted mainly in laboratories and at user sites. When we are speaking of computer applications that are intended to be used by masses of ordinary people there is also a need to study their usability with a broader set of users. Such research can be conducted within an *information kiosk*, i.e. a publicly accessible terminal connected to some information system (Perrochon, 1995). An information kiosk used in usability research is often called a *usability kiosk* as it then acts as a self-served usability laboratory and can be used as part of a hallway methodology (Nielsen, 1993). The number of subjects, or users, in a usability kiosk research is supposed to be large. Therefore, usability kiosks are located in public places with lots of people passing by: fairs and exhibitions, shopping centres, libraries, etc. (Gould et al., 1987; Salomon, 1990). There are texts about usability testing and assessment (Dumas & Redish, 1993; Hix & Hartson, 1993; Kirakowski & Corbett, 1990; Landauer, 1988; Lindgaard, 1994; Nielsen, 1993; Nielsen & Mack, 1994; Preece et al., 1993) but little is said about problems special to usability kiosks.

Usability kiosk users, such as fair visitors, are often in a hurry and they will use computer based services only a couple of minutes. There is not much time for learning details of the user interface. Thus, only services that can be used immediately without any additional instructions can reach high subjective satisfaction. All available functions must be clearly marked so that users can immediately see them and their meaning must correspond directly to concepts in normal life. It is, of course, not reasonable to think that all mass production services could be used with a few clearly marked buttons. Therefore, more complex services should be studied in other environments or they must be reprogrammed to offer a version with a very simple user interface. Information kiosks can be best exploited in usability research by studying services that are intended to be used in similar circumstances or are intended to be used only once. Such services include for example electronic timetables and museum information services. The amount and diversity of users that can be obtained in a usability kiosk exceed clearly that of other methods.

As the duration of sessions in a usability kiosk is on average only some minutes there is no sense in studying usability problems concerning complicated operations or cases. It is, however, possible to find immediate learning problems and to study differences in allurement. Thus, suitable questions to be studied must be limited to fulfill these criteria. With these restrictions in mind, usability kiosks can produce valuable information that is not easy to obtain in any other way. In a fair, for example, computer services are used by all kinds of people. Even people who normally avoid computers can be induced to use them. Such people are not typical participants in laboratory experiments but still their opinions of the services are important for the success of the multimedia industry.

We have conducted a usability research of three multimedia and telematic services in a housing fair where the services were publicly available. Our aim was to analyse usability of the services (Tossavainen & Sajaniemi, 1995) and to study research methods suitable for usability kiosks (Sajaniemi & Tossavainen, 1995). In this paper we will consider the connection between session length and subjective satisfaction in usability kiosks.

2 Overview

There are many possibilities to collect data in usability kiosk research. Users' actions can be logged automatically, users can be observed, and they can be interviewed. Automatic logs are easiest to obtain, and, provided suitable analysis programs can be created, to analyse. In this paper, we are interested in possible connections between session length, which is easy to extract from the logs, and users' subjective satisfaction, which is important for the success of a service.

The nature of a computer based service has an effect on the usage pattern and on session lengths. In the following, we will distinguish three types of services:

1. *discrete single-use* services which have a clear starting/ending point and which are used only once, e.g. a long quiz that is seldom gone through several times;
2. *discrete multiple-use* services which have a clear starting/ending point and which are often used several times, e.g. a short quiz or a database service where each turn consists of entering the search criteria, starting the search, and viewing the search results; and
3. *continuous services* that can be started and ended anywhere, e.g. an electronic newspaper or information service.

Usability of a service can be seen to be associated with the following attributes (Nielsen, 1993):

- Learnability: The service should be easy to learn.
- Efficiency: The service should be efficient to use.
- Memorability: The use of the service should be easy to remember.
- Errors: The service should prevent users from making errors, and it should be easy to recover from errors.
- Satisfaction: The users should be subjectively satisfied with the service.

We understand *subjective satisfaction* in this context: it is the user's overall opinion of a service. In multimedia and telematic services that are intended to be used by masses of people, the most crucial attributes, from the point of view of the producers and distributors of a service, are learnability and subjective satisfaction. If the use of a service is hard to learn initially then people will not start to use it even if it were the only service of its kind. Likewise, if people are satisfied with the service then they will continue to use it, even when another similar service becomes available.

By the *length of a session* we mean the amount of user activity. It can be measured by time, by the number of user actions, or by the volume of data a user goes

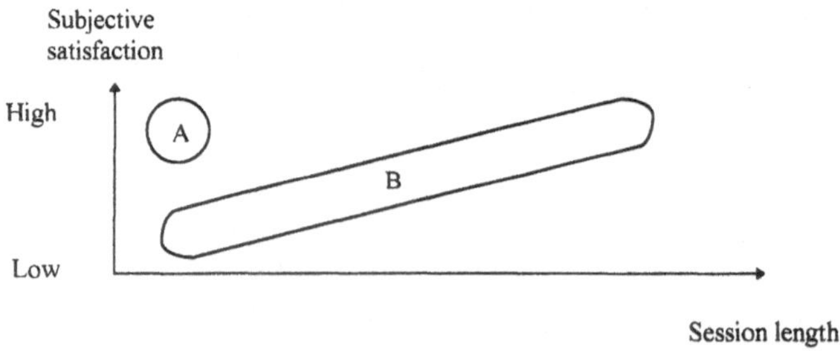

Figure 1: The expected distribution of subjective satisfaction vs. session length.

through. For example, in a database service, the length of a session could be simply the number of searches done. But care must be taken in selecting the measurement unit and interpreting its meaning. In a database service a single search carried out by a user may suggest that the quality of the result was so bad that the user did not consider it worthwhile to proceed, or it may indicate that the search was so successful that there was no need for further actions.

The research questions and the nature of differences among versions dictates what length measure to use. For example, if there are several versions of a service and they have different line speeds then users have to wait for computer output longer with some versions and, consequently, time is not a good measure for session length. Often the data volume is a good measure for the combination of learnability and subjective satisfaction.

The concept of session length in usability kiosks often differs from controlled experiments and user observations carried out in working places. In a controlled experiment the experimenter gives the subject some task to carry out. The duration of the task reflects in some sense the amount of work required for that task. Similarly, in working place observations subjects carry out their normal tasks (given to them by their management) and the time reflects again the laboriousness of the tasks. In a multimedia service there are, however, no predefined tasks. Users may quit a service whenever they want. Moreover, users' 'tasks' can have no exact goal that could be used to define size, as with entertainment services, or the size can vary dynamically, as with information services where an interesting finding may lead to more thorough exploration of the service.

The length of a session without any enforced or predefined goal does not describe how laborious it is to use the service but, more likely, how long the subject decided to use the service and play with it. It is, therefore, tempting to assume that a user who likes a service would use it longer than someone who finds the service inadequate, i.e. to assume that session length would correlate positively with subjective satisfaction.

There are also passers-by who just make a couple of mouse clicks to see what a service is about. They cannot form a real opinion of the service in such a short time, and when they are asked about the quality of the service, they may give a positive statement just to please the person making the interview. On these grounds the distribution of session length combined with subjective satisfaction could be expected to look like in Figure 1. Group A consists of people who have used the service superficially and Group B consists of users who quit early if they dislike the service and continue to use it longer if they like it. In the following we will see that this hypothesis is false.

3 Method

The usability research in the housing fair was conducted in normal booths that were mainly presenting communal services and attractions, such as services of the city of Joensuu. There were no special computer services dedicated for usability research, but all research was conducted in connection with computer services originally designed for the exhibitors. The usability research in the housing fair concerned three telematic multimedia services, two of which are important for the current paper: a quiz, and an information service.

The quiz consisted of a series of questions concerning knowledge of building houses. There were always 21 questions that were randomly selected among 63 possible questions for each user of the service. The quiz was implemented as a series of HTML (or WWW) pages which were presented to the user with the Netscape browser. In our study, the quiz represents discrete single-use services.

The information service was a collection of HTML pages presented to users with the Netscape browser. The pages contained information of local companies, communal services, colleges, and the University of Joensuu. Information service computers were also running another program all the time in background. If a user did not do anything for a certain period of time then the background program started to send commands to the Netscape browser so that the browser showed 'automatically' some preselected HTML pages. When a new user made some action with the mouse then the background program ceased sending these commands and started to watch for a long enough break in the user's actions. In our classification, the information service is a continuous service.

We collected data through four different methods: automatic logging of users' actions, user observations, interviews, and questionnaires. Data collected with different methods can be connected whenever they describe the same user.

4 Results

The use of the quiz was logged during 35 computer days (i.e. collected using several computers with a total of 35 days of use) consisting of 826 user sessions with 33,271 records in the log files. Figure 2 gives the distribution of session lengths as measured by the number of HTML pages seen by the user. Each question occupied its own page and there were, moreover, pages to start and end the quiz. The peak around 24 pages corresponds to users who answered all the questions. The peak has some width as some users did return the service to its beginning page at the end of their session while others did not. Figure 3 gives the distribution of quiz session lengths as measured by the number of mouse events (with 22 sessions having more than 120 mouse events). The peak is wider and lower than in Figure 2.

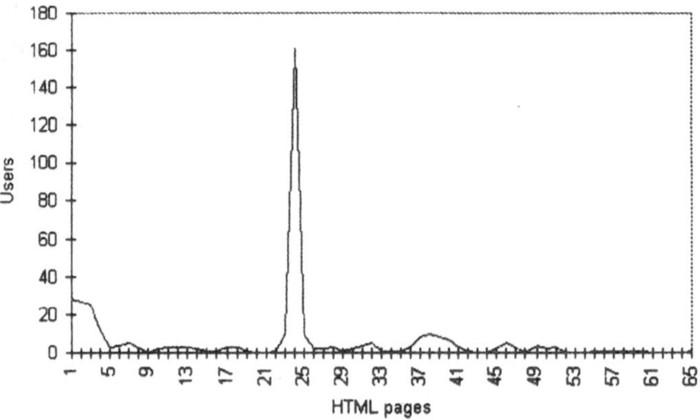

Figure 2: The distribution of quiz session lengths measured by the number of HTML pages.

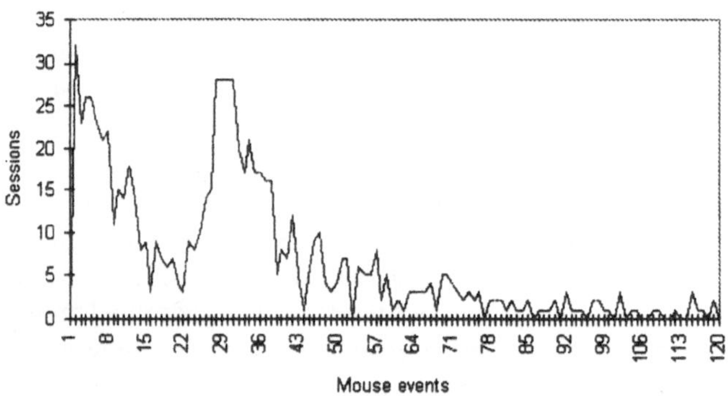

Figure 3: The distribution of quiz session lengths measured by the number of mouse events.

Figure 2 shows that there are some users with session length between 27 and 51, which seems to suggest that they have answered all the questions and then started a new quiz but not made it through. Protocol analysis reveals, however, that most of these users interrupted their first series of questions perhaps because of a wrong answer or because they wanted to ponder the alternatives more seriously.

Some quiz users were interviewed and as a part of the interview they evaluated the general impression of the service on scale from 1 (worst) to 5 (best). The average score among users that had seen 22–26 HTML pages was 4.1 (n = 8) and among users that had seen at least 27 pages it was 3.8 (n = 4).

The use of the information service was logged during 79 computer days consisting of 2,114 user sessions with 72,643 records in the log files. Figure 4 gives the distribution of session lengths as measured by session duration. The form of the distribution of session lengths does not change if session length is measured by the

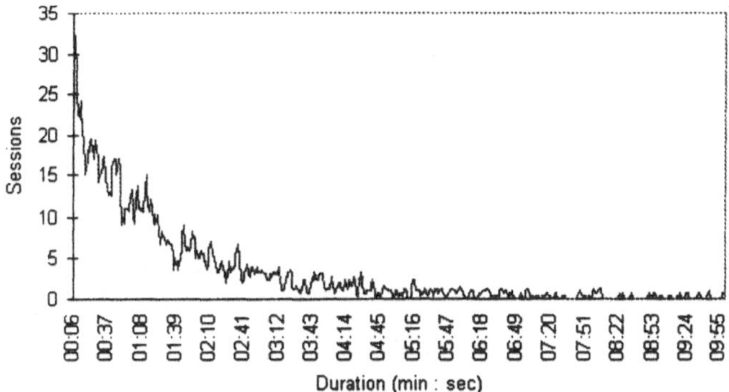

Figure 4: The distribution of information service session lengths measured by session durations (running average of three consecutive values).

---

number of HTML pages or by the number of mouse events. The general impression of the service as evaluated by users during interviews was on average 4.1 among users that used the service less than one minute (n = 8), 3.7 among users using the service at least one minute and at most five minutes (n = 10), and 3.7 among users having a session lasting at least five minutes (n = 7).

5 Discussion

The results do not support the hypothesis given by Figure 1. There is some evidence of the existence of Group A users who give a positive evaluation based on superficial use, but Group B cannot be found. There is no clear correlation between session length and subjective satisfaction. The data points are dispersed too uniformly in the subjective satisfaction scale and, moreover, there are gaps in the session length scale. This leads us to a more thorough analysis of the data and of user behaviour with different services.

5.1 Discrete Single-use Services

Let us first consider the case of discrete single-use services represented by the quiz. The selection of the length measure is not trivial with this service. Time is not a proper measure as it also includes thinking time. A user with an extensively long session may have troubles with the user interface but more probably the questions are difficult and the user ponders answers carefully. Moreover, some versions of the quiz included video sequences and the loading of these sequences increased total time. The number of questions describes better what proportion of the service the user has gone through and the number of mouse events describes the amount of her actions.

Figure 2 gives the number of users as a function of the number of HTML pages they went through. Figure 2 shows clearly the relatively small number of users having session length between 5 and 22. This gap suggests that there is a qualitative difference in the behaviour of the users in different sides of the gap. Let us consider this more thoroughly and in a more general sense.

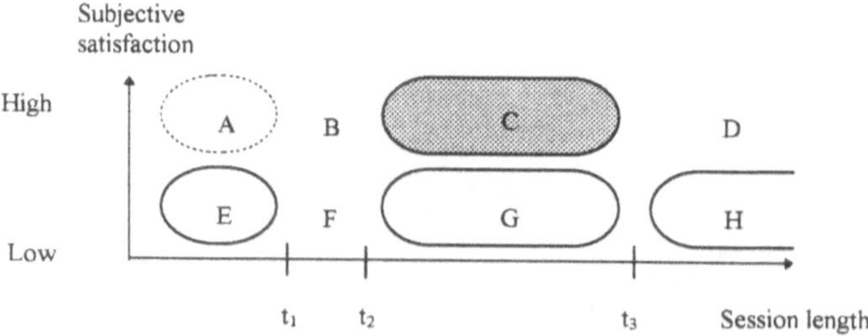

Figure 5: User groups in discrete single-use services.

Figure 5 introduces a new classification of user groups we expect to find in a discrete single-use service. Groups are, again, formed according to session length and subjective satisfaction. Group A is the same as in Figure 1 and it consists of 'carefree' people that give a positive evaluation of the service after a very brief session. As their opinions have no solid grounds we suggest that their opinions should not be regarded as a positive factor for the service, nor should they be considered negative. Therefore, this group should be removed from the data as emphasized by the dotted edge of Group A in Figure 5.

Group A includes people who do not intend to use the service in any real sense but just want to see what it is all about. If the purpose of the service is clearly explained to people passing by then they will understand that it takes some time to go through the service. Therefore, the number of users in Group A should be small.

Group E consists of users that give a negative opinion of the service after using it shortly. There may be carefree users in this group, also, but what is more important, it includes users who have not succeeded in climbing the learnability curve: the curve is too steep for them. Therefore, this group is most interesting in assessing the usability of the service.

The length limits t_2 and t_3 describe the lower and upper bound of session length for normal users. Thus, Groups C and G include people using the service in the way anticipated by its developers. The limits may be somewhat vague and they differ from service to service. With a proper session length measure they should, however, be easily identified in the data.

The limit t_1 can be thought to describe the impatience threshold. A user who is really interested in the service and has the patience to work with it so that she exceeds t_1, even if there are some problems, is likely to use the service for a normal length. Therefore, Group F should be nearly empty. One would not expect to see many users in Group B either, as the carefree users hardly use the service longer than an interested user who tries to struggle with the service. The fact that there should not be many users in these groups is emphasized by no edge around them. In the quiz, the small number of users having session length between $t_1 = 5$ and $t_2 = 22$ is a good example of this effect.

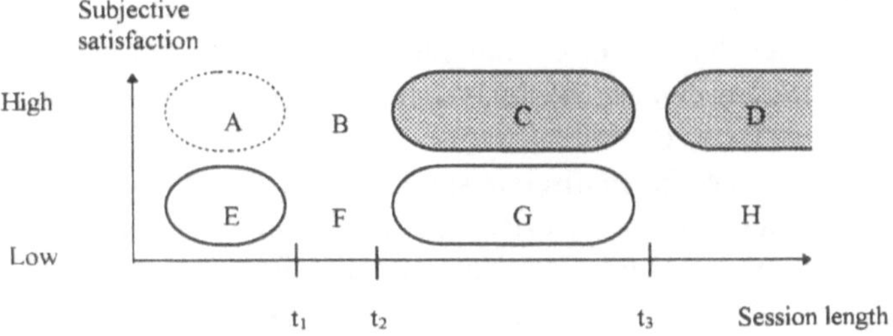

Figure 6: User groups in continuous services.

Groups D and H include users that have used the service noticeably long and there should be few of them (otherwise the selection of the limit t_3 or of the length measure is not correct). The service is, however, a discrete single-use service and thus there is in general no justification for extra long sessions. In the quiz, extra long sessions can, however, be explained by protocol analysis as discussed earlier.

Group H includes users who do not like a service but the session length is very high. If session length is measured by time then a long session can be explained by problems in the use of the service. A user of a discrete service wants to reach the end of the service, and if there are troubles it may take long to get through. In the quiz, session length was measured by the number of HTML pages seen by users, which does not distinguish Group G users from Group H users, and by the number of mouse events, which is a better measure in this respect.

Group D users do like the service and hence it is improbable that they have had serious user interface problems. As there is no good explanation for Group D usage patterns, we suggest that in general they be excluded from further analysis.

When usability problems in a single version of a service are analysed then attention should be paid to Groups E, G and H. Further, there is a qualitative difference in usability problems with these groups. Group E includes users that have problems in learning how to use the service or have wrong expectations of its contents. By analysing the problems of this group it is possible to find usability problems that make the starting threshold too high. Group G includes users that do not like the user interface or are disappointed by the detailed contents of the service. Finally, Group H includes users that have severe problems with the user interface but are supposedly satisfied with the contents of the service.

When several versions of a service are compared, there is a need to measure the success of each version. According to the previous discussion this can be done by counting the subjectively satisfied users in Group C and dividing it by the number of users in Groups C, E, G, and H. This excludes from the analysis users whose opinions are questionable.

5.2 Continuous Services

Let us next consider the case of continuous services. The basic grouping of users is the same as in the previous case but the interpretation of Groups A, D and H is somewhat different (see Figure 6).

Group A is the same as in discrete single-use services but one would expect to see more users with continuous services. As the use of a continuous service can be ended at any time, people can start to use it more easily.

Groups D and H include users that have used the service noticeably long and they should be nearly empty. If the service does not have an automatic restart mechanism then long sessions can occur if the user is involved for a while in another matter like extraneous discussions. If the service restarts automatically when the user has not done anything for a while then the pause will be considered a change of users.

In our research there was an automatic mechanism to restart the information service after 30 seconds of no user actions. Therefore, even the longest sessions describe active use (though there may be many consecutive users in a single session). Group H includes people who have used the service extraordinary long but still do not like it. There should not be many such users if the limit t_3 has been selected correctly. Users in Group D are satisfied with the service and they may just be so enthusiastic about the service that they have used it for an extended period. One would expect more cases in Group D than in Group H as there is no clear explanation for Group H users. Therefore we are willing to include Group D in further analysis but exclude Group H.

When several versions of a service are compared, the success of each version can thus be measured by counting the subjectively satisfied users in Groups C and D and dividing it by the number of users in Groups C, D, E, and G.

When usability problems in a single version of a service are analysed then attention should be paid to Groups E and G. As in discrete single-use services, Group E includes users that have problems in learning how to use the service or have wrong expectations of its contents. Similarly, Group G includes users that do not like the user interface or are disappointed by the detailed contents of the service.

The information service used in the housing fair is a continuous service. According to the previous discussion we expected that the session length distribution would be similar to that of Figures 2 and 3, but with an even broader and lower peak. Such an effect could not, however, be found. The length measure can be selected in many ways but the form of the distribution is always that of Figure 4. The lack of a peak associated with normal session length is due to the fact that users of the information service had no goal to achieve. They just jumped from page to page until they got bored. The distribution curves decline rapidly and thus practically all users belong to Groups A and E. As a consequence it is impossible to make any meaningful analysis of the results.

To make the analysis of a continuous service possible there must be some reason for the users not to quit too early. For example, there could be a contest consisting of one or two questions whose answers could be found through the service. The contest form could also ask for the users' opinion of the service and thus subjective satisfaction could be measured. Users in Group E will be a problem, though, as they have so many problems using the service that they will not find out the correct answers and, accordingly, they will not fill a form. If forms can be connected with log sessions then the form could have a question asking whether the user did quit the service right after finding the answers. This would give a possibility to make a distinction between different reasons for extra long sessions.

5.3 Discrete Multiple-use Services

Discrete multiple-use services are closer to continuous services than discrete single-use services in respect to session length. By a suitable selection for length measure it may be possible to obtain a series of length limits so that every other interval contains normal session endings and every other interval should be nearly empty. But if session length is measured, e.g. by time, then service cycles soon mix up and result in a continuous service type distribution.

6 Conclusions

Usability kiosks can be used to obtain valuable information of computer based services. However, the previous analysis of different kinds of services make it clear that there is no simple correlation between subjective satisfaction and session length. Therefore, subjective satisfaction must be determined by other means, e.g. by an interview or questionnaire. It is of course possible to include a questionnaire form as a part of the service at its end, but users having serious usability problems (Group E) never reach such a questionnaire. By a careful protocol analysis it may be possible to find such usability problems by looking at the logs of users who have quit the service very quickly. However, if it is not known which users are satisfied with the service, then such an analysis will also include the carefree users. The information service example above suggests that the number of Group A users may be many times over that of Group E. To avoid unnecessary work we suggest that the level of subjective satisfaction is obtained by interviewing users.

Low subjective satisfaction can be a result of problems in the user interface or in the information contents of the service. Session length does not provide any solution to making a distinction between these two cases. All low satisfaction groups can have problems in the user interface or in the information contents. Therefore, it is important to ask in interviews not only the level of subjective satisfaction but reasons for low satisfaction, also.

The qualitative differences among user Groups A, ..., H are important for usability analysis. We have seen that usability problems have different roots in different groups. Moreover, we have suggested that some groups should be excluded when different versions of a service are compared. It is therefore important that the limits t_1, t_2, and t_3 can be figured out. Figures 5 and 6 show that this can be done: the practically empty groups are located so that the limits should be visible in a length distribution containing all users.

The length limits can be decided after the service has been used in the information kiosk for a couple of days. After that it is possible to focus on different problems with different user groups. Moreover, it is then possible to diminish analysis work by excluding Group A altogether. Interviews with short session users can start with a question of subjective satisfaction and if it is high then the interview can be terminated.

Acknowledgements

We would like to thank Pertti Saariluoma, and Markku Tukiainen for their valuable comments on the first drafts of this paper, and Tuomo Kauranne (CRNet Oy) for providing access to the equipment and services in the housing fair. This work was supported by TEKES (Technology Development Centre Finland).

References

Dumas, J. S. & Redish, J. C. (1993), *A Practical Guide to Usability Testing*, Ablex.

Gould, J. D., Boies, S. J., Levy, S., Richards, J. T. & Schoonard, J. (1987), "The 1984 Olympic Message System: A Test of Behavioral Principles of System Design", *Communications of the ACM* **30**(9), 758–769.

Hix, D. & Hartson, H. R. (1993), *Developing User Interfaces: Ensuring Usability Through Product and Process*, John Wiley & Sons.

Kirakowski, J. & Corbett, M. (1990), *Effective Methodology for the Study of HCI*, North-Holland.

Landauer, T. K. (1988), Research Methods in Human–Computer Interaction, *in* M. Helander (ed.), "Handbook of Human–Computer Interaction", North-Holland, pp.905–928.

Lindgaard, G. (1994), *Usability Testing and System Evaluation: A Guide for Designing Useful Computer Systems*, Chapman & Hall.

Nielsen, J. (1993), *Usability Engineering*, Academic Press.

Nielsen, J. & Mack, R. L. (eds.) (1994), *Usability Inspection Methods*, John Wiley & Sons.

Perrochon, L. (1995), "Building a W3-Kiosk with Existing Products". W3-Based Online Kiosk Systems Workshop at Third International World-Wide Web Conference. http://www.igd.fhg.de/www/www95/workshops/work-b.html.

Preece, J., Benyon, D., Davies, G., Keller, L. & Rogers, Y. (1993), *A Guide to Usability: Human Factors in Computing*, Addison–Wesley.

Sajaniemi, J. & Tossavainen, I. (1995), Usability Research in a Housing Fair: Problems and Possibilities, Technical Report Series A A-1995-7, Department of Computer Science, University of Joensuu.

Salomon, G. B. (1990), Designing Casual Use Hypertext: The CHI'89 InfoBooth, *in* J. C. Chew & J. Whiteside (eds.), "Proceedings of CHI'90: Human Factors in Computing Systems", ACM Press, pp.451–458.

Tossavainen, I. & Sajaniemi, J. (1995), Kolmen telemaattisen palvelun käytettävyyden arviointi asuntomessuilla suoritetun testauksen perusteella (An Evaluation of the Usability of Three Telematic Applications Based on Testing in a Housing Fair), Raporttisarja B B-1995-1, Tietojenkäsittelytieteen laitos, Joensuun yliopisto.

Author Index

Keyword Index